Upright walking

In the African forests, apes evolve the ability to walk upright. This frees their hands for carrying and throwing. The first known ape which may have been bipedal (two-legged) is called *Sahelanthropus tchadensis*.

Australopithecines

Several species of bipedal ape, Australopithecines, spread across the grasslands of East Africa. The most famous Australopithecus is Lucy, a female whose 3.2 million-year-old bones were discovered in Ethiopia in 1974.

7–6 MYA (million years ago)

4 MYA

Human ancestors

Humans originated as African apes and are related to chimps and gorillas. Around 6 million years ago, our closest ape ancestors, called hominins, began to walk on two legs. Over time, they developed bigger brains and learned to make tools and control fire. As hominins evolved, they left Africa to settle all over the world.

Hand axe

Homo erectus moves out of Africa and into Asia. It invents a new kind of stone tool—a hand axe with a leaf-shaped cutting blade. This is the first tool made to a design.

1.8–1.75 MYA

Making fire

Homo erectus uses fire, allowing the species to cook, keep warm, and protect itself from wild animals. The earliest evidence of fire is a 1 million-year-old collection of charred animal bones found in a cave in South Africa.

Homo heidelbergensis

Homo heidelbergensis appears in Africa, later moving into West Asia and Europe. It is the first hominin species to build shelters and use spears to hunt animals.

1 MYA

700,000 YA (years ago)

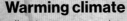

Warming climate

The climate warms, causing sea levels to rise. Big game animals, such as mammoths, die out. Humans adapt by eating new plant foods and catching more fish. The bow and arrow, a new invention, allows them to hunt small game such as deer.

First art

Humans in Europe and Asia produce the first works of art: paintings and carvings of animals and people. The paintings, created in caves, probably serve a ritual purpose, such as contacting animal spirits to bring about a successful hunt.

Last Neanderthals

Neanderthals die out, perhaps unable to adapt to the rapidly changing climate. Our own species (*Homo sapiens sapiens*) is now the last type of human on the planet. However, today, most of us carry some Neanderthal genes.

14,000–12,000 YA

35,000 YA

39,000 YA

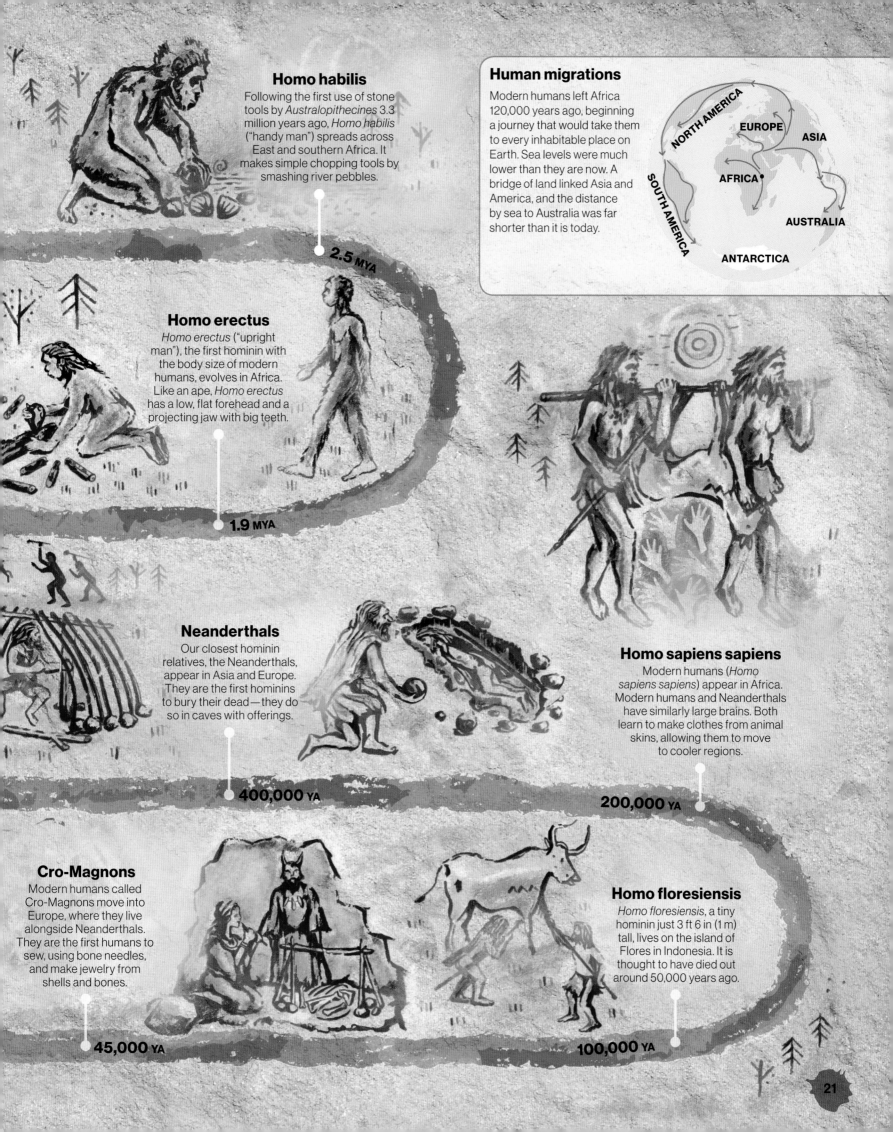

Homo habilis

Following the first use of stone tools by *Australopithecines* 3.3 million years ago, *Homo habilis* ("handy man") spreads across East and southern Africa. It makes simple chopping tools by smashing river pebbles.

2.5 MYA

Human migrations

Modern humans left Africa 120,000 years ago, beginning a journey that would take them to every inhabitable place on Earth. Sea levels were much lower than they are now. A bridge of land linked Asia and America, and the distance by sea to Australia was far shorter than it is today.

NORTH AMERICA
EUROPE
ASIA
SOUTH AMERICA
AFRICA
AUSTRALIA
ANTARCTICA

Homo erectus

Homo erectus ("upright man"), the first hominin with the body size of modern humans, evolves in Africa. Like an ape, *Homo erectus* has a low, flat forehead and a projecting jaw with big teeth.

1.9 MYA

Neanderthals

Our closest hominin relatives, the Neanderthals, appear in Asia and Europe. They are the first hominins to bury their dead—they do so in caves with offerings.

400,000 YA

Homo sapiens sapiens

Modern humans (*Homo sapiens sapiens*) appear in Africa. Modern humans and Neanderthals have similarly large brains. Both learn to make clothes from animal skins, allowing them to move to cooler regions.

200,000 YA

Cro-Magnons

Modern humans called Cro-Magnons move into Europe, where they live alongside Neanderthals. They are the first humans to sew, using bone needles, and make jewelry from shells and bones.

45,000 YA

Homo floresiensis

Homo floresiensis, a tiny hominin just 3 ft 6 in (1 m) tall, lives on the island of Flores in Indonesia. It is thought to have died out around 50,000 years ago.

100,000 YA

21

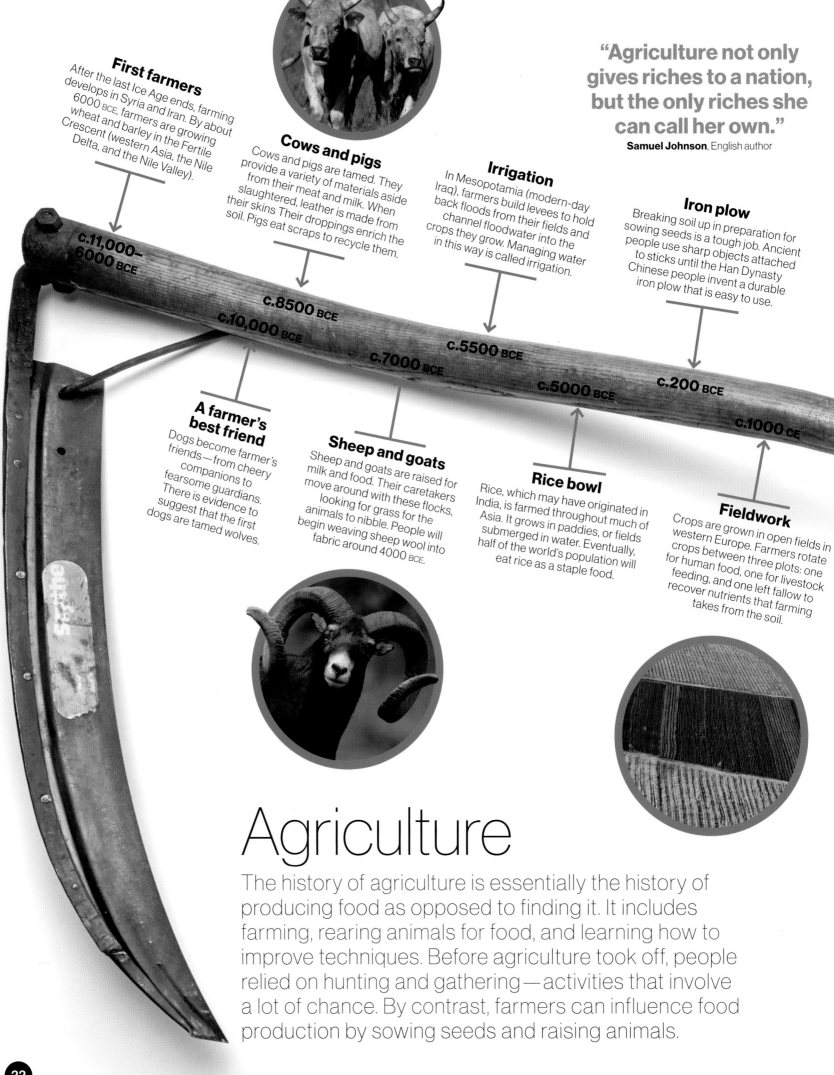

First farmers

After the last Ice Age ends, farming develops in Syria and Iran. By about 6000 BCE, farmers are growing wheat and barley in the Fertile Crescent (western Asia, the Nile Delta, and the Nile Valley).

Cows and pigs

Cows and pigs are tamed. They provide a variety of materials aside from their meat and milk. When slaughtered, leather is made from their skins Their droppings enrich the soil. Pigs eat scraps to recycle them.

Irrigation

In Mesopotamia (modern-day Iraq), farmers build levees to hold back floods from their fields and channel floodwater into the crops they grow. Managing water in this way is called irrigation.

Iron plow

Breaking soil up in preparation for sowing seeds is a tough job. Ancient people use sharp objects attached to sticks until the Han Dynasty Chinese people invent a durable iron plow that is easy to use.

> **"Agriculture not only gives riches to a nation, but the only riches she can call her own."**
> **Samuel Johnson**, English author

c.11,000–6000 BCE

c.10,000 BCE

c.8500 BCE

c.7000 BCE

c.5500 BCE

c.5000 BCE

c.200 BCE

c.1000 CE

A farmer's best friend

Dogs become farmer's friends—from cheery companions to fearsome guardians. There is evidence to suggest that the first dogs are tamed wolves.

Sheep and goats

Sheep and goats are raised for milk and food. Their caretakers move around with these flocks, looking for grass for the animals to nibble. People will begin weaving sheep wool into fabric around 4000 BCE.

Rice bowl

Rice, which may have originated in India, is farmed throughout much of Asia. It grows in paddies, or fields submerged in water. Eventually, half of the world's population will eat rice as a staple food.

Fieldwork

Crops are grown in open fields in western Europe. Farmers rotate crops between three plots: one for human food, one for livestock feeding, and one left fallow to recover nutrients that farming takes from the soil.

Agriculture

The history of agriculture is essentially the history of producing food as opposed to finding it. It includes farming, rearing animals for food, and learning how to improve techniques. Before agriculture took off, people relied on hunting and gathering—activities that involve a lot of chance. By contrast, farmers can influence food production by sowing seeds and raising animals.

Scythe

The scythe is an agricultural tool used to mow grass and reap crops. It is swung along the ground, and the sharp blade slices the grass or crop at the base. The first scythes may have been developed around 500 BCE.

Crop swap

As Europeans explore more of the world, crops are exchanged across the globe. Coffee, tea, sugar, and citrus fruits come from Asia; wheat, barley, and rye come from Europe; while tomatoes, corn, beans, potatoes, and chile peppers move from the Americas. Animals are exchanged, too.

Steel plow

Blacksmith John Deere invents a steel plow to keep the sticky soil of the American prairie from clogging up cast-iron plows. His invention is wildly successful.

Reaping rewards

Harvesting is slow and back-breaking work, done by hand with a scythe. Cyrus McCormick patents the reaper, a machine that aids in crop harvesting. His reaper cuts, threshes, and bundles grain as horses pull it along.

Selective breeding

Austrian friar and scientist Gregor Mendel conducts experiments with flowers and pea plants. Mendel describes how certain traits, such as color or size, are passed on through the generations. This knowledge is used by farmers to selectively breed crops.

1400s–1500s

1794

1831

1837

Cotton gin

US-born inventor Eli Whitney invents a machine that makes removing seeds from cotton much easier and faster. By the middle of the 19th century, the material will become America's biggest export.

Tractor

Steam-powered threshers that separate grain from cereal crops are expensive and hard to move. American inventor John Froelich invents a rudimentary tractor that can pull the thresher with ease.

GM crops

Genetically modified (GM) crops become common. They can increase yield, boost nutrition, and resist pests, but potential food safety risks from "tampering" with the natural ecosystem are a worry for many.

1866

1885

1890s

1940s

1990s

Combine harvester

Australian Hugh Victor McKay produces the first commercially successful combine harvester, a machine that cuts, threshes, and cleans crops with one pass of its mighty rotating blades.

Green Revolution

Farmers in Mexico lead a movement to update farming practices and produce more nourishing food. The technologies spread across the globe.

23

Working with metals

The use of metals was one of the greatest technological leaps in history. Unlike stone tools, metal ones can be molded or beaten into any shape, and metal blades are easy to resharpen. The first metal tools were made mostly with copper, a soft metal that was easy to find. Later, people discovered how to work iron—a much harder metal that had to be extracted from rock in a furnace.

Pouring bronze

Bronze is a soft metal that is relatively easy to melt and pour into a mold. Gold, silver, copper, tin, and lead are also soft metals. Iron is harder and melts at a much higher temperature.

Malachite is a copper-rich mineral found in rocks.

The Copper-Stone Age

The people of western Asia discover how to extract copper from copper-rich rocks by heating them in a fire (this is called smelting). They pour the molten copper into molds to make tools. Most people still use stone tools, so this period is called the Copper-Stone Age.

The Bronze Age

In western Asia and Central Europe, the use of bronze becomes widespread. Bronze is made by melting copper with a small amount of tin. This results in a much harder metal. A trade in tin, which is a rare metal, also develops.

c.9000 BCE   **c.4500 BCE**   **c.4500 BCE**   **c.3100 BCE**   **c.2200 BCE**

Metalworking begins

Metalworking begins in western Asia, where the world's first farmers live. Early farmers find naturally occurring copper nuggets and hammer them into beads. Soon after, they make objects from gold, silver, and lead.

Oldest gold treasure

In Varna, in what is now Bulgaria, people are buried with thousands of items of gold jewelry. The oldest gold treasure in the world, it will lie hidden underground for over 6,000 years before being discovered by accident in 1972.

Iron

Iron is first made by the Hittites of western Asia, who use it to make weapons. Although iron is the most common metal, it requires great heat to extract from rock. Instead of being poured into molds, it is softened and beaten into shape.

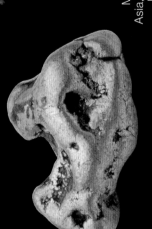

Chinese statues

The Sanxingdui people of China make large bronze statues with masklike faces. Their bronze includes lead, as well as tin and copper, making a stronger, heavier metal. The biggest statue, of a tree, stands almost 13 ft (4 m) high.

Iron-Age Europe

Iron working spreads throughout Europe, where readily available iron weapons lead to an increase in warfare. This 6th-century-BCE Greek vase shows blacksmiths using a forge (a powerful fire) to soften iron before shaping it with a hammer.

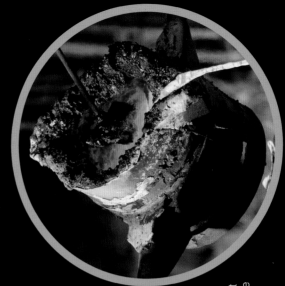

African iron

The Iron Age reaches sub-Saharan Africa, where the Nok people of Nigeria use iron to make spearheads, knives, and bracelets. The use of iron tools helps farming spread across Africa.

Cast iron

In China, people discover how to make iron in a blast furnace—a furnace powered by a blast of hot air. The resulting iron can be remelted and poured into molds to make cast iron. Blast furnaces will not be invented in the West for almost 2,000 years.

| c.1200 BCE | 1200–1101 BCE | 800–300 BCE | c.700 BCE | c.600 BCE | 6th century BCE | 5th century BCE | 13th century CE |

The Iron Age

The use of iron spreads from Western Asia to Europe, and India's Iron Age takes off at around the same time. Iron's hardness makes it ideal for tools, cooking pots, and nails, as well as weapons.

Peru and Bolivia

In Peru and Bolivia, people begin large-scale smelting of copper. They use gold, silver, and tumbaga (gold mixed with copper or silver) to make beautiful works of art in various colors.

Indian steel

Indian metalworkers make the highest quality steel in the ancient world. It is later exported to China and the West, where it is called "wootz." It is used to make exceptionally sharp, hard-wearing swords.

European blast furnaces

The first European blast furnaces begin operating in Germany, Switzerland, and Sweden. They use water wheels to power bellows that blow air into the furnace, and because of this, are built by rivers.

Prehistoric communities

9000–4000 BCE

Early farmers establish villages with basic buildings and shared structures. The first of these are found in Mesopotamia in West Asia. Gradually, they expand to become small towns with organized communities.

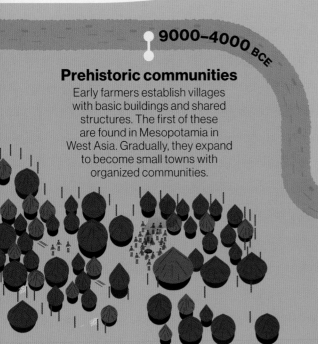

8000 BCE

Walled settlements

Communities begin to surround their settlements with protective walls. In the town of Jericho in Palestine, a huge stone wall is constructed for defense, surveillance, and flood protection, keeping the 3,000 inhabitants safe.

Byzantine bazaars

In the Byzantine Empire, around the Mediterranean, public areas and main roads in cities start to become closed off by shops. These eventually evolve into bazaars—covered markets where locals barter to get the best price for goods.

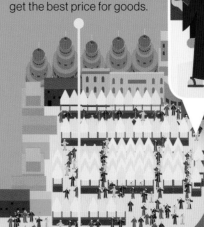

Towns and cities

The first settlements started in prehistoric times. Basic buildings provided shelter and safety as these communities grew into towns and villages. With more opportunities for trade and work, the populations of many increased, eventually resulting in the growth of major cities. The birth of new technologies enabled many of these towns and cities to develop even faster into the modern metropolises we know today.

500–700 CE

Replacement walls

King Philip II of France orders a new wall to be built around Paris, stretching beyond the outskirts of the city. It is 8 ft (2 m) wide with around 70 towers. Many other medieval European cities also rebuild their original walls to contain their growing centers.

1190

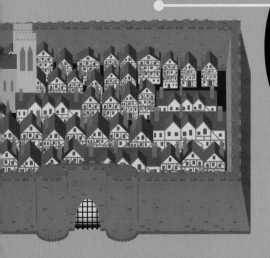

Factory towns

During the Industrial Revolution, people move to work in factories. New towns grow rapidly around the factories to house workers.

1750–1800

1807

Street lights

The first public street lighting that uses gas is demonstrated in London. This becomes the norm across towns and cities, solving the problem of limited light at night.

Early cities

The first great cities develop in Mesopotamia. These are each ruled by a king. Grand brick structures called ziggurats are built, containing shrines, staircases, and towers.

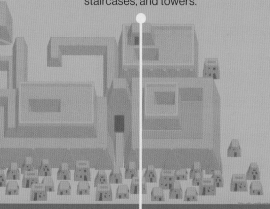

Trading hubs

Mesopotamia's cities become important trading centers, using rivers to transport goods. Long-distance trade takes place between cities in Mesopotamia and in the Indus Valley in Pakistan. Luxury items such as spices, textiles, metals, and precious stones are exchanged.

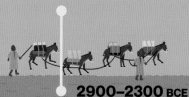

Sewer systems

The first sewer systems are constructed by the Indus Valley civilization. Underground tunnels carry water from place to place, allowing most homes to have a bath, toilet, and water supply.

4000–3000 BCE   **2900–2300 BCE**   **2600 BCE**

Record-breaking Rome

Rome becomes the first city to reach a population of 1 million people. Most Romans live in blocks of flats called *insulae* that are 6 or 7 stories high, maximizing space in the city.

City-states

In ancient Greece, cities establish themselves as independent states with their own political systems. Athens, Sparta, and Thebes are some of the most important city-states.

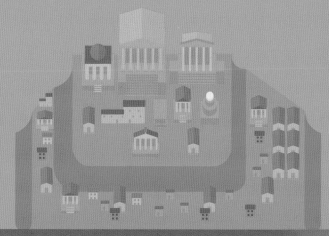

1 CE   **800 BCE**

Skyscrapers

The first high-rise building, nicknamed a "skyscraper," is built in Chicago, IL. Building upward saves space in the packed city center and is possible due to the invention of the elevator and sturdy steel.

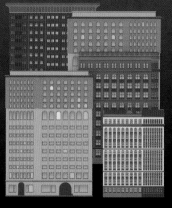

City slickers

Half of the world's population now lives in cities. Megacities, which have populations of more than 10 million, have become more common. Tokyo, Japan, is the biggest city in the world, with around 13 million people living there.

1863   **1885**   **2008**

Underground railway

The world's first underground railway system opens in London. Moving transportation underground saves space and provides a quicker way to get around the bustling city.

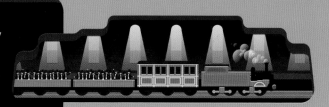

> **"What is the city but the people?"**
>
> **William Shakespeare**, *Coriolanus*, c. 1608 CE

The story of the wheel

Early humans realized that heavy objects could be moved more easily if they were rolled instead of dragged. It took thousands of years to develop the wheel. Many inventions developed over the past 3,500 years would not have been possible without it.

Inventing the wheel

Wheels can be seen in so many objects around us that it is tricky to imagine a time when they didn't exist. Nobody knows exactly how the wheel evolved to form the wheel we see today, but archaeologists think it all began thousands of years ago with simple log rollers and sleds.

Rolling along
The ancient Sumerians realized that they could move bulky objects more easily if they rolled them over round log rollers.

Simple sled
Rollers proved awkward to move around, so the Sumerians developed a sled with a curved front that could be pulled along more easily.

Teaming up
The Sumerians decided to combine the sled and roller, finding that the sled glided over the rollers more smoothly than over the ground.

Making grooves
Over time, the movement of the sled over the roller wore grooves in the log roller, which helped keep the sled in place.

Early wheels
To improve the design, the Sumerians chipped away at the log to create two wheels and an axle. Pegs fixed on the sled hooked it onto the axle.

The first cart
The Sumerians later fixed individual wheels onto an axle and attached the sled to it securely by drilling holes in its frame.

> **"The greatest inventors are unknown to us. Someone invented the wheel—but who?"**
> **Isaac Asimov,**
> science-fiction writer, 1988

Water wheel
The grinding of corn is transformed by the invention of the water wheel. This machine uses the water of a fast-flowing stream, rather than people, to power a mill. The windmill won't be invented for another 700 years, in 600 CE.

Archimedes' screw
Archimedes, an ancient Greek inventor, develops a rotating corkscrew that transforms irrigation by allowing water to be transferred from low ground to high ground.

c.100 BCE

Gears
Gears are toothed wheels that work together to increase the speed and force of a machine. The earliest examples appear in the 4th century BCE in China and will eventually be found in machines such as chariots, clocks, cars, and bicycles.

3rd century BCE

4th century BCE

Spoked wheel
The ancient Egyptians realize that wheels made lighter by cutting chunks from them. These spoked wheels allow the Egyptians to outrun their enemies in battle and trade goods more quickly.

c.2000 BCE

Wheels for transportation
The earliest wheels used for transportation are seen on Mesopotamian chariots and carts. They are built from solid wood and allow people to travel more easily than ever before.

c.3500 BCE

The first wheel
The first wheels are potters' wheels. They begin to appear in different cultures across the globe in around 3500 BCE. Made of hardened clay, the wheel allows people to create better bowls and jars.

c.3500 BCE

The Penny Farthing
The enormous front wheel enabled high speeds, but the Penny Farthing was dangerous. It lost popularity in the 1880s with the introduction of "safety bicycles."

Astrolabe
This astronomical calculator uses wheels to find the position of objects that can be seen in the night sky, helping navigators and astronomers identify stars and planets and use them to find their way.

c.500 CE

Flywheel
One of the most significant technological developments of the wheel, the flywheel is used in cars and spacecraft to store energy. This heavy wheel spins so it can increase a machine's momentum and store rotational energy.

c.1100

Mechanical clock
The invention of a mechanism that can control a gear's rotation leads to the development of the mechanical clock, where it is used to make the hands of the clock tick at regular intervals.

c.1300

Propeller
Leonardo da Vinci designs a helicopter that cleverly adapts the principles of the Archimedes screw to create an upward force called lift. Da Vinci's idea is developed into a propeller with blades that are now used to drive ships and planes forward.

1493

The Industrial Revolution
With the creation of many new technologies during the Industrial Revolution, the wheel becomes crucial to the development of mechanisms and inventions such as power looms, spinning machines, and steam engines.

1760

Electric motor
The first usable electric motor, created by Moritz Jacobi, converts electrical energy into mechanical energy. It paves the way for the motors we use in many machines today.

1834

Pneumatic tires
Until pneumatic tires were invented, travelers had to put up with uncomfortably bumpy journeys on vehicles with wooden or hardened rubber wheels. Pneumatic tires are filled with air, making for a much more comfortable ride.

1888

Tanks
The earliest tanks are built for World War I as armored, mobile weapons. The tank uses a continuous band of treads wrapped around two or more wheels on each side. This spreads its weight over a larger area which helps it move over soft, uneven ground.

1915

The written word

Spoken language has existed since prehistoric times. The need to keep records of trade led civilizations around the world to invent ways of writing language down. This allowed knowledge to be collected and passed on from person to person both reliably and over great distances. It's thanks to the written word that we know the thoughts and ideas of people who lived thousands of years ago.

c.3300 BCE

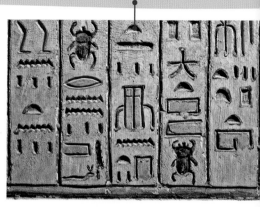

World's first writing
The Egyptians invent hieroglyphs, a system of around 700–800 picture signs, which stand for words, sounds, and ideas.

c.650 BCE

Roman alphabet
In Italy, the Romans adapt the Greek alphabet to write their own language, Latin. The Roman alphabet goes on to become the world's most widely used script.

c.800 BCE

Greek alphabet
The Greeks adapt the Phoenician alphabet, adding letters for vowels. It has 24 letters, and is usually written from left to right.

c.800 BCE

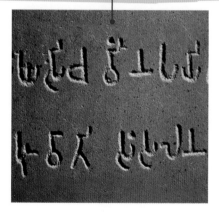

Brahmi script
This script is developed in India, using signs for consonants with additional markings for vowels. Brahmi is the ancestor of around 200 later Asian scripts.

c.300 BCE

Mayan writing
In Central America, the Mayan people develop a writing system with signs standing for syllables as well as ideas. They carve monumental inscriptions, paint text on vases, and write on fig tree bark.

c.150 BCE

Runes
In Scandinavia and modern-day Germany, people begin to use runes, with 24 signs. The system is inspired by contact with the Roman alphabet, but uses straight lines, so it can be easily carved onto wood or stone.

3rd century CE

Arabic script
Arabs create an alphabet with 28 letters, written from right to left. With the spread of Islam, the Arabic script is later adopted across North Africa and much of Asia.

c.3200 BCE

Cuneiform

The Sumerians of Mesopotamia (see pages 36–37) invent cuneiform, a writing system of shapes pressed into clay with a reed stylus.

c.2600 BCE

Indus script

The Indus people of India invent a script that remains undeciphered to this day. Evidence suggests it was written from right to left.

c.2500 BCE

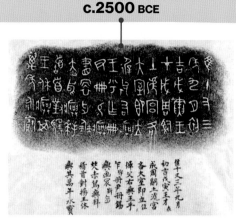

Chinese writing

The earliest surviving Chinese writing uses picture signs called "ideograms." Each picture stands for an idea or an object. The signs later develop into the script used in China today.

c.1200 BCE

Phoenician alphabet

Phoenicians (from the eastern Mediterranean coast) simplify the Proto-Sinaitic alphabet. They use 22 signs, all standing for consonants. The script later inspires the Hebrew, Arabic, and Greek writing systems.

c.1850–1650 BCE

First alphabet

To the east of Egypt, the first alphabet, Proto-Sinaitic (or Canaanite), is created. Based on Egyptian hieroglyphs, people only need to learn 30 signs to be able to write.

5th century

Japanese scripts

Japanese people adapt Chinese writing to create a script called *kanji*. They also invent two other scripts, *hiragana* and *katakana*, with signs standing for syllables. As a result, Japan has three writing systems.

c.860–880

Slavic scripts

Bulgarian churchmen adapt the Greek alphabet to create the Glagolitic and Cyrillic alphabets, which they use to translate the Bible into Slavic languages from Central and Eastern Europe. Cyrillic later evolves into the modern Russian alphabet.

The Rosetta Stone

The Rosetta Stone is an inscribed basalt block, discovered by French soldiers in Egypt in 1799. Carved in 196 BCE, the same text is written on it in Ancient Greek, hieroglyphs, and demotic (an everyday Egyptian script). In 1822, French linguist Jean-François Champollion used the inscriptions on the stone to work out how to read hieroglyphs, which until then had been impossible to decipher.

THE ANCIENT WORLD

3000 BCE-500 CE

The Ancient World

The earliest civilizations established their cultures around huge rivers that could support farming, such as the Tigris and Euphrates in West Asia, and the Nile in Egypt. As technology developed and trade expanded after 3000 BCE, great empires also sprang up across Europe and East Asia. As these new societies took shape, many of them came into conflict with one another in competition for land and resources.

c.2500 BCE
The first recorded war takes place, between the cities of Umma and Lagash in Mesopotamia.

c.950–612 BCE
The Assyrians of Mesopotamia create an empire stretching from Egypt across West Asia.

550 BCE
Cyrus the Great founds the First Persian Empire, based in West Asia.

490–479 BCE
The Persians make two unsuccessful attempts to conquer the cities of Greece.

336–323 BCE
Alexander of Macedon unites Greece and conquers the Persian Empire. Greek cities are founded as far east as India.

2589–2566 BCE
The Egyptians construct the Great Pyramid at Giza.

c.1900 BCE
The Amorites conquer most of Mesopotamia, which they rule from the city of Babylon.

c.509 BCE
The people of Rome in Italy overthrow their king, and begin to expand the city's influence.

508 BCE
The Athenians of Greece establish the first democracy.

c.450–50 BCE
The Celtic La Tène culture develops in modern-day Switzerland.

321–185 BCE
Chandragupta Maurya of South India invades the north and establishes the Maurya Empire.

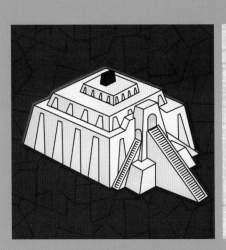

Mesopotamia
The earliest cities were built in West Asia, in a historical region known as Mesopotamia (see pages 36–37). The cultures of this area invented farming and the wheel.

Land of the Pharaohs
Ruled by kings known as pharaohs, the ancient Egyptians (see pages 40–41) built large monuments called pyramids to house their royal dead.

Ancient Greece
In Athens, one of the warring city-states of ancient Greece (see pages 52–53), great thinkers developed early philosophy and democracy.

The Celts
Spread across Central and Western Europe, the Celts (see pages 58–59) were warriors who shared a single culture. They were experts at crafting metal.

Pottery

The process of creating pottery was first discovered in prehistoric times, but in the ancient world, many cultures—particularly the Greeks—perfected pottery design as an art form. Objects such as this Greek amphora (jug) give historians many visual clues about the fashions, stories, and societies of the ancient world.

221 BCE
The king of Qin unites the kingdoms of China under his rule, becoming Shi Huangdi ("First Emperor").

27 BCE
After a civil war, Octavian becomes Rome's first emperor, taking a new name, Augustus.

c.320 CE
Chandra Gupta I conquers the Ganges Valley in northern India, founding the Gupta Empire.

202 BCE–220 CE
The emperors of the Han Dynasty rule China for more than 400 years.

30 BCE
Egypt is conquered by the Romans, bringing an end to the rule of the pharaohs.

79 CE
Mount Vesuvius in Italy erupts, destroying the towns of Pompeii and Herculaneum.

476 CE
Rome falls to Germanic invaders, but its empire survives in the east as the Byzantine Empire.

The Persian Empire
Centered in West Asia, the Persian Empire (see pages 60–61) was split into provinces, each one ruled by a regional governor known as a satrap.

Imperial China
Emperor Qin Shi Huang created the first of a series of imperial dynasties that would go on to rule China (see pages 68–69) for the next 2,000 years.

Rome
Beginning as a small hilltop town in Italy, Rome (see pages 72–73) became the capital of an empire that spanned much of Europe, North Africa, and West Asia.

Ancient India
Greatly influenced by the religions of Hinduism and Buddhism, a series of empires sprang up across the Indian subcontinent (see pages 82–83).

Mesopotamia

Mesopotamia means "the land between the two rivers," referring to the Tigris and the Euphrates in western Asia. It was here, more than 5,000 years ago, that the world's first cities were built. The Mesopotamians invented organized religion, royalty, armies, law, and many other fundamental features of civilization as we know it.

Early beginnings
Farming people in northern Mesopotamia develop systems to supply their fields with water. Fine Mesopotamian painted pottery is exported across southwest Asia.

c.6000–4000 BCE

Babylonians
The Amorites, a people from the western deserts, conquer most of Mesopotamia, which they rule from Babylon. They are known as the Babylonians, and their new empire is called Babylonia.

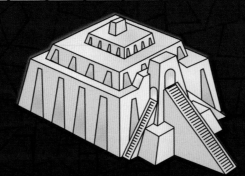

Ziggurat
The first ziggurats (stepped temples) are built in Ur, Eridu, Nippur, and Uruk. These huge stone structures were built as places of religious worship.

Akkadians
King Sargon of Akkad (a region in northern Mesopotamia) conquers all of Sumer, creating the world's first empire. The Akkadian language gradually replaces Sumerian in Mesopotamia.

c.1900 BCE

c.2100 BCE

c.2350 BCE

Hammurabi's law code
King Hammurabi reigns over Babylon. He is famous for his law code, which, although based on earlier codes, he claims to have received in person from Shamash, the god of justice.

Hittites and Kassites
The Hittites and Kassites invade Babylonia using iron weapons and fast chariots pulled by horses. The Kassites conquer Babylonia, which they rule for 500 years.

Assyrians
The Assyrians of northern Mesopotamia create an empire stretching from Egypt to western Persia. They speak Aramaic, which becomes the standard language used across southwest Asia.

1792–1750 BCE

c.1595–1530 BCE

c.950–612 BCE

Sumer

Northern Mesopotamians move into the flat southern plains, later called Sumer. They establish large villages, build the first temples, and invent the potter's wheel.

First city

Villages at Uruk join together to form the world's first city. It has walls, monumental architecture, and a society split into specialized classes, including priests, merchants and craftworkers.

Kings and writing

Around a dozen city-states emerge. Each is ruled by an *ensi* (king), who lives in a palace and claims to govern on behalf of the local god. Cuneiform writing (see page 31) is invented.

c.5000 BCE

c.4500 BCE

c.3300–3100 BCE

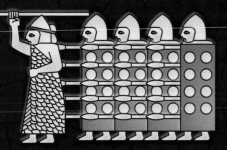

Warfare

The first recorded war in history takes place, between the cities of Lagash and Umma. A carving shows King Eannatum of Lagash leading his army to victory, marching over fallen enemies.

Royals tombs of Ur

Kings and queens of Ur are buried in tombs with treasures made of gold, silver, lapis lazuli, and carnelian. The tombs also contain the bodies of servants who have been sacrificed.

Bronze

Sumerians learn how to make bronze by mixing copper and tin. At first they use it to make tools and weapons, eventually creating sculptures with it.

c.2500 BCE

c.2750–2400 BCE

c.3000 BCE

Fall of Assyria

There are widespread rebellions against Assyrian rule, led by the Babylonians and the Medes. The Assyrian cities are burned, and Babylonia takes control of the Assyrian Empire.

Cyrus the Great

King Cyrus the Great of Persia conquers the Babylonian Empire. He claims to rule on behalf of Marduk, the chief god of the city of Babylon.

The Standard of Ur

This box was found in a royal tomb in the city of Ur. It was made around 2500 BCE and its mosaic decoration shows what life was like in early Mesopotamia. This side depicts warfare, while the other side shows life during peacetime.

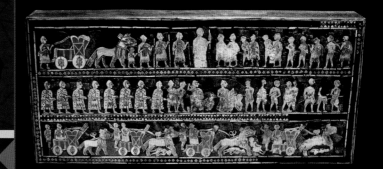

614–612 BCE

539 BCE

Senet

Board games are popular in ancient Egypt, with some royalty deciding to be buried with their games. A favorite game is senet, which is played on a board marked with 30 squares.

The royal game of Ur

This game is played on a board of 20 squares with four-sided dice and two sets of seven pieces. The aim is for a player to get their pieces from one end of the board to the other.

Tic-tac-toe

People all across the Roman Empire play a version of tic-tac-toe (also known today as noughts and crosses). The Roman version is called *terni lapilli* (meaning "three pebbles at a time").

Chess

This skill and strategy game is first played in either Northern India or Central Asia. As trade routes from India and Persia in West Asia expand, chess will reach Europe by 1000 CE.

c.3500 BCE

c.2600 BCE

1st century BCE

c.2800 BCE

Dice

People have been rolling objects as part of games for thousands of years, but the oldest known dice come from Shahr-e Sūkhté, a Bronze Age city in modern-day Iran. Dice soon become common.

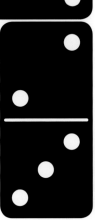

c.500 BCE

Go

Invented in China, go is played on a grid board, with players taking turns to place white and black stones at the grid intersections. It is one of the oldest board games that is still played today.

c.600

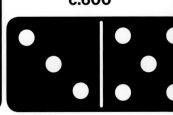

4th century CE

Pachisi

The Indian game of pachisi is played on a cross-shaped board. Six or seven cowrie shells are thrown to decide how many places a player moves their pieces. Emperor Akbar (1542–1605) has a gigantic board built, on which humans are moved around as game pieces.

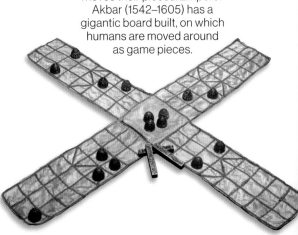

Fun and games

People have been sitting down to play games together for many thousands of years. Board games were popular in ancient Egypt, while card games were created in imperial China. Today, old favorites are enjoyed alongside new fantastical storytelling adventures. Games provide hours of entertainment and competition at every roll of the dice or choice of a card.

Snakes and ladders

Originally called mokshapat, this board game is invented by an Indian saint named Gyandev. It is meant to help children understand the difference between good and evil, with the ladders representing good and the snakes representing evil.

c.13th century

Monopoly

American Elizabeth Magie invents "The Landlord's Game" to warn children against pitfalls of capitalism. Magie's original board uses made-up street names, but later versions of the game (now called Monopoly) each use real place names from a city around the world.

In the 12th century, the Chinese created two-sided tiles with dots to represent numbers on each side. They were given the name "dominoes" in Italy and can be used to play a variety of games.

Modern board games

Families and groups of friends rediscover tabletop games as a fun group activity. There is a huge rise in people playing games and a surge in the production of new games. There are now many thousands of titles on the market to choose from.

21st century

Role play

Fantastical role-playing games become popular with the release of Dungeons and Dragons. With its nonhuman characters and magical narrative, the game soon spreads around the world.

1974

1904

9th century

Playing cards

The Chinese invent the earliest playing cards. When cards reach Europe, the suit markings are cups, gold coins, swords, and polo sticks. In about 1480, the French suits familiar today (hearts, diamonds, spades, and clubs) become standard.

1870

Mahjong

This tile-laying game is first developed in China and becomes popular across Asia. The game of skill and strategy is usually played with a set of 144 tiles featuring Chinese symbols.

1933

Scrabble

An American architect named Alfred Butts invents the word game Scrabble to mix spelling skills with a scoring system. During the 1950s, it becomes such a big hit that stores ration supplies per customer.

1944

Clue

This classic crime mystery board game is invented by British musician Anthony E. Pratt. Players are suspects who must follow clues to decide which of them is the murderer, where the crime was committed, and what weapon was used.

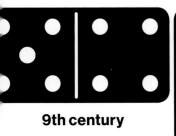

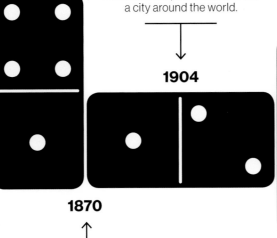

Ancient Egypt

Around 3000 BCE, the people of Egypt created the world's first united state. It was governed by a king known as a pharaoh, who was believed to be the representative of the gods on Earth. For 3,000 years, Egyptians wore similar white linen clothing, spoke the same language, and followed a regular cycle of work, governed by the annual flooding of the River Nile.

> **"Hail to you O Nile! ... Come, O Nile, come and prosper!"**
> *Hymn to the Nile*,
> c.2100 BCE

2181–2055 BCE

Dark period

The fall of the Old Kingdom after a period of political strife and widespread drought is followed by a time of disunity, called the First Intermediate Period. There are few monumental building projects during this time, as the power of royal authority was in decline.

2589–2566 BCE

Great Pyramid

At Giza, Pharaoh Khufu builds the Great Pyramid, which remains to this day the world's tallest pyramid. The whole nation takes part in the project, either hauling stone or growing food for the workforce.

2055–1710 BCE

Middle Kingdom

Egypt is reunited by Pharaoh Mentuhotep II, the founder of what historians would later call the Middle Kingdom. This period is remembered for its great achievements in art and literature, which leave behind clues about the daily lives of ancient Egyptians.

Mentuhotep II

1650 BCE

The Hyksos

A people from western Asia, the Hyksos, move into northern Egypt and destroy the Middle Kingdom. They bring with them the new technology of fighting from horse-drawn chariots. While the Hyksos rule the north, Egyptian pharaohs continue to govern in the south.

332–30 BCE

Ptolemaic Dynasty

Egypt is ruled by 15 Macedonian pharaohs, all called Ptolemy. The capital of Egypt during this period is Alexandria, founded by Alexander the Great on the Mediterranean coast. The last ruler is Queen Cleopatra (ruled 51–30 BCE). Egypt is then conquered by the Romans, bringing an end to the rule of ancient Egypt.

Coins showing Cleopatra

664–332 BCE

Foreign rulers

During the Late Period, Egypt is conquered by a series of foreign powers. The first invaders are the Nubians, followed by the Assyrians and the Persians. Finally, in 332 BCE, King Alexander the Great of Macedon, ruler of an empire that extends from Greece, takes control.

1279-1213 BCE

Ramesses the Great

Ramesses II rules for an astonishing 66 years and fathers around 100 children. He has many colossal statues built of himself, as well as a temple at Abu Simbel, where he is worshipped as a god.

c.4500 BCE

First settlements

Farming people settle in villages by the Nile. They grow wheat and barley, keep cattle and sheep, and make polished red pottery with blackened tops. This early culture is later called Badarian, after the site of El Badari, the remains of which were excavated in 1923.

c.3300 BCE

Early writing

Egyptians invent the world's first writing system: hieroglyphics. It uses hundreds of picture signs, standing for ideas, words, and sounds. These are carved on stone or painted on sheets of papyrus, a writing material made from the reeds along the Nile.

Early hieroglyphs on wooden labels

2667–2648 BCE

Stepped pyramid

Pharaoh Djoser, the first ruler of a period that historians call the Old Kingdom, builds the first pyramid. This is a royal tomb where the king's body, preserved as a mummy, is thought to live on after death. Djoser's pyramid has stepped rather than smooth sides and is Egypt's first monument to be built out of stone.

c.3100 BCE

A kingdom united

Egypt, previously two kingdoms, is united under one king. The first king we know of is called Narmer. He is shown in art as a warrior defeating enemies while wearing the crowns of Upper (southern) and Lower (northern) Egypt.

Narmer wears the white crown of Upper Egypt.

Narmer wears the red crown of Lower Egypt.

1550–1525 BCE

New Kingdom

Ahmose, ruler of Thebes, drives out the Hyksos and reunites Egypt, founding what would become known as the New Kingdom. Pharaohs are no longer buried in pyramids, but in hidden tombs in the Valley of the Kings, in the desert to the west of Thebes. The Theban god Amon-Re becomes chief Egyptian god.

Depiction of Amon-Re

1504–1425 BCE

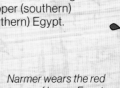

Egyptian Empire

Thutmose I aggressively expands Egyptian rule into Nubia, a country that lies to the south of Egypt, as well as into areas of western Asia. The Egyptian Empire continues to grow under his successors, Thutmose II (1492–1479 BCE) and Thutmose III (1479–1425 BCE).

Thutmose I

1336–1327 BCE

Tutankhamun

Under the rule of Pharaoh Tutankhamun, the old religion is restored. After his death at the age of around 18, Tutankhamun is buried in a tomb filled with treasures. Discovered in 1922, the tomb of Tutankhamun is the only unrobbed Egyptian royal tomb ever found.

1352–1336 BCE

Sun worship

Pharaoh Akhenaten makes sweeping changes to Egypt's religion, closing down the temples to the gods and introducing worship of the Aten, a disk that represents the Sun. He builds a new capital called Akhetaten (modern-day El Amarna), with open-air temples for the worship of the Sun.

Ancient monuments

For most of prehistory, people lived as nomadic hunter-gatherers and left behind little trace of their existence. It was only after people became settled farmers that they began to build monuments, such as tombs and temples. Most were simple structures, but some were built on an enormous scale that required hundreds of laborers—a sign they were built for powerful leaders.

Dolmens

In western Europe, people begin to build dolmens—tombs using three or more huge standing stones supporting a flat table-stone. These are covered with earth or rocks to form a mound called a barrow.

c.4000 BCE

10,000–9000 BCE

First temple

People in Göbekli Tepe in Turkey build the world's oldest religious structure, with more than 200 pillars arranged in 20 circles. Unusually, it seems to have been built by hunter-gatherers in the process of becoming farmers.

c.4500–2000 BCE

Standing stones

In Brittany in France, farming people set up more than 3,000 standing stones in long lines. Their purpose is a mystery, but it is possible that each one was placed in honor of a dead person.

Abu Simbel

At Abu Simbel in southern Egypt, Pharaoh Rameses II has a great temple carved out of solid rock. It is dedicated to three gods. Colossal statues of the pharaoh sit outside and line the temple's entrance hall.

1264–1244 BCE

Korean dolmens

In Korea, people begin to build dolmen tombs. Some stand above ground, but others have an underground burial chamber. About 45,000 are built, giving Korea the world's largest collection of dolmens.

700 BCE

c.250 BCE

Sanchi Stupa

At Sanchi in India, Emperor Ashoka builds a great stupa—a domed monument holding relics of the Buddha. Stupas are places of pilgrimage for Buddhists, who walk around them praying and meditating.

c.200 BCE

Great Pyramid of Cholula

The people of Cholula in Mexico build a pyramid temple to worship the god Quetzalcoatl. Over the next thousand years, it is rebuilt on a progressively bigger scale, until it is the largest pyramid in the world.

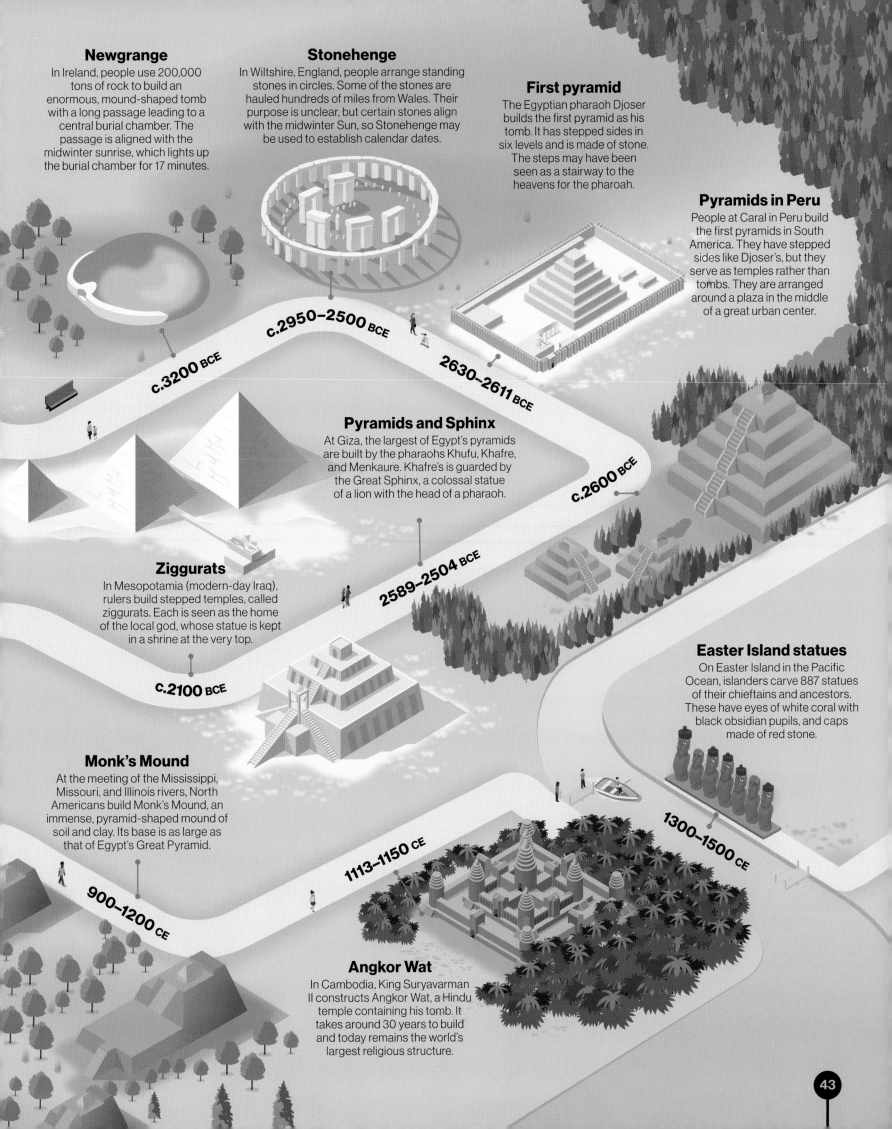

Newgrange

In Ireland, people use 200,000 tons of rock to build an enormous, mound-shaped tomb with a long passage leading to a central burial chamber. The passage is aligned with the midwinter sunrise, which lights up the burial chamber for 17 minutes.

Stonehenge

In Wiltshire, England, people arrange standing stones in circles. Some of the stones are hauled hundreds of miles from Wales. Their purpose is unclear, but certain stones align with the midwinter Sun, so Stonehenge may be used to establish calendar dates.

First pyramid

The Egyptian pharaoh Djoser builds the first pyramid as his tomb. It has stepped sides in six levels and is made of stone. The steps may have been seen as a stairway to the heavens for the pharoah.

Pyramids in Peru

People at Caral in Peru build the first pyramids in South America. They have stepped sides like Djoser's, but they serve as temples rather than tombs. They are arranged around a plaza in the middle of a great urban center.

c.3200 BCE

c.2950–2500 BCE

2630–2611 BCE

Pyramids and Sphinx

At Giza, the largest of Egypt's pyramids are built by the pharaohs Khufu, Khafre, and Menkaure. Khafre's is guarded by the Great Sphinx, a colossal statue of a lion with the head of a pharaoh.

c.2600 BCE

2589–2504 BCE

Ziggurats

In Mesopotamia (modern-day Iraq), rulers build stepped temples, called ziggurats. Each is seen as the home of the local god, whose statue is kept in a shrine at the very top.

c.2100 BCE

Easter Island statues

On Easter Island in the Pacific Ocean, islanders carve 887 statues of their chieftains and ancestors. These have eyes of white coral with black obsidian pupils, and caps made of red stone.

Monk's Mound

At the meeting of the Mississippi, Missouri, and Illinois rivers, North Americans build Monk's Mound, an immense, pyramid-shaped mound of soil and clay. Its base is as large as that of Egypt's Great Pyramid.

1300–1500 CE

1113–1150 CE

900–1200 CE

Angkor Wat

In Cambodia, King Suryavarman II constructs Angkor Wat, a Hindu temple containing his tomb. It takes around 30 years to build and today remains the world's largest religious structure.

The Great Sphinx

The ancient Egyptians built sphinx statues to guard important areas such as tombs and temples. The most famous sphinx is the Great Sphinx of Giza, situated on the west bank of the River Nile. It was carved out of a huge outcrop of limestone that sticks up above the desert floor to guard the pyramid of Khafre in Giza. It was built 4,500 years ago, and is one of the largest and oldest statues in the world. The Sphinx has a human head, probably that of Pharaoh Khafre, and the body of a lion.

Sharing stories

Many of the earliest stories were composed as poems, as the rhythm and repetition of poetry made it easier for storytellers to learn them. With the invention of writing around 6,000 years ago, these stories began to be written down. Drama and, much later, the novel developed as new forms of storytelling. Today, books are still a popular format for reading stories, but they are also available digitally as e-books or online.

In the story, the Monkey King had a magic staff that could shrink or grow in size.

13th century

13th–15th century

16th century

1623

Scandinavian sagas

Most Icelandic sagas are tales of historic voyages, battles, and kings of northern Europe. Some sagas tell of a legendary past full of dwarves and giants. As well as sagas, the Icelanders write down stories of Thor and Loki from Norse mythology.

Medieval romances

Tales of chivalrous knights going on quests and having heroic adventures are known in medieval Europe as romances. Old French and British legends of King Arthur and his Knights of the Round Table are written down as romances in the late Middle Ages.

Monkey magic

Journey to the West (also known as *Monkey*) is a Chinese novel based on the true story of a monk's journey to bring Buddhist scrolls from India to China. The novel adds characters from Chinese mythology, such as the Monkey King.

First Folio

Shakespeare adds many words to the English language and has a huge impact on the development of literature around the world. After his death, 36 of his plays are collected together for the first time in the *First Folio*.

1865

1884

1887

1914–1918

Wonderland

English clergyman Lewis Carroll's *Alice in Wonderland* is full of nonsense speech and fantastical characters. It brings about a "Golden Age" in which children's books focus on entertainment rather than education.

Great American Novel

US novelist Mark Twain's *Adventures of Huckleberry Finn* vividly portrays the American South and the language of its people. It is considered one of the "Great American Novels"—works that capture the spirit of America.

Elementary, my dear Watson

Scottish writer Sir Arthur Conan Doyle creates the world's best-known fictional detective, Sherlock Holmes, as well as his sidekick, Dr. Watson, in his novel *A Study in Scarlet*.

War poets

A number of British and French soldiers fighting on the front lines in World War I write about their horrific experiences in haunting poetry. Sadly, many of them never come home from the war.

The tale of Gilgamesh from Mesopotamia in modern-day Iraq is the oldest surviving epic.

Ancient Greek actors wore masks to identify the character they played.

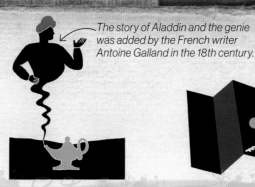

The story of Aladdin and the genie was added by the French writer Antoine Galland in the 18th century.

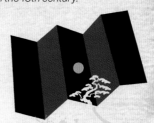

After 2100 BCE

Ancient epics

Societies of the ancient world produce long poems called epics. Performed by storytellers rather than written down, these epics celebrate a civilization's culture through stories of great heroes.

5th century BCE

Greek drama

Early Greek plays involve only a single actor and a chorus (a group of performers who comment on the action). Playwrights add a second and then a third actor to the stage, laying the foundations for Western drama.

8th–15th century CE

1001 stories

One Thousand and One Nights is a collection of popular stories from Arabia. Although they appear in Arabic folk tales, many of its well-known characters—Sinbad, Aladdin, and Ali Baba—will be added much later.

c.1000–1012

First novel

The *Tale of Genji* by the Japanese lady-in-waiting Murasaki Shikibu is maybe the world's first novel. Written on sheets of paper pasted and folded together, it tells the story of "Shining Genji," the son of an ancient Japanese emperor.

18th–19th century

Rise of the novel

The novel becomes an extremely popular form of literature. Many European and American writers produce their novels in serial form. They are published in sections as monthly parts to make them more affordable to the public.

1812–1822

Once upon a time

Brothers Jacob and Wilhelm Grimm collect traditional German folk tales such as Snow White and Hansel and Gretel, in *Children's and Household Tales*. The cruelty and violence of the original stories is toned down in future editions.

1818

Gothic horror

Mary Shelley writes *Frankenstein,* one of the greatest works of Gothic horror—a type of story that deals with the supernatural, ghosts, and haunted houses. One of the last examples of Gothic horror is *Dracula* (1897) by Bram Stoker.

1864

Science fiction

Science and fantasy meet in French writer Jules Verne's *Journey to the Center of the Earth* and, later, *20,000 Leagues Under the Sea* (1870). These stories are early masterpieces of what we now call science fiction.

1920s

Stream of consciousness

A new style of writing, called "stream of consciousness" attempts to show fragments of thoughts and feelings as they pass through a character's mind.

1950s

Postcolonial writing

As European powers lose hold of their international empires, writers from former colonies in Africa, South America, and Asia—particularly India—begin to write about the experience of being colonized.

1960s

Black voices

African-Americans inspired by the Civil Rights Movement (see pages 290–291) write about the experiences of their people. The decade also sees the rise of female African-American poets.

1997–2007

Harry Potter

British novelist J.K. Rowling's seven books about Harry Potter and the wizard school of Hogwarts become a worldwide phenomenon. The novels have since been translated into around 80 languages and have sold more than 450 million copies.

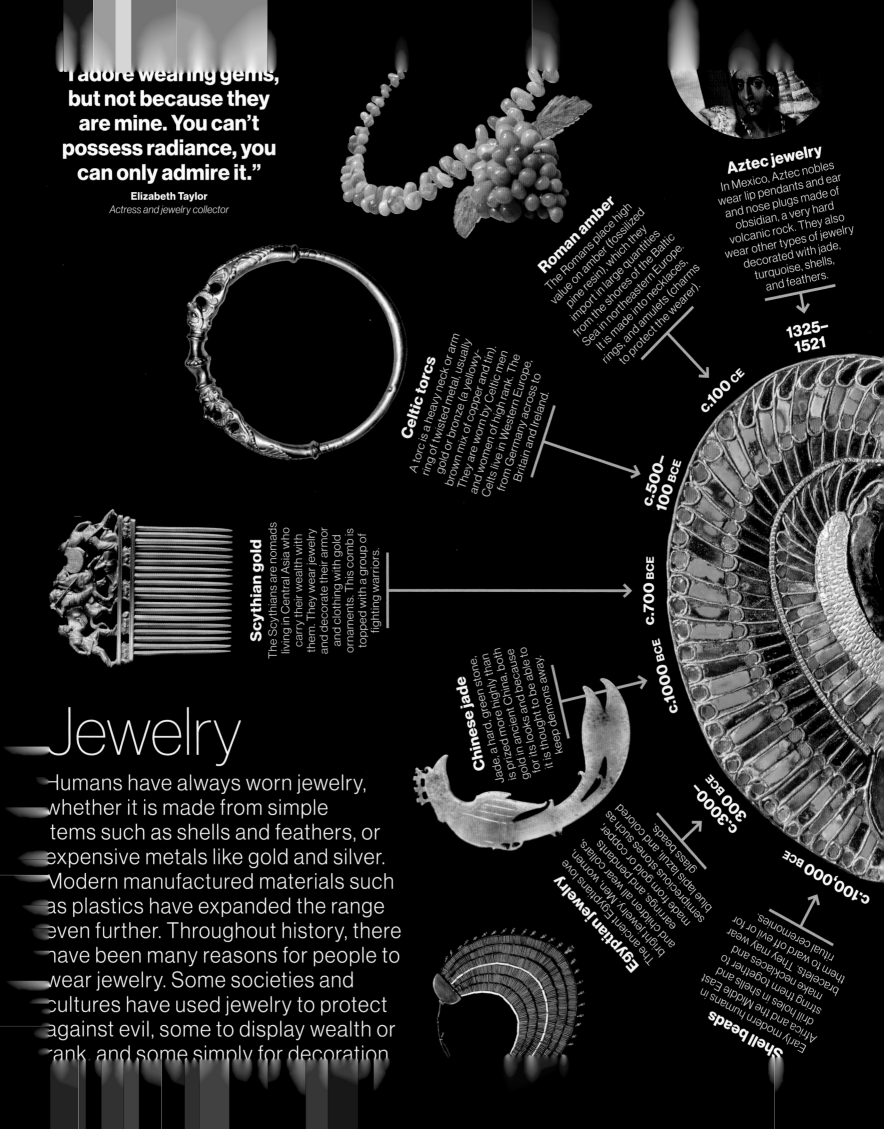

> "I adore wearing gems, but not because they are mine. You can't possess radiance, you can only admire it."

Elizabeth Taylor
Actress and jewelry collector

Aztec jewelry

In Mexico, Aztec nobles wear lip pendants and ear and nose plugs made of obsidian, a very hard volcanic rock. They also wear other types of jewelry decorated with jade, turquoise, shells, and feathers.

1325–1521

Roman amber

The Romans place high value on amber (fossilized pine resin), which they import in large quantities from the shores of the Baltic Sea in northeastern Europe. It is made into necklaces, rings, and amulets (charms to protect the wearer).

c.100 CE

Celtic torcs

A torc is a heavy neck or arm ring of twisted metal, usually gold or bronze (a yellowy-brown mix of copper and tin). They are worn by Celtic men and women of high rank. The Celts live in Western Europe, from Germany across to Britain and Ireland.

c.500–100 BCE

Scythian gold

The Scythians are nomads living in Central Asia who carry their wealth with them. They wear jewelry and decorate their armor and clothing with gold ornaments. This comb is topped with a group of fighting warriors.

c.700 BCE

Chinese jade

Jade, a hard, green stone, is prized more highly than gold in ancient China, both for its looks and because it is thought to be able to keep demons away.

c.1000 BCE

Jewelry

Humans have always worn jewelry, whether it is made from simple items such as shells and feathers, or expensive metals like gold and silver. Modern manufactured materials such as plastics have expanded the range even further. Throughout history, there have been many reasons for people to wear jewelry. Some societies and cultures have used jewelry to protect against evil, some to display wealth or rank, and some simply for decoration.

Egyptian jewelry

The ancient Egyptians love bright jewelry. Men, women, and children all wear collars, earrings and pendants, made from gold or copper, semiprecious stones such as blue lapis lazuli, and colored glass beads.

c.3000–300 BCE

Shell beads

Early modern humans in Africa and the Middle East drill holes in shells and string them together to make necklaces and bracelets. They may wear them to ward off evil or for ritual ceremonies.

c.100,000 BCE

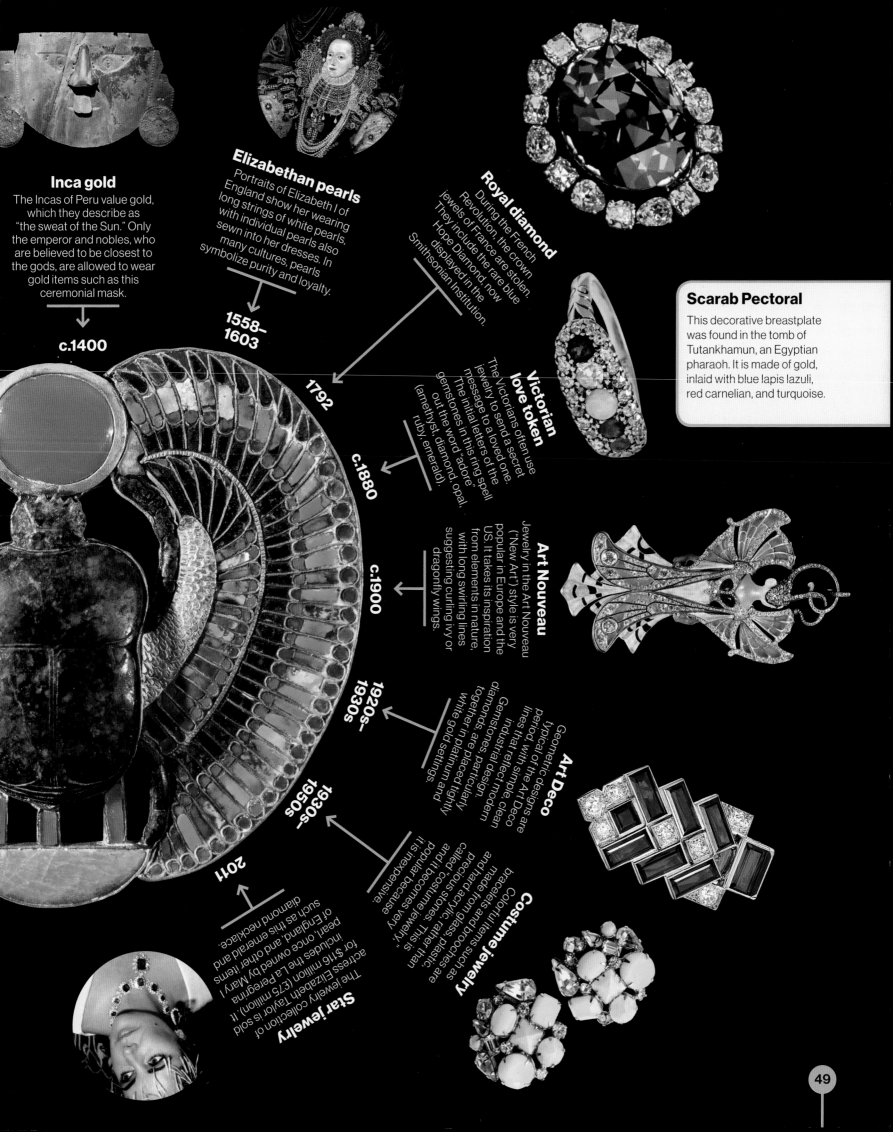

Inca gold

The Incas of Peru value gold, which they describe as "the sweat of the Sun." Only the emperor and nobles, who are believed to be closest to the gods, are allowed to wear gold items such as this ceremonial mask.

c.1400

Elizabethan pearls

Portraits of Elizabeth I of England show her wearing long strings of white pearls, with individual pearls also sewn into her dresses. In many cultures, pearls symbolize purity and loyalty.

1558–1603

Royal diamond

During the French Revolution, the crown jewels of France are stolen. They include the rare blue Hope Diamond, now displayed in the Smithsonian Institution.

1792

Victorian love token

The Victorians often use jewelry to send a secret message to a loved one. The initial letters of the gemstones in this ring spell out the word "adore" (amethyst, diamond, opal, ruby, emerald).

c.1880

Art Nouveau

Jewelry in the Art Nouveau ('New Art') style is very popular in Europe and the US. It takes its inspiration from elements in nature, with long swirling lines suggesting curling ivy or dragonfly wings.

c.1900

Art Deco

Geometric designs typical of the designs are lines that reflect the Art Deco period, with simple, clean Gemstones, particularly industrial design diamonds, are placed together modern white in platinum and placed tightly gold settings.

1920s–1930s

Costume jewelry

Colorful items such as bracelets and brooches are made from glass, plastic, and acrylic, rather than precious stones. This is called 'costume jewelry,' and it becomes very popular because it is inexpensive.

1930s–1950s

Star jewelry

The jewelry collection of actress Elizabeth Taylor is sold for $116 million (£75 million). It includes the La Peregrina pearl, once owned by Mary I of England, and other items such as this emerald and diamond necklace.

2011

Scarab Pectoral

This decorative breastplate was found in the tomb of Tutankhamun, an Egyptian pharaoh. It is made of gold, inlaid with blue lapis lazuli, red carnelian, and turquoise.

The story of sports

The story of sports began thousands of years ago, when ancient people first started playing ball games. As time passed, new sports emerged, along with competitions and international events at which to play them. In modern times, sports are a major source of exercise, entertainment for spectators, and a way for millions of professional athletes worldwide to test their skills.

Bowling beginnings

Discoveries of ancient balls and pins in an Egyptian grave date bowling back 5,000 years. Modern tenpin bowling will begin in 1841 in the US.

Ancient ball game

The Mayans play a speedy ball game called *pitz*. The objective is to pass a rubber ball through a stone hoop without using hands or feet. The Aztecs, Incas, and Olmecs play similar games.

3200 BCE

c.2000 BCE

World Series

The two US baseball leagues—the American League and the National League—compete for the end-of-year championship for the first time in what is today known as the World Series.

Modern Olympics

French aristocrat Pierre de Coubertin arranges a revival of the ancient Olympic Games. The competition is held in Athens, Greece with about 300 athletes from 14 countries. Events include swimming, cycling, weightlifting, wrestling, athletics, and the first marathon.

Soccer league

The world's first soccer league competition gets underway in England. Twelve teams take part, with Preston North End crowned champions at the end of the season.

Table tennis

During winters in Victorian England, houseguests make their own entertainment by turning their dining tables into mini tennis courts to play the first games of ping pong (also known as table tennis). Champagne corks are used as balls.

1903

1896

1888

1880s

Tour de France

The first Tour de France is held, lasting 19 days and covering 1,508 miles (2,428 km) along French roads. Although 60 competitors start the race, only 21 finish. The race was born to help boost the flagging sales of the cycling newspaper *L'Auto*.

Beach volleyball

This game is first played on the beach in Santa Monica, California. Today, the sport is played on beaches and artificial sand courts all around the world.

Football leagues

The National Football League begins with a meeting in Canton, Ohio. A second football league, named the American Football League, gets underway 40 years later. In 1967, the champions of the two leagues face each other in the first annual Super Bowl.

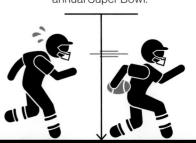

1903

1920s

1920

Ancient Olympics

At Olympia, a religious site in southwest Greece, the first recorded Olympic Games are held. They honor the protector of the people, Zeus. The Games are held every four years, with competitors often traveling long distances to participate.

Marathon message

When a messenger named Pheidippides runs from the Battle of Marathon to Athens, Greece with news of a victory, the distance of 25 miles (40 km) becomes the measurement for a marathon. In 1921, the distance will be standardized as 26.2 miles (42.195 km).

Hand tennis

European monks play the earliest version of tennis using their hands to hit the ball. By the 1870s, a similar game named *Sphairistike* is played in the UK with wooden rackets. Renamed tennis, the game's first championship will be played at Wimbledon in 1877.

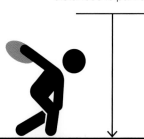 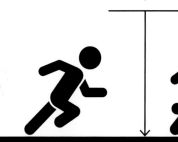 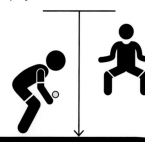

776 BCE   **490 BCE**   **1100s CE**

Boxing gloves

Wearing padded boxing gloves becomes compulsory for competitive fighters. However, similar attire had already been seen in ancient Greece, where fighters covered their hands in animal hide, and in ancient Rome, where gladiators used metal to really pack a punch!

Cricket

The Marylebone Cricket Club in London introduces rules to turn a 16th-century game into the sport we now call cricket.

Bicycle design

Italian artist and inventor Leonardo da Vinci sketches the first bicycle design, complete with pedals and a chain. Bicycles and competitive cycling sports do not develop until centuries later.

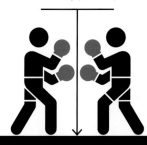 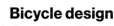  

1867   **1788**   **1490**

World Cup

The biggest soccer competition gets underway in Uruguay. Thirteen teams contest it, with the host nation emerging as the champions. The tournament has been held every four years since, except when World War II twice caused its postponement.

Paralympics

The first Paralympic Games takes place in Rome, Italy. More than 400 athletes take part in events including archery, swimming, table tennis, and basketball.

Women's World Cup

The first competition of the FIFA Women's World Cup is held in China, with the US beating Norway 2-1 in the final. The tournament has been held every four years since.

1930   **1960**   **1991**

Ancient Greece

The first great civilization in Europe began in ancient Greece. During the high point of Greek culture (800–300 BCE), the Greeks invented science, philosophy, theater, and democracy. They introduced the alphabet to Europe, and their art, architecture, and literature left a lasting legacy.

Minoans of Crete

On the island of Crete, the Minoan civilization builds large palaces and trades with the Greek mainland. Bulls are sacred animals in their religion.

From c. 2900 BCE

Greek colonies

The Greeks establish overseas settlements around the Mediterranean and Black Seas. These include Emporion (Empuries) in Spain, Neapolis (Naples) in Italy, Massilia (Marseilles) in France, Syracuse in Sicily, Naucratis in Egypt, Cyrene in Libya, and Olbia in the Ukraine.

750–500 BCE

Mycenaean civilization

On the Greek mainland, the Mycenaeans build fortified palaces at Mycenae, Thebes, and Athens. They are warlike people, fighting from chariots and wearing bronze armor with boar-tusk helmets.

From c. 1600 BCE

Iliad and Odyssey

Two epic poems are composed, according to tradition, by Homer. The *Iliad* tells of a mythical war against Troy, and the *Odyssey* is the story of one hero's journey home from the war.

c. 750 BCE

Greek pottery

Greek artists in Corinth begin to make "black figure" vases, with figures painted in black on the red or white background of the vase. Around 525 BCE, Athenians invent the "red figure" style, with outlines of figures left in the red of the clay while the background is painted black.

c. 700 BCE

Olympic Games

The first recorded Olympic Games are held at Olympia in honor of the god Zeus. Held once every 4 years, the games give the Greeks a common dating system.

776 BCE

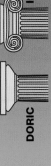

DORIC   **IONIC**

Greek architecture

The Greeks begin to build stone temples, replacing earlier timber buildings. Two main styles emerge— sturdy Doric on the mainland, and the more delicate Ionic in Ionia (in present-day Turkey).

c. 600 BCE

Athenian democracy

The Athenians drive out Hippias, a tyrant ruler, and establish the first democracy. All citizens can vote directly on laws—but women, slaves, and foreigners are not considered to be citizens.

508 BCE

Greek drama

The Athenian playwright Aeschylus writes his first recorded tragedy. Plays are performed in honor of Dionysus, god of wine, at first in the marketplace and later in an open-air theater.

Greek–Persian Wars

The Persians make two unsuccessful attempts to conquer Greece. Resistance is led by the cities of Athens and Sparta. The Persians sack Athens, but are then defeated at sea and on land.

Parthenon

The Athenians rebuild the temples on the Acropolis, a hilltop citadel in Athens. The Parthenon, a new marble temple to Athena, is constructed at the same site.

First history book

Herodotus writes the first history book, an account of the Greek–Persian Wars, together with descriptions of the customs of foreign peoples.

Pottery as history

Greek vases were painted with scenes from myths, warfare, sporting events, and daily life. Unlike bronze statues, which were mostly melted down for their metal by later civilizations, painted vases have survived because they were often buried as tomb offerings.

499 BCE

490–479 BCE

447 BCE

c. 440 BCE

"I believe that the Earth is very large and that we (Greeks) ... live in a small part of it, like ants or frogs about a pond."

Plato, *Phaedo* (c. 380 BCE)

Peloponnesian Wars

Athens and Sparta fight the Peloponnesian Wars, which end in a Spartan victory. Sparta replaces Athens as the dominant city-state.

Academy

The philosopher Plato founds the Academy, an exclusive "school" where he gives lectures and poses problems to be solved.

Alexander the Great

Uniting Greece under his rule, Alexander of Macedon conquers the Persian Empire. A new age begins, in which Greek cities are founded as far east as India.

431–404 BCE

387 BCE

336–323 BCE

Greek city-states

The Greeks were divided into scores of city-states. Each city-state, known as a polis, included the city and surrounding countryside. It operated as a small state with its own laws, calendar, public assemblies, and coins.

735–715 BCE
Sparta conquers the city-state of Messenia.

550 BCE
Sparta becomes the leader of a confederation of city-states.

478–454 BCE
The alliance led by Athens against Persia becomes the Athenian Empire.

431 BCE
Peloponnesian Wars begin between Sparta and the Athenian Empire.

404 BCE
Sparta finally defeats Athens, overthrowing its democracy.

Extent of influence
By 500 BCE, city-states controlled the entire Greek mainland, as well as coastlines across the Aegean Sea.

395–387 BCE
Sparta wins a war against Corinth, Argos, Thebes, and Athens.

378–362 BCE
Sparta wins a series of wars against Thebes for leadership of Greece.

338 BCE
Philip of Macedon defeats Thebes and Athens at the Battle of Chaeronea.

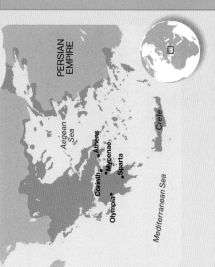

PERSIAN EMPIRE

Aegean Sea
Corinth
Athens
Mycenae
Sparta
Olympia
Mediterranean Sea
Crete

Mathematics

Since prehistoric times, people have been finding different ways to count and measure things in the world. In most cultures, mathematics soon developed far beyond basic counting, and historical artifacts such as books, drawings, and tools have helped us track the evolution of these mathematical ideas. Today, we use math in almost everything we do, from telling time to building things.

c.2560 BCE
Building the Great Pyramid

Ancient Egyptians' knowledge of right angles helps them to build the Great Pyramid, an architectural wonder whose construction involves precise measurements and the perfect alignment of at least 2.5 million stones. Present-day mathematicians are amazed by how complex the Egyptians' calculations are.

c.30,000 BCE
Ancient tallies

Before written numbers are invented, prehistoric people make marks in wood, clay, bone, or stone to count things such as passing days or animals in their herds.

c.3000 BCE
Ancient fractions

Ancient Egypt is one of the first civilizations to use fractions. This advancement is referred to in the *Rhind Papyrus*, an ancient mathematics textbook written around 1550 BCE that won't be discovered until thousands of years later in a tomb in Thebes in Egypt.

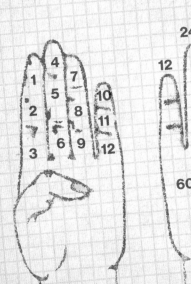

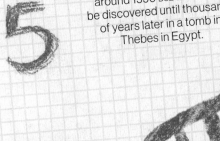

c.3500 BCE
First numbers

People in the Sumerian civilization in Mesopotamia (modern-day Iraq) devise the first system to use symbols to stand for the numbers of objects. The system is sexagesimal, meaning that it uses 60 as its base. This is based on the Sumerian method of counting on their hands. They count each finger segment on one hand to reach 12, and multipy that by five (the number of fingers on the other hand) to reach 60.

c.3000 BCE
Piece of Pi

The Babylonian people in Mesopotamia calculate that a circle's circumference is about three times the size of its diameter. This ratio is important as it applies to any circle of any size. We now know that this number is 3.141592..., with the numbers after the decimal point continuing forever. This number is represented by the Greek symbol pi (π).

c.500 BCE
The golden ratio
The ancient Greeks are fascinated by a ratio, known as the golden ratio, which they discover can be used to draw attractive patterns of rectangles. They build temples using this ratio, as it is said to create shapes that are pleasing to the eye.

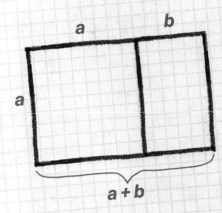

$a + b$

1655
To infinity
The concept of a number going on forever, known as infinity, has been discussed since ancient times. However, British mathematician John Wallis is the first person to come up with a symbol for infinity. ∞ is still used to represent infinity today.

10, 000, 000, 000, 000, 000
000, 000, 000, 000, 000, 000
000, 000, 000, 000, 000, 000
000, 000, 000, 000, 000, 000
000, 000, 000, 000, 000, 000
000, 000, 000, 000, = 1 googol

1920
Googol
US mathematician Edward Kasner asks his nine-year-old nephew what to call the number 1 followed by 100 zeros, and he suggests "googol." The number 1 followed by a googol of zeros is a googolplex, and 1 followed by a googolplex of zeros is a googolplexian, the biggest named number to date.

5
8
1
3
2

c.500 BCE
Triangle theory
Ancient Greek mathematician Pythagoras presents a theory of right-angled triangles, which can be used to work out the length of any unknown sides, and is used in many other math problems. It is known by the formula $a^2 + b^2 = c^2$, where the letters refer to the length of each side of the triangle.

1415
Artistic mathematics
Renaissance artists discover they can use math to make pictures look more three-dimensional by drawing distant objects smaller. This geometrical approach, known as perspective, is first adopted by Italian designer and artist Fillipo Brunelleschi.

1202
Fibonacci sequence
Italian mathematician Fibonacci devises a special sequence of numbers in which each number is found by adding together the two numbers before it: 0, 1, 1, 2, 3, 5, 8, 13, 21, and so on. This sequence can be used to draw a perfect spiral pattern, and will go on to be used to write computer programs, too.

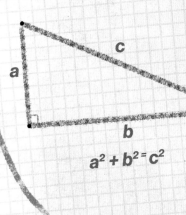

$$a^2 + b^2 = c^2$$

c.630 CE
Zero
The idea of zero to represent nothing is introduced in a manuscript by Indian mathematician Brahmagupta, written around 630 CE. The creation of zero is one of the greatest breakthroughs in math, as it allows us to write huge numbers without the need to create new digits.

c.800
Known numbers
Persian mathematician Al-Khwarizmi adapts a number system in which Hindu-Arabic symbols stand for the number of objects, to create the system most used today. In this, the numerals 0 to 9 are used to represent all numbers. In 300 years, these numbers will be introduced to Europe.

Democracy
had its origins in the
where citizens met in assemblies
important decisions. Democracy declined in the
different form: Voters could now choose representatives to make

The story of

Greek democracy

In the ancient world, important decisions were made by the wealthy. This all changes when a statesman from the Greek city-state of Athens named Cleisthenes revamps the system by giving ordinary citizens political rights. As a result, historians now refer to him as "the father of Athenian democracy." However, women, slaves, and foreigners are not part of the new democracy, which lasts two centuries.

A STATUE OF CLEISTHENES

507 BCE

Magna Carta

The Magna Carta ("Great Charter") is written by English barons after a period of heavy taxation by the king. This important document states that the monarch is not above the law, and promises to protect certain rights through a council of 25 barons, which gradually develops into a parliament. By 1265, the English parliament features ordinary people alongside nobles.

KING JOHN SIGNING THE MAGNA CARTA

1215 CE

US Constitution

Representatives of the 13 former British colonies that make up the newly formed United States of America meet to establish rules about how the new nation should be run. This leads to the drafting of the US Constitution, the supreme law of the United States, which among other rules, states that the country should have an elected president.

THE FIRST PAGE OF THE US CONSTITUTION

1787

Independence for Liberia

The colony of Liberia, settled by freed US slaves who had decided to emigrate to Africa, declares independence. Joseph Jenkins Roberts, a merchant and politician, becomes the first president of Liberia, which is the first democratic nation in the history of Africa.

JOSEPH JENKINS ROBERTS

1847

in the West
ancient city of Athens,
to cast their votes directly about
Middle Ages, and when it reappeared it took a
decisions on their behalf in gatherings called parliaments.

democracy

"I have a dream"

Civil rights campaigner Martin Luther King Jr. gives his famous "I have a dream" speech in Washington, DC. The government introduces the Civil Rights Act in 1964, keeping employers from discriminating against people on the grounds of race, religion, or nationality. The Voting Rights Act of 1965 gives most black people the right to vote.

Fall of the Berlin Wall

The wall that had split communist East Berlin from democratic West Berlin for 28 years is finally knocked down when East and West Germany are reunited. Democracy begins to return to all of Germany.

End to Apartheid

A blow against apartheid comes when prominent anti-apartheid campaigners are released from prison, including Nelson Mandela, who had been imprisoned for 27 years. The South African word for "separateness," *apartheid* refers to huge restrictions to the freedoms of black people in South Africa that were enshrined by law for more than four decades. Apartheid law is eventually abolished in 1991.

Electronic Voting

Estonia is the first country to hold elections using electronic voting machines. These are a way to encourage young and busy people to vote in governmental elections, creating a more democratic society.

**MARTIN LUTHER KING JR.
IN WASHINGTON, DC**

**KNOCKING DOWN
THE BERLIN WALL**

**NELSON
MANDELA**

**VOTING WITH AN
ELECTRONIC MACHINE**

1963

1989

1990

2005

Rise of the Celts

During the Iron Age, the people we now call Celts spread across most of Europe from their original homeland north of the Alps. Celtic peoples shared common religious beliefs and spoke related languages, which are still spoken today in parts of northwest Europe. The Celts were feared warriors and skilled metalworkers.

c.1300–800 BCE

Urnfield culture
The Urnfield culture, from present-day Italy and east-central Europe, spreads across the continent. When a wealthy person dies, they are cremated and buried, often with bronze ornaments and weapons.

c.800–500 BCE

People of Hallstatt
These Celtic people, from what is now Austria, bury their dead with bronze weapons, ornaments, and bowls, which are all decorated with geometric patterns. Hallstatt is the first clearly defined Celtic culture.

c.450–50 BCE

La Tène culture
People of the La Tène culture create metalwork covered with flowing decoration. The culture is later named after the La Tène site in modern-day Switzerland, where many artifacts from their culture have since been found.

c.400–390 BCE

Gauls in Italy
Celts move into what's now northern Italy. In 396 BCE, they raid the major Etruscan city of Melpum (modern-day Milan), and then settle across the Po Valley to the east of the Apennines. The Romans call them Galli (Gauls).

390 BCE

Gauls sack Rome
Gauls capture and ransack Rome, although they are prevented from capturing the important Capitol Hill when a flock of geese raises the alarm. The Romans pay the Gauls a huge ransom to make them leave.

> **"The whole race... is madly fond of war, high spirited, and quick to battle..."**
> **Strabo**, *Geographica*, early 1st century CE

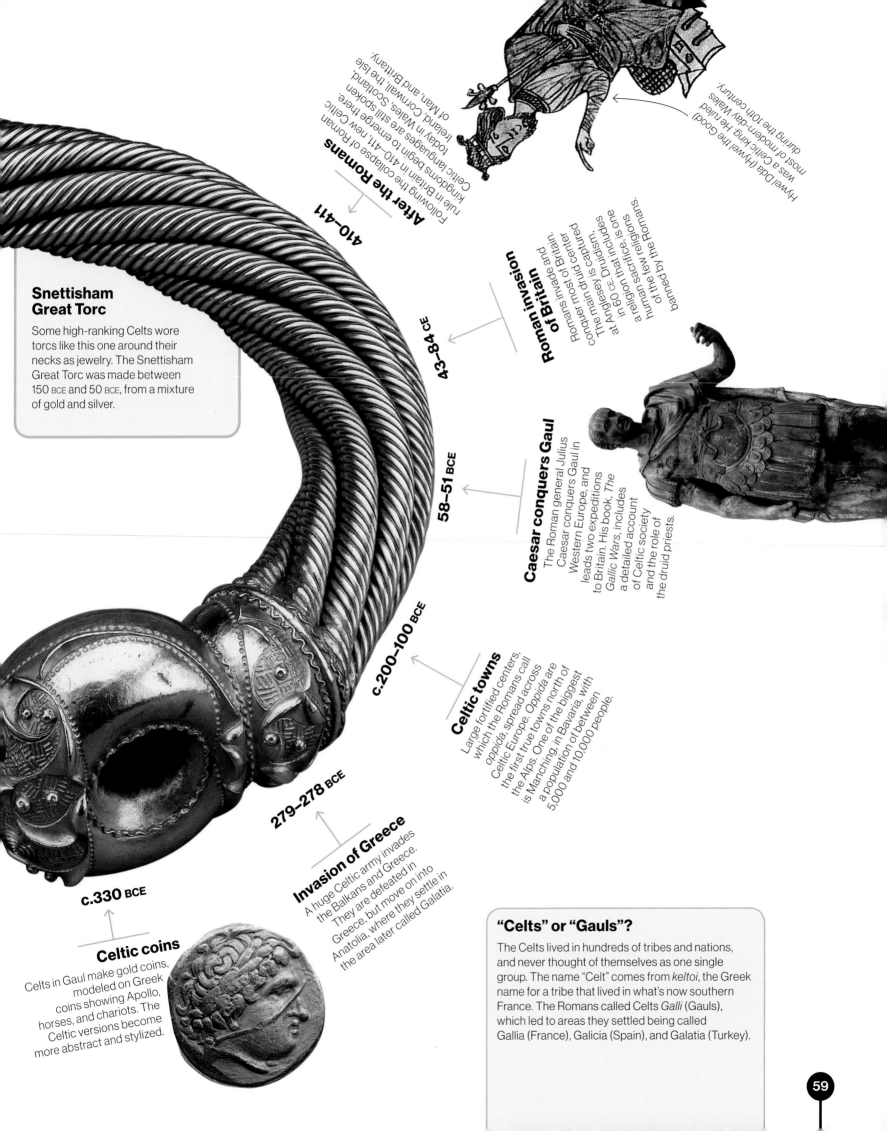

Snettisham Great Torc

Some high-ranking Celts wore torcs like this one around their necks as jewelry. The Snettisham Great Torc was made between 150 BCE and 50 BCE, from a mixture of gold and silver.

410–411

After the Romans

Following the collapse of Roman rule in Britain in 410–411, new Celtic kingdoms begin to emerge there. Celtic languages are still spoken today in Wales, Scotland, Ireland, Cornwall, the Isle of Man, and Brittany.

Hywel Dda (Hywel the Good) was a Celtic king. He ruled most of modern-day Wales during the 10th century.

43–84 CE

Roman invasion of Britain

Romans invade and conquer most of Britain. The main druid center at Anglesey is captured in 60 CE. Druidism, a religion that includes human sacrifice, is one of the few religions banned by the Romans.

58–51 BCE

Caesar conquers Gaul

The Roman general Julius Caesar conquers Gaul in Western Europe, and leads two expeditions to Britain. His book, *The Gallic Wars*, includes a detailed account of Celtic society and the role of the druid priests.

c.200–100 BCE

Celtic towns

Large fortified centers, which the Romans call *oppida*, spread across Celtic Europe. *Oppida* are the first true towns north of the Alps. One of the biggest is Manching, in Bavaria, with a population of between 5,000 and 10,000 people.

279–278 BCE

Invasion of Greece

A huge Celtic army invades the Balkans and Greece. They are defeated in Greece, but move on into Anatolia, where they settle in the area later called Galatia.

c.330 BCE

Celtic coins

Celts in Gaul make gold coins, modeled on Greek coins showing Apollo, horses, and chariots. The Celtic versions become more abstract and stylized.

"Celts" or "Gauls"?

The Celts lived in hundreds of tribes and nations, and never thought of themselves as one single group. The name "Celt" comes from *keltoi*, the Greek name for a tribe that lived in what's now southern France. The Romans called Celts *Galli* (Gauls), which led to areas they settled being called Gallia (France), Galicia (Spain), and Galatia (Turkey).

The Persian Empire

The Achaemenid Persian Empire, which lasted from the 6th to the 4th century BCE, was the world's first major empire. It was vast and powerful and, at its height, stretched from Egypt to northwest India. Unlike many other ancient empires, the Persians showed respect for the customs of the people they ruled.

Darius's palace at Susa
Darius the Great had several palaces, including one at Susa (in modern-day Iran). The walls were decorated with brightly colored glazed bricks and showed an imperial guard of archers as well as mythical animals.

550 BCE

547–546 BCE

539 BCE

525 BCE

Cyrus the Great
King Astyages of Media (a region of modern-day northwest Iran) is overthrown by his subject Cyrus. Cyrus founds the Achaemenid Empire, also known as the First Persian Empire.

Lydia and Lycia
King Croesus of Lydia (a region in modern-day western Turkey) sees the fall of Media as a chance to invade the region. Cyrus counterattacks, and eventually conquers Lydia and Lycia (in modern-day southern Turkey).

Babylon
Cyrus conquers the Babylonian Empire (see page 36). He makes his capital Babylon, whose Ishtar Gate is shown above. Cyrus allows the Jews, who have been exiled in Babylon, to return home to Jerusalem.

Cambyses II
Cyrus's son, Cambyses II, conquers Egypt. Cambyses captures the Egyptian pharaoh Psamtik III. Psamtik is initially well treated, but is later executed for secretly trying to act against the Persians.

492 BCE

490 BCE

480–479 BCE

C.457 BCE

Darius's conquests
Darius conquers Macedonia and Thrace. He sends ambassadors to all Greek cities, demanding they accept him as king. In Athens and Sparta, the ambassadors are executed.

Defeat at Marathon
Darius sends an army by sea to invade Greece. The Persians capture many Greek islands, and loot and destroy Eretria. They are then defeated at Marathon by an army from Athens.

Second Persian invasion
Darius's son Xerxes I makes a second attempt to conquer Greece. The Persians ransack Athens, but are then defeated at Salamis and, a year later, at Plataea (see page 154).

Artaxerxes I
The son of Xerxes, Artaxerxes I, allows the Jews to rebuild the Jerusalem Temple, which had been destroyed by the Babylonians. This is described in the Torah and the Bible.

How the Persians ruled

The Persian Empire was too large to be ruled directly by a single king. It was therefore divided into 20 provinces, called satrapies. Each had a satrap (governor), usually a Persian noble appointed by the king. The provinces paid tribute (taxes) to the king, provided soldiers for his armies, and were punished if they rebelled. Otherwise, they were free to manage their own affairs, preserving their languages, customs, and religions.

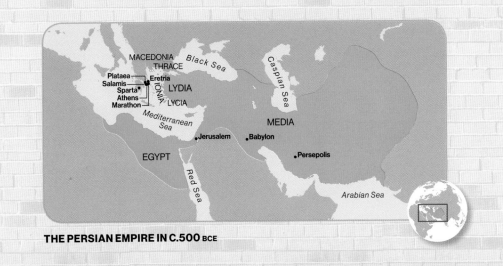

THE PERSIAN EMPIRE IN C.500 BCE

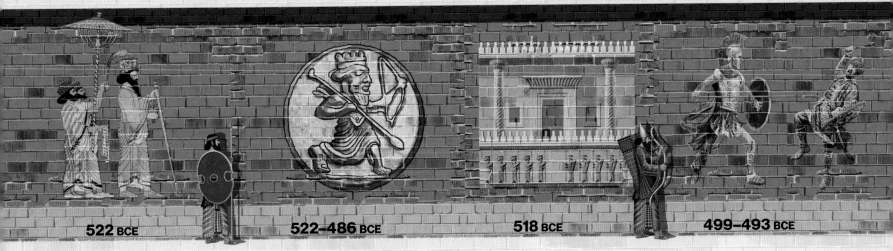

522 BCE

522–486 BCE

518 BCE

499–493 BCE

Darius the Great
After Cambyses' death, a Persian nobleman named Darius seizes power. At first he does not have the support of the people, but with his loyal army, he is able to suppress any revolts in his first year.

Organizing the empire
Darius the Great reorganizes government, creating the satrapies (see panel), a civil service, and a network of roads for official use. He issues a gold coin called a daric to be used as money across the empire.

Persepolis
Darius builds a new capital at Persepolis (called Parsa in Persian). His great palace has walls covered with stone relief sculptures, showing the citizens of the empire bringing gifts in tribute to him.

Greek rebellion
The eastern Greek cities of the region of Ionia rebel against Persian rule. They are helped by western Greeks, from Athens and Eretria. After the rebels are defeated, Darius vows to punish Athens and Eretria.

c.440 BCE

424–423 BCE

401 BCE

336–330 BCE

First historian
Herodotus, a Greek living in the Persian Empire, writes *The Histories*, the first-known history book. He describes the rise of the Persians and the customs within the empire.

Three kings
After Artaxerxes' death, three of his sons proclaim themselves king. Xerxes II is murdered by his brother Sogdianus, who is then killed by Ochus. Ochus then rules as Darius II.

The Greeks in Asia
Cyrus the Younger tries and fails to seize power from his brother, Artaxerxes II, using 10,000 Greek soldiers. After Cyrus's death, the Greeks fight their way home from Asia.

The fall of the empire
Alexander the Great of Macedonia conquers the Persian Empire. He defeats Darius III in two great battles, at Issus and Gaugamela, and burns down the palace at Persepolis.

The Battle of Issus

This Roman floor mosaic from around 100 BCE was discovered during excavations at the buried city of Pompeii in southern Italy. It is made out of around a million small mosaic tiles. The artwork is thought to illustrate the Battle of Issus between the armies of Alexander the Great and Darius III of Persia in the year 333 BCE. Alexander, seen on horseback (above), leads his army into battle. King Darius of Persia, riding in a chariot drawn by horses, is preparing to flee, only turning to glance back at his opponent.

Prehistory

The period before written records were invented around 5,000 years ago is known as prehistory. Most of what we know about this time comes from remains left behind, such as tools, bones, and ruined buildings. Until recently, it was difficult to tell how old these objects were, but scientific advances have allowed us to put together a much clearer picture of not only human history, but also the origin of life on Earth, and even of the Universe itself.

13.5 billion years ago
The first stars are born.

4.3 billion years ago
Life begins on Earth.

252 million years ago
Dinosaurs become the dominant life form on Earth.

1 million years ago
The ancestors of humans begin to use fire.

13.8 billion years ago
The Universe comes into existence with the Big Bang.

4.6 billion years ago
The Sun, planets, and other objects that make up our solar system are formed.

66 million years ago
The dinosaurs die out in a mass extinction event.

7–6 million years ago
Apes in Africa evolve the ability to walk upright.

200,000 years ago
Modern humans first appear in Africa.

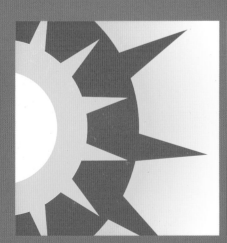

The Big Bang
The Universe started with the Big Bang (see pages 12–13). Over billions of years, stars, galaxies, and eventually our own solar system were formed.

Early life
The first forms of life on Earth were simple organisms, but they evolved over time into the many varieties of plants and animals known today (see pages 14–15).

Dinosaurs
Millions of years ago, dinosaurs walked, swam, or flew on Earth (see pages 16–17). Until they became extinct, they were the dominant animals on the planet.

Early humans
The ancestors of humans, known as hominins, evolved from tree-dwelling apes (see pages 20–21). Over time, they began to use tools and make fire.

PREHISTORY

Before 3000 BCE

AFTER 1914

1750–1914

THE AGE OF REVOLUTION

BEFORE 3000 BCE

PREHISTORY

CONTENTS

Senior Art Editor Smiljka Surla
Senior Editor Sam Atkinson
Project Editors Steven Carton, Ben Ffrancon Davies, Sarah Edwards, Sarah MacLeod,
Ben Morgan, Sophie Parkes, Laura Sandford, Pauline Savage, Amanda Wyatt
US Editors Kayla Dugger, Christy Lusiak
Project Designers Sunita Gahir, Alex Lloyd, Gregory McCarthy,
Stefan Podhorodecki, Michelle Staples, Jacqui Swan, Sadie Thomas
Illustrators Acute Graphics, Peter Bull, Edwood Burn, Sunita Gahir, Clare Joyce,
KJA Artists, Arran Lewis, Alex Lloyd, Maltings Partnership, Gus Scott
DK Media Archive Romaine Werblow
Picture Researchers Sarah Hopper, Jo Walton
Managing Editor Lisa Gillespie
Managing Art Editor Owen Peyton Jones
Producers, Pre-Production David Almond, Andy Hilliard
Senior Producers Alex Bell, Mary Slater
Jacket Designers Surabhi Wadhwa-Gandhi, Juhi Sheth, Smiljka Surla
Jackets Design Development Manager Sophia MTT
Jackets Editor Amelia Collins
Publisher Andrew Macintyre
Art Director Karen Self
Associate Publishing Director Liz Wheeler
Design Director Phil Ormerod
Publishing Director Jonathan Metcalf
Consultant Philip Parker
Contributors Laura Buller, Peter Chrisp, Alexander Cox, Susan Kennedy,
Andrea Mills, Sally Regan

DK Delhi
DTP Designers Jaypal Singh Chauhan, Syed Mohammed Farhan
Senior DTP Designers Neeraj Bhatia, Jagtar Singh
Jackets Designer Juhi Sheth
Jacket Senior DTP Designer Harish Aggarwal
Jacket DTP Designer Rakesh Kumar
Jackets Editorial Coordinator Priyanka Sharma
Managing Jackets Editor Saloni Singh

First American Edition, 2018
Published in the United States by DK Publishing
1450 Broadway, Suite 801, New York, NY 10018

Copyright © 2018 Dorling Kindersley Limited
DK, a Division of Penguin Random House LLC
18 19 20 21 22 10 9 8 7 6 5 4 3 2 1
001–306015–Oct/2018

DK books are available at special discounts when purchased in bulk for sales promotions,
premiums, fund-raising, or educational use. For details, contact: DK Publishing Special Markets,
1450 Broadway, Suite 801, New York, NY 10018
SpecialSales@dk.com
Printed and bound in China

A WORLD OF IDEAS:
SEE ALL THERE IS TO KNOW

www.dk.com

Smithsonian

THE SMITHSONIAN
Established in 1846, the Smithsonian—the world's largest museum and research complex—includes
19 museums and galleries and the National Zoological Park. The total number of artifacts, works of art, and
specimens in the Smithsonian's collection is estimated at 154 million. The Smithsonian is a renowned research
center, dedicated to public education, national service, and scholarship in the arts, sciences, and history.

Traveling through time

The earliest events in this book took place a very long time ago. Some dates may be followed by BYA, short for "billion years ago," MYA, short for "million years ago," or YA, short for "years ago." Other dates have BCE and CE after them. These are short for "before the Common Era" and "Common Era." The Common Era dates from when people think Jesus was born. Where the exact date of an event is not known, "c." is used. This is short for the Latin word *circa*, meaning "around," and indicates that the date is approximate.

TIMELINES OF EVERYTHING

TIMELINES OF EVERYTHING

The wheel

One of the most important technological developments of the prehistoric era was the wheel (see pages 28–29). Invented independently by different cultures around the world, the wheel revolutionized transportation. It was also crucial to later advancements in farming, construction, industry, and engineering.

c.9000 BCE
Metalworking begins in Mesopotamia in West Asia.

9000–4000 BCE
Early farmers establish the first villages.

c.4000 BCE
The first great cities arise in Mesopotamia.

c.3500 BCE
The first wheels used for transportation appear in Mesopotamia.

c.11,000–9000 BCE
The development of farming allows people to produce their own food.

c.8000 BCE
Communities begin to construct walls around their settlements.

c.3300 BCE
The Egyptians develop hieroglyphs, the first system of writing.

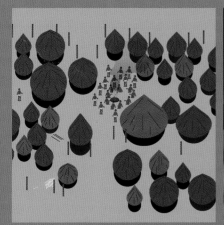

Settling down

Early humans moved from place to place in search of food. With the development of farming (see pages 22–23), people built villages and worked the land.

Working with metal

As humans discovered the technology of creating items from copper, bronze, and iron (see pages 24–25), they crafted stronger tools and weapons.

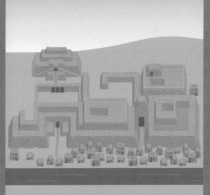

The first cities

Some villages continued to grow, becoming towns and eventually cities (see pages 26–27). These population hubs were bustling centers of trade.

Writing

With the invention of writing (see pages 30–31), people could leave records to be read by later generations. The period known as prehistory came to an end.

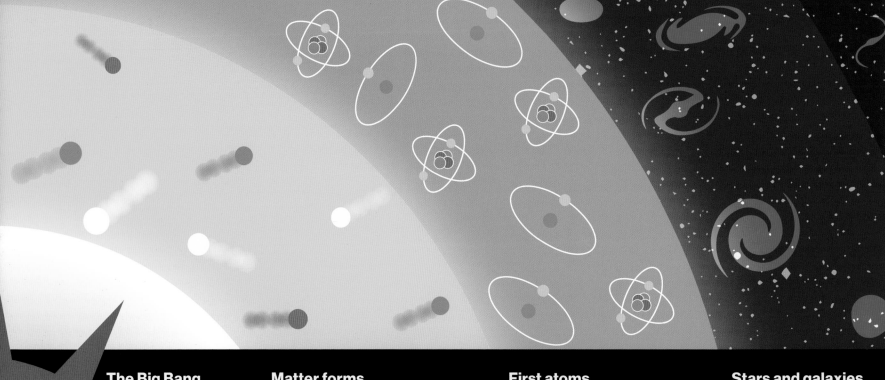

The Big Bang

The Universe materializes out of nothing. It is smaller than an atom but has all the energy and mass it will ever have. In the first trillionth of a trillionth of a trillionth of a second, it expands to the size of a football—a process known as inflation.

13.8 billion years ago

Matter forms

Within a second, the incredible energy of the expanding Universe produces tiny particles of matter. Most of these collide, destroy each other, and vanish, but a tiny fraction remain. These leftovers build up to form larger particles called protons and neutrons—the building blocks of atoms.

1 second later

First atoms

It takes 300,000 years for the Universe to cool sufficiently for protons and neutrons to form the first atoms: hydrogen and helium. These gases form a thin cloud that fills the Universe. Light can now travel freely, making space transparent. This ancient light can still be captured by astronomers today.

13.7997 billion years ago

Stars and galaxies

Gravity pulls thicker areas of gas into clumps that get tighter and tighter. This heats their cores, triggering nuclear reactions, and so giving birth to stars. The newborn stars cluster by the billion in vast whirlpools—galaxies.

13.5 billion years ago

The story of the Universe

The Universe began 13.8 billion years ago in an event called the Big Bang. The Big Bang was not an explosion of matter in space, but the sudden appearance and expansion of space itself. The expansion has continued ever since, creating a cosmos of unimaginable vastness. Although light travels extremely quickly, it still takes it billions of years to cross the Universe. This means that peering into deep space allows us to look back in time and study the Universe's early years.

The Solar System

Our local star, the Sun, forms from a cloud of gas and dust left by dying stars. Not all the material is absorbed by the new star though—a gigantic disk of dust and gas is left in orbit around it. Over time, the particles of matter in this disk stick together to form the planets, moons, asteroids, and comets of our Solar System.

4.6 billion years ago

Life begins

Farther from the Sun than scalding Venus but not as far as freezing Mars, planet Earth is just the right temperature for liquid water to settle on its surface. A random chemical reaction between carbon-based chemicals in the water produces a molecule that can make copies of itself, as DNA can today. It is the first form of life.

4.3 billion years ago

The Sun dies

About 5 billion years in the future, the Sun will turn into a red giant star as its supply of fuel begins to run out. It will swell in size, its outer layers engulfing the planets Mercury, Venus, and probably Earth. The heat will vaporize any water left on Earth, and possibly our planet's crust, too, making life impossible.

5 billion years in the future

The Big Freeze

The Universe may continue expanding forever. Matter and energy will become ever more thinly dispersed, preventing new stars from forming. After the last star burns out, the Universe will be permanently dark and freezing cold—an endless void with no activity.

Over 100 trillion years in the future

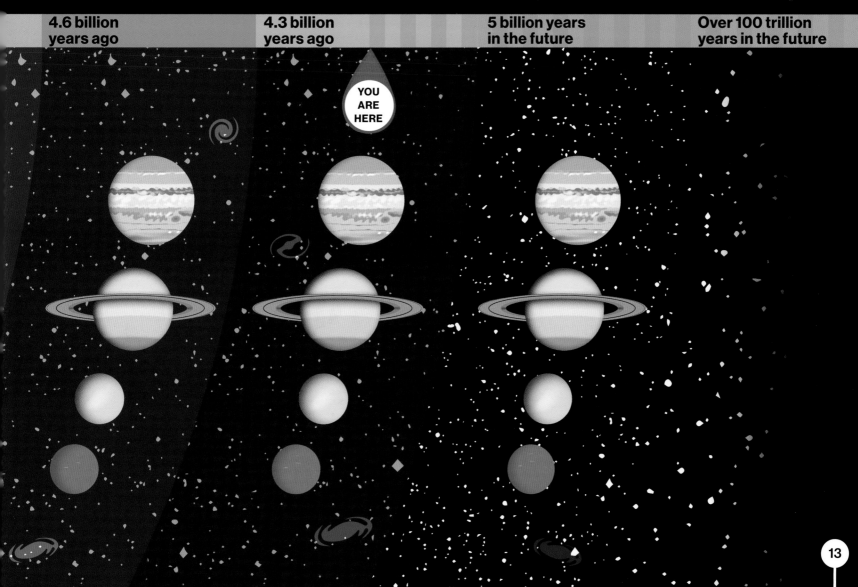

YOU ARE HERE

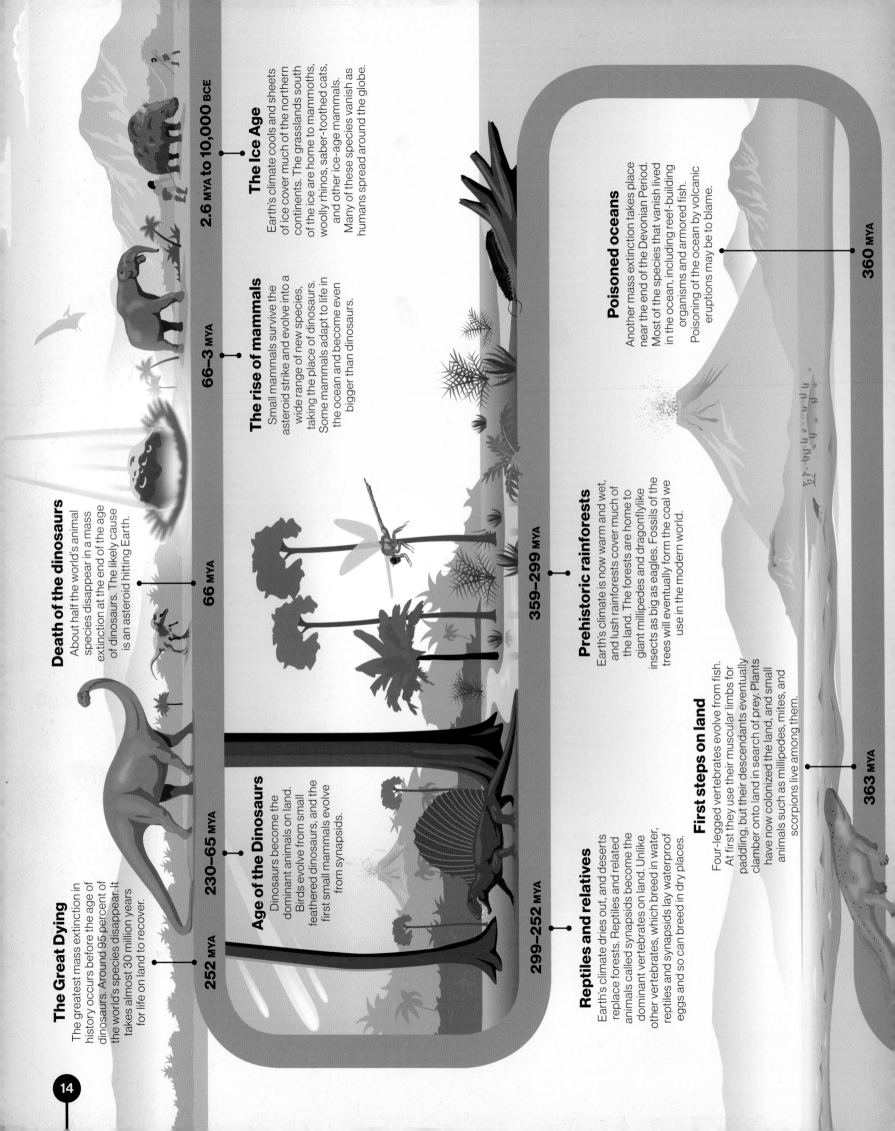

The Great Dying

The greatest mass extinction in history occurs before the age of dinosaurs. Around 95 percent of the world's species disappear. It takes almost 30 million years for life on land to recover.

252 MYA

Death of the dinosaurs

About half the world's animal species disappear in a mass extinction at the end of the age of dinosaurs. The likely cause is an asteroid hitting Earth.

66 MYA

2.6 MYA to 10,000 BCE

The Ice Age

Earth's climate cools and sheets of ice cover much of the northern continents. The grasslands south of the ice are home to mammoths, woolly rhinos, saber-toothed cats, and other ice-age mammals. Many of these species vanish as humans spread around the globe.

66–3 MYA

The rise of mammals

Small mammals survive the asteroid strike and evolve into a wide range of new species, taking the place of dinosaurs. Some mammals adapt to life in the ocean and become even bigger than dinosaurs.

230–65 MYA

Age of the Dinosaurs

Dinosaurs become the dominant animals on land. Birds evolve from small feathered dinosaurs, and the first small mammals evolve from synapsids.

299–252 MYA

Reptiles and relatives

Earth's climate dries out, and deserts replace forests. Reptiles and related animals called synapsids become the dominant vertebrates on land. Unlike other vertebrates, which breed in water, reptiles and synapsids lay waterproof eggs and so can breed in dry places.

359–299 MYA

Prehistoric rainforests

Earth's climate is now warm and wet, and lush rainforests cover much of the land. The forests are home to giant millipedes and dragonflylike insects as big as eagles. Fossils of the trees will eventually form the coal we use in the modern world.

First steps on land

Four-legged vertebrates evolve from fish. At first they use their muscular limbs for paddling, but their descendants eventually clamber onto land in search of prey. Plants have now colonized the land, and small animals such as millipedes, mites, and scorpions live among them.

363 MYA

Poisoned oceans

Another mass extinction takes place near the end of the Devonian Period. Most of the species that vanish lived in the ocean, including reef-building organisms and armored fish. Poisoning of the ocean by volcanic eruptions may be to blame.

360 MYA

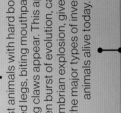

Dunkleosteus

Life on Earth

After oceans first formed on Earth, it didn't take long for life to appear on the planet. How life began remains one of the great mysteries of science, but most scientists believe the first living things developed from carbon-based chemicals in water. No trace of these remains, but the animals and plants that evolved from them left numerous fossils behind. The fossil record shows that the story of life on Earth has had twists and turns, with occasional mass extinctions wiping out the dominant species and allowing new forms of life to emerge.

An explosion of life

The first animals with hard body cases, jointed legs, biting mouthparts, and gripping claws appear. This apparently sudden burst of evolution, called the Cambrian explosion, gives rise to all the major types of invertebrate animals alive today.

541 MYA

First vertebrates

The first vertebrates—animals with backbones—appear. They are fishlike animals that swim like tadpoles and have simple mouths for sucking. Later, their descendants evolve hinged jaws, allowing them to grab prey and tear flesh.

525 MYA

First animals

Soon after the Snowball era ends, complex organisms that may be the first living animals appear. They are soft-bodied, leaf-shaped creatures with no obvious organs, limbs, or mouthparts. They probably live on the ocean floor and feed on particles of food absorbed through their skin.

600 MYA

Death in the ocean

Around 85 percent of all marine species disappear in a series of major extinctions. The cause is unknown, but some scientists suspect climate change is to blame.

419–359 MYA

444 MYA

Snowball Earth

Earth's surface freezes and a thick layer of ice encases the whole planet for millions of years. Life on the surface is wiped out during this "Snowball Earth" period, but microorganisms survive under the ice in the ocean.

780–630 million years ago (MYA)

First cells

Single-celled organisms evolve. They will be the only forms of life on Earth for most of the planet's history. Many grow in mounds on the ocean floor, using sunlight to photosynthesize. They release the gas oxygen as a waste, changing Earth's atmosphere.

3.7 BYA

The age of fish

Fish rule the ocean in the Devonian Period, which is also called the age of fish. Sharks are now common, but the most fearsome predator is *Dunkleosteus*, a 20 ft (6 m) long predator with an armored body and huge jaws equipped with a flesh-cutting beak.

Origin of life

Life begins in water, possibly near hot volcanic springs in the deep ocean. The first life forms are carbon-based molecules that have the ability to make copies of themselves. Once they start multiplying, the process of evolution begins, and the self-copying molecules become more complex.

4.3 billion years ago (BYA)

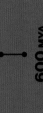

The age of dinosaurs

Modern humans have existed for about 200,000 years, but dinosaurs dominated life on Earth for nearly 200 million years. This vast span of time is called the Mesozoic Era and is divided into three distinct periods. The reign of the dinosaurs and other giant reptiles came to an abrupt end in a mass extinction 66 million years ago, but not every kind of dinosaur was wiped out.

Rhamphorhynchus

Eudimorphodon

Plateosaurus

Cryolophosaurus

Isanosaurus

Stegosaurus

Eoraptor

Scelidosaurus

Coelophysis

Anchiornis

240 million years ago   220   210   200   190   180   170   160

Triassic Period

The first dinosaurs appear in the middle of the Triassic Period. They are small, nimble animals that scamper on powerful hind legs, using their stiff tails to balance and their small arms to handle food. This successful formula soon leads to variations. Some dinosaurs evolve into plant-eaters, growing longer necks that help them reach leaves or armored skin for protection. Others specialize in hunting. While dinosaurs rule the land, other prehistoric reptiles adapt to life in the ocean and air.

Jurassic Period

In the Jurassic Period, plant-eating dinosaurs reach gigantic sizes, making them the largest animals ever to walk on Earth. Exactly why this happens isn't clear, but one theory is that predators target smaller animals, driving a process of natural selection that makes both prey and predator become larger and larger. Meanwhile, the smallest dinosaurs evade predators by taking flight—they evolve into the first birds.

Nothosaurus

Mixosaurus

Liopleurodon

Diplodocus

Argentinosaurus

Quetzalcoatlus

Pteranodon

Therizinosaurus

Confuciusornis

Allosaurus

Tyrannosaurus

Sauropelta

Triceratops

Velociraptor

Struthiomimus

Iguanodon

50   140   130   120   110   100   90   80   70

Cretaceous Period

During the Cretaceous Period, Earth's continents slowly drift toward their current configuration, moving about as fast as human toenails grow. There are now more kinds of dinosaurs than ever, including flightless, feathered giants and small but ferocious carnivores with hooklike foot claws that might be used to disembowel prey. At the end of the Cretaceous, all types of giant prehistoric reptiles disappear in a mass extinction, perhaps victims of a catastrophic asteroid strike, but birds survive.

Albertonectes

Mosasaurus

From 632 CE

Islamic philosophy

The religion of Islam spreads through parts of Asia and North Africa after the death of the prophet Muhammad. Islamic philosophy deals with questions about the nature of the universe, but also involves science, logic, and mathematics.

From 1100

East meets West

The Islamic philosopher Averroes studies the work of the ancient Greek thinker Aristotle, and brings together the theories of Western philosophy with the religious beliefs of Islam.

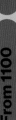

From 1100

Medieval philosophy

Philosophy and religious belief combine in a system of thought called Scholasticism. Medieval philosophers such as the Italian priest Thomas Aquinas seek to bring together the teachings of ancient philosophy and their Christian faith.

2nd century CE

Nothing is certain

Sextus Empiricus of the Roman Empire writes down the ideas of the ancient Greek Skeptics, who believed that nothing can be known for certain.

From c.4th century BCE

Following "the Way"

Also known as "the Way," Daoism is based on ideas written down in a book called the *dao de jing*. It teaches that a force called the *dao* connects all living things, and that people must live in harmony with this force.

4th–3rd century BCE

Accept your reality

The Stoic philosopher Zeno of Citium from Cyprus argues that the Universe is governed by natural laws. People must accept the existence of cruelty and injustice.

5th–4th century BCE

An ideal world

A student of Socrates, Plato believes that things in the real world are only shadows. He imagines there is a perfect "ideal form" of things that exists outside our knowledge.

The real world

Plato's student Aristotle disagrees with his teacher. He believes that knowledge is gained only through experience of the real world—we know a horse is a horse because we have seen horses before.

From 5th century BCE

Respect for tradition

Chinese philosopher Confucius believes in an ordered society and the importance of tradition. People should honor their ancestors, and those with power over others should use that power with respect for those they rule.

From 6th–4th century BCE

The middle path

Siddhartha Gautama, later known as the Buddha, is an Indian prince who gives up his life of luxury for one of poverty. The religion he inspires teaches that following a middle path between these extremes leads to enlightenment (true happiness).

Question everything

The first great thinker to examine abstract ideas—concepts such as goodness and justice—is Socrates. He asks a series of questions to explore these subjects. Socrates is famous for saying that "the only thing I know is that I know nothing."

6th–5th century BCE

Natural philosophy

Early philosophers in ancient Greece are "natural philosophers" who try to explain the world around them. For instance, Thales of Miletus theorizes that everything that exists is made of water.

From 7th–6th century BCE

Good and evil

The religion of Zoroastrianism is started by the prophet Zoroaster in Persia in West Asia. It has ideas concerning the nature of God and the concept of evil that will influence many later religions.

"Philosophy begins in wonder."

Socrates, as quoted in Plato's *Theaetetus,* c.369 BCE

65

The story of sculpture

Sculptures are three-dimensional works of art created from materials such as stone, wood, metal, or plastic. They have been created since the earliest times and can be small enough to be held or so large that they take up the side of a mountain. A sculpture can be a personal object or a grand public work to celebrate status or achievement.

Venus figurines
Small female statuettes may have been fertility goddesses thought to help women conceive.

Egyptian giants
The ancient Egyptians place massive statues of their pharaohs outside temples and tombs. The figures are carved from hard granite rock and have stiff postures, giving the appearance of great power.

Chinese craft
Artists of the Shang Dynasty in China make bronzes (a mix of copper and tin), often in the shape of animals, to be filled with food and buried with the dead.

Greek sculpture
Sculptors in Greece portray the human body in a lifelike manner never seen before. Their bronze and marble statues are brightly painted, although the colors will gradually fade away.

c.35,000 BCE

c.1550–1070 BCE

1500 BCE

450 BCE

First figures
Small sculptures of humans, usually female, and of animals are made throughout Europe. Some are carved from stone, bone, or ivory. Others are molded from clay, which is then fired.

The Terracotta Army
More than 8,000 life-size statues of clay soldiers, each one individually modeled, protect the enormous burial tomb of Qin Shi Huang, the first emperor of China.

210 BCE

Rialto Bridge
This late-Renaissance bridge in Venice, Italy, is lined with colorful shops.

Arch of Titus
This Roman arch, dedicated to the Emperor Titus, is decorated with carved panels of his military triumphs.

c.100 CE

Roman sculpture
Roman houses, gardens, and public spaces are filled with sculptures. They range from realistic portrait busts of ancestors and famous citizens to large marble statues depicting stories of gods and heroes.

Medieval saints
The walls of Gothic cathedrals in Europe are decorated with statues of Christian saints and figures from the Bible.

Guardians in stone
The Rapa Nui people, the Polynesian inhabitants of Easter Island in the Pacific Ocean, carve large stone figures to represent their ancestors. They stand on platforms facing out to sea.

c.1200

Buddha statues
Robed statues of Buddha from Gandhara (in modern-day northern Pakistan and Afghanistan) are naturalistic in style, reflecting Greek and Roman art.

200–500

1150–1400

Modernism

Romanian-born sculptor Constantin Brancusi starts carving directly in marble and wood. These smooth outlines and simple geometric forms influence modern sculpture in the 20th century.

1907

1927–1941

Mount Rushmore

Gutzon Borglum carves the giant heads of four American presidents (George Washington, Thomas Jefferson, Theodore Roosevelt, and Abraham Lincoln) on the face of Mount Rushmore in the US.

1902

The Thinker

Frenchman Auguste Rodin is the most important sculptor in Europe at this time. His most famous work is a statue of a man deep in thought.

The Three Graces

Neoclassical works, such as this by Italian sculptor Antonio Canova, refer back to the order and harmony of Greek and Roman sculpture.

1814

Abstract forms

In Britain, sculptors Barbara Hepworth and Henry Moore begin to create abstract sculptures and semi-abstract figures inspired by landscape and natural shapes, such as shells and pebbles.

1930s

Gian Lorenzo Bernini

Bernini transforms Rome by creating dramatic statues and spectacular fountains with figures that seem full of movement. This highly decorative style is typical of the Baroque era in art.

Fountain of the Four Rivers
Bernini's fountain in the Piazza Navona surrounds an ancient Egyptian obelisk.

1932

Moving sculptures

American sculptor Alexander Calder suspends colorful shapes of steel on wires to create abstract mobiles, sculptures that move by motor power or with the flow of air.

c.1640–1660

c.1300–1600

1999

Giant spider

Louise Bourgeois's giant sculpture of a female spider is called *Maman* (*Mummy*). It is balanced on spindly legs and stands 30 ft (9 m) high.

2006

The Renaissance

Sculpture enters a new golden age in Renaissance Italy. Donatello's magnificent statue of a horse and rider (1453) in Padua is the first bronze of its kind to be created since Roman times.

Public sculpture

Anish Kapoor's *Cloud Gate* in Chicago, IL, is one of the world's largest outdoor sculptures. It is made of 168 highly polished stainless-steel plates that reflect and distort the city around it.

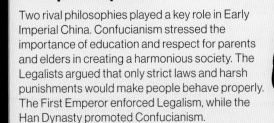

Rival philosophies

Two rival philosophies played a key role in Early Imperial China. Confucianism stressed the importance of education and respect for parents and elders in creating a harmonious society. The Legalists argued that only strict laws and harsh punishments would make people behave properly. The First Emperor enforced Legalism, while the Han Dynasty promoted Confucianism.

Standardization

The emperor introduces standard weights, measurements, and coins, and a common writing system. His coins are circular with a square hole in the middle, representing a square earth encircled by the dome of the heavens.

Book burning

In an attempt to suppress free thought, the emperor orders a large-scale burning of books, including the histories of the kingdoms he has conquered and works of Confucian philosophy and poetry. Only texts supporting Legalism are permitted.

Great Wall

The emperor sends 300,000 soldiers north to build the first Great Wall, protecting China against northern raiders. He also unifies China by knocking down the internal defensive walls that had previously separated the warring states.

Fall of the Qin

The second Qin emperor, Qin Er Shi, is a weak ruler who can't prevent widespread revolts. After his death in 207 BCE, the dynasty collapses in the face of rebellion. Two former rebel leaders, Xiang Yu and Liu Bang, will engage in a war to decide who will rule China.

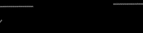

Han founder

Liu Bang defeats Xiang Yu and establishes the Han Dynasty, ruling as Emperor Gaozu. He builds a new capital at Chang'an and recruits Confucian scholars to serve in his government.

First Emperor

The teenage Ying Zheng comes to the throne of the western kingdom of Qin. Between 230 and 221 BCE, his armies conquer all six rival kingdoms. He takes a new title, Shi Huangdi, or "First Emperor."

246–221 BCE   **220 BCE**   **215 BCE**   **213 BCE**   **210–207 BCE**   **202–195 BCE**

Early Imperial China

In 221 BCE, China, previously divided into warring kingdoms, was united by the king of Qin, who became the First Emperor. He used force to impose the same way of life throughout China, but his rule was so harsh that the Qin Dynasty quickly collapsed after his death in 210 BCE. It was followed by the Han Dynasty, which ruled more leniently and created the First Golden Age of China.

Emperor Wudi
Emperor Wudi reigns, and extends Chinese rule into Central Asia, Korea, and modern-day Vietnam. He makes Confucianism the state philosophy, but still imposes Legalist punishments.

Central Asia
Zhang Qian, a Chinese diplomat, travels to Central Asia, returning in 125 BCE. His reports lead to Han expansion in Central Asia. Long distance trade begins between China and the West, along the Silk Road.

Fall of the Han
Han rule collapses as China breaks up into three kingdoms: Shu, Wei, and Wu. The ruler of each kingdom uses the title emperor, claiming to be descended from the Han. It is a time of constant warfare.

Civil service exams
Emperor Wen introduces examinations for government appointments. Previously, civil servants have been appointed on recommendations from nobles and senior officials.

Grand historian
Sima Qian, a Han court official, writes a monumental history of China. To later generations, the book will be known as *The Records of the Grand Historian*.

Counting China
A Han census records the population of China as 58 million people.

Paper
A court official named Cai Lun manufactures the first paper, from bark and rags. It is cheaper to write on than bamboo or silk.

| 165 BCE | 141–87 BCE | c.85 BCE | 138–c.50 BCE | 2 BCE | c.105 CE | 220 CE |

Terracotta Army
After his death, the First Emperor was buried in a vast tomb with an army of 7,000 life-size terracotta warriors buried in nearby pits. The emperor believed that these soldiers would protect him in the afterlife.

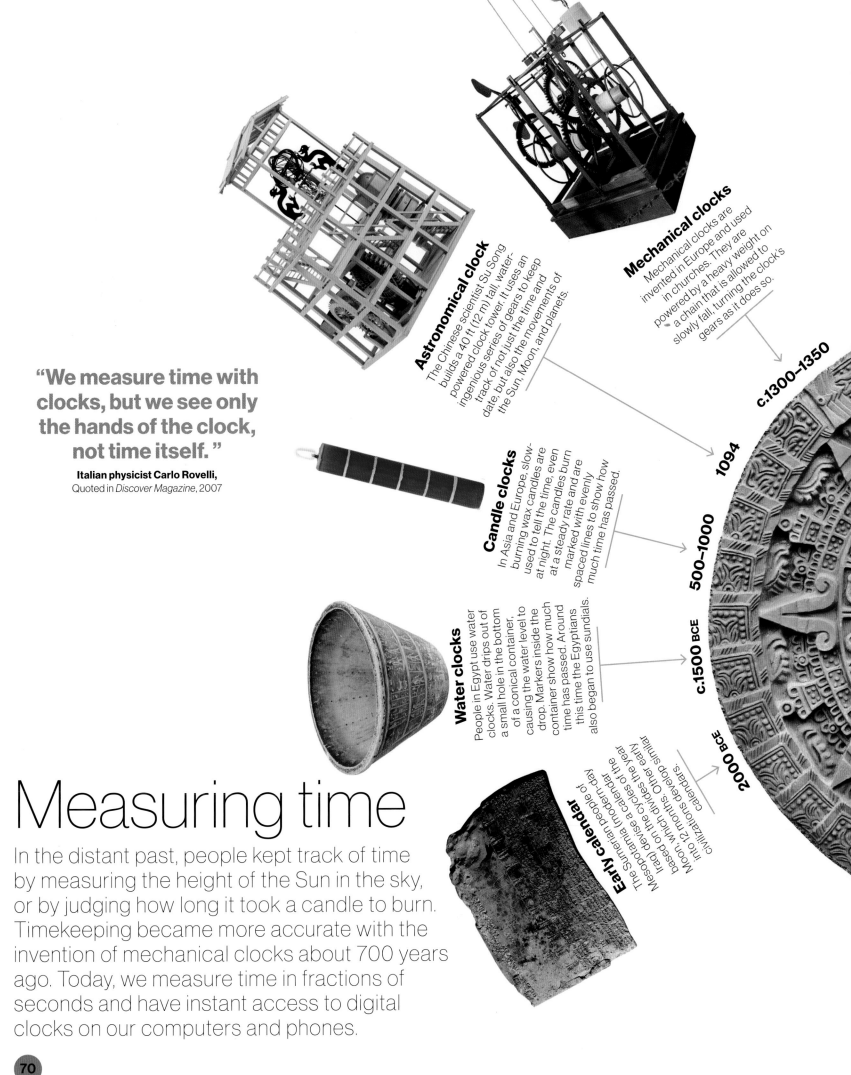

Astronomical clock
The Chinese scientist Su Song builds a 40 ft (12 m) tall, water-powered clock tower. It uses an ingenious series of gears to keep track of not just the time and date, but also the movements of the Sun, Moon, and planets.

Mechanical clocks
Mechanical clocks are invented in Europe and used in churches. They are powered by a heavy weight on a chain that is allowed to slowly fall, turning the clock's gears as it does so.

Candle clocks
In Asia and Europe, slow-burning wax candles are used to tell the time, even at night. The candles burn at a steady rate and are marked with evenly spaced lines to show how much time has passed.

Water clocks
People in Egypt use water clocks. Water drips out of a small hole in the bottom of a conical container, causing the water level to drop. Markers inside the container show how much time has passed. Around this time the Egyptians also began to use sundials.

Early calendar
The Sumerian people of Mesopotamia devise the year (modern-day Iraq) based on the cycles they see in the Sun and Moon, which divides into 12 months. Other early civilizations develop similar calendars.

c.1300–1350

1094

500–1000

c.1500 BCE

2000 BCE

> "We measure time with clocks, but we see only the hands of the clock, not time itself."
>
> **Italian physicist Carlo Rovelli,**
> Quoted in *Discover Magazine*, 2007

Measuring time

In the distant past, people kept track of time by measuring the height of the Sun in the sky, or by judging how long it took a candle to burn. Timekeeping became more accurate with the invention of mechanical clocks about 700 years ago. Today, we measure time in fractions of seconds and have instant access to digital clocks on our computers and phones.

Pocket watch

German clockmaker Peter Henlein makes mechanical clocks that are small enough to fit into pockets. They are driven by a steel spring that turns the clock's wheels as it unwinds.

1524

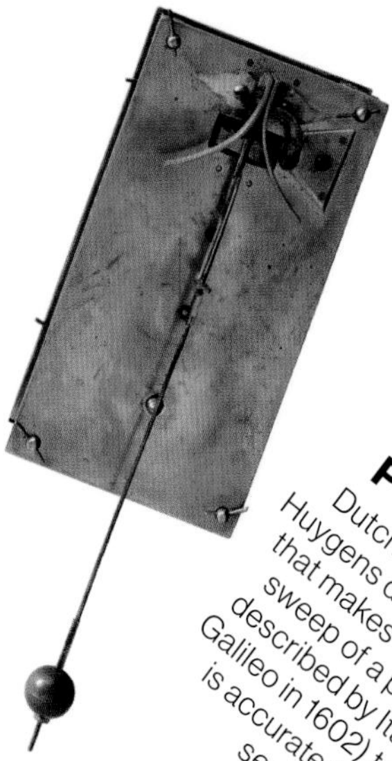

Pendulum clock

Dutch scientist Christiaan Huygens designs the first clock that makes use of the regular sweep of a pendulum (first described by Italian scientist Galileo in 1602) to keep time. It is accurate to within a few seconds a day.

1656

Marine chronometer

After 45 years' work, English clockmaker John Harrison completes the marine chronometer H4, a pocket watch so accurate that sailors can use it to calculate how far east or west of London they've sailed by comparing the local noon to London time. It is accurate to within three seconds a day.

1759

Railroad time

Railroad stations in Britain synchronize their clocks and timetables with Greenwich Mean Time, a standard time set by the Royal Observatory in London. Before this, each town had kept its own local time, based on the Sun.

1847

Wristwatches

The first wristwatches are items of jewelry—decorative bracelets incorporating clocks. Pocket watches on chains remain more common until World War I, when military style wristwatches become popular.

1910

Atomic clocks

Scientists invent clocks that are regulated by the rapid vibration of electrons inside atomic clocks lose less than one second in a million years. An atomic clock loses less than one second in a million years.

1950s

Aztec calendar

The Aztec people of Central America used calendars carved in stone. The 20 days of a month were represented by 20 symbols around the central face. There were 18 months in a year, making 360 days—5 days short of a full year. The remaining five days were considered unlucky days.

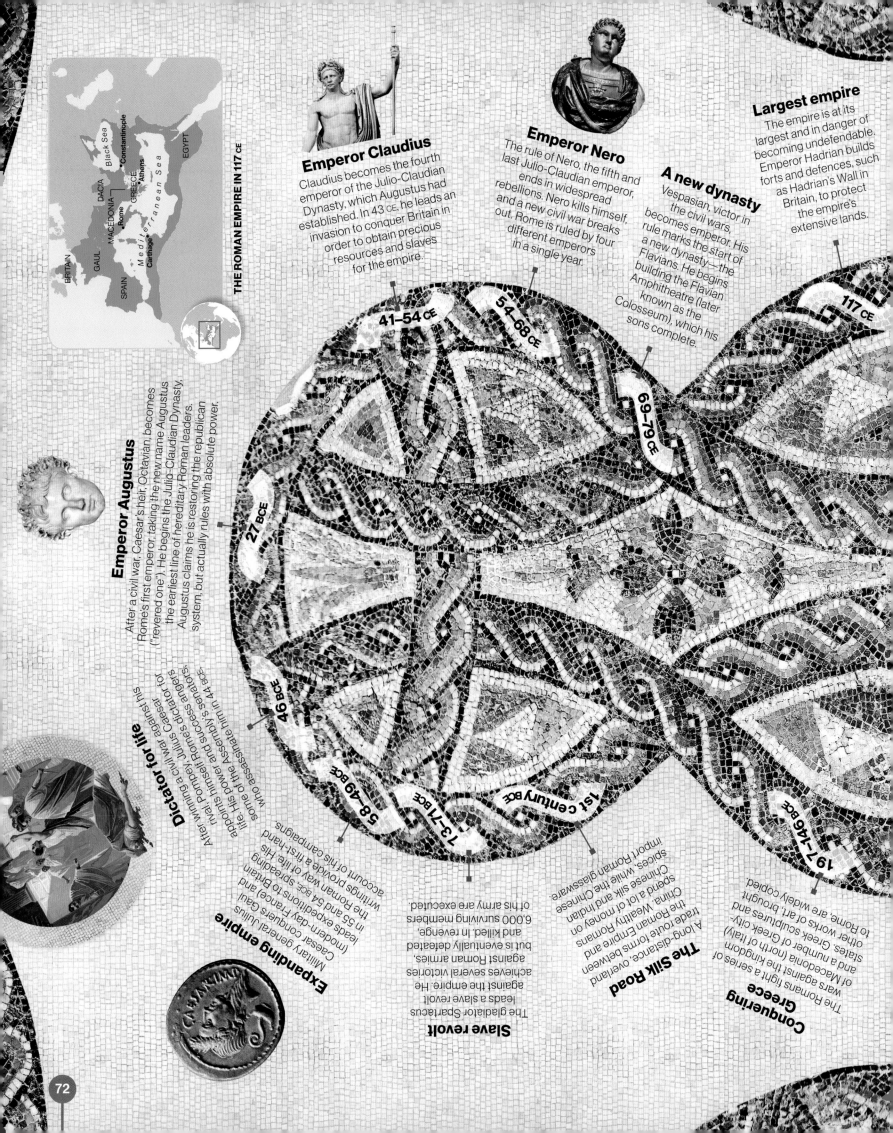

THE ROMAN EMPIRE IN 117 CE

Map labels: BRITAIN · GAUL · SPAIN · Rome · Carthage · MACEDONIA · GREECE · Athens · Mediterranean Sea · DACIA · Black Sea · Constantinople · EGYPT

Emperor Claudius

41–54 CE

Claudius becomes the fourth emperor of the Julio-Claudian Dynasty, which Augustus had established. In 43 CE, he leads an invasion to conquer Britain in order to obtain precious resources and slaves for the empire.

Emperor Nero

54–68 CE

The rule of Nero, the fifth and last Julio-Claudian emperor, ends in widespread rebellions. Nero kills himself, and a new civil war breaks out. Rome is ruled by four different emperors in a single year.

A new dynasty

69–79 CE

Vespasian, victor in the civil wars, becomes emperor. His rule marks the start of a new dynasty—the Flavians. He begins building the Flavian Amphitheatre (later known as the Colosseum), which his sons complete.

Largest empire

117 CE

The empire is at its largest and in danger of becoming undefendable. Emperor Hadrian builds forts and defences, such as Hadrian's Wall in Britain, to protect the empire's extensive lands.

Emperor Augustus

27 BCE

After a civil war, Caesar's heir, Octavian, becomes Rome's first emperor, taking the new name Augustus ("revered one"). He begins the Julio-Claudian Dynasty, the earliest line of hereditary Roman leaders. Augustus claims he is restoring the republican system, but actually rules with absolute power.

Dictator for life

46 BCE

After winning a civil war Caesar for against his rival, Pompey, Julius dictator's success angers appoints himself Rome's senators. His power and Assembly's for life. Some of the 44 BCE who assassinate him in

Expanding empire

58–49 BCE

Military general Julius Caesar conquers Gaul (modern-day France) and leads expeditions to Britain in 55 and 54 BCE, spreading the Roman way of life. His writings provide a first-hand account of his campaigns.

Slave revolt

73–71 BCE

The gladiator Spartacus leads a slave revolt against the empire. He achieves several victories against Roman armies, but is eventually defeated and killed. In revenge, 6,000 surviving members of his army are executed.

The Silk Road

1st century BCE

A long-distance, overland trade route forms between China and the Roman Empire and spices, while the Chinese import Roman glassware. Chinese silk and Indian spend a lot of money on the wealthy Romans

Conquering Greece

197–146 BCE

The Romans fight a series of wars against the kingdom of Macedonia (north of Italy) and a number of Greek city-states. Greek sculptures and other works of art, brought to Rome, are widely copied.

The Roman Empire

The ancient Romans created one of the largest and best organized empires in history. At its height, the empire stretched 2,500 miles (4,000 km) from east to west and 2,300 miles (3,700 km) from north to south. For the only time in history, all the lands around the Mediterranean Sea belonged to a single state, ruled from Rome. By the 1st century CE, the city had more than a million inhabitants.

Imperial crisis

During this troubled period, the empire is attacked by Persians in the east and Germanic tribes in the north. Several regions break away, and a plague erupts in 249 CE. Many emperors rule briefly; almost all die violently.

235–284 CE

Restoring stability

Emperor Diocletian seeks to re-establish strong government by splitting the empire into a western and eastern half, each ruled by a senior emperor (the Augustus) and a junior (the Caesar).

284–305 CE

West versus east

Emperor Constantine takes power in the west. After winning a civil war against Licinius, he reunites the eastern emperor, empire. He establishes a new capital in the east, later called Constantinople.

312–330 CE

476 CE

Fall of Rome

In the west, Emperor Romulus Augustulus is overthrown by Odoacer, a Germanic chieftain who makes himself king of Italy. In the east, the empire survives for 1,000 more years, but it is now called the Byzantine Empire.

Under attack

The Romans fight and win three wars against the Carthaginian Empire of North Africa. During the second war, the Carthaginian general Hannibal crosses the Alps and invades Italy from the north. He fails to capture Rome.

264–146 BCE

Republic

The Romans expel their king and establish a republic, in which power is held by state leaders. Romans citizens elect two heads of state each year, known as consuls, who rule alongside an assembly called the Senate.

510/509–27 BCE

Rome established

According to legend, Rome is founded by twin brothers Romulus and Remus in the 8th century BCE. They were sons of the war god Mars. In fact, the city originated on one of the settlement built during the city's seven hills, raised by a she-wolf. In the 10th century BCE.

753 BCE

Roman technology

Under the Romans, Europe and the Mediterranean world saw great technological advances. Often the Romans used the inventions of earlier peoples, but on a greater scale. For example, they did not invent arches, but used them for support in many buildings. Thanks to arches, mass-produced bricks, and concrete, the Romans constructed hundreds of massive structures, many of which remain standing today.

Glass blowing
Glass blowing is invented in Roman Syria. It allows a skilled worker to make a glass container in minutes. As a result, glassware is no longer a luxury item for the wealthy.

Late 1st century BCE

Public toilets
Romans build public toilets across the empire. These have stone seats over a channel of flowing water. The keyhole shape allows users to clean themselves with a wet sponge held on a stick.

2nd century BCE

Concrete buildings
Romans start using concrete, a building material made by mixing gravel with water and minerals that set solid when wet. Concrete allows them to build cheaply on a massive scale. The Basilica of Maxentius (c. 310 CE) was one of the empire's largest concrete structures.

2nd century BCE

Roman roads
The Via Appia — the first long road for the Roman army — is built, linking Rome with southern Italy. Later, the whole empire will be connected by long, straight roads along which soldiers can march long distances quickly.

312 BCE

Aqueducts
Romans build their first aqueduct, the Aqua Appia, to carry water 10 miles (16 km) to Rome, almost completely underground. Later aqueducts, such the 40–60 CE Pont du Gard in France, use arches to span rivers and valleys.

312 BCE

Measuring tools

The Romans were able to plot the routes of dead-straight, long-distance roads and figure out the precise yet incredibly gentle slope of aqueducts that carried water for many miles. Before these structures were built, surveyors used simple tools to make careful measurements.

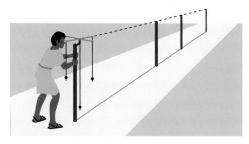

Planning roads

Roman surveyors ensured roads were straight by using a tool called a groma. This had a cross with weights hanging from it that helped keep it upright and level when lining up distant points.

Measuring slopes

The chorobates was a wooden table with a trough on top, filled with water. Keeping the water level allowed surveyors to check that structures were built to the right height.

Underfloor heating

Roman engineer Sergius Orata invents underfloor heating. Hot air from a furnace is fed through the space under a raised floor that is supported on columns of tiles.

c.90 BCE

Steam engine

In Roman Egypt, a scientist named Hero invents a steam engine. A curiosity with no obvious purpose, it consists of a spherical water boiler that spins around when steam emerges from two nozzles.

c.80 CE

Screw press

Romans invent the screw press, a simple machine that crushes objects when a large screw is turned. It is used to press olives for oil and grapes for wine.

1st century CE

First books

Books with pages made of animal skin or papyrus (a kind of reed) are created. These are much more convenient than long scrolls and eventually replace them.

Late 1st century CE

Pantheon

The Roman emperor Hadrian builds the Pantheon, a temple in Rome. Its concrete dome still stands and remains the world's largest unreinforced concrete dome.

126 CE

The Colosseum

The Romans built amphitheaters to watch gladiators fight. Unlike earlier amphitheaters, which were dug out of hillsides, the Colosseum in Rome was a free-standing structure, with three stories supported by 80 arches made of brick and concrete.

Buddhism

In eastern India, a wealthy prince named Siddhartha Gautama renounces luxury and embarks on a quest to overcome human suffering. His quest ends when he reaches nirvana (blissful enlightenment) while meditating. He becomes known as Buddha and dedicates his life to guiding others, founding the religion of Buddhism.

6th century BCE

Jainism

In northern India, a wandering holy man named Mahavira establishes Jainism. Followers of the faith, which has no god, reject worldly pleasures and lead nonviolent, vegetarian lives. They believe in an endless cycle of reincarnation.

6th century BCE

Confucianism

The teachings of Confucius, a Chinese scholar and philosopher, are compiled in five books. Confucianism is a way of life based on values such as kindness and respect for family. Unlike most other religions, it is not based on supernatural beliefs.

6th–5th century BCE

Zoroastrianism

In Persia (modern-day Iran), a priest named Zarathustra has a series of visions that inspire a new religion— Zoroastrianism. He teaches followers that there is a single god and an eternal battle between good and evil.

7th–6th century BCE

Religion

Religious ideas have existed since prehistoric times, when our ancestors began to bury their dead with precious items—a sign they believed in an afterlife. Since then, hundreds of religions have developed, many growing from older ones. Nearly all religions teach belief in life after death, but not all religions involve a supernatural being such as a god or goddess.

C.1500 BCE

Hinduism

The Vedas—a collection of hymns and chants that form the oldest texts of Hinduism—are written in northwestern India. Hindus follow many gods and goddesses and believe in reincarnation after death.

C.2000 BCE

Judaism

The first major religion based on a single god develops among the Hebrews, a group of seminomadic farmers and herders in Israel. They record the laws laid down by God on scrolls, forming the Bible.

Cao Dai

Ngo Van Chieu, a government official in Vietnam, creates the religion of Cao Dai after being contacted by a spirit during a seance. Cao Dai combines aspects of Christianity and Buddhism and promotes peace, tolerance, and vegetarianism.

1926

Shinto

Shinto becomes the state religion of Japan. Followers of the ancient religion, which is thousands of years old, worship invisible spirits at shrines, believing them to bring good luck. Shinto spirits are everywhere, and shrines can be natural features such as rocks, trees, or mountains.

1868

Daoism

Chinese philosopher Laozi writes the *Dao de jing*, the main book followed by Daoists. Daoists believe there is an invisible force—the Dao—running through the Universe and controlling it. Followers try to live in harmony with this natural force and lead peaceful, unselfish lives.

c. 4th century BCE

> **"Our greatest glory is not in never falling, but in rising every time we fall."**
>
> Chinese philosopher **Confucius**

1853

Baha'i

Mirza Husayn-Ali, a nobleman in Persia (modern-day Iran), has a religious revelation that inspires a vast body of religious writings, creating the main scriptures of the Baha'i faith. Baha'is believe in the unity of all religions and the equality of all people, whatever their nationality or faith.

1st century CE

Christianity

In Judea (modern-day Israel), the Jewish preacher Jesus of Nazareth is executed by the Roman government, who see him as a threat. His teachings, which emphasize forgiveness and peace, give rise to the religion of Christianity. It will eventually spread to become the world's biggest religion.

7th century

Islam

An Arab merchant, Muhammad, establishes the religion of Islam after an angel appears to him in a series of visions, reciting the word of God. The angel's commandments are recorded in the Qur'an, the holy book that all Muslims follow.

1499

Sikhism

Guru Nanak, the founder of Sikhism, has a mystical experience after bathing in a river in northwestern India. He renounces Hinduism and begins teaching a new faith that combines elements of Hinduism and Islam. Sikhs believe in a single god and reincarnation after death.

THE DESTRUCTION OF POMPEII

Mount Vesuvius erupts

As the Roman Empire rose to power, bustling towns and cities, including Pompeii and Herculaneum in southern Italy, grew and flourished around the base of the sleeping Mount Vesuvius. Then, on August 24, 79 CE, the mountain unexpectedly erupted, shrouding 15,000 unsuspecting Roman citizens in darkness and death.

An active mountain

Around **62 CE**, the Bay of Naples experiences a series of destructive earthquakes as gas builds up inside Mount Vesuvius. The violent tremors are felt in the nearby towns of Herculaneum, 4.3 miles (7 km) to the west, and Pompeii, 6 miles (10 km) to the southeast. Seventeen years later, in **August 79 CE**, molten lava hardens inside Vesuvius's main cone and more gas builds up, leading to several days of violent earth tremors.

A cloud in the sky

On **August 24**, in the port of Misenum, 18 miles (30 km) west of Mount Vesuvius, the 18-year-old scholar Pliny the Younger spots a towering cloud rising from the quiet mountain. Just after **noon**, a tall column of hot ash, rock, and gas rises to more than 12.5 miles (20 km) in the sky. Winds start to carry the super-hot ash and rocks southeast toward Pompeii. Later, harmful gas spurts from the rumbling mountain as lightweight volcanic rock, known as pumice, rains down on the surprised Pompeii citizens. They start to panic, grabbing their valued possessions as they flee toward the beach looking for a way to escape.

Darkness descends

By the **afternoon**, a thick layer of ash and pumice builds up in Pompeii, causing buildings to collapse. The ash from the fiery mountain blocks out the Sun and the Bay of Naples descends into an early night. The darkness and crumbling buildings add to the panic as citizens gather at the shore.

The lightweight pumice floats in the water, making it hard for the overcrowded boats to flee the horror. As **evening** sets in, boiling hot, fist-sized rocks fly down through the ashy darkness and the terrified people of Pompeii scramble for shelter among the ruined buildings.

The towering inferno

At **midnight**, the eruption cloud reaches its highest peak at around 18.5 miles (30 km) in the air. The towering column of ash and gas collapses and a cloud of scorching gas and debris, known as a pyroclastic flow, rushes down from the mountain toward the town of Herculaneum. The super-hot cloud moves at speeds close to 435 mph (700 kph) and reaches a searing temperature of 750°F (400°C). The citizens have nowhere to hide and perish instantly as the volcanic cloud gusts through the city streets.

The dust settles

Overnight and into the darkness of a volcanic morning, the eruption cloud collapses several times, launching more terrifying pyroclastic flows down from the mountain. This time they also head southeast toward Pompeii, adding to the thousands of victims that have already perished. Pliny the Younger and thousands of survivors head inland away from the fiery disaster. As they look back into the bay, they notice that Herculaneum has vanished, buried under 65 ft (20 m) of ash, pumice, and volcanic rock. The Bay of Naples is shrouded in darkness for several days as the volcanic cloud finally settles, and Mount Vesuvius is quiet once more.

> "Ashes were already falling, hotter and thicker... followed by bits of pumice."
>
> **Pliny the Younger**, *Letters VI 16*

Fun and festivals

The first museums, zoos, and festivals were already drawing crowds in ancient times. Rulers and royalty also created spectacular shows to reflect their own power and wealth. Singing and storytelling have been important for a long time in many cultures, and theaters and music halls put performers on stage in front of paying audiences. Over the centuries, millions of people have gathered to enjoy the greatest shows on the planet.

The first zoo
The first historically recorded zoo is created in the Egyptian city of Nekhen. Visitors come to see baboons, leopards, hippos, gazelles, and crocodiles. The mummified remains of these animals will be discovered thousands of years later.

Early museums
The oldest known museum, devoted to Mesopotamian history, is built by the Babylonian princess Ennigaldi in her palace in Ur (in modern-day Iraq). Many museums begin as private collections of art or artifacts displayed in wealthy homes.

c.3500 BCE

c.530 BCE

Fireworks
First invented in China in about 600 CE, Italian explorer Marco Polo brought fireworks to Europe in 1295. When the first colored fireworks are invented in Italy in the 1830s, public displays become even more spectacular.

Circus
English stunt rider Philip Astley holds a horse show, performing tricks inside a ring. Eventually, he adds clowns, musicians, and other performers, resulting in circus. By the 18th century, the popularity of the circus spreads from Europe to the US.

Opera house
The world's oldest opera house opens in the Italian city of Naples. The Real Teatro Di San Carlo showcases the work of leading composers, orchestras, and singers. The building later survives a fire and bombings during World War II.

1830s

1768

1737

World's Fair
The first international World's Fair is held at the Crystal Palace in London. Industrial, scientific, and cultural exhibits are displayed for months at a time. Thousands of visitors have since enjoyed more than 100 of these festivals in 20 different cities.

Public aquarium
The world's first public aquarium, called The Fish House, opens at the London Zoo. Around 300 different types of marine life are on display. This is the first time aquatic creatures have been kept and displayed in enclosed tanks.

Big screens
The first public cinema screening shown to a paying audience is presented by the French brothers Auguste and Louis Lumière in Paris, France. They show 10 short clips they had filmed.

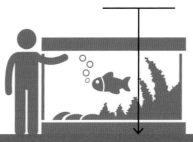

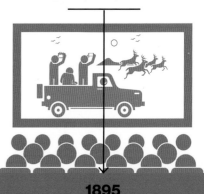

1851

1853

1895

Mayan festivals

In Mayan culture, there is a festival every 20 days. Huge crowds gather at the local central plaza for religious rituals, live music, and intricate dances. Performers entertain the crowds by dressing up as gods and mythical creatures.

Colosseum

This great Roman amphitheater opens with 100 days of games, including gladiator battles and fights between wild animals. The games are watched by up to 50,000 spectators at a time, and continue to be held until the 5th century.

India's Golden Age

The Gupta Empire is called the Golden Age in Indian entertainment. People gather to watch a variety of dance, theater, and musical spectacles. The classical music and dance styles from this era are still practiced in Asia today.

c.250 BCE–900 CE

c.80 BCE

c.320–550 CE

Carnival

Based on a spring festival from ancient Greece, the world's largest carnival celebration opens in Brazil. More than half a million people celebrate on the streets and beaches of Rio de Janeiro every year.

Royal festivities

French king Louis XIV stages grand entertainment at the Palace of Versailles, near Paris in France. The program includes operas, concerts, fireworks, light displays, and theater.

The Globe Theatre

The home of Shakespeare's plays opens in London. The Globe Theatre accommodates 1,500 people on the inside, while crowds gather outside to enjoy the atmosphere.

1723

1674

1599

Radio

Canadian-American engineer Reginald A. Fessenden invents an electric generator that can produce continuous sound waves. His first public radio broadcast is from Brent Rock in Massachusetts on Christmas Eve.

Theme parks

The first theme park opens in Indiana. Santa Claus Land features rides and attractions with a festive theme. Theme parks soon become popular across the country, with Disneyland becoming the world's leading theme park by the 1950s.

Pride

Joyful crowds gather in New York to celebrate the first gay pride event. Pride carries an important message to promote the equality and rights of the gay community. Annual celebrations have since been held in cities around the world.

Rock spectacular

A record-breaking audience for a rock concert attends Rod Stewart's performance on Copacabana Beach in Rio de Janeiro. More than 3.5 million people gather there on New Year's Eve for the free concert.

1906

1946

1970

1994

Kushan Empire

The Kushans, a nomadic people from Central Asia, conquer northwest India and modern-day Afghanistan. They follow a new form of Buddhism called Mahayana (meaning "great vehicle"), which spreads to Central and East Asia.

c.30 CE

Dharma wheel
The Buddha's first sermon, entitled Setting in Motion the Wheel of the Law *("Dharma"), was shown in art by a wheel.*

Shunga Empire

Brihadratha, the last Mauryan king, is assassinated by Pushyamitra Shunga, the chief of his guard. Shunga founds an empire in his own name that covers the central area of the Maurya Empire.

185 BCE

Peace pillars

After conquering Kalinga in eastern India, Ashoka decides to stop waging war. He sets up pillars across the empire, topped by sculptures of lions, elephants, and bulls. The pillars are inscribed with apologies for his previous actions. He also warns those who will rule after him not to conquer new territory.

c.260 BCE

Bodhi tree
The Buddha is thought to have found enlightenment (true wisdom) while sitting under a bodhi (fig) tree.

Ashoka the Great

Following Bindusara's death, civil war breaks out. The victor is Ashoka the Great. He converts to Buddhism and promotes the religion by sending missionary monks to Sri Lanka and Central Asia and building many stupas (mounds holding relics of the Buddha and other holy leaders).

268 BCE

Mauryan expansion

Bindusara, the second Mauryan king, expands the empire into southern India. He is also known as Amitraghata, which means "destroyer of enemies." Bindusara maintains good diplomatic relations with the Greeks and enjoys the sweet wine and figs they bring.

c.297–273 BCE

Elephant exchange

Chandragupta defeats an invading Macedonian army, led by King Seleucus. In a peace treaty, Seleucus gives Chandragupta the Punjab (in modern-day northern India and Pakistan) in exchange for 500 war elephants.

305–303 BCE

Maurya Empire

Inspired by Alexander the Great's invasion of the Indian subcontinent, Chandragupta Maurya conquers the Nanda Empire of northern India. He establishes the Maurya Empire, whose capital is Pataliputra.

c.321 BCE

Ancient Indian empires

From 321 BCE, a series of great empires arose in the Indian subcontinent (modern-day India, Pakistan, and Bangladesh). The era also saw the rise of a new world religion, Buddhism, promoted by Mauryan emperors. The religion continued to thrive under the later Guptas, though they were Hindus. The Gupta period is considered to be India's Classical Age, when the arts and sciences flourished.

Buddha statues
c.75
Art flourishes under the Kushans. Inspired by Greek art, sculptors in Gandhara make statues of the Buddha, who in previous times had been represented only by symbols such as the dharma wheel.

Southern trade
c.103–130
The Satavahana Dynasty reaches its height under Gautamiputra Satakarni. It controls the Deccan plateau of southern India and trades by sea with the Roman Empire, exchanging spices and exotic animals for Roman gold.

Gupta Empire
c.320
Chandra Gupta I conquers the Ganges Valley in northern India, founding the Gupta Empire. The Guptas are Hindus who build the first stone temples to Hindu gods, such as Vishnu, Shiva, and the elephant-headed Ganesha.

Gupta expansion
c.330–380
Samudra Gupta expands the empire, conquering more than 20 kingdoms. The defeated kings are allowed to continue ruling, but must send tribute to Gupta. On his inscriptions, he boasts that he is "invincible."

Classical Age
c.380–415
The Gupta Empire is at its peak under Chandra Gupta II, a patron of art, literature, and science. It is thought that Kalidasa, the greatest poet and playwright in the Sanskrit language, may have been one of the court poets.

Math and astronomy
c.499
Aryabhata, the mathematician-astronomer, writes the *Aryabhatiya*, the earliest-surviving Indian book about mathematics. He correctly argues that Earth is a rotating sphere, and that the Moon and planets shine because of reflected sunlight.

Reclining Buddha
Some of the earliest Buddha statues show him lying on his deathbed. This style later spreads across East Asia.

Indian sculptures
Hindu and Buddhist temples throughout the subcontinent are covered with intricate carvings of people, animals, and nature. The sculptures are full of activity, giving an impression of what life was like in ancient India.

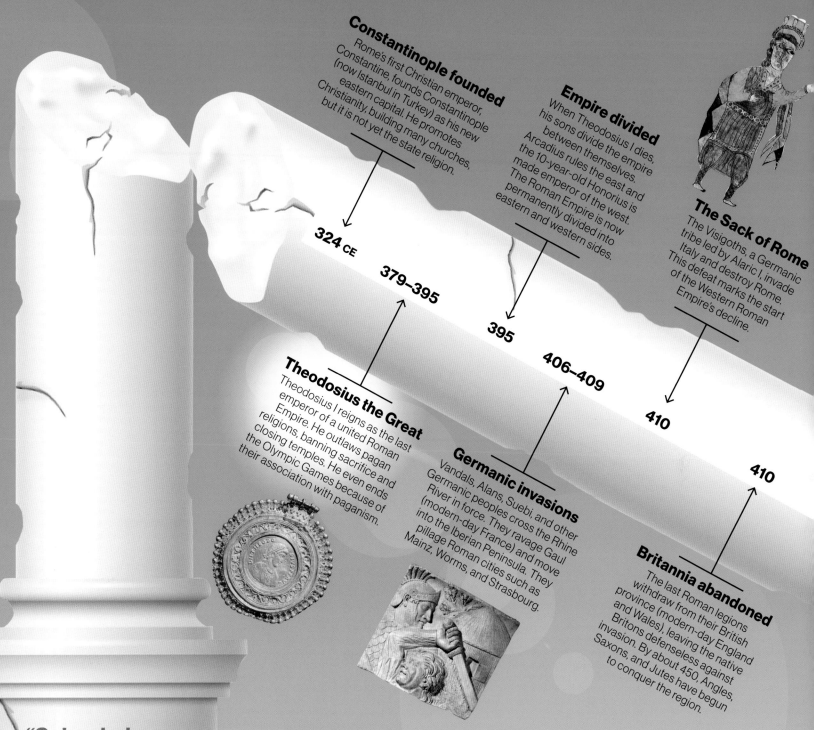

Constantinople founded
Rome's first Christian emperor, Constantine, founds Constantinople (now Istanbul in Turkey) as his new eastern capital. He promotes Christianity, building many churches, but it is not yet the state religion.

Empire divided
When Theodosius I dies, his sons divide the empire between themselves. Arcadius rules the east and the 10-year-old Honorius is made emperor of the west. The Roman Empire is now permanently divided into eastern and western sides.

The Sack of Rome
The Visigoths, a Germanic tribe led by Alaric I, invade Italy and destroy Rome. This defeat marks the start of the Western Roman Empire's decline.

324 CE

379–395

395

406–409

410

410

Theodosius the Great
Theodosius I reigns as the last emperor of a united Roman Empire. He outlaws pagan religions, banning sacrifice and closing temples. He even ends the Olympic Games because of their association with paganism.

Germanic invasions
Vandals, Alans, Suebi, and other Germanic peoples cross the Rhine River in force. They ravage Gaul (modern-day France) and move into the Iberian Peninsula. They pillage Roman cities such as Mainz, Worms, and Strasbourg.

Britannia abandoned
The last Roman legions withdraw from their British province (modern-day England and Wales), leaving the native Britons defenseless against invasion. By about 450, Angles, Saxons, and Jutes have begun to conquer the region.

> "Sobs choke my speech. The city which had taken the whole world was itself taken."
>
> **St. Jerome**, in a letter upon hearing of the sack of Rome, written in 412.

The transformation of the Roman Empire

From the 4th century, the Roman Empire started to fall apart as Germanic invaders swept into western Europe. These Germanic conquerors established new kingdoms there, but preserved many Roman institutions and customs. In the east, the Roman Empire survived as the Greek Byzantine Empire.

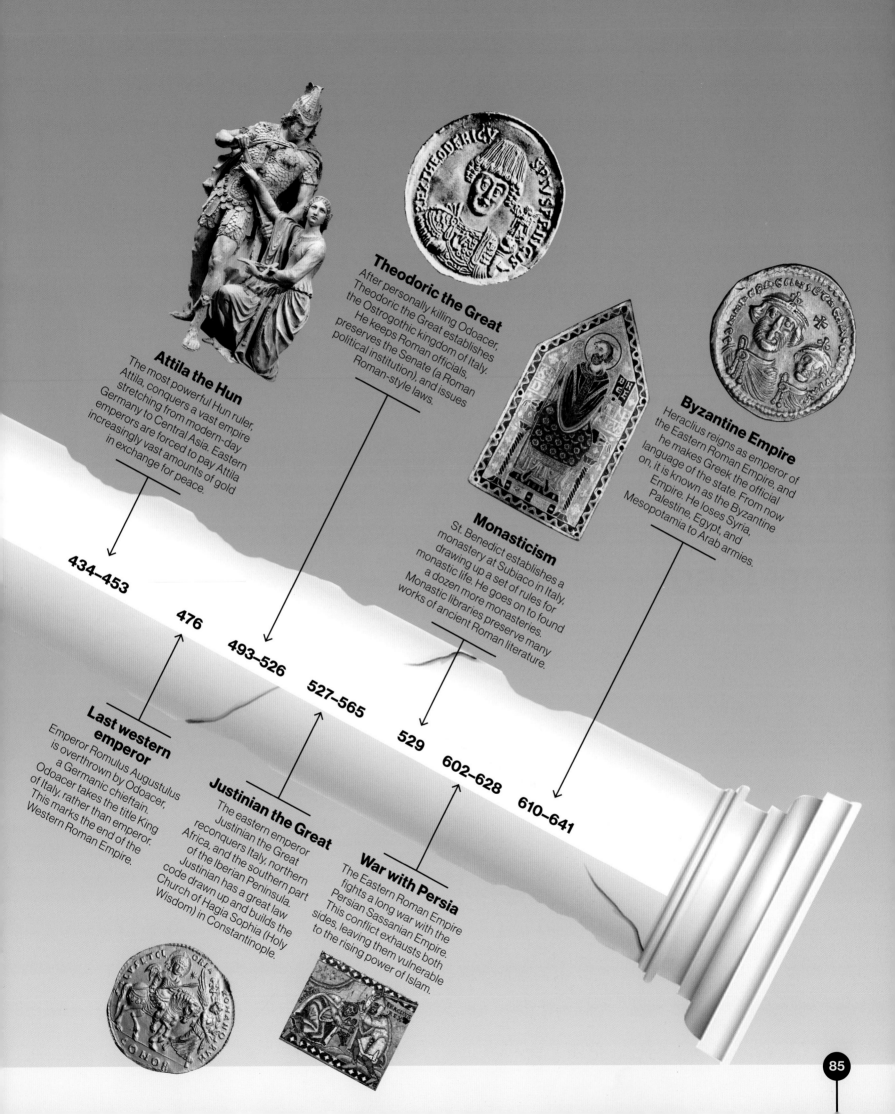

Attila the Hun
The most powerful Hun ruler, Attila, conquers a vast empire stretching from modern-day Germany to Central Asia. Eastern emperors are forced to pay Attila increasingly vast amounts of gold in exchange for peace.

Theodoric the Great
After personally killing Odoacer, Theodoric the Great establishes the Ostrogothic kingdom of Italy. He keeps Roman officials, preserves the Senate (a Roman political institution), and issues Roman-style laws.

Byzantine Empire
Heraclius reigns as emperor of the Eastern Roman Empire, and he makes Greek the official language of the state. From now on, it is known as the Byzantine Empire. He loses Syria, Palestine, Egypt, and Mesopotamia to Arab armies.

Monasticism
St. Benedict establishes a monastery at Subiaco in Italy, drawing up a set of rules for monastic life. He goes on to found a dozen more monasteries. Monastic libraries preserve many works of ancient Roman literature.

434–453

476

493–526

527–565

529

602–628

610–641

Last western emperor
Emperor Romulus Augustulus is overthrown by Odoacer, a Germanic chieftain. Odoacer takes the title King of Italy, rather than emperor. This marks the end of the Western Roman Empire.

Justinian the Great
The eastern emperor Justinian the Great reconquers Italy, northern Africa, and the southern part of the Iberian Peninsula. Justinian has a great law code drawn up and builds the Church of Hagia Sophia (Holy Wisdom) in Constantinople.

War with Persia
The Eastern Roman Empire fights a long war with the Persian Sassanian Empire. This conflict exhausts both sides, leaving them vulnerable to the rising power of Islam.

THE MEDIEVAL WORLD

500-1450

The Medieval World

After the fall of the Roman Empire in 476 CE, Europe was divided into squabbling kingdoms, but civilizations in Asia continued to flourish and expand. China developed many technological and artistic innovations. In the Middle East, the new religion of Islam took hold, and scholars made great strides in the study of math, astronomy, and medicine. During this period, advanced cultures also appeared across the Americas, Africa, and Southeast Asia.

618–907
The Tang Dynasty rules in China.

750
The Islamic Abbasid Dynasty establishes a new capital at Baghdad in modern-day Iraq.

800
The Frankish king Charlemagne is crowned Holy Roman Emperor.

960
The Song Dynasty takes control of China.

1066
William of Normandy in France becomes king of England after his victory at the Battle of Hastings.

c.610
According to Islamic belief, the Prophet Muhammad receives revelations from God, and founds the religion of Islam.

711
An Islamic army begins the conquest of most of Spain and Portugal.

802
King Jayavarman II is the first ruler of the Khmer Empire in modern-day Cambodia.

841
Vikings settle on the coast of Ireland, founding modern-day Dublin.

1050
The Inuit people begin to settle in the Arctic regions of North America.

Rise of Islam
Islamic empires (see pages 92–93) spread across the Middle East, North Africa, and Spain, bringing the teachings of this new religion to many cultures.

The Americas
In Central and South America, a series of civilizations grew (see pages 94–95). These cultures dominated the continent until the arrival of Europeans.

Medieval Europe
After the fall of Rome, new kingdoms rose and fought for power across Europe (see pages 98–99). Christianity spread over the whole continent.

The Crusades
As both religions grew in power, Christianity and Islam clashed in a series of bloody wars known as the Crusades (see pages 104–105).

Chain mail

Armor made from chain mail was constructed from small iron or steel rings linked together to form a mesh. Chain mail offered protection against blades, and was popular throughout medieval Europe and other parts of the world. It was cheap enough that soldiers other than knights could afford it, and the mesh made it very flexible and easy to wear.

c.1100–1400
Great Zimbabwe in southeast Africa emerges as a trading empire.

1205–1206
Genghis Khan unites the Mongol tribes under his rule.

1280
A Polynesian people known as the Maori settle in New Zealand.

1346
The Battle of Crécy during the Hundred Years' War ends in an English victory against the French.

c.1540
The Inca city of Machu Picchu is established in modern-day Peru.

1095
Pope Urban II launches the first of eight Crusades—holy wars to take the city of Jerusalem from Muslim control.

1192
Minamoto Yoritomo is named shogun (military leader) of Japan. This begins an era of rule by the samurai class.

1264–1368
Mongol conquerors found the Yuan Dynasty in China.

1325–1521
The Aztec people create an empire in modern-day Mexico.

1347–1352
The Black Death plague spreads across Europe, killing between 30 and 60 percent of its population.

Rise of the samurai
A series of conflicts across Japan saw the rise to power of the samurai (see pages 110–111). These were elite warriors who lived by a strict code of honor.

Settling the Pacific
Polynesian people settled previously uninhabited Pacific islands (see pages 116–117). They created cultures on Hawaii, New Zealand, and Easter Island.

African kingdoms
South of the Sahara desert, rich and powerful kingdoms appeared in Africa (see pages 118–119). Trade with North Africa brought with it the religion of Islam.

The Mongols
Under the leadership of the warrior Genghis Khan, nomadic Mongol tribes from northern Asia (see pages 120–121) invaded as far as Europe and China.

China's Golden Ages

China went through two Golden Ages during the Tang and Song dynasties. Under the Tang (618–907), China was a great imperial power, with a sophisticated culture open to foreign ideas. In the 8th century, the Tang capital, Chang'an, was the largest city in the world. The Song Dynasty (960–1269) was a time of economic transformation, when the population doubled from 50 to 100 million.

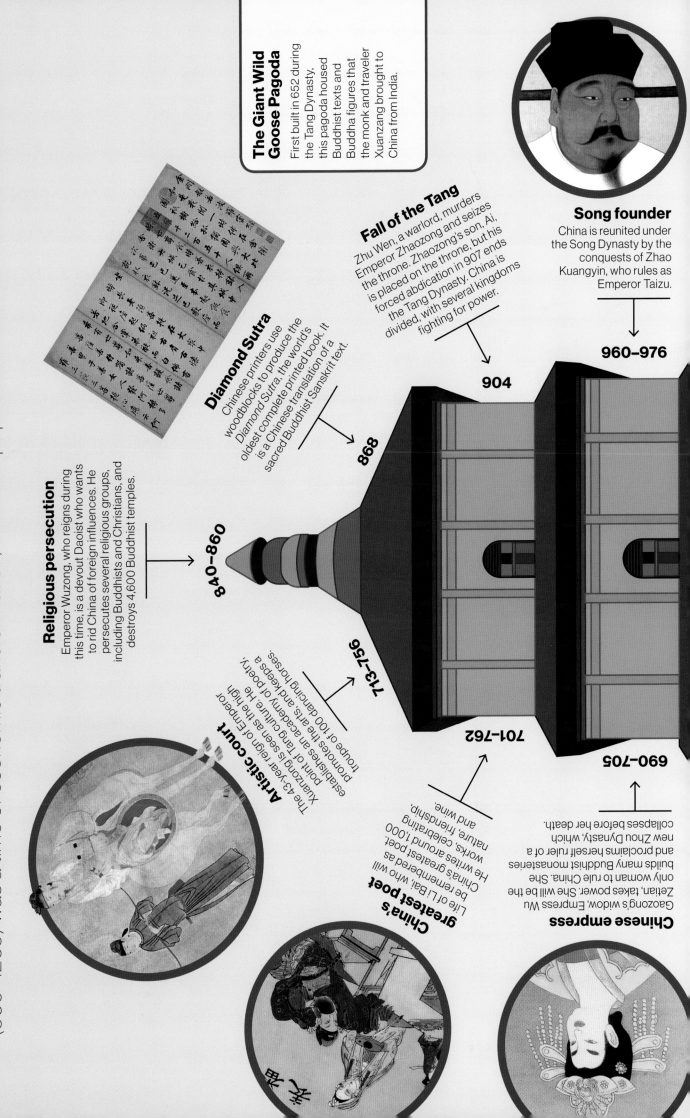

The Giant Wild Goose Pagoda

First built in 652 during the Tang Dynasty, this pagoda housed Buddhist texts and Buddha figures that the monk and traveler Xuanzang brought to China from India.

Fall of the Tang

Zhu Wen, a warlord, murders Emperor Zhaozong and seizes the throne. Zhaozong's son, Ai, is placed on the throne, but his forced abdication in 907 ends the Tang Dynasty. China is divided, with several kingdoms fighting for power.

904

Song founder

China is reunited under the Song Dynasty by the conquests of Zhao Kuangyin, who rules as Emperor Taizu.

960–976

Diamond Sutra

Chinese printers use woodblocks to produce the Diamond Sutra, the world's oldest complete printed book. It is a Chinese translation of a sacred Buddhist Sanskrit text.

868

Religious persecution

Emperor Wuzong, who reigns during this time, is a devout Daoist who wants to rid China of foreign influences. He persecutes several religious groups, including Buddhists and Christians, and destroys 4,600 Buddhist temples.

840–860

Artistic court

The 43-year reign of Emperor Xuanzong is seen as the high point of Tang culture. He establishes an academy of poetry, promotes the arts, and keeps a troupe of 100 dancing horses.

713–756

China's greatest poet

Life of Li Bai, who will be remembered as China's greatest poet. He writes around 1,000 works, celebrating nature, friendship, and wine.

701–762

Chinese empress

Gaozong's widow, Empress Wu Zetian, takes power. She will be the only woman to rule China. She builds many Buddhist monasteries and proclaims herself ruler of a new Zhou Dynasty, which collapses before her death.

690–705

90

Paper money

The Song Dynasty issues the world's first paper money, called *jiaozi*.

1023

Wonder crop

China adopts a new variety of early ripening rice from Champa (modern-day Vietnam), which can produce up to three harvests a year. It is drought-resistant and can grow on higher ground.

11th century

Jin-China wars

Nomads (travelers) from the north called the Jurchen Jin invade and conquer northern China, forcing the Song Dynasty to move south. The Southern Song Dynasty will survive until its conquest by the Mongols (see pages 120–121) in 1279.

1125–1234

Tang law code

Emperor Gaozong issues a great law code with 502 laws, listing penalties such as death, forced labor, and flogging. It lays the basis for later law codes across East Asia.

652

Islam in China

Saad ibn Waqqas, uncle of Prophet Muhammad, travels to China as an ambassador for Islam. Although he fails to persuade Emperor Gaozong to become a Muslim, the emperor builds China's first mosque, in the city of Canton.

650

Central Asia conquered

Li Shimin rules China as Emperor Taizong, conquering Central Asia and parts of Korea and modern-day Vietnam. He will be remembered as one of China's wisest rulers.

626–649

Tang founder

Li Yuan, a regional governor, takes power as emperor and establishes the Tang Dynasty. In 626, his son, Li Shimin, forces him to retire, but gives him the title Gaozu (high founder).

618–626

Impressive inventions

During its Golden Ages, China was technically far ahead of the West. Chinese inventions of the time included printed books, gunpowder weaponry, and water-driven mechanical clocks.

747
Emperor Xuanzong builds a "cool hall" in the imperial palace with fan wheels and water sprays.

984
The first canal lock is invented, with gates that can capture water.

c.1090
The inventor Su Song builds a water-driven mechanical clock tower.

9th century
The development of woodblock printing leads to the widespread distribution of printed books.

c.11th century
1044 sees the earliest description of gunpowder weaponry, in a Chinese military manual.

c.1115
The use of the maritime compass for navigation is recorded for the first time.

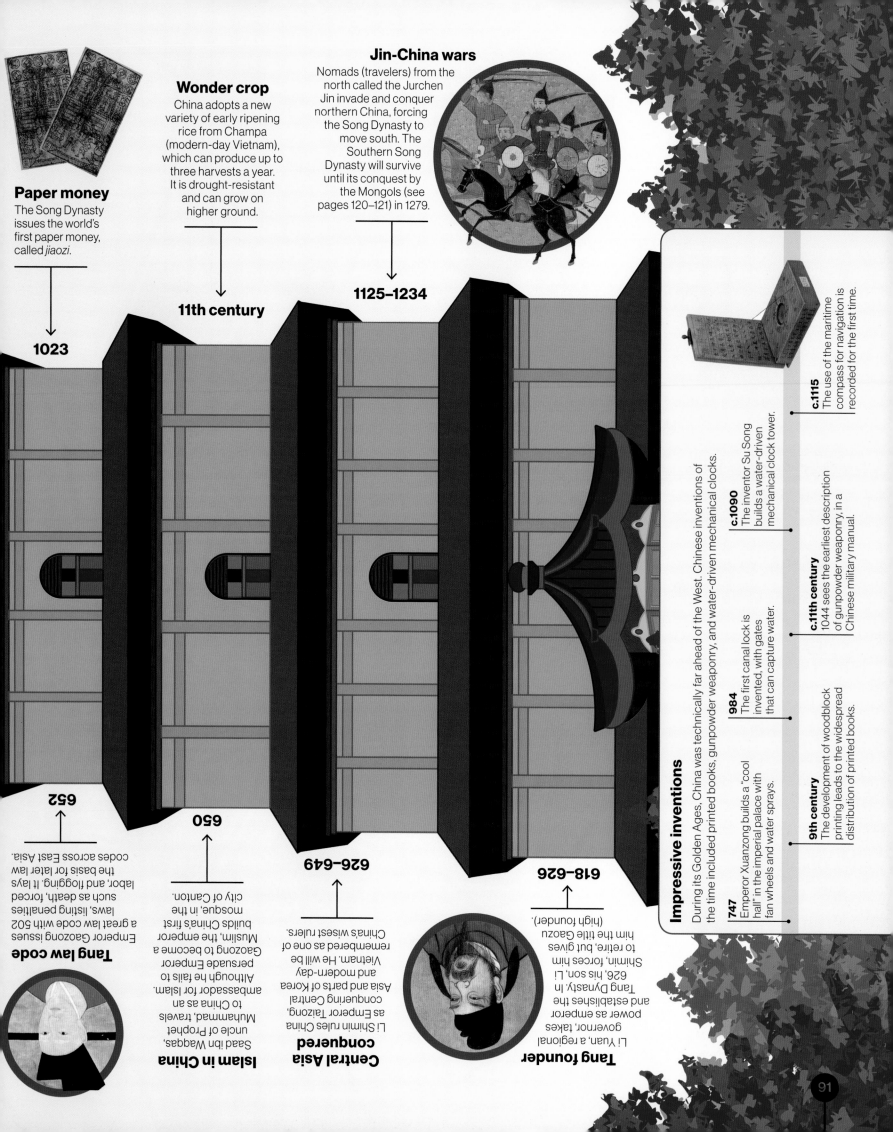

Early Islamic empires

The religion of Islam began early in the 7th century in Arabia in southwest Asia. According to its teachings, the archangel Jibril (Gabriel) first revealed God's Word to the Prophet Muhammad. Within a hundred years, Arab armies had carried their religion to other parts of Asia, North Africa, and Spain, creating powerful Islamic empires. Meanwhile, Arab scholars began to further the study of science and medicine, influenced by the civilizations they conquered.

Study of medicine

The Persian Islamic scholar ibn Sina (also known as Avicenna) publishes *The Canon of Medicine*. The book's fame spreads beyond the Islamic world, and it becomes the standard medical textbook for doctors in medieval Europe.

First university

Fatima al-Fihri, the daughter of a wealthy merchant, founds a mosque and *madrasa* (school) called al-Quaraouiyine at Fez in Morocco. It is now regarded as the first-ever university and is still in existence today.

Abbasid Dynasty

The Abbasids become caliphs after overthrowing the Umayyads. They establish a new capital at Baghdad in modern-day Iraq. In 751, the Abbasids defeat a Chinese army to win control of Central Asia.

Conquest of Spain

A Muslim army crosses from Morocco to conquer most of Spain and Portugal, which they call al-Andalus, which bring with them their distinctive architectural style. Their Muslim rule in Spain lasts until the fall of Granada in 1492.

Umayyad Dynasty

After the assassination of Ali, the fourth caliph, Mu'awiya becomes caliph and founds the Umayyad Dynasty. He makes the ancient city of Damascus in Syria the new capital of Islam. Its Great Mosque is completed by 715.

Early Arab Conquests

Islam spreads rapidly out of Arabia under the early caliphs (leaders of Islam) as Muslim armies overrun present-day Iran, and Persia (modern-day Iran). They go on to conquer Egypt and North Africa as far as Morocco.

1025

859

750

711

661

634–669

EXTENT OF THE ISLAMIC WORLD, 750 CE

Black Sea

AL-ANDALUS

Tangier • • Granada

Fez

MOROCCO

ANATOLIA

Mediterranean Sea

SYRIA

Damascus • PERSIA

• Baghdad

AFGHANISTAN

PALESTINE

EGYPT

Red Sea

• Medina

ARABIA

• Mecca

S A H A R A

Seljuk Empire

A Muslim Turkish dynasty called the Seljuks, originally from Central Asia, creates a vast empire from Afghanistan to Syria and Anatolia (modern-day Turkey). The Seljuks capture Baghdad in 1055. Malik-Shah I is the greatest of their rulers.

Almoravid Empire

Moroccan tribesmen, the Almoravids, extend Muslim power south of the Sahara desert to western Africa. Marrakesh in Morocco becomes their capital in 1062. They also take control of Islamic Spain for a time.

Omar Khayyam

Persian mathematician Omar Khayyam calculates the length of a year to devise an accurate calendar. He is said to be the author of a famous collection of poetry, The Rubaiyat of Omar Khayyam.

Ismail al-Jazari

A water clock shaped like an elephant is among the ingenious machines created by the Muslim world engineer al-Jazari.

Destruction of Baghdad

A Mongol army from Central Asia captures Baghdad, killing thousands of people and loots famous libraries. The destruction brings an end to the Abbasid Dynasty.

Muslim traveler

Ibn Battuta: first of many journeys to holy places that will make in his lifetime. He is said to have traveled more than 75,000 miles (120,000 km) and visited most of the Islamic world.

1037
1054
c.1073
1206
1258
1325

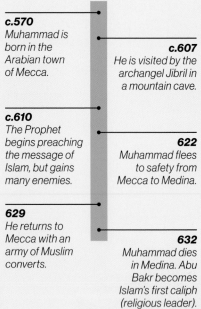

The Life of Muhammad

Muhammad, the Prophet of Islam, is said to have received his revelation from the archangel Jibril in the form of the verses of the Qu'ran (an Islamic sacred book). By the time of his death, Muhammad had united the whole of Arabia under Islam.

c.570
Muhammad is born in the Arabian town of Mecca.

c.607
He is visited by the archangel Jibril in a mountain cave.

c.610
The Prophet begins preaching the message of Islam, but gains many enemies.

622
Muhammad flees to safety from Mecca to Medina.

629
He returns to Mecca with an army of Muslim converts.

632
Muhammad dies in Medina. Abu Bakr becomes Islam's first caliph (religious leader).

Geometric patterns

Islamic teaching does not allow pictures of humans or animals in holy places. Mosques and other religious buildings throughout the Islamic world are richly decorated with geometric patterns of tiles.

93

Empires of the Americas

The first humans arrived in Central and South America many thousands of years ago. Crossing an ice bridge from Siberia, they traveled south. There they built thriving civilizations on strong foundations of religious beliefs and artistic crafts. These great empires eventually fell at the hands of European conquerors.

c.500 BCE
Zapotec
The Zapotec people create acentral site for their ceremonies at present-day Monte Albán in Mexico. Also known as the "Cloud People," they pray and make offerings and sacrifices to their many gods.

c.900–200 BCE
Chavín de Huántar
Chavín de Huántar becomes an important center for politics and religion in the Andes mountains. Locals decorate their pottery with carvings of animals, such as jaguars and eagles.

c.2800 BCE
Norte Chico
The first South American civilization, Norte Chico, establishes the first big towns in modern-day Peru, where pottery and farming become commonplace. This ancient civilization flourishes until 1800 BCE.

c.100–600 CE
Teotihuacan
The biggest city in the ancient Americas was Teotihuacan in present-day Mexico. The Temple of the Sun, shown here, is an enormous structure stretching 207 ft (63 m) high. Trade flourishes until a fire in 600 CE destroys the city.

c.900 BCE
First pyramids
Stepped towers, similar to pyramids, are built all around Central and South America as part of temple complexes. The first known example is created by the Olmec people at La Venta in modern-day Mexico.

c.1200–400 BCE
The Olmec
In the jungles of what is now Mexico, the Olmec people build temples and make sculptures of their rulers and gods. Although not much is known about the Olmec today, they do influence later Mayan, Aztec, and Inca Empires.

Double-headed turquoise serpent

Double-headed turquoise serpents were featured in Aztec religious ceremonies. Snakes symbolized the serpent god Quetzalcoatl, while the mineral turquoise was highly prized at the time.

987–1187
Toltecs

The Toltecs, from what is now northern Mexico, seize the great Mayan city of Chichen Itza and take charge for two centuries.

400–650 CE
Nasca lines

People inhabiting what's now known as the Nasca desert in Peru draw huge pictures on the ground of birds and other shapes. They do this by taking away the ground's top layer to reveal the light soil beneath.

1325–1521
Aztec Empire

The Aztec people arrive in what's now Mexico. Legend says that they built their capital city, Tenochtitlán, on Lake Texcoco, where an eagle held a snake in its beak while perched on a flowering cactus.

1438
Inca Empire

Inca ruler Pachacutec expands the Inca Empire, which now stretches from present-day Ecuador to Chile. The Inca city of Machu Picchu is established high in the Andes mountains, and remains undiscovered until 1911.

AFTER

The arrival of Spanish conquerors during the 16th century brought an end to the Aztec and Inca Empires. Driven by greed and with little concern for the natives, the Spanish soon destroyed both civilizations. Hernán Cortés took over the Aztec Empire, while Francisco Pizarro overthrew the Incas.

250 CE
Mighty Mayans

The Mayans reach their peak, building temples and expanding cities. Tikal, in present-day Guatemala, is one of the biggest Mayan cities, is home to 100,000 people. Other great cities include Chichen Itza and Uxmal. By 800 CE, many Mayan cities are ruined by famine.

c.1325
Ancient game

The people of Central and South America played ball games as far back as 1400 BCE, and the Aztecs develop their own version, which they call *ullamaliztli*. The court represents the world, while the ball is the Sun and Moon.

Germanic peoples

The Germanic peoples lived in many different tribes east of the River Rhine and north of the River Danube. From the 4th century, they began a mass migration into the Western Roman Empire, hoping to find land to settle on and to share in its wealth. They eventually brought down the Western Roman Empire, replacing it with new Germanic kingdoms.

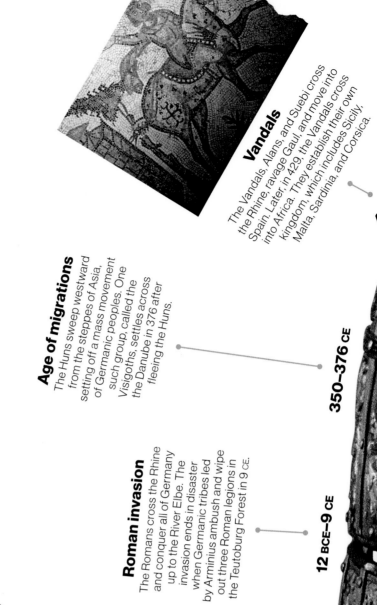

Vandals

The Vandals, Alans, and Suebi cross the Rhine, ravage Gaul, and move into Spain. Later, in 429, the Vandals cross into Africa. They establish their own kingdom, which includes Sicily, Malta, Sardinia, and Corsica.

406 CE

Age of migrations

The Huns sweep westward from the steppes of Asia, setting off a mass movement of Germanic peoples. One such group, called the Visigoths, settles across the Danube in 376 after fleeing the Huns.

350–376 CE

Roman invasion

The Romans cross the Rhine and conquer all of Germany up to the River Elbe. The invasion ends in disaster when Germanic tribes led by Arminius ambush and wipe out three Roman legions in the Teutoburg Forest in 9 CE.

12 BCE–9 CE

Roman Germany

The Romans occupy the west bank of the Rhine, where they offer protection to loyal Germanic tribes. The first German towns are built here by the Romans. Later on, the region is divided by the Romans into Germania Inferior, (with its capital in Cologne) and Germania Superior (with Mainz as its capital).

c.50 BCE

First Germanic invasion

Three Germanic peoples, the Cimbri, Teutons, and Ambrones, launch a large-scale invasion of the Roman Empire. They ravage Gaul and Spain, but are finally defeated by the Roman general Gaius Marius.

113–101 BCE

Sutton Hoo helmet

This is a replica of a helmet that was buried with a 7th century Anglo-Saxon king at Sutton Hoo, England. Based on late-Roman cavalry helmets, its decoration is Germanic in style.

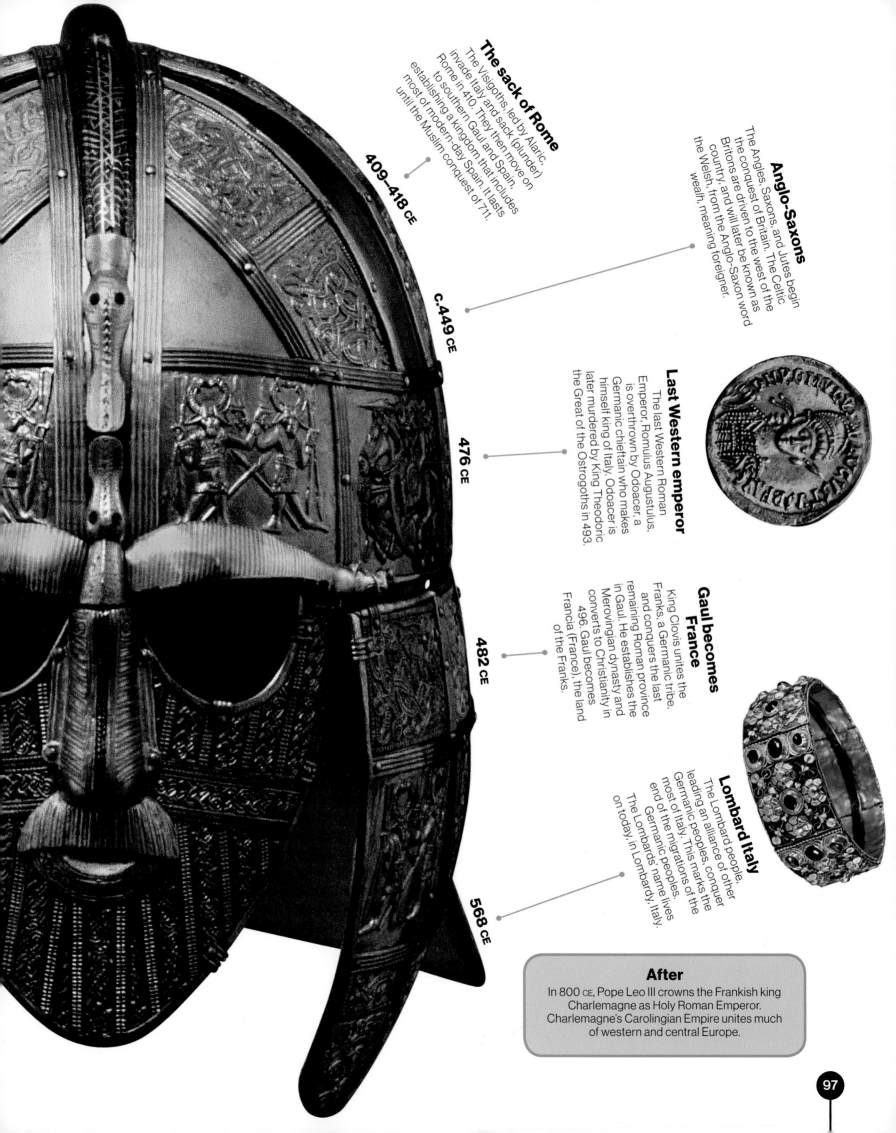

The sack of Rome

The Visigoths, led by Alaric, invade Italy and sack (plunder) Rome in 410. They then move on to southern Gaul and Spain, establishing a kingdom that includes most of modern-day Spain. It lasts until the Muslim conquest of 711.

409–418 CE

Anglo-Saxons

The Angles, Saxons, and Jutes begin the conquest of Britain. The Celtic Britons are driven to the west of the country, and will later be known as the Welsh, from the Anglo-Saxon word wealh, meaning foreigner.

c.449 CE

Last Western emperor

The last Western Roman Emperor, Romulus Augustulus, is overthrown by Odoacer, a Germanic chieftain who makes himself king of Italy. Odoacer is later murdered by King Theodoric the Great of the Ostrogoths in 493.

476 CE

Gaul becomes France

King Clovis unites the Franks, a Germanic tribe, and conquers the last remaining Roman province in Gaul. He establishes the Merovingian dynasty and converts to Christianity in 496. Gaul becomes Francia (France), the land of the Franks.

482 CE

Lombard Italy

The Lombard people, leading an alliance of other Germanic peoples, conquer most of Italy. This marks the end of the migrations of the Germanic peoples. The Lombards' name lives on today, in Lombardy, Italy.

568 CE

After

In 800 CE, Pope Leo III crowns the Frankish king Charlemagne as Holy Roman Emperor. Charlemagne's Carolingian Empire unites much of western and central Europe.

BEFORE

As the Western Roman Empire broke apart, Germanic invaders founded new kingdoms across Europe (see pages 84–85). Their leaders quickly became Christian, and they gained authority from the Church, which taught that rulers were chosen by God.

Charlemagne crowned

In Rome, Pope Leo III crowns the Frankish King Charlemagne as the first Holy Roman Emperor. Charlemagne (ruled 800–814) unites much of western Europe in his Carolingian Empire.

Vikings found Dublin

After raiding Ireland, the Vikings build a fortified camp by the Liffey River. This permanent settlement becomes the town of Dublin. The Vikings go on to found settlements at Limerick, Wexford, Waterford, and Cork.

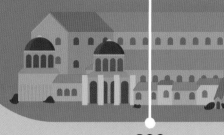

800

841

Medieval Europe

In Europe, the Medieval period, or Middle Ages, lasted from the 5th to the 15th centuries. It followed the fall of the Western Roman Empire (see pages 84–85). Medieval Europe was dominated by the Catholic Church (headed by the pope in Rome), and by ruling classes of warriors. The majority of the population was made up of peasant farmers.

The First Crusade

Pope Urban II proclaims a crusade (holy war), against the Muslims, who rule the Middle East. In 1099, the crusaders capture Jerusalem, founding four Christian states in the Middle East. Seven more crusades follow.

1095

Franciscan order

St. Francis founds an order of friars, whose role is to spread Christianity by preaching. Unlike monks, who live apart from the world in monasteries, friars live in towns among ordinary people.

1209

Battle of Las Navas de Tolosa

The Almohad Muslims of southern Spain suffer a crushing defeat in a battle against a Christian army. The Christian reconquest of Spain from Muslim control is under way.

1212

Hanseatic League

Hamburg, which has salt mines, and Lubeck, which has a herring fishery, form a trading alliance to produce salted herring. This marks the start of the Hanseatic League, a great trading association of northern German towns.

1241

Hundred Years' War

Edward III of England proclaims that, as the son of a French princess, he has more right to rule France than the new king, Philip of Valois. This begins more than a century of on-and-off warfare between England and France.

1337–1453

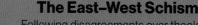

Vladimir the Great

Prince Vladimir the Great of Kievan Rus in Eastern Europe adopts a branch of Christianity known as the Eastern Orthodox Church. He orders a mass baptism of his people.

988

The East–West Schism

Following disagreements over theology (beliefs) and methods of worship, the Roman Catholic Church and the Eastern Orthodox Church fully separate. The Orthodox leaders reject the Pope's claim to have authority over them.

1054

Humbled emperor

After a quarrel, Pope Gregory VII excommunicates Henry IV, the Holy Roman Emperor, denying him Church membership. To earn the pope's pardon, Henry stands barefoot in the snow for three days at Canossa in Italy.

The Battle of Hastings

Duke William of Normandy invades England, where he defeats and kills Harold Godwinson, the last Anglo-Saxon king, at Hastings. In 1085, William orders a huge survey of his kingdom, which is later called the Domesday Book.

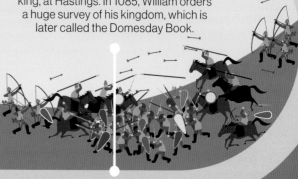

1077

1066

Joan of Arc

Joan of Arc, a farmer's daughter who claims to hear the voices of saints, leads the French to victory over the English. She is eventually captured by the English, accused of heresy, and burned at the stake for it.

Black Death

A deadly plague is carried to Europe from Central Asia on merchant ships. It spreads everywhere, killing between 30 and 60 percent of Europe's population.

Gutenberg Bible

In Germany, Johannes Gutenberg uses his printing press, invented around 1439, to produce the first printed Bible. As more people are able to read the book for themselves, many begin to question the teachings of the Catholic Church.

AFTER

At the end of the 15th century, Medieval Europe is shaken by a series of events. Christopher Columbus lands in the Americas in 1492, changing Europeans' view of the world. New theories spread by printing also lead to the rejection of many long-held ideas and beliefs.

1347–1352

1429–1431

c.1439

THE BATTLE OF CRECY

The longbow strikes back

On August 26, 1346, in Normandy in northern France, an invading English army gathered for battle on high ground near the town of Crécy and faced a French army that outnumbered them by more than two to one. However, as the combat-hungry French prepared to charge at the English defenses, the English king, Edward III, prepared a strategy that would surprise and overwhelm the dominant force of his attackers.

The Hundred Years' War

In **February 1328**, the death of the French king Charles IV leads to a succession dispute between the kingdoms of France and England. King Philip VI of France lays claim to the throne, as does the English monarch, Edward III. This power struggle leads to the beginning of the epic conflict that will become known as the Hundred Years' War in **May 1337**. Other disputes between the French and English keep the fighting going for more than 100 years. These include the control of the valuable wool trade and disputes over areas of land. On **June 24, 1340**, Edward III and his navy are victorious against the cumbersome French fleet at the Battle of Sluys. The English navy dominates the English Channel, allowing invading forces to be transported efficiently to the continent.

The English invade

In **July 1346**, an invading English army lands in Normandy and takes the town of Caen. Philip VI rallies his troops and with the assistance of King John of Bohemia, who is blind, and a regiment of around 6,000 mercenary crossbowmen from Genoa, they move north to engage the English. In **August**, Edward III and his invading army of about 14,000 men gather in preparation for battle on the hills between the towns of Crécy and Wadicourt. Word of the marching French army arrives, so the English dig trenches and construct staked barricades to protect their position. Edward III orders his knights to dismount, and the English divide into three units of spearmen, knights, and longbowmen. They are under the command of the king, his son (known as the Black Prince), and the Earl of Northampton.

The battle commences

On **August 26**, Philip VI and his 30,000-strong army of mounted knights, infantry, and crossbowmen arrive at the Crécy battlefield. At **noon**, a unit of horsemen report back to the king about the English position and recommend that his army rests and attacks the following day. With dominant numbers and an eagerness to prove the might of their army, the French noblemen persuade Philip VI to attack immediately. At around **4:00 p.m.**, as the French army marches toward the English, a rainstorm hits the battlefield and the Genoese crossbowmen are unable to shield their crossbows from the pouring rain. On the hill, the English longbowmen are prepared and protect their bowstrings from the downpour. The crossbowmen launch an attack, but their arrows land short as their range is reduced by their damp weapons.

The French retreat

The English longbowmen step forward and bombard the misfiring crossbowmen with their arrows. Their much greater range and their ability to reload faster creates chaos in the enemy ranks. Many crossbowmen fall, and in a state of panic, the French army starts to flee the battlefield. The cowardice of the Genoese is punished by the mounted French knights who slay their retreating allies. In the mud and chaos, the French cavalry charges up the hill. Again, the English archers bombard their attackers with arrows and many horses tumble, taking their riders with them. A second charge on the English is led by blind King John, who is tied to his horse and pointed in the direction of his foes. This charge is more successful, beating back the Black Prince's troops, but help from the Earl of Northampton neutralizes the French offensive and the English manage to hold their position.

Victory of the longbowmen

Throughout the **evening**, Edward III watches from the top of the hill as charge after charge by the French fails to break through his troops' defenses. The English longbowmen dominate the battle as more French soldiers fall on the muddy battlefield, including Philip's brother Charles II of Alençon. Just before **midnight**, the wounded Philip VI abandons the battlefield and seeks refuge at the castle of Labroye. The French soldiers and remaining knights follow suit, leaving more than 21,500 dead on the battlefield. The English, who count their losses at fewer than 100 men, hold their position on the hillside throughout the night before continuing their invasion of Normandy. In **1347**, after a year of besieging, King Edward III takes the port of Calais and secures a strategic foothold in northern France that will serve the English army in its ongoing war against the French for the next 200 years.

Vinland

Leif Ericsson, son of Eric the Red, sets up a settlement called Vinland in modern-day Newfoundland in Canada. Leif is probably the first European ever to set foot in the Americas.

1002

Danish domination

English king Ethelred is forced to flee as the Viking king of Denmark, Sweyn Forkbeard, conquers England. By 1016, Forkbread's son, Canute, is king of England and Denmark.

1013

Viking treasure

A huge haul of Viking treasure was found in 2007, more than 1,000 years after a Viking leader buried it for safekeeping. The Vale of York Hoard contained 617 silver coins, along with various ornaments and other treasure. The coins were found inside a large cup made during the 9th century in modern-day France or Germany. It's made of solid silver, covered with a thin layer of gold.

End of an era

As the raids end, the Viking age is over. King Harald Hardrada of Norway dies while trying to conquer part of England. In the same year, the Battle of Hastings and is William of Normandy wins crowned king of England.

1066

The Danegeld

English king Ethelred is the first to pay a new annual ransom payment to keep the Danish Vikings from raiding England. This ransom came to be known as the Danegeld.

991

Grass is greener

Viking explorer Eric the Red gathers them west to Viking people from Iceland to and takes them to settle there Greenland. The weather there is suitable and raising cattle. colony. The for growing crops

986

Christian conversion

King Harald Bluetooth of Denmark converts to Christianity. Christian priests travel around Viking settlements to encourage other people to convert. Most Vikings give up their traditional beliefs and become Christians.

960

Keeping cool

Viking settlers reach Iceland. In 930, they establish a parliament called the Althing, which still exists today. Although the location has changed, it is the oldest surviving parliament in the world.

c.870

Viking capital

The 'Great Army' conquers most of the Anglo-Saxon kingdoms that make up present-day England. In 866, they capture the important city now known as York in northern England, and make it their new capital, Jorvik.

865-866

Novgorod

Swedish Vikings establish themselves in the trading settlement at Novgorod in present-day Russia. They use the great rivers down to the Black Sea to trade with foreign emperors.

862

The Vikings

Originally from Denmark, Norway, and Sweden, the Vikings were farmers and traders. From the 8th century onward, they left their homelands to invade territories far and wide, raiding and ransacking their way around Europe. They were master craftspeople, building huge wooden longships to travel, and making fine jewelry to trade with other populations. By the 11th century, they had established themselves in settlements across the continent.

860

Constantinople

Viking raids reach as far as the city of Constantinople, now known as Istanbul in modern-day Turkey. They catch the city off guard, sailing in on 200 longboats to loot monasteries and homes.

841

Emerald isle

Norwegian Vikings establish a trading settlement in Ireland. Built on marshland, this settlement goes on to become the city of Dublin. From this new base, they launch further attacks on the south and west of the island.

793

First raids

The first known Viking raid occurs suddenly in northeast England. The terrible attack on the Lindisfarne monastery. The Vikings continue their rampage, with further raids in Ireland, and France.

The Crusades

In the 11th century, a Christian army set off to regain Jerusalem, a sacred site in both Christianity and Islam, from Muslim control in a military expedition known as a crusade. This was the first of eight crusades that would take place over the next 200 years. The Christians were ultimately unsuccessful.

Crusading call

Pope Urban II declares the First Crusade, calling upon European Christian knights to help take Jerusalem from Muslim control. Hundreds take a holy vow to join the crusade and wear a cross as a sign of their commitment.

1095

Capture of Jerusalem

The army of the First Crusade sets off in 1096, reaching the walls of Jerusalem three years later. It captures the city amid terrible scenes of slaughter, and the Crusaders set up four Christian kingdoms in the Middle East.

1099

Second Crusade

After a Muslim army captures the Crusader city of Edessa in 1144, a leading French churchman, St. Bernard of Clairvaux, launches the Second Crusade to win it back. The crusade ends in failure for the Christians.

1147–1149

Battle of Hattin

Saladin, a Muslim warrior, revitalizes the Muslim forces in the Middle East. They defeat a Christian army at the Battle of Hattin, and storm most of the Crusader kingdoms, including Jerusalem.

1187

Third Crusade

Led by King Richard I the Lionheart of England and King Philip II Augustus of France, the Third Crusade recaptures the trading port of Acre from Saladin's forces, but fails to retake Jerusalem.

1189–1192

LANDS OF THE CRUSADES

Fourth Crusade

This crusade sets off to recapture Jerusalem, but ends in disaster. A Christian army reaches the Orthodox Christian city of Constantinople, the capital of the Byzantine Empire. Instead of carrying on to Jerusalem, the soldiers sack Constantinople and steal its treasures.

1204

Fifth Crusade

The Fifth Crusade makes a new attempt to regain Jerusalem, this time by first conquering the powerful Muslim state of Egypt. The Crusaders are trapped by the annual flood of the Nile River and forced to retreat.

1217–1221

Sixth Crusade

Frederick II, the German emperor, launches the Sixth Crusade. It involves very little fighting, and he makes a treaty with the Sultan of Egypt that restores Jerusalem to the Christians for a short time.

1228–1229

Saintly Crusader

King Louis IX of France leads two unsuccessful crusades. Captured in Egypt in 1254 during the Seventh Crusade, he dies in Tunisia in 1270 while on the Eighth Crusade. He is later made a saint.

1248–1270

End of the Crusades

Acre, the last major Crusader-controlled stronghold in Palestine, falls to a Muslim army. It marks the end of Crusader influence in the Middle East. No further crusades are organized to Jerusalem.

1291

First emperor of Nam-Viet

With the fall of China's Qin Dynasty, former general Zhao Tuo makes himself king of Nam-Viet (modern-day northern Vietnam and southern China). Some Vietnamese consider him to be their first emperor.

207 BCE

Chinese conquer Nam-Viet

Emperor Wu of China's Han Dynasty invades and conquers Nam-Viet. Chinese rule will last for more than 1,000 years, as the Han extend their influence throughout the region.

111 BCE

Funan

The state of Funan is created in modern-day southern Cambodia and the Mekong Delta of South Vietnam. Influenced by trade with India, the Funanese become Hindus and use the Sanskrit language.

c.50 CE

Champa

The Champa Kingdom of modern-day South Vietnam, influenced by Funan, adopts Hinduism and uses Sanskrit. Champa becomes a great naval power, controlling the spice trade in the South China Sea.

c.350

Srivijaya Empire

Rulers of Srivijaya in Sumatra take over the Malay peninsula, Java, and West Borneo, and many islands. The Srivijaya Empire is a great coastal power. Srivijaya kings follow Mahayana Buddhism and establish monasteries in India.

650–c.1300

Khmer Empire

King Jayavarman II, who is traditionally seen as the founder of the Khmer Empire in modern-day Cambodia, unites the region under his rule. The state religion is Hinduism, based on worship of Vishnu and Shiva.

802

Kingdoms of Southeast Asia

Southeast Asia lies at one of the world's great crossroads, in the middle of a trade and pilgrimage route between India and China and the Spice Islands. From the 1st century CE, wealthy kingdoms emerged here. Rulers took Indian names, and adopted both Hinduism and Buddhism. Later, Muslim traders brought Islam to the region.

BEFORE

From 600 BCE, people living by the Red River in modern-day northern Vietnam created the Dong Son culture. They were fishers and rice farmers, as well as skilled metalworkers of bronze and iron.

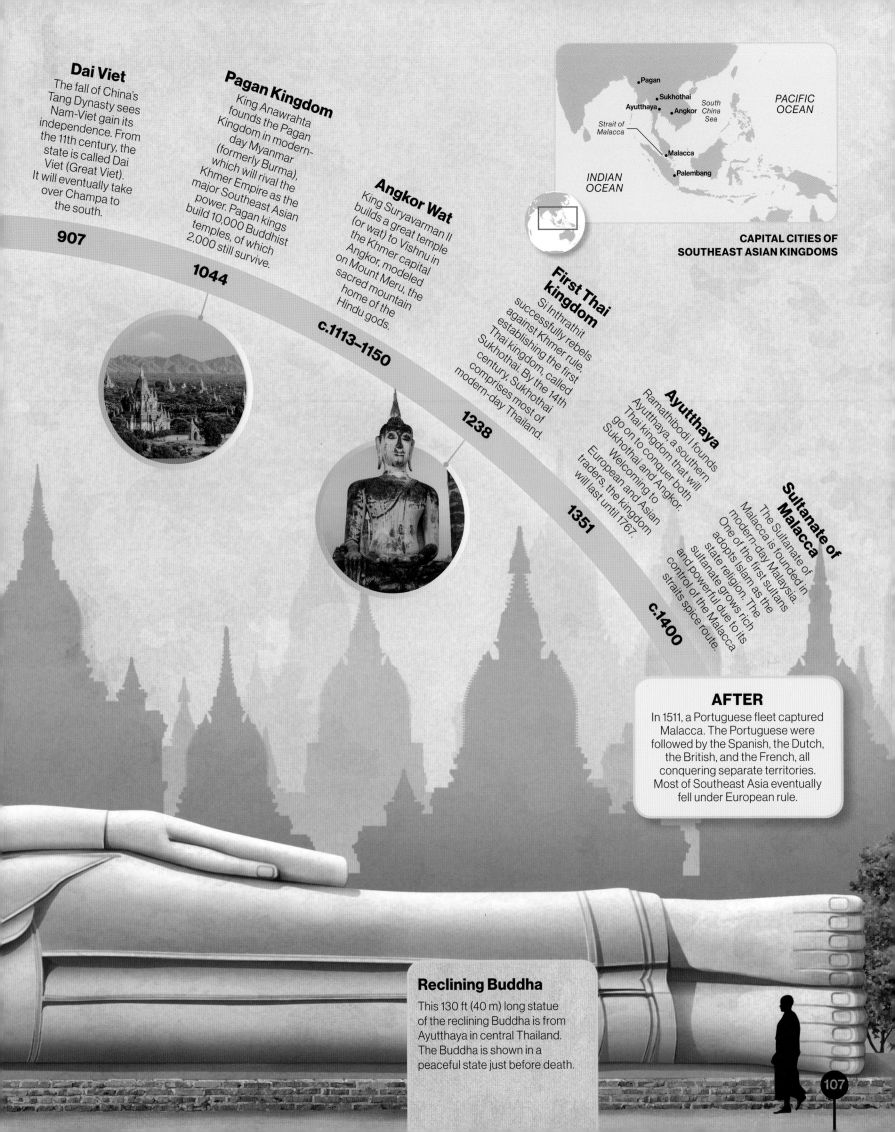

Dai Viet

The fall of China's Tang Dynasty sees Nam-Viet gain its independence. From the 11th century, the state is called Dai Viet (Great Viet). It will eventually take over Champa to the south.

907

Pagan Kingdom

King Anawrahta founds the Pagan Kingdom in modern-day Myanmar (formerly Burma), which will rival the Khmer Empire as the major Southeast Asian power. Pagan kings build 10,000 Buddhist temples, of which 2,000 still survive.

1044

Angkor Wat

King Suryavarman II builds a great temple (or wat) to Vishnu in the Khmer capital Angkor, modeled on Mount Meru, the sacred mountain home of the Hindu gods.

c.1113–1150

First Thai kingdom

Si Inthrathit successfully rebels against Khmer rule, establishing the first Thai kingdom, called Sukhothai. By the 14th century, Sukhothai comprises most of modern-day Thailand.

1238

Ayutthaya

Ramathibodi I founds Ayutthaya, a southern Thai kingdom that will go on to conquer both Sukhothai and Angkor. Welcoming to European and Asian traders, the kingdom will last until 1767.

1351

Sultanate of Malacca

The Sultanate of Malacca is founded in modern-day Malaysia. One of the first sultans adopts Islam as the state religion. The sultanate grows rich and powerful due to its control of the Malacca straits spice route.

c.1400

CAPITAL CITIES OF SOUTHEAST ASIAN KINGDOMS

Pagan
Sukhothai
Ayutthaya
Angkor
South China Sea
PACIFIC OCEAN
Strait of Malacca
INDIAN OCEAN
Malacca
Palembang

AFTER

In 1511, a Portuguese fleet captured Malacca. The Portuguese were followed by the Spanish, the Dutch, the British, and the French, all conquering separate territories. Most of Southeast Asia eventually fell under European rule.

Reclining Buddha

This 130 ft (40 m) long statue of the reclining Buddha is from Ayutthaya in central Thailand. The Buddha is shown in a peaceful state just before death.

Angkor Wat

The largest religious monument in the world, Angkor Wat (meaning "temple city") was originally built as a Hindu place of worship. It was constructed in the early 12th century in the reign of Suryavarman II of the Khmer Empire (in modern-day Cambodia). Hidden for centuries by jungle, it was rediscovered by Europeans in 1860. The outer walls represent the edge of the world, and the moat the cosmic ocean. The lotus bud designs on the towers are important Hindu symbols.

Rise of the samurai

According to legend, the first emperor of Japan, Jimmu, came to power in the 7th century BCE. His descendants controlled the country for more than 1,800 years. But in the late 12th century, the elite warrior class known as the samurai became the real power behind the throne. This began a time of conflict between warlords that would only end with the unification of Japan in 1603.

> **"Respect, Honesty, Courage, Rectitude, Loyalty, Honor, Benevolence."**
>
> **Yamamoto Tsunetomo** on the virtues of a samurai,
> *Hagakure: The Book of the Samurai,* 1716

Kamakura Shogunate

Yoritomo is formally recognized as shogun. His base of operations is at the city of Kamakura. The transfer of power from the emperor's capital at Kyoto is the beginning of an era in which the samurai class would become Japan's military and social elite.

Ashikaga Shogunate

Two years after seizing control, Ashikaga Takauji is formally recognized as shogun. He then founds his own dynasty, the Ashikaga Shogunate.

Genkō War

The Kamakura Shogunate is brought down with the help of one of its former generals, Ashikaga Takauji. Emperor Go-Daigo restores imperial power for a short time.

1185 1192 1274 1333 1338

First shogun

At the battle of Dan-no-ura, the Minamoto clan defeats the imperial favorites, the Taira clan. Minamoto Yoritomo is named shogun (military dictator), and the Japanese emperor becomes a powerless figurehead.

Divine wind

Two attempts by China to invade Japan, in 1274 and 1281, fail when their navies run into typhoons (tropical storms). On both occasions, the *kamikaze* ("divine wind") is credited with saving Japan from foreign invasion.

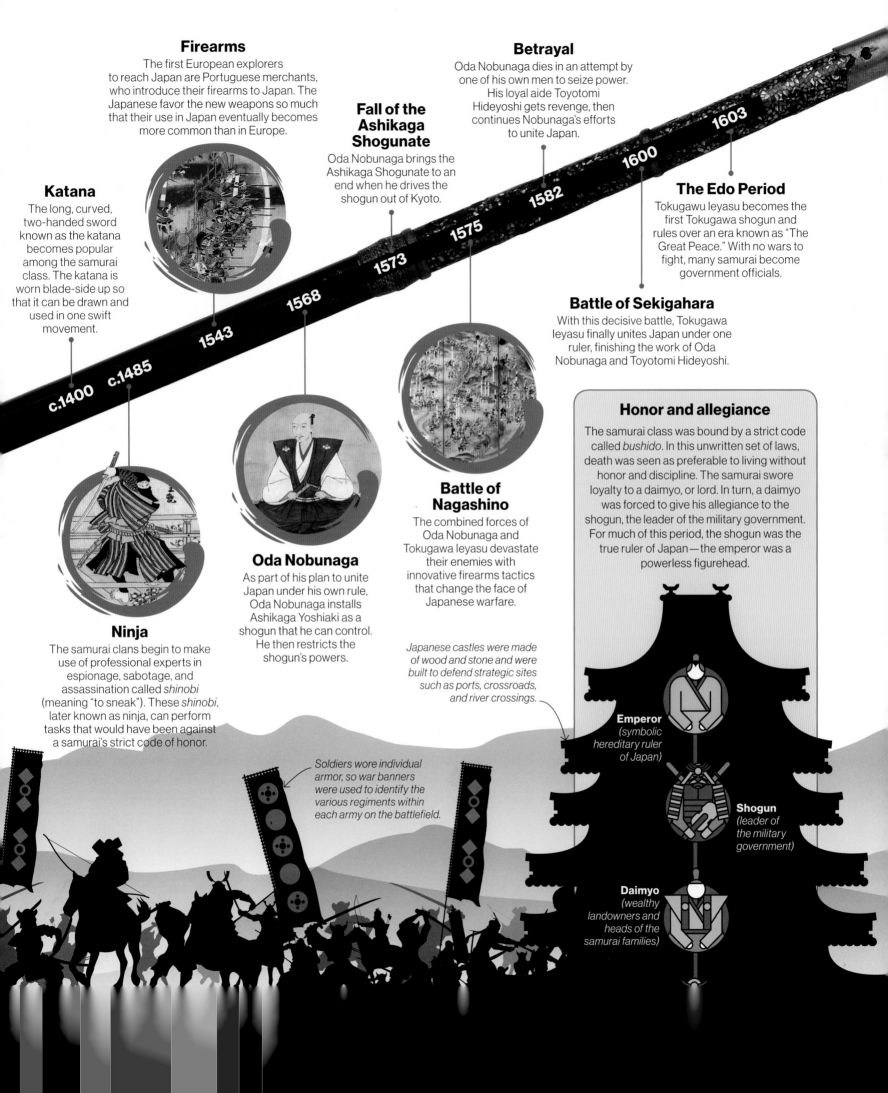

Firearms

The first European explorers to reach Japan are Portuguese merchants, who introduce their firearms to Japan. The Japanese favor the new weapons so much that their use in Japan eventually becomes more common than in Europe.

Fall of the Ashikaga Shogunate

Oda Nobunaga brings the Ashikaga Shogunate to an end when he drives the shogun out of Kyoto.

Betrayal

Oda Nobunaga dies in an attempt by one of his own men to seize power. His loyal aide Toyotomi Hideyoshi gets revenge, then continues Nobunaga's efforts to unite Japan.

Katana

The long, curved, two-handed sword known as the katana becomes popular among the samurai class. The katana is worn blade-side up so that it can be drawn and used in one swift movement.

The Edo Period

Tokugawu Ieyasu becomes the first Tokugawa shogun and rules over an era known as "The Great Peace." With no wars to fight, many samurai become government officials.

Battle of Sekigahara

With this decisive battle, Tokugawa Ieyasu finally unites Japan under one ruler, finishing the work of Oda Nobunaga and Toyotomi Hideyoshi.

1603
1600
1582
1575
1573
1568
1543
c.1485
c.1400

Ninja

The samurai clans begin to make use of professional experts in espionage, sabotage, and assassination called *shinobi* (meaning "to sneak"). These *shinobi*, later known as ninja, can perform tasks that would have been against a samurai's strict code of honor.

Oda Nobunaga

As part of his plan to unite Japan under his own rule, Oda Nobunaga installs Ashikaga Yoshiaki as a shogun that he can control. He then restricts the shogun's powers.

Battle of Nagashino

The combined forces of Oda Nobunaga and Tokugawa Ieyasu devastate their enemies with innovative firearms tactics that change the face of Japanese warfare.

Japanese castles were made of wood and stone and were built to defend strategic sites such as ports, crossroads, and river crossings.

Honor and allegiance

The samurai class was bound by a strict code called *bushido*. In this unwritten set of laws, death was seen as preferable to living without honor and discipline. The samurai swore loyalty to a daimyo, or lord. In turn, a daimyo was forced to give his allegiance to the shogun, the leader of the military government. For much of this period, the shogun was the true ruler of Japan—the emperor was a powerless figurehead.

Emperor *(symbolic hereditary ruler of Japan)*

Shogun *(leader of the military government)*

Daimyo *(wealthy landowners and heads of the samurai families)*

Soldiers wore individual armor, so war banners were used to identify the various regiments within each army on the battlefield.

Castles

Ancient civilizations built walls around their towns and settlements to protect them from attack, but castles as we think of them today only developed around 1,000 years ago. With their tall towers, strong walls, and wide moats to hold off attackers, they dominated the landscape of medieval Europe and elsewhere.

Roman fort

The Roman army construct stone forts, or camps, throughout their empire. They build them all to a similar layout, containing barracks, workshops, baths, and stores. Each fort is called a *castrum*, which is where the word "castle" comes from.

c.27 BCE–300 CE

Motte-and-bailey castle

In Europe, powerful lords pay to build castles out of earth and wood to keep attacking armies out. They consist of a mound (motte) topped by a tower (keep), and a yard (bailey) at the foot of the mound, all protected by a wooden fence.

c.950–1070

Stone keep

Castles throughout Europe are now being built of stone. Keeps are three or four stories high. At first the towers are square in shape, but later they become circular as this means they are more difficult to attack.

c.1070–1150

Strong defenses

Knights returning from the Crusades (see pages 104–105) bring back new ideas about castle building. Castles are now built on cliff tops or surrounded by moats to make them stronger. They have thick walls, tall towers, and defensive, fortified gatehouses at the entrance.

c.1200–1300

Inside the castle

Castles are home to the lord, his family, and their servants. The hall, where meals are served, has a large fireplace. There are bedchambers, a chapel, a kitchen, and even toilets (called "garderobes").

1100–1400

The story of philosophy

Philosophy means "love of wisdom" in Ancient Greek, and it describes a way of thinking about the world. Philosophers ask questions about the nature of reality, and the meaning of life itself. Two traditions of philosophy appeared in the ancient world. In Europe, the Greeks attempted to answer these questions without relying on religion. In Asia, philosophy and religion were seen as two parts of a single subject.

From 1921
The language of philosophy
Analytic philosophers question how philosophy itself is affected by the rules of language. Austrian Ludwig Wittgenstein says that we can only talk or write about things that we can experience.

From 1843
Individual meaning
The existentialists place the individual person at the center of their philosophy. The earliest existentialist is Danish philosopher Søren Kierkegaard, who says that each individual must give meaning to their life by living it sincerely.

From 1960
Examine the background
The post-structuralists believe that to study a thing, you must also study the environment around it. For example, Bulgarian thinker Julia Kristeva argues that the feminist movement is influenced by ideas from the male-dominated society that it is attempting to resist.

From 1756
Political philosophy
In the 18th and 19th centuries, political philosophers write about the best way for people to live and work together. Anglo-Irish politician Edmund Burke argues that societies exist to help us fulfil each other's needs.

From 1781
The world as we know it
Idealist philosophies all feature the belief that true reality cannot be known. Immanuel Kant says that knowledge comes from the senses. This means we cannot experience things as they are, only as we see, feel, hear, taste, or smell them.

From 1637
All in the mind
The rationalists believe that reason (the mind's ability to understand) is the foundation of all knowledge. French philosopher René Descartes concludes that because he knows he can think, he must really exist.

From 1689
World of experience
The empiricists believe that experience is the foundation of all knowledge. English philosopher John Locke says that it is impossible to know anything beyond what we can discover though our senses.

15th–16th century
Renaissance ideas
Dutchman Desiderius Erasmus and the humanists of the Renaissance (see pages 136–137) reject organized religion in favor of individual relationships with God. They place people themselves at the center of their philosophy.

End of the dinosaurs

Almost 66 million years ago, a catastrophic event occurred that wiped out more than half of life on Earth, including the dinosaurs. Most experts believe this mass extinction was caused by an enormous meteorite crashing into Earth. Such a huge impact would have created a worldwide cloud of dust and fumes, choking animals and blocking out the Sun's light and warmth. The planet's climate would have changed dramatically, making life impossible for many species.

Indian hill fort

Shivaji, the founder of the Maratha empire in India (see pages 162–162), builds and restores more than 300 hill forts in his war against the Mughals. Their huge stone walls exploit the natural features of the land.

1660–1680

Vauban forts

During the reign of King Louis XIV of France, the great military engineer Sébastien de Vauban constructs hundreds of fortresses and towers along the borders of France.

1667–1707

A bastion

Star fort

Tall towers and walls are easily destroyed by cannon fire, so a new type of fortification called a star fort is developed in Italy. They are low in height, and protected by sections called bastions coming off the center.

c.1500–1600

c.1570–1600

Japanese castle

Rival warlords (*daimyo*) in Japan build themselves strong castles as symbols of their authority. These castles are mostly made of wood, standing on tall stone platforms surrounded by rings of moats.

Built for show

Castles are now being built for show as much as for defense. Living quarters are becoming luxurious and spacious. Towers are covered with battlements to make them look impressive, and they have round holes to fire guns through.

c.1400

Brick castle

Because of a lack of stone in the plains of northern Europe, castles there are often built of brick. Malbork Castle, in present-day Poland, is built by the Teutonic Knights, a religious crusading order. It is still the largest castle in the world today.

c.1300

Early North America

The first people to arrive in North America no doubt did so without realizing it. Like their ancestors, they were hunting mammoths and other animals, following them along the Siberian coast and across the land bridge between Asia and North America. Once in Alaska, over the following thousands of years, these people gradually spread across what is now North America. By 10,000 BCE, life was well established there.

> "As long as the Sun shines and the waters flow, this land will be here to give life to men and animals."
> **Crowfoot Chief Siksika**

Bridge closed

Sea levels start to rise and Beringia is submerged. By now, hunter-gatherers have reached the prairies of modern-day Canada and the eastern side of the modern-day US.

c.25,000 BCE	c.22,000 BCE	c.10,000 BCE	9500 BCE	9000 BCE

Land bridge

During the last Ice Age, Asia and America are connected by a flat, grassy, treeless landscape (tundra) called Beringia. Hungry humans hunt animals and follow them across the tundra. Some historians believe people also arrive by boat.

Home in Beringia

People make their homes in Beringia for generations. According to some scientists, they are trapped there by huge ice sheets, but when the ice melts, they will move south into modern-day Canada and the US.

Moving south

Hunters spread throughout the North American grasslands into the American Southwest. They make sharp, stony spearheads (Clovis points) to hunt big animals such as the mastodon (a prehistoric relative of the modern-day elephant).

Amazing maize

In the Eastern Woodlands (a large part of modern-day eastern Canada), people hunt, fish, and gather, while in the desert regions of the Southwest, people learn how to grow corn (maize) and other crops. They also make tools, such as hammers and grinding gear, as well as pottery.

Adena culture

The Adena people use plants to make shoes, clothes, and bags. They also build amazing land sculptures such as Ohio's Serpent Mound with only baskets, digging sticks, and manual labor. Mounds such as these were probably used to bury important tribe members.

Pueblo culture

The Pueblo people in the Southwest use earth bricks, stone slabs, and mud and sticks to build their homes. Soon, they construct large apartmentlike structures. They weave cloth from cotton, grow a range of vegetable crops, and use coal.

Cahokia

The impressive city of Cahokia is near modern-day St. Louis. Its people build huge mounds topped by temples, surrounded by city streets, suburbs, and then farmland. It is as large as London or Paris at the same time.

| 8500 BCE | c.800 BCE | c.100 BCE | c.700 | c.800 | 1050 | 1050 |

Hopewell culture

These hunter-gatherers and farmers live in villages of rectangular houses with thatched roofs. They grow sunflowers, squash, and other seed-bearing plants. They also make pottery in new shapes such as bowls and jars, and pipes that are decorated with models of animals.

Mighty Mississippians

The people of the Mississippian culture build giant earth pyramids and set up huge trading networks connecting the eastern half of North America. They exchange pottery, woven items, copper, rare crystals, and shells.

Hunting bison

People living on America's Great Plains have hunted mammoths for a very long time, but as these die out, bison become the main target. Hunters make "buffalo jumps" to kill large numbers of bison at once. They build funnels from trees, rocks, poles, and people. Stampeding herds of bison rush through the funnels and over cliff edges.

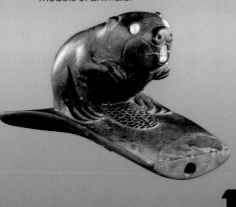

Inuit ancestors

The ancestors of the Inuit people arrive in the frozen lands of the Canadian Arctic. These hunter-gatherers live in groups of around 100 people, moving camps season by season to follow whales, caribou (reindeer), seals, and other prey.

Settling the Pacific

Many thousands of years ago, European ships never sailed far from land. But skilful sailors in the Pacific Ocean made voyages of up to 3,000 miles (4,800 km) to settle on tiny islands.

1600–500 BCE Lapita people
The Lapita people spread through Micronesia and part of Polynesia. They are traders and expert sailors. Their descendants, the Polynesians, will venture even further out in the Pacific Ocean.

1025–1121
Polynesians set out
Polynesians begin to sail east, settling an area of the Pacific from the Society Islands to the Gambier Islands.

1280
New Zealand
Polynesians reach New Zealand, which they call *Aotearoa* ("Land of the Long White Cloud"). The settlers, who are called Maori people, adapt to the cooler climate in New Zealand. They hunt large flightless birds, such as moa (above).

1330–1440 Extinction
Ten species of moa become extinct in New Zealand, caused by Maori hunting, deforestation, and the introduction of rats, which eat the birds' eggs. Many other small animals also go extinct.

c.50,000 BCE Melanesia
Melanesia is first settled by people from Southeast Asia. Sea levels are relatively low at this time, so there is more land. People can travel to these new regions by a combination of sailing and walking.

800 CE Cook Islands
People from Tahiti, Tonga, and Samoa colonize the Southern Cook Islands. These people are skilled at carving wood and stone. All of the Pacific voyagers use canoes that have one or more supports, called outriggers. These boats are fast, but can also sail in rough waters.

1200–1290
Social systems
Different social systems evolve on different islands. On densely populated islands, such as Tahiti and Hawaii, chiefs have great power, receiving tribute and labor from ordinary people. More equal societies are created on the thinly populated smaller islands.

1300–1500 Easter Island
Easter Islanders set up 887 huge stone statues of their ancestors and chiefs, called Moai. Modern-day experiments show they were probably transported upright from quarries using ropes and log rollers.

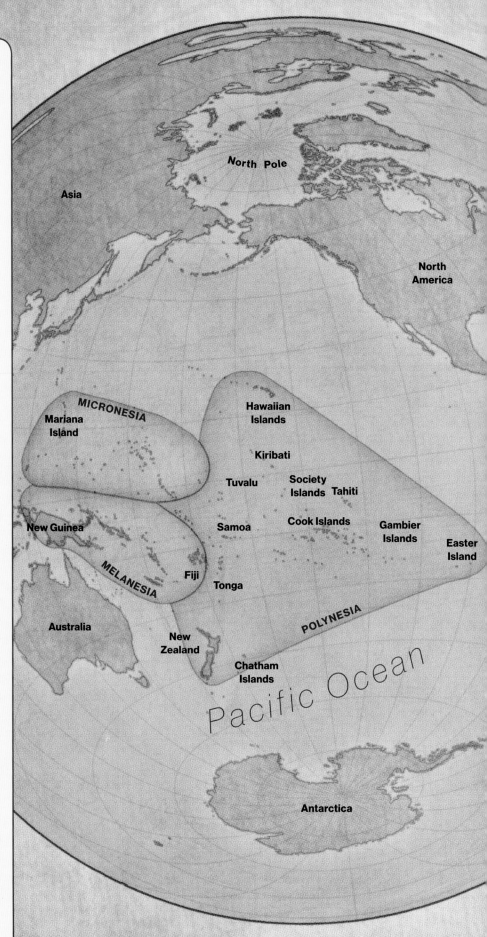

Pacific settlements

The three subregions of Melanesia, Micronesia, and Polynesia were first settled by people from Asia. As explorers ventured out into the ocean, each island within these subregions developed its own distinct culture, but all worshipped the same gods.

Intrepid explorer

English captain James Cook's voyages prove to be pivotal in European understanding of the geography and inhabitants of the Pacific Ocean. On his three voyages, he maps the east coast of Australia, New Zealand, and the Hawaiian Islands, and records a string of places previously unknown to Europeans.

The colonization of the Pacific

By 1300 CE, Polynesians had settled a vast area of the Pacific, from the Hawaiian Islands to New Zealand and Easter Island. When Europeans arrived later, they were amazed to find such widespread islands inhabited by Polynesians.

1722 Easter Island visit
Jacob Roggeveen from the Netherlands is the first European to visit Easter Island. He finds a thriving society, where the Moai are still standing, and people are still using canoes.

1642 Tasman
Dutch explorer Abel Tasman visits New Zealand, where his boats are attacked by Maori war canoes. After four sailors are killed, Tasman sails off.

1767 Tahiti
British naval officer Samuel Wallis arrives in Tahiti. At first, he is attacked by warriors in war canoes, but the Tahitians soon make peace. Tahiti is seen as a paradise by European visitors.

1769 Secrets of navigation
British explorer James Cook asks Tahitians how they managed to navigate across the vast ocean on their simple canoes. He hears that the islanders used the Sun, Moon, and stars to navigate, and gains very valuable information about the ocean.

1774 Easter Island collapse
Cook reaches Easter Island and finds that the statues have been neglected. He sees only three canoes, all unseaworthy. Easter Island society had collapsed— one theory states that the islanders' way of life ruined the island's environment.

1778–1779 Last voyages
James Cook makes two visits to Hawaii. He is killed in a quarrel after islanders steal a rowboat.

1828–1900 Colonization
European, Asian, and American powers race to seize control of the Pacific islands. During this time, France colonizes Tahiti, and Fiji, Kiribati, and Tuvalu come under British control. By 1900, the US controls Hawaii, and Germany has claimed Samoa.

1835 Massacre
A seal-hunting ship arrives in New Zealand with news of the peaceful society of the Chatham Islands, whose people do not know how to fight. Nine hundred Maori warriors then sail to the Chatham Islands, where they kill or enslave the local population.

1840 Treaty of Waitangi
The British Empire signs the Treaty of Waitangi with Maori chiefs, which recognizes Maori ownership of their lands. The treaty brings the country into the British Empire.

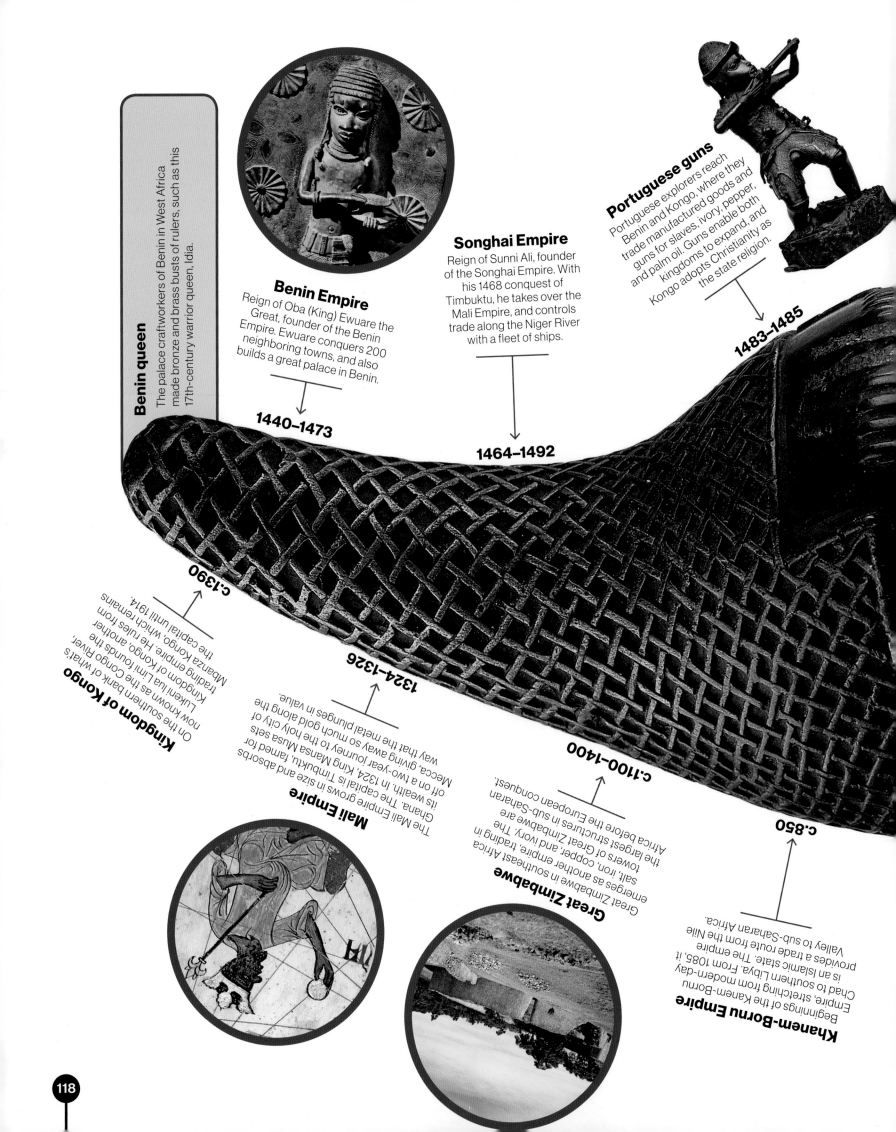

Benin Empire

Reign of Oba (King) Ewuare the Great, founder of the Benin Empire. Ewuare conquers 200 neighboring towns, and also builds a great palace in Benin.

1440–1473

Songhai Empire

Reign of Sunni Ali, founder of the Songhai Empire. With his 1468 conquest of Timbuktu, he takes over the Mali Empire, and controls trade along the Niger River with a fleet of ships.

1464–1492

Portuguese guns

Portuguese explorers reach Benin and Kongo, where they trade manufactured goods and guns for slaves, ivory, pepper, and palm oil. Guns enable both kingdoms to expand, and Kongo adopts Christianity as the state religion.

1483–1485

Kingdom of Kongo

On the southern bank of what's now known as the Congo River, Lukeni lua Nimi founds the trading empire of Kongo, another Kingdom of Kongo. He rules from Mbanza Kongo, which remains the capital until 1914.

c.1390

Mali Empire

The Mali Empire grows in size and absorbs Ghana. The capital is Timbuktu, famed for its wealth. In 1324, King Mansa Musa sets off on a two-year journey to the holy city of Mecca, giving away so much gold along the way that the metal plunges in value.

1324–1326

Great Zimbabwe

Great Zimbabwe in southeast Africa emerges as another empire, trading in salt, iron, copper, and ivory. The towers of Great Zimbabwe are the largest structures in sub-Saharan Africa before the European conquest.

c.1100–1400

Khanem-Bornu Empire

Beginnings of the Kanem-Bornu Empire, stretching from modern-day Chad to southern Libya. From 1085, it is an Islamic state. The empire provides a trade route from the Nile Valley to sub-Saharan Africa.

c.850

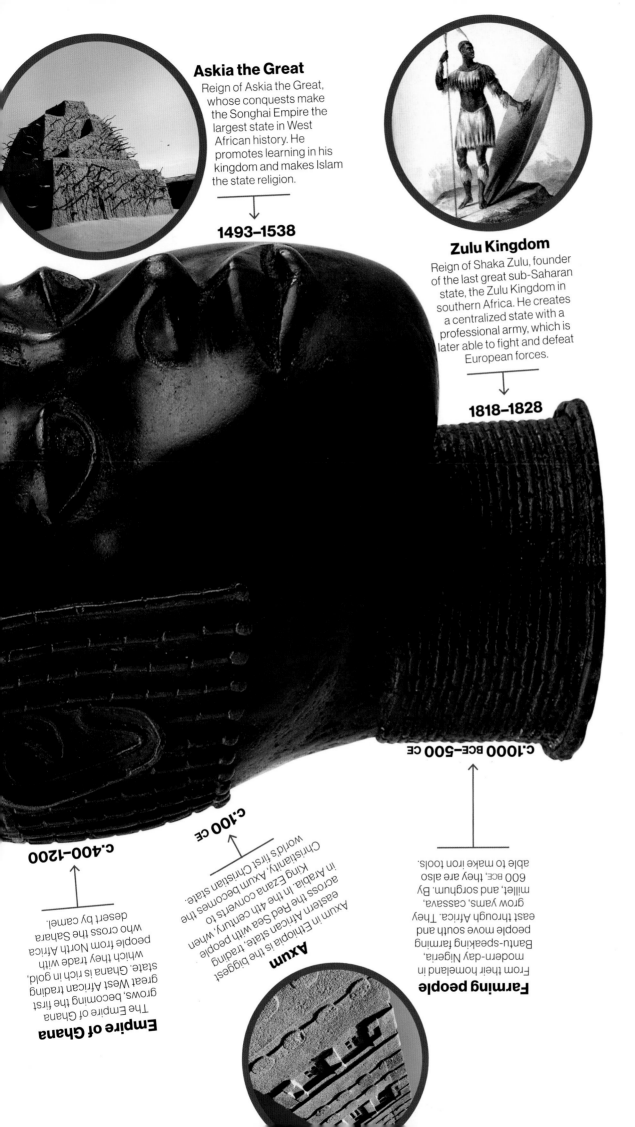

Askia the Great

Reign of Askia the Great, whose conquests make the Songhai Empire the largest state in West African history. He promotes learning in his kingdom and makes Islam the state religion.

1493–1538

Zulu Kingdom

Reign of Shaka Zulu, founder of the last great sub-Saharan state, the Zulu Kingdom in southern Africa. He creates a centralized state with a professional army, which is later able to fight and defeat European forces.

1818–1828

AFTER

King Leopold of Belgium claims personal ownership of the Congo in order to get its mineral wealth. This begins a "scramble for Africa" among the European powers, which ends in the conquest of all the African states, except for Liberia and Ethiopia.

African kingdoms

Sub-Saharan Africa has seen a series of powerful kingdoms and empires rise and fall. While ordinary Africans were mostly farmers, the wealth of the kingdoms was based on trade, mostly of gold, ivory, salt, and slaves. Trade was conducted across the Sahara by camel caravans, and by boat along the great rivers such as the Niger and the Congo.

c.1000 BCE–500 CE

Farming people

From their homeland in modern-day Nigeria, Bantu-speaking farming people move south and east through Africa. They grow yams, cassava, millet, and sorghum. By 600 BCE, they are also able to make iron tools.

c.100 CE

Axum

Axum in Ethiopia is the biggest eastern African state, trading across the Red Sea with people in Arabia. In the 4th century, when King Ezana converts to Christianity, Axum becomes the world's first Christian state.

c.400–1200

Empire of Ghana

The Empire of Ghana grows, becoming the first great West African trading state. Ghana is rich in gold, which they trade with people from North Africa who cross the Sahara desert by camel.

The Mongol Empire

The nomadic tribes known as the Mongols joined together to build the largest land empire in history, stretching across Europe, the Middle East, and Asia. The founder of the empire was the invincible Genghis Khan. He was skilled in military strategy and led his army, which consisted almost entirely of horsemen armed with bows and arrows, to many victories.

Horse trouble

Genghis's horsemen lead his rise to power, but in early 1227, he falls off of his horse. He never really recovers, and dies in August. Afterward, his heirs, including Batu, Ogedei, and Kublai, continue to build the empire.

Tribes united

By relying on fearsome fighters instead of family members, Temujin forms a loyal band of warriors. By 1205, he rules his rivals. He holds a meeting with other Mongol leaders from all over the territory to form a nation. He names himself Genghis Khan, which means "universal ruler."

Early life of Genghis Khan

Temujin (later named Genghis Khan) is born somewhere between modern-day Mongolia and Siberia. The nomadic tribes here are always fighting. After his clan leaves his family to fend for themselves or else starve to death, Temujin goes on to gather his own tribe of followers.

On to China

The Mongol army, almost entirely on horses armed with bows and arrows, targets China. They battle the Xi Xia Empire in central China, then attack the Jin Dynasty of the north. In 1214, the Mongols take the Jin capital city, Zhongdu (modern-day Beijing).

First attack on Russia

Genghis's grandson Batu Khan leads attacks to the west of Mongol territory. Rus' (in modern-day Russia) becomes part of his empire. It is known as the Golden Horde, perhaps because of the Mongol rulers' yellow tents.

c.1162

c.1200

1205–1206

c.1206

1207–1214

1227

1237

Arrows in warfare

Mongol warriors fill the skies with deadly arrows. These can hit targets up to 1050 ft (320 m) away, and so the victims never see them coming. Hollow whistle arrows sing like flutes, so commanders can send signals to troops across a noisy battlefield.

Postal system

Genghis and his warrior leaders across the huge new empire need to communicate with each other quickly, so they set up a relay messenger and delivery service called Yam, meaning "checkpoint."

Conquest of the Song Dynasty

In their last big show of military power, Kublai's forces attack southern China. They capture most of the territory and Kublai brings nearly all of China together.

Moving west

Batu Khan seeks to expand the Golden Horde into Western Europe. One by one, new territories fall, but when he hears about his uncle Ogedei's death, he gives up his quest.

Defeat in the west

The Mamluks of Egypt under their general, Baybars, work out a clever strategy to outsmart the Mongols. The underdogs win at the Battle of Ain Jalut, which ends the Mongol expansion to the west.

1241   **1257**   **1260**   **1264**   **1274**   **1279**   **1368**

Invasion of Vietnam

Under Kublai Khan, the Mongols hope to smash their way into power in Dai Viet (part of modern-day Vietnam). Three invasions fail, but the Tran Dynasty rulers decide to surrender anyway, in order to put an end to the fighting.

Kublai Khan

One grandson of Genghis, Kublai Khan, argues with his brothers about who will rule. Kublai names himself the new Great Khan. In China, he founds the Yuan Dynasty and is the country's first non-Chinese ruler.

Invasion of Japan

Kublai invades Japan with a fleet of ships. On the ground, his army throws grenades—metal jars filled with gunpowder. In a second invasion, typhoon winds wreck most of Khan's fleet. The Japanese call the storm *kamikaze*, meaning "divine winds."

End of rule in China

The Mongols are harsh rulers, and a series of natural disasters make things even worse for the Chinese. Rebel Zhu Yuanzhang attacks the Mongols and drives them out of the country to start the Ming Dynasty.

The Silk Road and the Pax Mongolica

An ancient network of routes, known as the Silk Road, connected travelers and traders from East Asia to the West. When the Mongols took control of this route at the beginning of the 13th century, they made sure people could travel safely. This peaceful and stable time was known as the Pax Mongolica. Some less welcome visitors made the journey, too: fleas. These pests carried the Plague from the East to Europe, wiping out about 25 percent of the population.

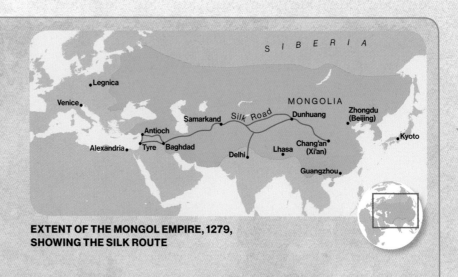

EXTENT OF THE MONGOL EMPIRE, 1279, SHOWING THE SILK ROUTE

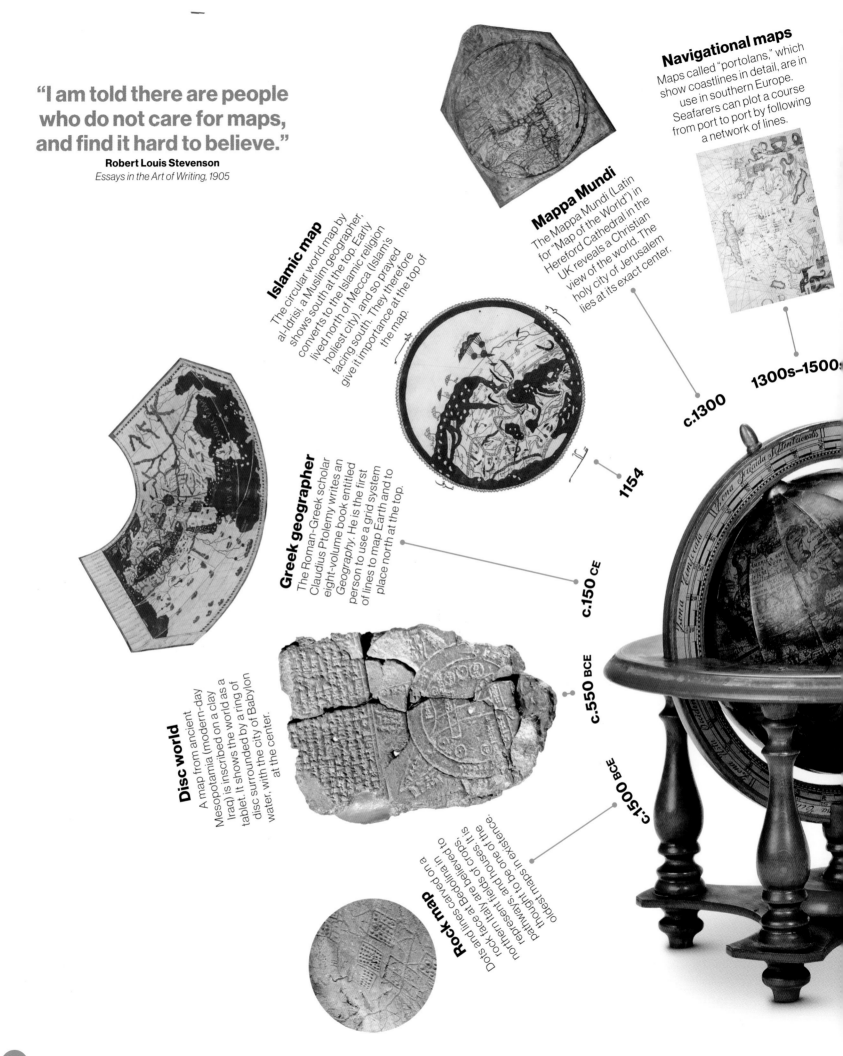

> **"I am told there are people who do not care for maps, and find it hard to believe."**
>
> **Robert Louis Stevenson**
> *Essays in the Art of Writing, 1905*

Navigational maps

Maps called "portolans," which show coastlines in detail, are in use in southern Europe. Seafarers can plot a course from port to port by following a network of lines.

1300s–1500s

Mappa Mundi

The Mappa Mundi (Latin for "Map of the World") in Hereford Cathedral in the UK reveals a Christian view of the world. The holy city of Jerusalem lies at its exact center.

c.1300

Islamic map

The circular world map by al-Idrisi, a Muslim geographer, shows south at the top. Early converts to the Islamic religion lived north of Mecca (Islam's holiest city), and so prayed facing south. They therefore give it importance at the top of the map.

1154

Greek geographer

The Roman–Greek scholar Claudius Ptolemy writes an eight-volume book entitled *Geography*. He is the first person to use a grid system of lines to map Earth and to place north at the top.

c.150 CE

Disc world

A map from ancient-day Mesopotamia (modern-day Iraq) is inscribed on a clay tablet. It shows the world as a disc surrounded by a ring of water, with the city of Babylon at the center.

c.550 BCE

Rock map

Dots and lines carved on a rock face at Bedolina in northern Italy are believed to represent fields or crops, pathways, and houses. It is thought to be one of the oldest maps in existence.

c.1500 BCE

Maps and mapmaking

The earliest maps did not portray the world as it was, but instead reflected the beliefs of those who made them. As people learned more about the world around them, maps became more realistic. By the Age of Exploration in Europe, mapmaking, or cartography, was used extensively by ocean explorers to chart unfamiliar shores. Today, advances in modern technology ensure that no part of Earth's surface remains unmapped.

America named

German mapmaker Martin Waldseemüller produces the first map of the world that shows America as a separate continent. He supposedly names the land mass after Italian explorer Amerigo Vespucci.

1507

Aztec map

In this Aztec map, Tenochtitlán, the capital city destroyed by the Spanish in 1521, is represented by an eagle landing on a cactus. Today, this symbol appears on the flag of modern-day Mexico.

1542

Scientific mapping

Three generations of the Cassini family are employed in making the Map of France, the first complete cartographic survey of a nation using modern surveying techniques.

1750–1815

Transportation map

Harry Beck's map of the London Underground shows the transit network as a diagram. It does not reflect actual directions and distances, but it is very clear, which makes it easier to follow.

1931

Ocean floor map

Geologists Marie Tharp and Bruce Heezen create the first scientific map of Earth's ocean floor. It reveals a previously unknown landscape of marine ridges and trenches.

1950s–1977

Google Earth

The computer program Google Earth is launched. It maps Earth by superimposing images obtained from satellites or aircraft and allows users to zoom in on cities and landscapes on their mobile phone, tablet, or computer.

2005

Representing the globe

Cartographers (people who draw maps) use a map projection to display Earth's sphere on a flat piece of paper—like flattening the rounded peel of an orange. It is impossible to do this without some distortion. In 1569, Gerardus Mercator devised a projection that still dominates the way we see the shape of the world. His projection exaggerates the size of countries near the poles at the expense of those at the Equator.

MERCATOR'S PROJECTION

Plagues and epidemics

Before the importance of cleanliness and hygiene was fully understood, many diseases were uncontrollable killers that could devastate entire populations. Although several infectious illnesses remain problematic, modern medicine has wiped out many threats to human health.

Mexican epidemic

When the New World is invaded by Spanish and Portuguese explorers, local people are exposed to new diseases. A smallpox epidemic kills many millions of people in what is now Mexico and the Andes over the next 2 years.

Communal living

As people begin living in towns and villages, cramped conditions and poor sanitation help diseases to spread. With limited medical knowledge, people blame evil spirits or angry gods.

Rat fleas were responsible for spreading many historic plagues.

First cases of the bubonic plague

A mysterious disease is first reported in China. Symptoms are bleeding sores, high temperature, and vomiting, leading to a rapid and painful death.

c.3000 BCE

430–427 BCE

165–180 CE

541–542

1334

1347–1351

1519

1665

Antonine Plague

This Roman plague takes its name from Marcus Aurelius Antoninus, the ruler at the time. About 5 million die over 15 years, and experts now believe the disease was smallpox.

The Black Death

The bubonic plague, or Black Death, wipes out half the population of Europe (around 40 million people) in just 4 years. Millions also die across Africa and Asia. The disease resurfaces every few decades in the following years.

Great Plague

The Great Plague of London kills 100,000 people. As the city is rebuilt following the Great Fire of London a year later, rules are introduced to improve sanitation and congestion.

Plague of Justinian

Disease spreads through the city of Constantinople (now Istanbul), killing 40 percent of the population. It had been carried over by rats coming over from Egypt on grain ships.

Ancient plague

The city of Athens in ancient Greece is hit by a plague that kills more than 30,000 people. The writer Thucydides describes terrible symptoms that lead to death within a week.

Plague doctors wore beaked masks containing herbs and flowers. They believed these would restrict contact with the disease.

Life-saving discovery

Scottish scientist Alexander Fleming accidentally discovers penicillin, which becomes the first ever antibiotic. This discovery saves millions of people from bacterial infections that would once have been fatal.

Ebola outbreak

Ebola is a fast-spreading virus causing fever and bleeding. An outbreak starts in Guinea, and soon becomes a 3-year epidemic throughout West Africa.

Final outbreak

The bubonic plague hits Europe again, this time in the busy port of Marseille in France. This final outbreak in Europe is over by 1722.

Clean-up operation

Cleanliness finally becomes a priority. Carbolic acid is used to kill bacteria in wounds. Doctors and surgeons begin washing their hands to stop infections from spreading, and sanitation standards improve.

1720–1722   **1829**   **1860s**   **1918**   **1928**   **1980**   **1981–**   **2013–2016**   **2015**

Eradication of smallpox

Following the last known natural case of smallpox in Somalia in 1977, the disease is officially declared eradicated by the World Health Assembly after an effective immunization program.

Cholera pandemic

People become ill after drinking water polluted with sewage and cholera bacteria. The outbreak begins in India, arrives in Europe on merchant ships, and later reaches the Americas.

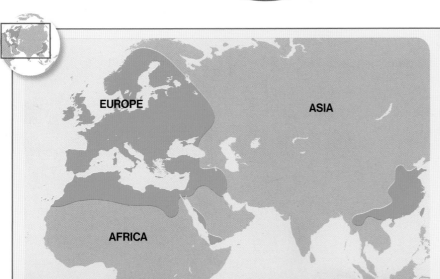

Spanish flu

More deadly than the Black Death, Spanish flu is a strain of influenza that kills at least 50 million people, or about 3 percent of the global population.

Mosquito malaria

Malaria is a killer disease spread by mosquitoes. It is eliminated in the developed world in the 1980s but still has a devastating impact in Africa and Asia, killing 2 million people every year.

HIV/AIDS

An unknown disease that destroys the immune system starts to spread. It becomes known as AIDS (acquired immunodeficiency syndrome), and is later discovered to be caused by the human immunodeficiency virus (HIV). More than 20 million people die from AIDS, but drugs are later developed to control it.

Spread of the Black Death

The Black Death quickly made its mark across Europe, Africa, and Asia. Bacteria contracted from flea bites was the reason for its rapid spread. Rats carried fleas along streets and aboard ships, passing the fatal disease to populations far and wide around the world. Recent studies also suggest that human fleas and body lice helped to spread the epidemic.

EUROPE

ASIA

AFRICA

Weapons and armor

The earliest weapons and armor were designed to help humans hunt animals, but it is very likely they could have been used to attack humans, too. The histories of weapons and armor have been intertwined ever since, with an advance in one leading to improvements in the other, and back again.

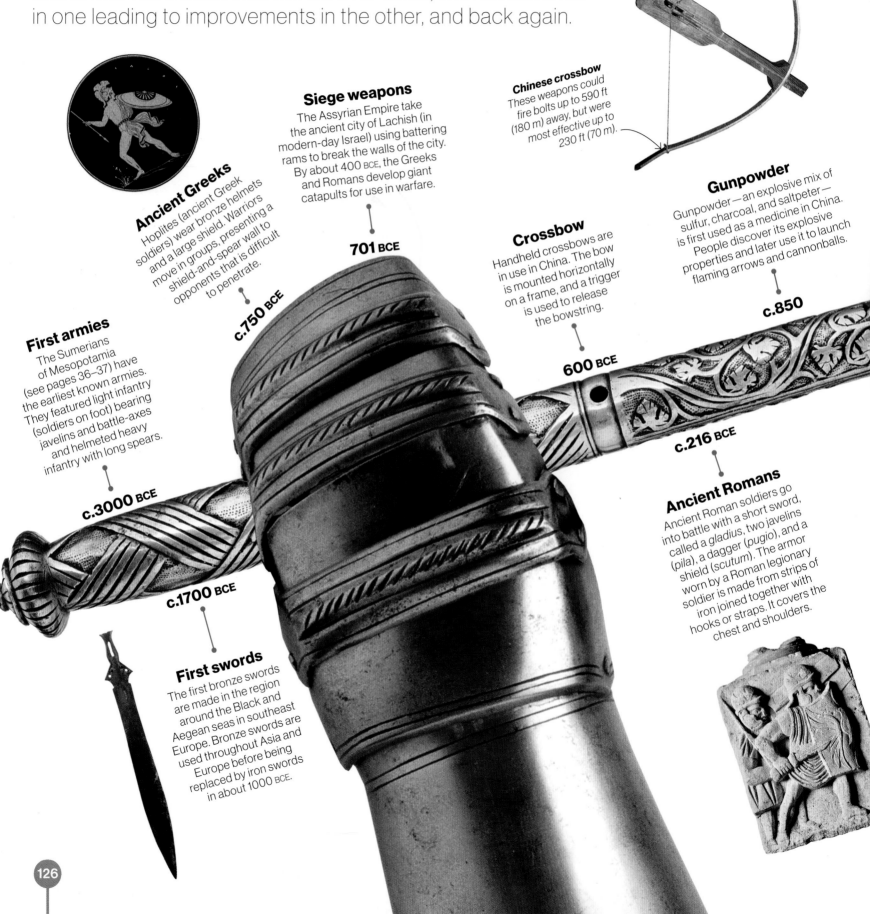

Chinese crossbow
These weapons could fire bolts up to 590 ft (180 m) away, but were most effective up to 230 ft (70 m).

Siege weapons
The Assyrian Empire take the ancient city of Lachish (in modern-day Israel) using battering rams to break the walls of the city. By about 400 BCE, the Greeks and Romans develop giant catapults for use in warfare.

701 BCE

Gunpowder
Gunpowder—an explosive mix of sulfur, charcoal, and saltpeter— is first used as a medicine in China. People discover its explosive properties and later use it to launch flaming arrows and cannonballs.

c.850

Ancient Greeks
Hoplites (ancient Greek soldiers) wear bronze helmets and a large shield. Warriors move in groups, presenting a shield-and-spear wall to opponents that is difficult to penetrate.

c.750 BCE

Crossbow
Handheld crossbows are in use in China. The bow is mounted horizontally on a frame, and a trigger is used to release the bowstring.

600 BCE

First armies
The Sumerians of Mesopotamia (see pages 36–37) have the earliest known armies. They featured light infantry (soldiers on foot) bearing javelins and battle-axes and helmeted heavy infantry with long spears.

c.3000 BCE

c.216 BCE

Ancient Romans
Ancient Roman soldiers go into battle with a short sword, called a *gladius*, two javelins (*pila*), a dagger (*pugio*), and a shield (*scutum*). The armor worn by a Roman legionary soldier is made from strips of iron joined together with hooks or straps. It covers the chest and shoulders.

c.1700 BCE

First swords
The first bronze swords are made in the region around the Black and Aegean seas in southeast Europe. Bronze swords are used throughout Asia and Europe before being replaced by iron swords in about 1000 BCE.

Atomic bomb
The most devastating weapon ever—the atomic bomb—is developed by the US, and ends the war when dropped on Japan in 1945.

World War II
The US army produces the first portable rocket launcher, which allows infantry troops to destroy tanks. It is fired from the shoulder. The V-2 rocket, the first long-range missile, is made in Germany. It can hit a target 200 miles (320 km) away.

1939–1945

Gun
The flintlock gun comes into use, and will be popular for more than 200 years in the age of large infantry armies. In 1862, the Gatling gun, developed during the American Civil War, is the first hand-driven machine gun, operated by a crank.

1620

Japanese armor
Samurai warriors in Japan wear body armor made of leather or metal scales laced together with colored cords, with a separate apron covering the thighs. Together with the high-crested helmet (*kabuto*), it is designed to terrify the enemy. Samurai armor changes very little over time.

c.1000

1973

Drones and Kevlar
The first unmanned aerial vehicles, commonly called "drones" are used by the US in the Vietnam War. In 1978, Kevlar—a high-strength synthetic fiber—becomes the new standard armor. It is 10 times stronger than steel, and is bullet- and stab-proof.

c.1300

1914–1918

Plate armor
European knights start to wear a solid breastplate made of iron or steel over their chain mail for better protection. As more pieces are added to protect the head, arms, and legs, complete suits of armour develop.

World War I
World War I brings about a new era of weapons and armor. Poison gas, tanks, airplanes, and Zeppelins are all used for the first time. Soldiers are issued with steel helmets and new types of armor that prove to be ineffective.

Zeppelin
Used to bomb Britain during World War I, huge Zeppelin airships were filled with hydrogen gas, which allowed them to float. They fell out of use when the British learned to shoot at the aircraft's skin in order to ignite the hydrogen gas inside.

c. 900

Vikings
Although the Vikings had spears and swords, the long-handled battle-axe is their most effective weapon. Vikings use wooden shields and round helmets, and either a shirt of mail or possibly small sheets of metal linked together for protection.

Viking battle-axe
Deadly weapons, Viking battle-axes could be wielded with one hand, but larger ones like this were swung with two hands to inflict terrible injuries.

Mamluk heavy cavalry
During the Middle Ages, heavily armored knights, such as this Arabian Mamluk, rode into battle on armored horses.

Warhorses
The earliest warhorses were used in Europe and Asia about 5,000 years ago. Using horses in battle became easier when saddles, stirrups, and the horse collar emerged. Later on, the Mongol Empire's military power rested on the success of its light cavalry and riders, who could fire arrows with great accuracy from horseback. As developments in distance weapons continued, the use of horses in battle declined.

THE AGE OF EXPLORATION

1450-1750

The Age of Exploration

In the late 15th century, ancient texts that had been lost to Europe were rediscovered through contact with the Middle East. This refound knowledge inspired a spirit of curiosity about the world. New inventions and discoveries led to the birth of modern science, and voyages of discovery sailed to uncharted lands. European nations built mighty overseas empires to rival the older empires that continued in the Middle East, China, and India.

1497–1499
Vasco da Gama makes the first sea voyage from Europe to India.

1517
Martin Luther accuses the Catholic Church of corruption in his 95 "theses" (complaints).

1522
The first voyage around the world (circumnavigation) is completed.

1529
Suleiman the Magnificent of the Ottoman Empire fails to take the city of Vienna in a siege.

1492
Christopher Columbus lands in the Americas, opening up a "New World" to European explorers.

1504
Michelangelo unveils his statue of David, a masterpiece of the Renaissance.

1521
Hernán Cortés destroys the Aztec Empire's capital city of Tenochtitlán.

1526
Babur founds the Mughal Empire in northern India.

The Renaissance
In Europe, the Renaissance (French for "rebirth") was a period of great artistic achievement in painting, architecture, and literature (see pages 136–137).

European explorers
Voyages to find new sea routes led to the exploration of lands in the Americas, Africa, and Asia that were previously unknown to Europe (see pages 138–139).

The Reformation
Martin Luther's protest against corruption in the Catholic Church led to an era of religious upheaval known as the Reformation (see pages 144–145).

The Ottoman Empire
The Islamic Ottoman Empire (see pages 150–151) dominated the Middle East for over 600 years. Its power extended into Eastern Europe and North Africa.

Backstaff

Voyages of discovery throughout this period were made possible by advancements in navigation technology. The backstaff was invented by John Davis around 1594. It allowed sailors to measure the angle of the Sun or the Moon above the horizon to work out their location.

1543
Nicolaus Copernicus argues that Earth travels around the Sun.

1618–1648
The Thirty Years' War marks the end of a period of religious conflict in Europe.

1619
The first shipment of African slaves to America arrives in Jamestown.

1644
After more than 200 years of rule, the Ming Dynasty of China collapses. The Qing Dynasty later takes control.

1603
Japan is unified and enters a period known as the "Great Peace."

1607
Jamestown becomes the first permanent English settlement in North America.

1632
Mughal emperor Shah Jahan orders the construction of the Taj Mahal as a mausoleum (tomb) for his wife.

1666
Isaac Newton formulates his ideas on the theory of gravity.

Colonial America

European nations such as Spain, France, and Britain quickly took control of the lands of the "New World" in the Americas (see pages 160–161).

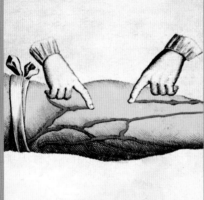

The rise of science

A revolution in scientific thought (see pages 162–163) followed the Renaissance. It challenged and changed accepted views about the Universe.

Mughal India

Spread across the Indian subcontinent, the Islamic Mughal Empire (see pages 166–167) produced some of South Asia's finest monuments.

Qing China

The Qing people take control of China from the declining Ming Dynasty (see pages 168–169). They will be the last imperial dynasty to rule over China.

Technology of writing

The technology that allows people to write things down is as important as the invention of scripts and alphabets themselves. Thanks to technological advances such as the inventions of paper, ink, and printing, more and more people have become literate. Today, 86 percent of adults worldwide can read and write.

Inks

As far back as the 3rd millenium BCE, the Chinese and Egyptians made inks using soot, water, and gum. From the 4th century BCE, a richer, more durable black ink was made from iron sulphite and tannic acid (taken from growths on parasite-infested trees). Neither kind was suitable for printing. When Gutenberg built his printing press, he invented a new oil-based ink, made from soot, turpentine, and walnut oil.

Printing

The Chinese invent printing, with carved woodblocks. It is used first to print pictures on silk, and later for words on paper. The oldest surviving printed book with a clear date is the Chinese Diamond Sutra, shown below, which was printed back in 868 CE.

Clay tablets

The Sumerians of Mesopotamia in modern-day southern Iraq begin to write on soft clay tablets, making marks with a piece of reed. The use of clay tablets later spreads across western Asia and the eastern Mediterranean.

Paper

The Chinese invent paper made from plant fibers and rags. Paper production spreads west to the Arabs around 750 CE, reaching Italy in 1270. Modern paper, made from wood pulp, will not be invented until the 1840s.

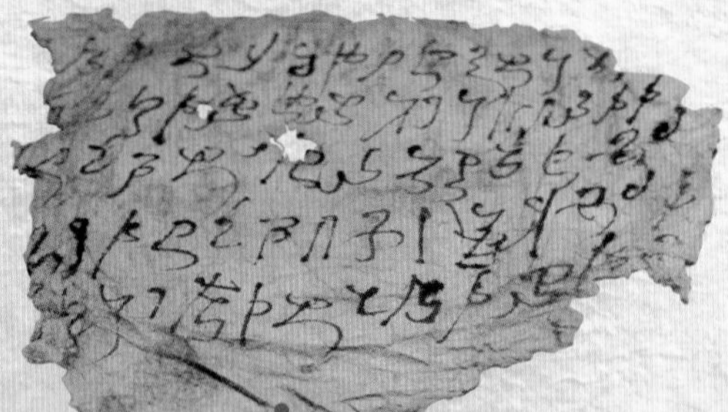

c.3300 BCE

c.3200 BCE

6th century BCE

2nd century BCE

1st century CE

c.200

Writing begins

The earliest evidence of Egyptian writing is of hieroglyphs carved on ivory and bone tablets. Egyptians also write on papyrus, using a reed brush, with ink made from soot, water, and gum from trees.

Parchment

Writing on parchment made from dried, stretched animal skin becomes common across the eastern Mediterranean. Writers use a reed pen and ink made from iron sulphite and tannic acid.

Books with pages

The Romans make the first books with separate pages. Each book is called a codex, and is more portable and easier to use than a long scroll.

Ballpoint pens

Laszlo Bíró, a Hungarian newspaper editor, creates the first effective ballpoint pen. It combines quick-drying ink with a ball-and-socket mechanism, which prevents the ink from drying out inside the pen.

1938

1868

Fountain pens

In France, the Romanian inventor Petrache Poenaru patents "a never-ending portable pen." This first fountain pen has a barrel made from a swan's quill. By the 1880s, fountain pens will be mass-produced.

1827

Typewriters

US inventor Christopher Latham Sholes patents the first commercially successful typewriter. It has the QWERTY layout that is still used today. E. Remington and Sons, formerly firearms manufacturers, begin producing the new typewriter in 1874.

Word processors

The first successful word processor program, WordStar, is released. People can now type onto a digital screen instead of directly onto paper.

1979

Pencils

Nicholas Jaques-Conte, a French army officer and scientist, invents the modern pencil. It is made of powdered graphite mixed with clay, pressed between two half cylinders of wood.

1795

1450

Personal printers

The US company Hewlett-Packard (HP) produce their first desktop laser printer. It allows individuals with word processor programs to produce high-quality printed documents on demand.

1984

Moveable type

In China, Bi Sheng invents the first printing system to use movable type, where each letter or symbol can be moved and reused to make different words. The letters are made from baked clay. The Koreans improve this technology with metal letters, cast from bronze, in the 1230s.

1040s

Gutenberg's printing press

In Germany, Johannes Gutenberg invents a printing press with moveable metal type, using oil-based ink. The press rapidly spreads across Europe and, by 1500, 20 million books will have been printed.

7th century

Quill pens

Western Christian monks begin to use goose feather quill pens, which replace the earlier calamus (reed pens). Using a quill allows swifter, smaller writing. Our word "pen" comes from the Latin word *pinna*, which means "feather."

Ships

The oceans were first navigated by ancient people on wooden rafts. Travelers from Asia arrived in Australia on rafts around 50,000 years ago. Many centuries of design and development have improved our waterways and made our ships more safe and stable. Today, ships continue to be important for travel and trade.

Setting sail

The first boats to replace rafts are built by the ancient Egyptians for transporting cargo along the Nile. Sails are also invented to harness the power of the wind.

c.3100 BCE

Steaming ahead

The first steamboat to offer a public passenger service is the *Clermont*, which travels from New York City to Albany, NY. Steam powers the engines, and giant paddle wheels propel the boats through the water.

Fast clippers

The biggest sails at sea belong to clippers. These fast-moving ships have multiple sails and narrow hulls to cruise the waters faster. Clippers transport cargo from Asia to Europe and North America.

Cruise liners

The world's first cruise liner, called *Prinzessin Victoria Luise* launches. As the century continues, cruise liners become increasingly luxurious, providing expensive accommodation, entertainment, and swimming pools.

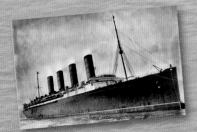

1900

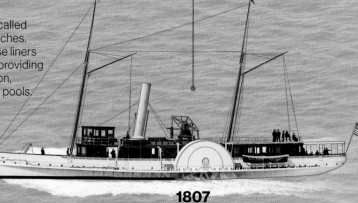

1807

1800s

Battleships

At the turn of the 20th century, naval conflict advances with the development of battleships. They are protected by armor plating and equipped with gun turrets to blast shells long distances.

c.1900

Aircraft carriers

American flight pioneer Eugene Ely is the first pilot to take off from the deck of a ship—the US armored *Birmingham*. As aircraft become important military weapons, huge military ships with runways are designed.

1910

Greek galleys

The ancient Greeks craft huge shallow boats called galleys, equipped with multiple sails and oars. These warships feature a heavy beam, called a battering ram, to attack enemy vessels.

c.750–700 BCE

Viking longboats

The Vikings launch raids from Scandinavia in longboats. These feature overlapping planks for superior strength, sturdy bases called keels, and carvings of scary creatures to ward off attackers.

c.800 CE

Junk boats

Chinese sailors brave storms in the South China Sea. The Chinese junk—Malayan for "boat"—has a strong hull, multiple masts, and concertina sails. Merchant junks carry trade goods far and wide.

c.1000

Fighting ships

European conflict leads to advances in the design of sailing ships. Vessels are now heavily armed and ready to destroy the enemy. Some have spikes to make holes, while others use cannons.

Fast galleons

The basic galleon is developed by English navigator and slave-trader John Hawkins. These sailing ships sit deeper in the water and move very fast. They are first used as warships and later for trade.

First lifeboat

The first lifeboat is constructed in England. *The Original* has its maiden voyage on the River Tyne before being used for rescue missions later in the year.

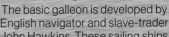

1790

1650

1600

Container ships

The American SeaLand line is the first to use containerized shipping between the US and Europe. Steel boxes of the same size are stacked up, so a huge quantity of goods can be transported together.

1950s

Catamarans

The high-speed, long-distance watercraft called a catamaran is a great engine-powered vessel that moves through turbulent water effectively. Its two parallel hulls of equal size keep it steady.

1970s

Luxury yachts

The ultimate yachts feature the latest technology, onboard entertainment systems, sleek and stylish designs, and luxurious decor. These floating mansions are built for comfort.

21st century

c.1305

New style of painting

Giotto di Bondone (known as "Giotto") begins painting in a more realistic style. His masterpiece is a fresco in the Scrovegni Chapel in Padua, Italy.

1308

Literary masterpiece

Writer Dante Alighieri begins *The Divine Comedy*, a long poem that describes a journey through the afterlife. It is still considered one of the major works in world literature.

1453

Classical revival

When Constantinople (modern-day Istanbul), capital of the Byzantine Empire, is captured by the Ottomans, many scholars flee to Italy. They bring along ancient Greek and Roman texts, which have long been lost in the West.

1455

The power of print

Johannes Gutenberg, a German goldsmith, introduces printing to Europe with his invention of moveable type (metal letters that can be used again). Printed books help spread new knowledge throughout Europe.

c.1485

Flying machine

Leonardo da Vinci, the great artist, scientist, and inventor, is ahead of his time with a design for a flying machine with mechanical wings, even if it could never work in practice.

1504

Statue of David

Michelangelo's life-like statue of the Biblical figure of David is put on display in Florence's main square. It is carved from a single block of marble and is more than 17 ft (5 m) high.

1511

Philosophy lessons

The artist Raphael paints *The School of Athens*, a fresco for the Pope's rooms in the Vatican in Rome. It shows a gathering of Greek philosophers, and is one of four representing the different branches of knowledge.

1513

Devious politics

Niccolò Machiavelli, a diplomat from Florence, writes *The Prince*. The book is intended as a guide for rulers. The term "Machiavellian," from the author's name, comes to be associated with gaining political power by clever but dishonest methods.

Architectural feat

Filippo Brunelleschi's impressive dome for the cathedral in Florence is the first of its size to be built since Roman times. It is still the largest brick dome in the world.

Perspective in painting

Artists work out how to show three-dimensional objects on a flat (two-dimensional) surface. This is described in Leon Battista Alberti's book, *On Painting.*

1469

Patron of the arts

Lorenzo de' Medici, known as the Magnificent, becomes the most powerful man in Florence. He uses his vast wealth to sponsor great artists such as Sandro Botticelli and Michelangelo.

Renaissance

In 14th-century northern Italy, a number of artists, architects, and scholars became interested in the styles and ideas of Ancient Greece and Rome. This revival of classical knowledge became known as the "Renaissance" (French for "rebirth"). Painting moved away from the stiff forms of medieval Christian art to a more realistic style. Renaissance ideas spread throughout Europe, starting a revolution in thought.

1509

Humanism

The Dutch humanist Desiderius Erasmus publishes his best-known work, *In Praise of Folly.* Renaissance humanists looked to ancient texts rather than religion, creating a philosophy that championed the human individual.

1532

1543

Northern Renaissance

The Renaissance spreads from Italy to influence art and literature across Europe. *The Ambassadors* by German artist Hans Holbein, then working in England, is one of the greatest works of the Northern Renaissance.

New science

Polish astronomer Nicolaus Copernicus argues that Earth travels around the Sun, rather than the other way around. His ideas begin a revolution in science.

Fresco painting

A fresco is a wall painting made on fresh wet plaster. The colors sink in, allowing the pictures to stay very bright for hundreds of years.

Exploring the world

In the 15th and 16th centuries, many explorers set sail from Europe in the hope of finding new lands, great riches, and exotic goods. The arrival of Europeans in the Americas, Asia, and Africa, helped by new navigational techniques and ship design, opened up trade between the continents for the first time. This exciting era was considered to be the golden age of exploration.

Henry the Navigator

Prince Henry of Portugal, known as "the Navigator," becomes governor of the southernmost part of Portugal, an ideal departure point for the exploration of new lands. He orders ships to venture into the Atlantic Ocean to follow the African coastline.

Scared sailors

Prior to this time, Prince Henry's crews will not sail beyond Cape Bojador (in modern-day Western Sahara) because they think it marks the end of the world. After Captain Gil Eannes urges them to face their fears, the exploration of Africa truly begins.

Cape of Good Hope

The southernmost tip of Africa is finally passed by Portuguese nobleman Bartolomeu Dias and his crew. King John II of Portugal calls this the "Cape of Good Hope." Europeans now have an ocean route by which to trade directly with India.

Arrival in the Americas

Italian seafarer Christopher Columbus sails west across the Atlantic Ocean, heading for India. He accidentally encounters America instead. He is given the title "Admiral of the Ocean Sea" and makes three more voyages, sailing along the coastlines of Central and South America.

Amazing Africa

Portuguese navigator Diogo Cão is the first European to discover the mouth of the Congo River. He reaches modern-day Namibia, erecting stone crosses to mark his route, and now realizes that Africa is far bigger than was originally thought.

1419   **1434**   **1480s**   **1488**   **1492–1504**

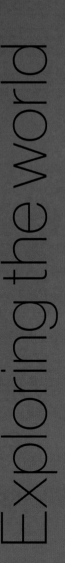

Newfoundland

Italian John Cabot sails across the Atlantic Ocean on a mission for King Henry VII of England. He arrives in Newfoundland in modern-day Canada, but mistakenly believes it is Asia.

Blown to Brazil

Portuguese sailor Pedro Álvares Cabral plans to sail to India, but the Atlantic Ocean winds blow him to modern-day Brazil. He claims the territory for Portugal and returns home loaded up with spices and gems.

North and South America

Italian explorer Amerigo Vespucci discovers that North and South America are separate continents. In 1507 German mapmaker Martin Waldseemüller supposedly names the lands "America" after him.

Crossing the Pacific

Portuguese sailor Ferdinand Magellan sets sail from Spain, determined to reach the Spice Islands (in Southeast Asia) by heading west instead of east. He rounds the southern tip of South America (known as Cape Horn) as the first European to cross the Pacific Ocean.

First circumnavigation

Magellan dies in the Philippines in a battle with locals. The fleet continues its around-the-world journey. King Charles V of Spain gives new captain Juan Sebastián de Elcano a coat of arms: a globe with the motto "You went around me first."

1497   1497   1500   1501   1519   1521

Caravel ships

Exploration would not have been possible without the caravel. These new ships were lightweight and topped by two or three masts, with plenty of sails to catch the ocean winds. These features enabled navigators to sail long distances.

Indian adventure

King Manuel I of Portugal arranges an expedition to India, captained by nobleman Vasco da Gama. The winds of the Atlantic Ocean help da Gama cross the Indian Ocean. The Portuguese trade their honey, hats, and beads, returning with spices stacked up on their ships.

The technology of exploration

As the Age of Exploration got underway, sailors soon realized that they needed to plan a course without being able to see land. New instruments were invented to aid navigation—the art of piloting a ship along a route—enabling explorers to cross vast oceans.

Early 1400s
Caravel ships have triangular sails instead of square ones, allowing them to use the wind on either side to sail the oceans.

c.1418
Prince Henry of Portugal founds the first school for oceanic navigation.

1470s
Spanish astronomer Abraham Zacuto develops a device to help sailors discover how far north or south they are.

1570
Belgian mapmaker Abraham Ortelius publishes the first modern atlas, *Theatre of the World*, which includes 70 maps.

c.1594
The backstaff is invented by English navigator John Davis to measure the height of the Sun and Moon above the horizon.

A ROUTE TO INDIA

Da Gama sails east

In the late 15th century, King Manuel I of Portugal wanted to discover a maritime route to India, longing to secure the trade of valuable Asian spices and textiles. The expedition was led by explorer Vasco da Gama, who would have to overcome the treacherous task of being the first captain to sail around Africa and beyond, into unchartered and hostile waters.

The fleet sets sail

On **July 8, 1497**, a fleet of four ships carrying around 170 sailors sets sail from the port of Lisbon in Portugal. Led by Vasco da Gama, with the help of his brother Paulo, the expedition heads south down the west coast of Africa. Da Gama follows a similar route that was plotted by the great Portuguese sailor Bartolomeu Dias, but instead of closely following the west coast, da Gama heads out into the open Atlantic Ocean. After four months at sea and using the Atlantic's strong prevailing winds and currents, da Gama passes the Cape of Good Hope, rounds the tip of southern Africa, and sails into the unknown waters of the Indian Ocean beyond.

African enemies

In **December 1497**, da Gama's fleet heads north along the east coast of Africa, and makes landfall in Mozambique. Da Gama and his men are met with hostility from the local Muslim sultan. After fleeing to his ship and bombarding the port, da Gama then heads north along the coast to Mombasa. Da Gama loots several unarmed Arab trading vessels and angers the local Mombasa people. After torturing several Muslim sailors, da Gama learns of a plot to avenge his actions in Mozambique, so he flees north to continue his search for India.

Unchartered waters

In **April 1498**, da Gama keeps heading north and finally makes an ally at the port of Malindi on **April 14**. Malindi is at war with Mombasa, and its leader offers to help da Gama with his expedition. Da Gama and Malindi sign a trade treaty and, as a sign of friendship, the east Africans give da Gama a local navigator to help the Portuguese fleet through the unchartered and treacherous waters of the Indian Ocean.

Indian shores

On **May 20**, after several weeks crossing the Indian Ocean and more than 10 months at sea, Vasco da Gama and his fleet sail into the port of Calicut (modern-day Kallicote) on the southwest coast of India. Da Gama meets the Zamorin (ruler) of Calicut and offers a selection of gifts. The Zamorin is unimpressed with the presents and, as tensions rise between the local Muslim traders and the Christian explorers, the Hindu ruler becomes less receptive to da Gama's trade offerings. After three months, in **August 1498**, da Gama and his men leave without a trade agreement, but carrying cargo worth nearly 60 times the cost of the expedition.

Homeward bound

The journey home is ill-fated as monsoons, scurvy, and exhaustion take their toll on da Gama's crew. Paulo da Gama and 117 of the 170-man crew die on the journey. In **September 1499**, two years and 24,000 miles (38,500 km) after he first left home, Vasco da Gama sails into the port of Lisbon. To celebrate his historic achievement, the king of Portugal honors Vasco da Gama with the title "Admiral of the Indian Seas."

A return to India

After Vasco da Gama's first expedition, Pedro Alvares Cabral, a Portuguese navigator and explorer, is immediately sent to establish a trading post in India. However, an uprising by local Muslim traders destroys the encampment and Cabral is forced to leave. In **1502**, da Gama sets sail for India for a second time to re-establish Portugal's trading post in the region. This time da Gama uses excessive force to persuade the Zamorin of Calicut to sign a trade treaty. Da Gama is seen as a villain in the Indian Ocean, but when he returns home once again with more precious cargo, he is celebrated as a hero. Twenty-two years later, in **1524**, Vasco da Gama makes his final journey to India, which also happens to be his last-ever voyage. During the journey, da Gama contracts malaria and gets sick. He arrives at Cochin in India, but eventually dies on **December 24, 1524**.

The story of painting

People have been painting pictures for tens of thousands of years. In the past, they painted them directly onto the walls of their caves, temples, or houses. Artists have since experimented with different styles of painting. They developed vibrant paints and created engaging images on paper and canvas. Painters continue to be inspired and influenced by artists from the past.

Enter

1601

Baroque painting

Dramatic use of light and shade (chiaroscuro) and depth perspective are typical of the Baroque style of art. *The Supper at Emmaus* by Caravaggio shows Jesus after he has risen from the dead.

c.1503

Renaissance masterpiece

Italian Renaissance painter Leonardo da Vinci paints the *Mona Lisa*, a hauntingly lifelike portrait of a young Italian woman. Da Vinci is one of the most influential artists of all time.

c.1430

The Arnolfini Portrait
by Jan van Eyck,
1434

Painting with oils

Oil paints, made by mixing pigments with flaxseed or walnut oil, are introduced in Europe, possibly from Asia. One of the first Europeans to paint with oils is Flemish painter Jan van Eyck.

c.1610–1620s

Squirrels in a Plane Tree
by Abu'l Hasan,
c.1610

Mughal miniatures

As the Mughal Empire flourishes in India, miniature paintings full of color and detail become popular. They are made as book illustrations, personal portraits, or for keeping in art albums.

1642

Dutch Golden Age

Rembrandt van Rijn is the most famous painter of the Dutch Golden Age, a time of prosperity in the Netherlands. His painting *The Night Watch* is characteristic of art at the time, full of color and realistic detail.

2002

Contemporary art

British artist Lucien Freud is one of the leading painters of the late 20th century. He enjoys painting friends and family, and exploring how to paint skin tones, such as in this portrait, *Woman with Eyes Closed*.

1928

American Modernism

Georgia O'Keeffe is a significant American Modernist artist, best known for her studies of flowers and cityscapes such as *East River from the 30th Story of the Shelton Hotel*.

c.1910

Composition
by Piet Mondrian,
1921

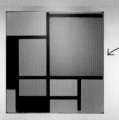

Abstract art

Artists begin to move away from depicting reality, finding a new kind of art that reflects the changes that are occurring in science and technology. They use simple shapes, colors, and lines to create effects.

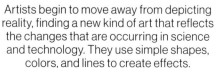

142

c.30,000 BCE

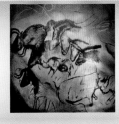

Animal cave art

Stone Age hunters paint the walls of caves with images of animals such as lions, bulls, and rhinos, possibly as part of hunting rituals. These horse images are from Chauvet Cave in France.

c.3,000–300 BCE

Sennefer's burial chamber
Nobleman Sennefer is depicted with his wife.

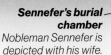

Egyptian tomb painting

In Ancient Egypt, paintings cover the walls and ceilings of the tombs of pharaohs and nobles. Deceased people are portrayed performing everyday tasks or making offerings to the gods.

c.100 BCE –100 CE

Portrait of Venus
This wall painting was buried during the eruption of Mount Vesuvius in 79 CE.

Roman wall paintings

The Romans brighten the rooms of their houses with wall paintings, known as murals. These are sometimes painted to give the illusion of looking through a window at a scene beyond.

c.1305

The Last Supper by Giotto, c.1305

Italian fresco

Italian artist Giotto paints a series of religious frescoes (wall paintings made on fresh plaster before it dries) in a softer, more realistic style than the stiff, flat images found in earlier medieval art.

c.1100

Our Lady of Vladimir, artist unknown, c.1100

Medieval icons

Icons are painted images of holy Christian figures such as Jesus. They are common in the Eastern Orthodox Christian Church, a Catholic religion practiced in Eastern Europe and Asia.

960–1279 CE

Snowy Landscape by Fan Kuan, c.960–1030

Chinese landscapes

During the Song Dynasty in China, artists paint beautiful landscapes, often of mountains or water, expressing love of the natural world.

1700s

The Death of General Wolfe by Benjamin West, 1770

History painting

Great scenes from history or from Greek and Roman legends, painted in a neoclassical style that looks back to the past, are popular topics in 18th-century Europe and the US.

c.1780–1850

Romanticism

Artists of the Romantic era are inspired by nature and how it makes them feel. British painter Turner is admired for his depictions of the shimmering effects of sunlight, as in his 1839 painting *The Fighting Temeraire.*

c.1860–1890s

The Japanese Footbridge by Claude Monet, 1899

Impressionism

Artists in Paris paint scenes of everyday life outdoors. They do so spontaneously, rather than in a studio from sketches. They come to be known as Impressionists, and include Monet, Renoir, and Degas.

c.1907–1908

Juan Legua by Juan Gris, 1911

Cubism

Spanish artist Pablo Picasso creates a way of showing objects from different angles all at once, known as Cubism. This style is a forerunner of Abstract art.

c.1886–1905

Sunflowers by Vincent van Gogh, 1888

Post-Impressionism

Artists like Van Gogh, Cézanne, and Gauguin add their own ideas to those of the Impressionists. They experiment with using bold blocks of color, often applying paint very thickly.

The Reformation

After hundreds of years, the Catholic Church was very powerful, both within the community and in political life. In 15th-century Europe, this power led to corrupt practices, such as the sale of "indulgences" (forgiveness for sins) to increase the Church's wealth. German priest and professor Martin Luther, angry at this greed, started a movement to change the Church. The Reformation spread across Europe, but brought with it war and religious persecution.

1524
Peasants' War

Once people begin to question the Church, they start thinking about the unfairness of other institutions. Poor farmers in Germany revolt against high taxes, but their protest is crushed two years later.

Marauding peasants
Mobs of angry farmers attack and burn homes of the rich.

1527
Lutheranism spreads

Luther's movement reaches Sweden. King Gustav I reforms the Church following Luther's ideas. In 1536, the movement spreads to the kingdom of Denmark-Norway and becomes the national religion.

1536
Calvinism

French theologist John Calvin is told to leave Paris because of his Reformation group in support of the Protestant make the starts his own Protestant

1519
Swiss reformers

In Zurich, Switzerland, priest Ulrich Zwingli leads a Bible-based reform movement of the Catholic Church. Zwingli and his followers translate the Old and New Testaments of the Bible into German for the first time.

God's Word is law
Zwingli teaches that the Bible is God's law, and that the state and Church are both under His rule.

1517
Martin Luther

German monk Luther writes a list of 95 "theses" (complaints) about the Catholic Church. He posts them on a church door for everyone to see. The invention of the printing press means that Luther's words can be printed and shared quickly across Europe.

1545

Council of Trent

The Catholic Church, alarmed by the spread of the Reformation, meets in Trent in northern Italy. They create the Roman Inquisition, a court of law to convict and punish nonbelievers. The Pope puts the Jesuits in charge of the Counter-Reformation.

1555

Peace treaty

Fighting between the Church and the reformers comes to an end with the Peace of Augsburg. The leader of each German empire is allowed to choose between the Catholic or the Lutheran faith for the people.

Religious harmony
Charles V signs the treaty that creates tolerance for two faiths.

1559

Church of England

England's Queen Elizabeth I turns England into a Protestant country by re-establishing the Church of England, which had been dismantled by Mary I. She tries to encourage tolerance between the two faiths to avoid wars with Catholic countries.

1562–1598

...rs of Religion

...on people die
...ts between
...cs and
...1572, on
...ew's Day,
...000 people are
...dict of Nantes
...vs Protestant
...ough religious
...tinues.

1618

Defenestration of Prague

Catholic officials in Prague in the modern-day Czech Republic shut down Protestant churches even though they are protected. Enraged Protestants throw two officials out of the window (this is known as defenestration).

Safe landing
Luckily for them, the ejected officials land in a pile of garbage and are not seriously hurt.

> ## "Whatever your heart clings to and confides in, that is really your God."
>
> **Martin Luther**, 1483–1546
> *professor, composer, priest, and monk*

1618–1648

Thirty Years' War

Religion and politics are tightly linked. When the emperor of Bohemia limits Protestant religious freedom, wars break out in Denmark, Sweden, France, Spain, and the Netherlands. They last for 30 years and bring devastation to Germany.

Huge losses
About 20 percent of the German population is killed.

1648

End of religious wars

A series of treaties ends religious conflict in Europe, but not before around eight million people have been killed.

Spanish America

Following the exploration of the Americas in the 15th century, Spanish conquistadors (meaning "conquerors") began to arrive to seek their fortune. Conflicts resulted as these settlers and American Indians battled over land, leadership, and local resources. Almost two million Spaniards moved to the Americas in the 300 years that followed, and Spanish influences are still present in North, Central, and South America today.

BEFORE
Explorer Christopher Columbus reached America in 1492 and returned to Spain with tempting tales of great riches. Many more Spanish explorers were lured overseas by the promise of gold in what they called the "New World."

American Indian rights
Spanish priest Bartolomé de las Casas sends a report to Charles V, outlining the harsh treatment of American Indians. The King orders the conquests to stop, and the government creates new laws in 1550 to protect the natives, but few conquistadors obey.

Silver source
The conquistadors find the world's largest silver supply in Potosí in modern-day Bolivia. Silver is shipped back to Spain to pay for its wars in Europe.

Weapons mismatch
American Indian weapons are no match for the swords of the Spanish conquistadors.

Continuing conquests
The Spanish gain the northern Yucatán Peninsula in 1546 and, over time, modern-day Guatemala. They also win a number of wars throughout the region of modern-day Mexico.

Rich mountain
The mountain in Potosí is sometimes called "Cerro Rico" ("rich mountain"), because it is thought to be made of silver.

Spanish colonization
Large numbers of Spanish settlers come to South America. By the 17th century, the Spanish empire spreads across the continent, the Caribbean islands, Central America, Mexico, and North America.

Beans as currency
Cocoa beans are used like money by both the Maya and the Aztec peoples of Central America.

Cocoa beans
Beans from the cacao tree are shipped to Spain from the forests of South America. These are used to make a sweet chocolate drink, which becomes very popular throughout Europe.

Trade triangle
Slaves from Africa are sold in the Americas for items such as sugar and tobacco. These are sent to Europe and exchanged for guns and nails, which are then sold in Africa for slaves. See also page 164.

NORTH AMERICA
ATLANTIC OCEAN
MEXICO
Tenochtitlán
Yucatán Peninsula
Caribbean Sea
GUATEMALA
Cajamarca
PERU
Vilcabamba
Potosí
BRAZIL
SOUTH AMERICA
PACIFIC OCEAN

Portuguese
Spanish

THE SPANISH EMPIRE

Columbian Exchange

An exchange of goods is established between the New and Old Worlds. New foods, flowers, and animals arrive from the Americas. Europeans introduce livestock. Sadly, they also bring with them diseases such as measles, smallpox, and influenza.

1493

New foods
Pineapples, chiles, potatoes, and turkeys are seen in Europe for the first time.

Encomienda

The Spanish introduce a system called "encomienda," in which settlers receive gold, labor, and (in practice) land, as long as they protect the American Indians and convert them to the Christian religion.

1503

"We Spaniards know a sickness of the heart only gold can cure."

Hernán Cortés, 1485–1547
Spanish conquistador

Portuguese progress

In 1500, Portuguese navigator Pedro Álvares Cabral set sail for India. Instead of traveling east, Cabral was blown westward across the Atlantic, ending up on the coastline of modern-day Brazil. He claimed the land for Portugal, beginning a widespread colonization of the country by the Portuguese.

1518

The slave trade begins

Spain's King Charles V gives permission for 4,000 Africans to be forcibly brought to the New World to work as slaves in the booming mining and sugar industries. This marks the start of the large-scale African slave trade.

Disease and hardship

By now, the American Indian population is drastically reduced, as they cannot fight the new illnesses brought by the Spanish. Those who survive are treated like slaves, working long hours in poor conditions for little or no pay.

1540s

1519

Aztec defeat

When Spanish nobleman Hernán Cortés and his army reach Mexico, they are welcomed by Aztec ruler Montezuma II. However, Cortés takes him prisoner and rules through him. In 1521, Cortés destroys the Aztec capital Tenochtitlán.

Gold treasures
Many items in Aztec culture are made from gold, such as this ceremonial mask.

1532

Inca entrapment

At Cajamarca in modern-day Peru, Francisco Pizarro and his army invite the Inca emperor Atahualpa and 5,000 of his unarmed men to a feast, where they kill all but Atahualpa himself. The following year, Pizarro kills him, too, and seizes control of the Inca Empire.

1687

Catholic missions

Father Eusebio Francisco Kino is one of many religious figures to introduce Christianity to the colonies. By the time of his death, he has founded more than 20 missions (centers for religious and humanitarian work).

AFTER

The four principal territories in the Americas—New Spain, New Granada, Peru, and River Plate—continued to be ruled by Spain. By the early 1800s, they started to declare their independence. Today, Spanish is still widely spoken in the region.

The fall of Tenochtitlán

The 79-day siege of Tenochtitlán, the capital city of the Aztec Empire, is illustrated in this 17th-century painting. The Aztecs surrendered on August 13, 1521, when an army of Spanish and Tlaxaclan warriors, led by the Spanish explorer Hernán Cortés, captured the Aztec ruler of Tenochtitlán, Cuauhtémoc. The destruction of Tenochtitlán was an important event in the Spanish conquest of Mexico and a critical stage in Spanish colonization of the Americas.

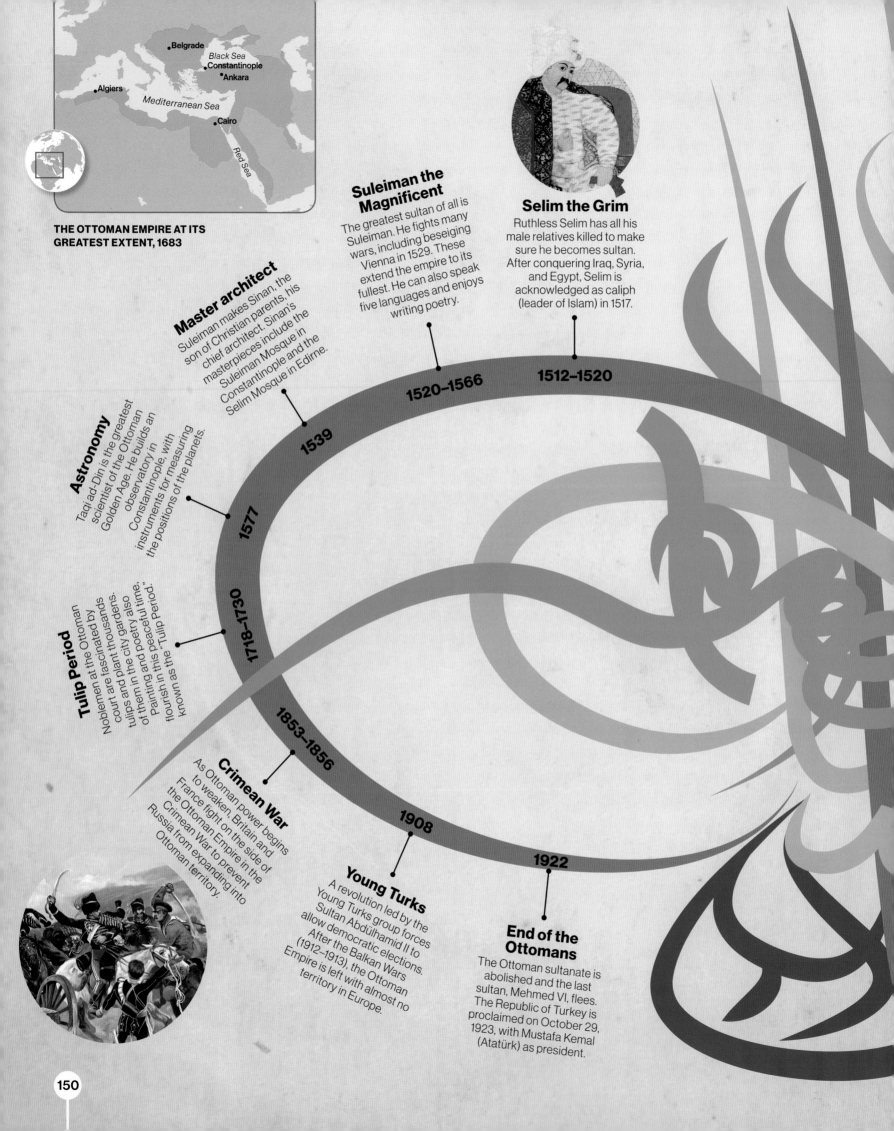

THE OTTOMAN EMPIRE AT ITS GREATEST EXTENT, 1683

Belgrade
Black Sea
Constantinople
Ankara
Algiers
Mediterranean Sea
Cairo
Red Sea

Suleiman the Magnificent
The greatest sultan of all is Suleiman. He fights many wars, including beseiging Vienna in 1529. These extend the empire to its fullest. He can also speak five languages and enjoys writing poetry.

Selim the Grim
Ruthless Selim has all his male relatives killed to make sure he becomes sultan. After conquering Iraq, Syria, and Egypt, Selim is acknowledged as caliph (leader of Islam) in 1517.

Master architect
Suleiman makes Sinan, the son of Christian parents, his chief architect. Sinan's masterpieces include the Suleiman Mosque in Constantinople and the Selim Mosque in Edirne.

Astronomy
Taqi ad-Din is the greatest scientist of the Ottoman Golden Age. He builds an observatory in Constantinople, with instruments for measuring the positions of the planets.

Tulip Period
Noblemen at the Ottoman court are fascinated by tulips and plant thousands of them in the city gardens. Painting and poetry also flourish in this peaceful time, known as the "Tulip Period."

Crimean War
As Ottoman power begins to weaken, Britain and France fight on the side of the Ottoman Empire in the Crimean War to prevent Russia from expanding into Ottoman territory.

Young Turks
A revolution led by the Young Turks group forces Sultan Abdülhamid II to allow democratic elections. After the Balkan Wars (1912–1913), the Ottoman Empire is left with almost no territory in Europe.

End of the Ottomans
The Ottoman sultanate is abolished and the last sultan, Mehmed VI, flees. The Republic of Turkey is proclaimed on October 29, 1923, with Mustafa Kemal (Atatürk) as president.

1512–1520
1520–1566
1539
1577
1718–1730
1853–1856
1908
1922

How to read a tughra

A tughra is read from right to left because it is in the Arabic language. The words of the sultan's title, shown here by different colors, have been combined with the shapes that make a tughra, each of which reflects a feature of the Ottoman Empire.

Key
- Mahmud
- Khan
- son of
- Abdülhamid
- victorious forever
- decorative feature

Beyze ("Egg")
Some think these symbolize the two seas controlled by the Ottomans (the Black Sea and the Mediterranean).

Tugh ("Flagpole")
Each vertical line signifies independence.

Zülfe ("Fringe")
Three S shapes indicate the Ottoman winds, which blow from east to west.

Sere ("Stand")
The base represents the Ottoman throne.

Hançer ("Arms")
These lines are a sign of power and strength.

Tughra

This decorative design is called a tughra. It was used by the sultan as a seal or signature on important documents. This one belonged to Sultan Mahmud II.

The Ottoman Empire

The Ottoman Empire began in the late 13th century when Osman, a Muslim warrior, founded a small state in Anatolia (modern-day Turkey). The powerful empire that later emerged lasted for 600 years. At its height, it stretched from Eastern Europe and the Black Sea to Arabia and North Africa. The rulers of the Ottoman Empire were known as sultans.

Topkapı Palace
Mehmed II orders the construction of the Topkapı Palace in his new capital, Constantinople. It is a large complex of buildings where the sultan lives and also runs his empire.

1459

Fall of Constantinople
Sultan Mehmed II conquers Constantinople (now called Istanbul) and ends the 1,000-year-old Byzantine Empire. He turns the cathedral of Hagia Sophia ("Holy Wisdom") into a mosque.

1453

Forced service
The Ottomans begin a system in which Christian boys from conquered territories are forced to convert to the Islamic religion and to work for the sultan as clerks, soldiers, or bodyguards.

Origins of the empire
Osman I is the ruler of a small Muslim state in northwest Anatolia. He regularly attacks the neighboring Byzantine Empire, the eastern remains of the Roman Empire.

1402 **c.1400** **1389** **1299–1326**

Battle of Ankara
The Ottoman Empire almost collapses when the Central Asian ruler Timur defeats Sultan Bayezid I at the Battle of Ankara and takes him prisoner. Legend has it that Timur kept the sultan in a golden cage.

Battle of Kosovo
Osman's grandson, Sultan Murad I, leads an army against Prince Lazar of Serbia at the "Field of the Blackbirds" (in modern-day Kosovo). Both leaders are killed, but the Ottomans win the battle, giving them control of southeastern Europe.

Astronomy

People have always looked up at the night sky and wondered about the nature of the Universe. Early astronomers found patterns in the stars and tried to follow and predict their movements. Nowadays, very powerful telescopes allow scientists to study the Sun, Moon, planets, and other galaxies, helping us to know more about our own planet and leading to theories about the beginning of the Universe.

Constellations

A constellation is a group of stars that form a pattern or outline of a recognizable shape. This one is Eridanus, known as the "Celestial River." It is the sixth-largest of the 88 constellations.

c.1420
Islamic astronomy

Central Asian ruler and astronomer Ulugh Beg builds an observatory in Samarkand. It is the largest and best of its kind in the Islamic world, and several famous astronomers visit it.

1543
Sun at the center

Nicolaus Copernicus, a Polish astronomer, disputes previous theories by suggesting that the Sun, rather than Earth, is the center of the Universe. He is not entirely correct, but his work provides ideas for future scientists to build on.

c.150 CE
Center of the Universe

Claudius Ptolemy of Greece writes in the *Almagest* that Earth sits at the center of the Universe. People believe this to be true for the next 1,400 years.

240 BCE
Broom stars

Chinese astronomers record the comets they see. They refer to them as "broom stars" or "long-tailed pheasant stars" because of their appearance.

c.330 BCE
Curved Earth

Ancient Greek philosophers start to think that Earth may be a sphere instead of flat. This is because the stars seen in southern lands are different from those seen in the north.

c.400 BCE
Mayan calendar

The Mayans are skilled astronomers who can measure vast periods of time. They create a calender that marks the beginning of time as 3114 BCE, according to their calculations.

700 BCE
Early patterns

The Babylonians use mathematics to predict and record the times and patterns of the eclipses of the Sun and Moon and the positions of planets.

1600 BCE
Star disk

The Bronze Age Nebra Sky Disk, found in Germany, is the oldest-known representation of the Universe, showing the Sun, Moon, and several stars.

c.2500 BCE
Stonehenge

A circle of giant standing stones is built in England. Many think it was used to mark the rising and setting points of the Sun at the summer and winter solstices.

Hawaii observatory
The observatory on top of the Mauna Kea volcano in Hawaii is the largest in the world.

"Astronomy compels the soul to look upward and leads us from this world to another."

Plato, *The Republic*, c.380 BCE

1608
Distant stars

Hans Lippershey of the Netherlands is the first to try to register a telescope design. This invention reveals that stars are much farther away from Earth than the planets in the Solar System.

2006
Properties of a planet

The International Astronomical Union agrees to a new definition of a planet. This downgrades Pluto from a planet to a dwarf planet.

1610
Jupiter's moons

Italian Galileo Galilei discovers moons orbiting Jupiter, which proves part of Copernicus's earlier theory that not all objects in the sky orbit Earth. This offends the Catholic Church, because it goes against some statements in the Bible.

1992
Exoplanets

The first exoplanets (planets outside the Solar System) are discovered. Today, more than 3,700 have been documented. Six have the right temperature for water to exist, which means that they could support life.

1687
Gravity

Isaac Newton, an English scientist, uses his understanding of the laws of motion and gravity to claim that the Moon is kept in orbit around Earth by gravity.

1774
Messier Catalog

A French scientist, Charles Messier, catalogs deep-sky objects, including comets, nebulae, and star clusters. They are known as "Messier objects," and today the Messier Catalog contains 110 of them.

1990
Hubble telescope

The Hubble Space Telescope is launched, the first time a telescope has been sent into space. It looks deep into space to take stunning photographs of the objects within our galaxy and the Universe.

1929
Expanding Universe

American Edwin Hubble, using the Hooker Telescope, finds that the Milky Way is not the only galaxy in the Universe. He shows that all galaxies are moving apart, which means that the Universe is expanding.

1912
Variable stars

American Henrietta Leavitt notices that certain stars, known as "Cepheid variables," change in brightness in a predictable way. Her discovery enables astronomers to calculate the distances between Earth and faraway galaxies.

Life of a star

Stars can live for millions of years, with smaller stars living the longest. The largest ones use up their fuel more quickly and die sooner by exploding, when they are called "supernovas." These explosions spread material around the Universe that can form new stars.

Protostar
Huge clouds of dust and gas bond to make a new star.

Red giant
The high temperature causes the star to expand.

Supernova
A very large red giant explodes. Its iron core becomes a black hole or a neutron star.

White dwarf
The outer gas layers are shed, leaving a dense core.

Main sequence star
A dense core is formed. Its temperature rises to 180° million Fahrenheit (100° million Celsius).

Planetary nebula
A red giant from a smaller star creates a glowing shell of gas.

Black dwarf
A white dwarf has no source of energy, so it cools and fades away.

Big battles

Even before the earliest civilizations began, families and tribes went to war with each other. As cities and states appeared, rose, and fell over many thousands of years, decisive battles fought on land, at sea, and in the air changed the course of history again and again.

Salamis

Invading Greece, the Persian navy is defeated by the Athenians, led by Themistocles, in a naval battle off Salamis. The following year, an alliance of Greek cities defeats the Persian army at Plataea.

Gaugamela

After invading the Persian Empire, Macedonian Alexander the Great wins a decisive victory over Darius III of Persia. The Persian army greatly outnumbers the Macedonians, but Alexander's men are better trained and led. Alexander goes on to conquer the whole Persian Empire.

Actium

The Roman politician Octavian defeats his enemies, Cleopatra of Egypt and Mark Antony, in a naval battle off Greece. The victory allows Octavian, now renamed Augustus, to take sole control of the Roman Empire and become emperor of Rome.

1274 BCE

September 480 BCE

280–279 BCE

October 331 BCE

260 BCE

August 216 BCE

September 2, 31 BCE

October 14, 1066

Kadesh

This great chariot battle is fought between the Egyptian army of Pharaoh Rameses II and the Hittites, led by Mutawalli II. Rameses claims victory in inscriptions on Egyptian temples, which provide the earliest detailed account of a battle. The real outcome of the battle is unknown.

Changping

The Chinese state of Qin defeats the state of Zhao at Changping. After 450,000 Zhao soldiers surrender, Bai Qi, the Qin general, massacres all but 240 of them, whose lives are spared so they can pass on the news. The Qin state goes on to unify China.

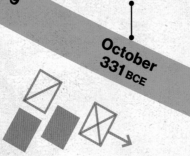

Pyrrhic victories

King Pyrrhus of Epirus invades Italy and wins two victories over the Romans, at Heraclea and Asculum. Pyrrhus loses so many men that his victory is as bad as a defeat. People use the phrase "Pyrrhic victory" to mean a hollow triumph.

Cannae

The Carthaginian general Hannibal invades Italy by crossing the Alps with an army, including his war elephants. At Cannae, he uses envelopment to destroy an army of 80,000 Roman soldiers.

Hastings

Duke William of Normandy defeats and kills Harold, the Anglo-Saxon king, at Hastings. Mounted Norman knights fight the charging Anglo-Saxons, who fight on foot, standing in a shield wall. French-speaking Normans take control of England.

Waterloo

The troops of British Duke of Wellington and Prussian Marshal Blucher defeat Napoleon Bonaparte in a major battle that brings the Napoleonic Wars to an end. Wellington fights a defensive battle, holding off repeated French attacks until Blucher arrives with reinforcements.

"I've seen thousands of men lying on the ground, their dead faces looking up at the skies. I tell you, war is hell!"

US General William Tecumsah Sherman, speech at the Michigan Military Academy, June 19, 1879

Stalingrad

The German army fights a major battle to seize the Russian city of Stalingrad. In November, when the Germans have almost captured the city, the Russians mount a counteroffensive. The trapped Germans surrender.

Gettysburg

This three-day battle, the largest ever fought in America, sees the Union army of George Meade, 94,000 strong, defeat the Confederate army of Robert E. Lee, numbering 72,000 men.

The Somme

During World War I, the British and French launch a major attack, but fail to break through the German lines at the Somme. More than three million men take part, and one million are killed.

October 7, 1571

June 18, 1815

July 1–3, 1863

July 1 – November 18, 1916

June 4–7, 1942

July 17, 1942 – February 2, 1943

January 1968

The Tet Offensive

Viet Cong and North Vietnamese forces launch a massive offensive against the cities of South Vietnam. US and South Vietnamese troops win a decisive victory. But in the US, the scale of the attack shakes public support for the war.

Lepanto

The Holy League, an alliance of Catholic Mediterranean states, wins a great victory over the Ottoman navy (see pages 150–151), in the waters off Greece. This is the last major naval battle to be fought entirely with rowing vessels (galleys).

Midway

The US defeats Japan in a great World War II ocean battle in the Pacific, fought mostly by planes launched from aircraft carriers. Japan loses all four of its carriers, while the Americans lose just one. The Japanese navy never recovers.

The Battle of Lepanto

This painting shows the Battle of Lepanto, between the Ottoman Turks and the Holy League of Spain, Venice, Genoa, and the Pope. The battle took place on October 7, 1571, and was the last battle to be fought entirely from rowing vessels called galleys. The Holy League damaged or captured about 200 of the Ottoman ships, losing only 12-17 of their own.

Edo Japan

After a long period of war (see pages 110–111), in 1603, Japan was finally unified under the leadership of Tokugawa Ieyasu. A golden age of peace, prosperity, and production followed, known as the Edo period, which saw new forms of Japanese art flourish. During this time, Japan cut contact with the rest of the world, and it would remain isolated from the West for most of the next three centuries.

1603
Edo capital
Shogun (military leader) Tokugawa Ieyasu moves away from the emperor's seat of influence in Kyoto. He establishes his headquarters in Edo (modern-day Tokyo), making it the base of real power in Japan.

c.1603
Kabuki theater
The Japanese dancer Okuni creates an art form known as kabuki. It combines drama, dance, and comedy to entertain audiences. In early kabuki theater, women play all the roles.

1614
Religious ban
The shogun bans Christianity throughout Japan, and any Christians who do not flee the country are publicly executed. The ban remains in place until 1867.

1620s
Art of ukiyo-e
Woodblock prints of scenes from everyday Japanese life become popular. Depicting local landscapes and urban entertainers, they become known as ukiyo-e ("pictures of the floating world").

1635
Closed country
Japan closes its ports to all Western nations apart from the Netherlands, who are still allowed to trade. The Japanese people are also not allowed to leave the country. This ban remains in effect until 1853.

The Great Peace

The Edo period marked an era of stability in Japan that became known as the Great Peace. The major cities of Edo, Kyoto, and Osaka catered for the wealthy, who could spend their money on new entertainments and luxury goods.

City streets during the Edo period became bustling shopping lanes.

1684
Sumo wrestling
Professional sumo wrestling begins in the Tomioka Hachiman Shrine. The first professional wrestlers are often samurai warriors who need a new source of income during the peaceful Edo period.

1833–1834
Tokaido
The Fifty-Three Stations of the Tōkaidō is a series of prints by Utagawa Hiroshige following his trip along the Tokaido road. With foreign travel banned, internal journeys within Japan become popular.

1850
Geishas
Professional female performers, called geishas, wear elaborate costumes and striking make-up. Trained in the arts of conversation, dance, and music, they are popular entertainers of the Edo period.

1854
Trade treaty
When the ban on contact with other countries is finally lifted, the Tokugawa Shogunate and the US agree to their first treaty, with Japanese ports opening up to American trade.

1868
Meiji Restoraion
The last Tokugawa shogun hands power back to the emperor, who takes the name Meiji (meaning 'enlightened rule'). With the Meiji Restoration, Japan fully opens its borders, and the Edo period ends.

Colonial America

As soon as Europeans became aware of the existence of the Americas, many were eager to visit what they called the "New World." Lots of people imagined a land of untold riches, others saw an opportunity for a new life away from religious persecution. The lands were already home to communities of native peoples who suffered displacement and destruction at the hands of European colonists.

1497

ENGLAND claims land in THE NEW WORLD

King Henry VII of England sponsors the Italian explorer John Cabot to find a new sea route to Asia. Cabot instead reaches what is now Newfoundland in Canada. He claims it for Henry VII, making it England's first claim to land in the New World.

1513

SPANISH TERRITORY claimed across the Atlantic

Spanish explorer Juan Ponce de León reaches land and claims it for Spain. He names it *La Florida*, Spanish for "the place with many flowers." This later becomes the Spanish colony of Florida.

1534

FRENCH

JOIN SURGE FOR LAND ACQUISITION

Jacques Cartier first explores the eastern edge of what is now Canada, going on to claim the land for France. In 1604, two more French explorers, Pierre de Monts and Samuel de Champlain, build a settlement on the St. Lawrence River, in present-day Québec City. French America eventually stretches from the Hudson Bay to the Gulf of Mexico.

1587

The missing townsfolk of ROANOKE: a mystery unsolved.

More than 100 men, women, and children from England settle in Roanoke, Virginia. Virginia Dare is born, the first English baby to be born in the Americas. In 1590, their settlement leader John White returns from a three-year trip back to England to find everyone gone. Their disappearance remains a mystery.

1607

JAMESTOWN STRUGGLES ON DESPITE HARDSHIP AND DIFFICULTY

This Virginia town is the first permanent English settlement in North America. The colony faces frequent food shortages, especially during the winter of 1609–1610. Known as "The Starving Time," this famine nearly wipes out the colony.

Virginia plants the seed for a GOOD HARVEST

The Virginia colonists plant cotton seeds for the first time. Cotton, tobacco, rice, and indigo (a plant used to make blue dye) become the major crops in the southern English colonies.

1619

AFRICAN SLAVES sold to English colonists

About 20 African slaves are brought to Jamestown, the first slaves in the English colonies. They are put to work on the tobacco and rice plantations. The economies of the southern English states becomes reliant on slave labor, which fuels the slave trade (see pages 164–165).

1626

DUTCH *deal* secures NEW AMSTERDAM

The Dutch colonist Peter Minuit buys Manhattan from American Indians and establishes New Amsterdam at the southern tip of the island. The English will capture the colony in 1664 and rename it New York.

1675

KING PHILIP'S WAR *rages on*

American Indians wage a 14-month-long battle against colonists in modern-day Massachusetts, Rhode Island, and Connecticut. Several tribes join together, led by tribal leader Metacom, also known as King Philip. They are eventually defeated, and this is the last major American Indian uprising against colonists in New England.

1732

Yet another new COLONY *in the* NEW WORLD

The British establish a new colony in North America and name it Georgia after King George. There are now 13 British colonies: Virginia, Georgia, Massachusetts, New York, Maryland, Rhode Island, Connecticut, Delaware, New Hampshire, North Carolina, South Carolina, New Jersey, and Pennsylvania.

1754

FRENCH AND SPANISH *losses reported*

Two European nations, France and Britain, battle over claims to land in the American colonies. Through the conflict, Britain gains control of Canada from the French, and Florida from the Spanish.

1620

THE MAYFLOWER SAILS FOR NEW ENGLAND

About a hundred settlers sail from England aboard the *Mayflower.* They land in what is now Massachusetts and establish the Plymouth colony there.

1773

No taxation *without* representation!

Fed up with being taxed by the British without having a say in how those taxes are spent, colonists board British ships and dump 342 chests of tea leaves (which were heavily taxed) into Boston harbor. The act triggers the American Revolution (see pages 190–191).

The Mayflower

Setting off from Plymouth, England in 1620, the *Mayflower* carried passengers over to the New World. Upon arrival, they established a settlement and named it Plymouth after the English town that they had sailed from.

The Scientific Revolution

During the 16th and 17th centuries, Europe was the scene of rapid and revolutionary scientific progress. Established ideas were rejected and religious thinking was challenged. Pioneering thinkers introduced new methods of experimentation and observation, and made major scientific breakthroughs, many of which have stood the test of time.

Pumping blood
English anatomist William Harvey investigates the valves and chambers of the heart and reveals how it pumps blood around the human body.

New methods
English scientist Francis Bacon writes *Novum Organum Scientiarum*, in which he argues that scientists should gather data by experimenting and observing.

First thermometer
Italian physicist Galileo Galilei invents an early form of thermometer, meaning "hot measure" in Greek. This device detects and indicates changes in temperature.

Orbiting the Sun
Polish astronomer Nicolaus Copernicus uses mathematical ideas to prove that Earth orbits the Sun. His work angers the Church, which says Earth is at the center of the Universe.

Anatomy pioneer
Flemish scientist Andreas Vesalius writes *De Humani Corporis Fabrica* after dissecting (cutting up) dead human bodies for research. His textbook revolutionizes the study of biology.

Natural history
Swiss naturalist Conrad Gessner writes *Historiae Animalium*. This 4,500-page encyclopedia features detailed drawings of animals and fossils.

First telescope
Galilei designs a telescope and uses it to study the Sun and planets. He observes the moons of Jupiter, sunspots, and mountains on the Moon.

1628

1620

1610

1593

1551–1558

1543

1543

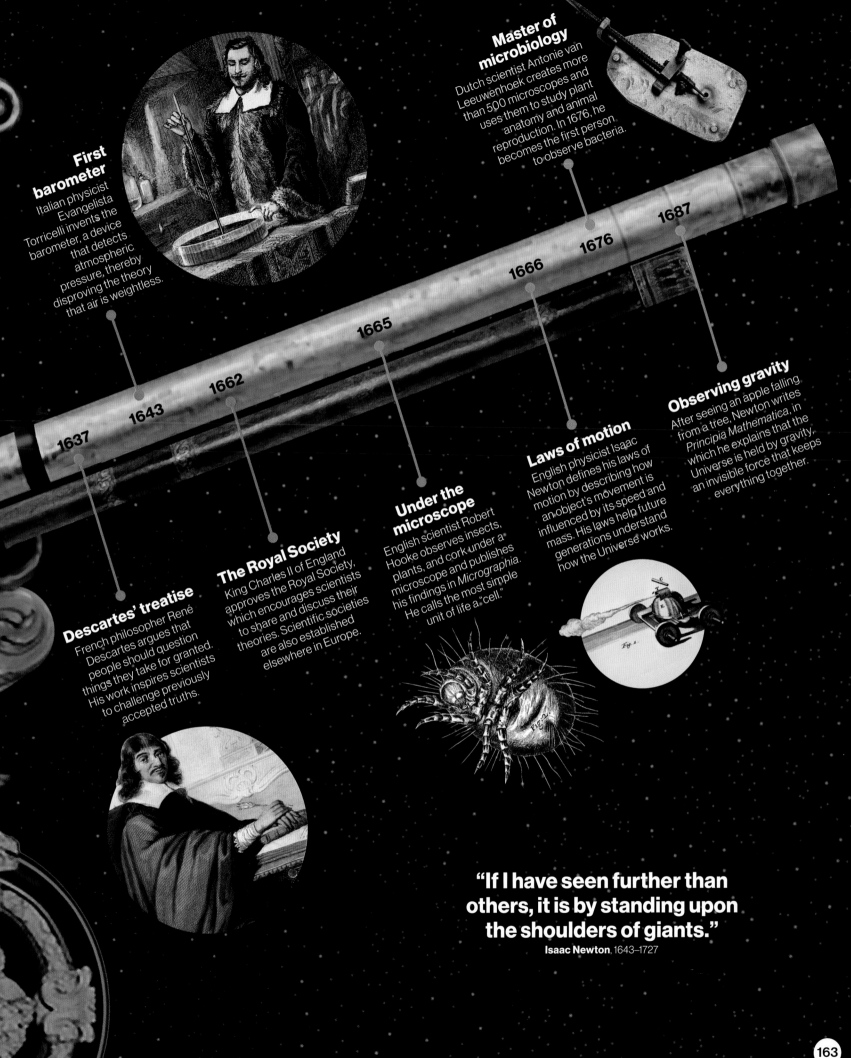

First barometer

Italian physicist Evangelista Torricelli invents the barometer, a device that detects atmospheric pressure, thereby disproving the theory that air is weightless.

Master of microbiology

Dutch scientist Antonie van Leeuwenhoek creates more than 500 microscopes and uses them to study plant anatomy and animal reproduction. In 1676, he becomes the first person to observe bacteria.

1637

1643

1662

1665

1666

1676

1687

Descartes' treatise

French philosopher René Descartes argues that people should question things they take for granted. His work inspires scientists to challenge previously accepted truths.

The Royal Society

King Charles II of England approves the Royal Society, which encourages scientists to share and discuss their theories. Scientific societies are also established elsewhere in Europe.

Under the microscope

English scientist Robert Hooke observes insects, plants, and cork under a microscope and publishes his findings in *Micrographia*. He calls the most simple unit of life a "cell."

Laws of motion

English physicist Isaac Newton defines his laws of motion by describing how an object's movement is influenced by its speed and mass. His laws help future generations understand how the Universe works.

Observing gravity

After seeing an apple falling from a tree, Newton writes *Principia Mathematica*, in which he explains that the Universe is held by gravity, an invisible force that keeps everything together.

"If I have seen further than others, it is by standing upon the shoulders of giants."

Isaac Newton, 1643–1727

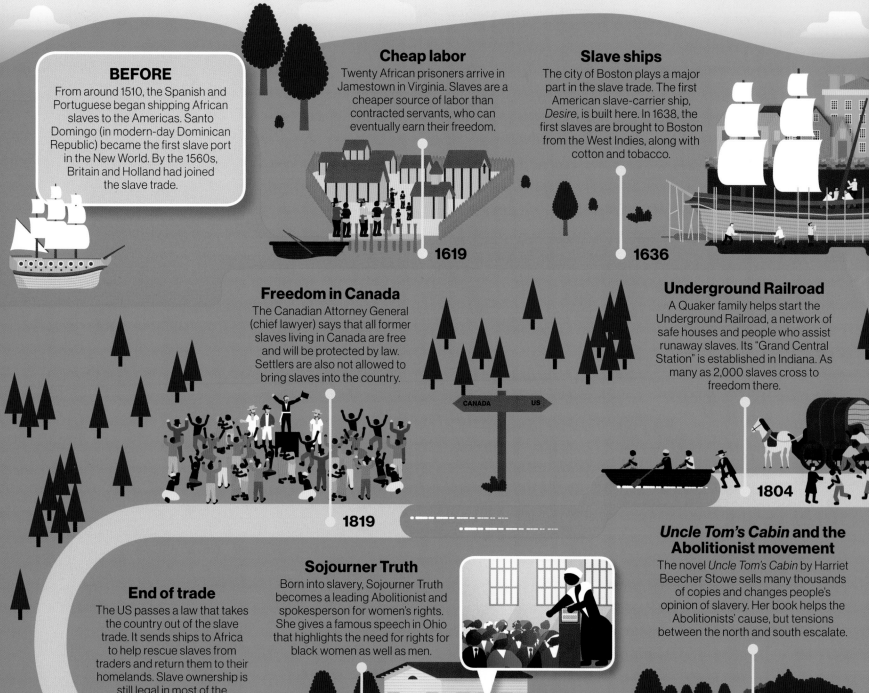

BEFORE

From around 1510, the Spanish and Portuguese began shipping African slaves to the Americas. Santo Domingo (in modern-day Dominican Republic) became the first slave port in the New World. By the 1560s, Britain and Holland had joined the slave trade.

Cheap labor

Twenty African prisoners arrive in Jamestown in Virginia. Slaves are a cheaper source of labor than contracted servants, who can eventually earn their freedom.

1619

Slave ships

The city of Boston plays a major part in the slave trade. The first American slave-carrier ship, *Desire*, is built here. In 1638, the first slaves are brought to Boston from the West Indies, along with cotton and tobacco.

1636

Freedom in Canada

The Canadian Attorney General (chief lawyer) says that all former slaves living in Canada are free and will be protected by law. Settlers are also not allowed to bring slaves into the country.

CANADA — US

1819

Underground Railroad

A Quaker family helps start the Underground Railroad, a network of safe houses and people who assist runaway slaves. Its "Grand Central Station" is established in Indiana. As many as 2,000 slaves cross to freedom there.

1804

End of trade

The US passes a law that takes the country out of the slave trade. It sends ships to Africa to help rescue slaves from traders and return them to their homelands. Slave ownership is still legal in most of the southern US states.

1819

Sojourner Truth

Born into slavery, Sojourner Truth becomes a leading Abolitionist and spokesperson for women's rights. She gives a famous speech in Ohio that highlights the need for rights for black women as well as men.

1850

Uncle Tom's Cabin and the Abolitionist movement

The novel *Uncle Tom's Cabin* by Harriet Beecher Stowe sells many thousands of copies and changes people's opinion of slavery. Her book helps the Abolitionists' cause, but tensions between the north and south escalate.

1852

Slavery in the US

Slavery was a part of life in the United States from its colonial beginnings, and slave owners used forced labor to build the young nation and its booming economy. By the 19th century, Abolitionists were campaigning to free all slaves, in the face of opposition from many American states. This resulted in civil war, with the north fighting to end slavery against the south, who wished to retain it.

> **"Whenever I hear anyone arguing for slavery, I feel a strong impulse to see it tried on him personally."**
> **Abraham Lincoln**,
> 16th president of the United States, 1861–1865

A life of slavery

In Virginia, the General Assembly passes a law stating that any child born to an enslaved mother will also become a slave for life. Most slave-holding colonies or states go on to enact similar laws that discriminate by race.

Quaker protest

In Pennsylvania, Quakers protest against slavery. The Quakers are Christians, who believe in treating others fairly. Later, the Quaker Church prevents members from profiting from the slave trade and from owning slaves.

Plantations of rice

Rice is introduced in South Carolina. It takes a lot of work to grow, so European settlers need slave labor to tend the crops and help them make it profitable. By around 1710, there are more enslaved Africans in the state than Europeans.

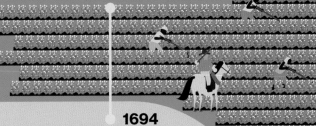

1662   **1688**   **1694**

The life of a slave

The first slave narrative, a story written by an ex-slave about the experience of slavery, is written in New York. Many more slave narratives follow, one of the most famous of which is written by Frederick Douglass in 1845.

Freedom Florida

Runaway slaves get their freedom in the Spanish territory of Florida. They must give their loyalty to Spain and join the Catholic Church. Many settle in St. Augustine, the oldest European city in the US.

1772   **1731**

Civil War

The debate over whether or not new states should use slaves splits the country in two. Northern victory in this 4-year conflict ends slavery, but more than 600,000 people lose their lives (see page 222).

Emancipation Proclamation

All slaves in the south are declared free on January 1 in President Abraham Lincoln's Emancipation Proclamation. This marks a turning point for the war, as Lincoln knows that ending slavery is the only way to keep the union of US states together.

Slavery abolished

The Emancipation Proclamation frees slaves but does not end slavery itself. The 13th Amendment to the US Constitution brings a permanent end to slavery in all of the United States, including new territories.

1861   **1863**   **1865**

Slave triangle

About 6 million Africans were taken to the Americas in a triangle of trade. Ships from Britain carried manufactured goods such as cloth, ironware, and guns to West Africa. These were exchanged for men, women, and children. The sea crossing to the West Indies was brutal, and many slaves did not survive. Those who did were sold at auctions, and the profits were used to buy sugar, cotton, rum, and tobacco to take back to Britain.

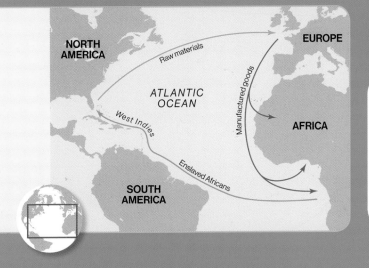

NORTH AMERICA

Raw materials

EUROPE

ATLANTIC OCEAN

Manufactured goods

West Indies

AFRICA

Enslaved Africans

SOUTH AMERICA

AFTER

Four million slaves were freed, but the challenges for African Americans remained. Lincoln had announced plans to help the South rebuild, but his assassination meant that his plans were never realized. Southern states went on to introduce laws to limit the civil rights of African Americans.

The Mughal Empire

The Mughals were rulers of an Islamic empire in what is now modern-day India, Pakistan, and Bangladesh. The empire lasted for more than 300 years and saw the construction of some of South Asia's finest monuments. The Mughals were originally from Central Asia and claimed to be descended from the Mongol leaders Genghis Khan and Timur the Great.

1526
Babur the Lion
The ruler of Kabul (in modern-day Afghanistan), Babur, invades northern India. Babur, whose name means "lion," defeats the sultan of Delhi to take control of a small area of land, founding the Mughal Empire.

1530–1556
Humayun
Babur's son Humayun loses his empire by 1540 and spends most of his reign in exile in Persia (modern-day Iran). He dies soon after regaining control of Delhi in 1555 and is succeeded by his 13-year-old son Akbar.

1560s–1590s
Akbar the Great
Akbar strengthens Mughal power by extending the empire into much of northern and central India. He is a devout Muslim, but encourages religious tolerance among his people. Hindu princes from the Rajput clans are given positions at court.

1590
Book of memoirs
Akbar has his grandfather Babur's memoirs translated into Persian, the language of the Mughal court. They show that Babur had a great love of poetry, culture, natural history, and gardens.

1658
Power struggle
When Shah Jahan falls ill, his sons fight each other for power. Aurangzeb, the third son, wins. He imprisons his father and makes himself emperor. Shah Jahan dies in prison in 1666.

1660s–1670s
Strict ruler
Aurangzeb introduces laws banning music, singing, and dancing. He destroys hundreds of Hindu temples and forces his Hindu subjects to pay high taxes in order to meet the cost of his endless wars.

1674
Hindu revival
Shivaji, a Maratha warrior from Maharashtra in western India, is crowned as a Hindu king. It is the start of a Hindu rise to power. The Marathas gradually extend northward into the territory of the Mughals.

1605–1627

Jahangir
Akbar's eldest son Salim becomes emperor and takes the name of Jahangir ("world-seizer"). The Mughal Empire grows even more during his reign, but his wife, Nur Jahan, is the real power behind the throne.

1620s

Mughal art
Jahangir has a love of art, especially painting, and this attracts many highly skilled artists to his court. They are famed for their carefully observed, lifelike studies of animals, birds, and flowers.

1632

Taj Mahal
Shah Jahan, the fifth Mughal emperor, begins building the Taj Mahal as a memorial to his wife, Mumtaz Mahal. It takes 20 years to complete and is considered the high point of Mughal architecture.

1635

Peacock Throne
Shah Jahan installs the Peacock Throne in the Red Fort in Delhi. It is made of gold and silver and decorated with precious stones, including the fabulous Koh-i-Noor diamond.

1707

End of an era
When Aurangzeb dies, aged 88, the Mughal Empire is at its greatest extent, reaching deep into southern India. It has been severely weakened by rebellion and war, however, and goes into rapid decline.

1739

Capture of Delhi
The Persian ruler Nadir Shah invades India and captures Delhi. He steals the Peacock Throne, taking it back to Persia. It is a humiliating blow, symbolizing the end of real Mughal authority.

1858

Last of the Mughals
The British take direct control of half of India. They depose and exile the last Mughal emperor, Bahadur Shah II, as punishment for his support of the Indian Revolt of 1857 against the British East India Company (see page 220).

Ming founder

Following the collapse of the Mongol Yuan Dynasty, Zhu Yuanzhang, a peasant turned warlord, seizes power. He declares himself Hongwu Emperor of the new Ming (Shining) Dynasty. His capital is Nanjing. He executes thousands of officials who are accused of plotting against him.

Yongle Emperor

The Ming Dynasty is at the height of its power under the Yongle Emperor. He repairs China's Grand Canal and restores the system of Civil Service exams, which the Mongols had discontinued.

"Why are the Western nations small and yet strong? Why are we large and yet weak?... We must search for the means to become their equal."

Feng Guifen, Chinese reformer, 1861

The Forbidden City

The Yongle Emperor moves the capital from Nanjing to Beijing in the north, where he oversees the building of the Purple Forbidden City. The Beijing dialect of Mandarin is adopted as the official state language at this time.

Yongle Encyclopedia

The emperor commissions the Yongle Encyclopedia. Compiled by 2,169 scholars, it consists of 22,937 manuscript rolls, covering agriculture, art, astronomy, geology, history, literature, medicine, religion, science, and many other subjects.

1368

1402–1424

1403–1408

1405–1433

1406–1420

1513

Portuguese explorer

Jorge Alvares, the Portuguese explorer, reaches Guangzhou, becoming the first European to sail to China. A new era of trade with the West begins. Christian missionaries begin to arrive in the 1550s.

Ming and Qing China

Following the fall of Mongol rule (see pages 120–121) in the 1360s, a new Chinese dynasty, the Ming, took over. Under the Ming (1368–1644), China became a superpower, and there was a global demand for Chinese porcelain and tea. During the Qing Dynasty that followed (1644–1912), the population increased from 160 to 450 million, but China was still technologically undeveloped and couldn't compete with Western powers.

Zheng He's voyages

Admiral Zheng He leads seven voyages of exploration to the Indian Ocean, East Africa, and the Red Sea. Their aim is to display the power of the Ming Dynasty. He returns with many exotic gifts, including an African giraffe.

Ming tombs

The Wanli Emperor is buried in a great tomb outside Beijing, which holds thousands of items of silk, porcelain, and jewelry. The tomb will be excavated in 1956—the only one of thirteen Ming royal tombs to be excavated to this day.

Last emperor

Military revolts lead to the proclamation of a Republic of China under President Sun Yat-sen. On February 12, 1912, the last Qing emperor, a six-year-old named Puyi, abdicates, ending more than 2,000 years of Chinese imperial history.

Dowager Empress Cixi

Dowager Empress Cixi controls the Chinese government. She is traditional and resists attempts to modernize China with Western-style industrial production of ships, railroads, and firearms.

First Opium War

The Daoguang Emperor's ban on the British opium trade leads to war with Britain. China suffers a humiliating defeat and is forced to sign a treaty giving Hong Kong to Britain. After losing a Second Opium War, in 1856–1860, China will have to legalize opium.

c.1861–1908

1911–1912

Imperial conquests

China conquers the Dzungar Khanate, the last remaining state from the former Mongol Empire. With the seizure of Tibet, Mongolia, and present-day Xinjiang (Turkestan), the Qing Empire is at its height.

1899–1901

1850–1864

Boxer Rebellion

In northern China, peasant rebels, called Boxers, rise up against foreigners and Christians. When the empress sides with the rebels, eight foreign nations intervene. After another humiliating defeat, China gives further concessions to foreign powers.

1839–1842

1620

1644

1645

1755–1757

Taiping Rebellion

In southern China, Hong Xiuqang, a Christian convert, leads a rebellion against Qing rule. He declares himself king of the Taiping Heavenly Kingdom. It takes 14 years to crush the rebellion, and 20 to 30 million people die during the fighting.

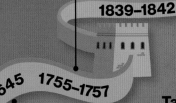

The Ming Great Wall

The Great Wall of China that people see today was mostly built between 1570 and 1583. The rebuilding was overseen by the Ming general Qi Jiguang, who wanted to keep out the Mongols.

Fall of the Ming

An army of peasant rebels led by Li Zicheng, a former Ming official, captures Beijing and overthrows the last Ming emperor. Li Zicheng declares himself emperor of the Shun Dynasty.

Qing Dynasty

Claiming to avenge the dead emperor, Manchu invaders from the north overthrow Li Zicheng and establish a new dynasty, the Qing. The new Shunzhi Emperor orders Chinese men to adopt the Manchu hairstyle, shaving their heads and wearing a pigtail. In China, the Manchus are resented as foreigners.

Ming ceramics

The Ming Dynasty is famous for milky blue and white porcelain, which they produced on an industrial scale. The imperial kilns at Jingdezhen made enough porcelain to supply not just the whole country, but the rest of the world. In the West, porcelain became so identified with the country that we still call it china.

Chemistry

Chemistry is the study of the matter that makes up our world. The foundations for this branch of science were laid in ancient Greece, as philosophers began to explore the properties and reactions of different substances. Following the discovery of atoms, today's chemists are able to study substances in incredible detail.

Four elements

450 BCE Greek philosopher Empedocles (495–430 BCE) claims everything is made up of differing amounts of four elements: earth, water, air, and fire. This theory is believed right up until the 17th century.

Amazing atoms

400 BCE Greek philosopher Democritus (460–370 BCE) states that everything is made up of tiny moving particles known as atoms, meaning "indivisible" in Greek. This marks the start of the atomic theory of the Universe.

Clay pieces
Democritus thought that a piece of clay split into smaller and smaller pieces would eventually become so tiny it couldn't be divided.

Atom C ←

Gas and fizz

1772 English chemist Joseph Priestley (1733–1804) presents his discovery of oxygen, carbon monoxide, and nitrous oxide. He invents the first carbonated fizzy water after seeing a reaction between gases at a local brewery.

1778

Fixed air

1754 Scottish chemist Joseph Black (1728–1799) shows that a gas called "fixed air" is exhaled by people. Made of one part carbon and two parts oxygen, it becomes known as carbon dioxide.

> **"Chemistry begins in the stars. The stars are the source of the chemical elements, which are the building blocks of matter and the core of our subject."**
>
> **Peter Atkins**, English chemist, 1940–

Boyle's Law

Irish chemist Sir Robert Boyle (1627–1691) studies the behavior of gases under pressure. At constant temperatures, he discovers that increasing the pressure on a gas squeezes it and decreases its volume.

Early alchemy

900 Arab scientist Al-Razi (854–925) completes experiments on and carefully observes metals, classifying them into groups. He studies alchemy, an early form of chemistry that explores what substances are made of and how they can be altered.

1662

Low pressure   **High pressure**

Elements list

Known as "the father of modern chemistry," French chemist Antoine Lavoisier (1743–1794) studies and names oxygen. He compiles the first list of chemical elements (pure substances that cannot be broken down into anything else), in what becomes the first true chemistry textbook.

Teamwork
Marie-Anne Lavoisier was also a chemist. She contributed to her husband's work.

New designs
Lavoisier made his own equipment to study chemicals in closed environments.

1803

Atomic theory

As scientists continue to experiment with gases, English chemist John Dalton (1766–1844) advances atomic theory by proposing that each element, or pure substance, has a different type of atom.

Carbon atom

Carbon dioxide
A compound is a mixture of at least two different elements. Carbon dioxide is formed by carbon and oxygen.

1869

Atomic bond

American scientist Linus Pauling (1901–1994) explains how the number of electrons in an atom's outer shell affects the way it bonds with other atoms.

1954

2016

New elements

The periodic table receives an update with the inclusion of four new elements, officially completing the seventh row. Nihonium, Moscovium, Tennessine, and Oganesson are among the heaviest elements ever found.

113 **Nh** Nihonium	115 **Mc** Moscovium
117 **Ts** Tennessine	118 **Og** Oganesson

Crystal structures

British chemist Dorothy Crowfoot Hodgkin (1910–1994) uses X-ray beams to study the arrangement of atoms inside different solids. She works out the structure of medications and proteins, helping to improve healthcare.

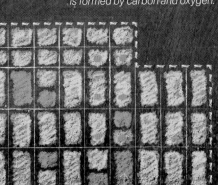

First periodic table

Russian chemist Dmitri Mendeleev (1834–1907) creates the first version of the periodic table of elements. It is so accurate that he leaves gaps in the right places for elements still to be discovered.

Mendeleev's table
Each element is positioned according to the size of its atoms.

1945

Atomic model
An atom has a nucleus full of protons at its center, which is orbited by electrons.

Acid test

The pH scale to measure acidity is invented by Danish chemist S.P.L. Sørensen (1868–1939). pH stands for "power of hydrogen" because acidic or alkaline levels depend on hydrogen ions—particles produced by atoms that are electrically charged.

1909

pH scale
The pH scale ranges from 0, very acidic (red), to 14, very alkaline (purple).

1917

Splitting the atom

New Zealander Ernest Rutherford (1871–1937) works out the structure of the atom and splits it apart. Inside the atom's nucleus, he proves the existence of protons—subatomic particles with a positive charge.

The story of dance

The urge to dance is as old as human life. People danced to honor their gods, to celebrate important moments, or simply for the sheer joy of it. Many styles of dance have emerged over the centuries, evolving from, and combining, traditional dance steps. Some forms of dance, such as ballet, take many years of training.

Indian dance

According to Hindu myth, dance is a gift from Lord Brahma, the creator god. He inspires scholar Bharat Muni to write the *Natyashastra*. This ancient book describes the elements of Indian classical dance.

c.200 BCE

Secret dance

Forbidden from following their own customs and traditions, African slaves living in Brazil develop a dance they call the capoeira. Combining martial arts with music and dance allows them to secretly practice combat moves.

c.1600

The galliard

Popular at royal courts throughout Europe is a lively dance with kicks, leaps, and hops, called the galliard. Queen Elizabeth I of England is said to dance six galliards every morning in order to keep fit.

1500s CE

Classical ballet

Swan Lake is first performed at the Bolshoi Theatre in Moscow, Russia. It is choreographed by Marius Petipa and features typical elements of classical ballet, such as turnout of the leg from the hip, high leg lifts, and dancing *en pointe*.

The tango

Ballroom dancers around the world are thrilled by the tango, a close-contact dance originally from Argentina and Uruguay. Like many dance styles, it blends African and European influences.

1913

Modern dance

American Isadora Duncan, a pioneer of modern dance, creates a sensation by performing barefoot and wearing a simple tunic. Her free, flowing dance movements are supposedly based on classical Greek dance.

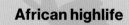

1900

1895

Ballet outrage

A new ballet, *The Rite of Spring*, causes a near riot at its first performance in Paris. It stars Russian dancer Vaslav Nijinsky and has music by Igor Stravinsky. The audience is outraged by the daring choreography and shocking sounds.

1913

African highlife

A popular new style of dance and music, known as "highlife," emerges in the dance halls of West Africa. Influenced by American jazz music, it combines Western dance steps with local rhythms.

c.1920

1923

The Charleston

After featuring in the musical theater show *Runnin' Wild*, the Charleston—a quick, energetic dance with swinging arm and leg movements—becomes an instant success with the fun-seekers of the 1920s.

Court ballet

King Louis XIV of France, who is himself a ballet dancer, establishes the Royal Academy of Dance in Paris to train dancers. At this time, male dancers are the leads in ballet performances.

Social dances

In European high society, men and women dance side by side at balls, seldom touching. They perform dances such as the minuet, which has intricate steps. Such dances are often based on traditional country dances.

1700s

c.1775

1661

Flamenco

The first written accounts of flamenco, the traditional dance of Andalusia in southern Spain, date from this time. These routines involve hand-clapping, singing, and guitar music, too. The origins of flamenco may be much earlier.

Ballerina

Marie Taglioni dances the ballet *La Sylphide* "en pointe" (on the tip of the toes), and shortens the length of her skirt to show off her footwork. Over time, this skirt style becomes even shorter, and is known as a tutu.

The waltz

The craze for the waltz, originally from Vienna, Austria, spreads rapidly through the ballrooms of Europe. It causes great scandal because couples dance face to face, with the man's arm around the woman's waist.

c.1840

1832

c.1800

Salsa

Originating in the Caribbean and brought to New York City by immigrants from Puerto Rico and Cuba, salsa evolves as a modern freestyle dance that mixes African, French, and Spanish dance steps and music.

Tap dance

In the US, metal is attached to the toe and heel of the shoes to create a tapping sound. Tap dance fuses two traditions: an African-American dance called juba, and the Irish jig.

Do the twist

The twist becomes the first worldwide teenage dance craze after singer Chubby Checker's rock and roll song *The Twist* reaches the top of the charts. Dancers swivel their hips as if drying their backs with a towel.

1970s

1933

1960

Dance in film

American dancer Fred Astaire partners with Ginger Rogers in *Flying Down to Rio*, the first of 10 musical films they make together. They bring Hollywood glamour to the world of dance.

Bollywood

Lively dance routines on a large scale feature in Bollywood films from Mumbai, India. They combine the classical dance traditions of India with the disco dance styles of the West.

c.1972

Breakdance

On the streets of New York City, young African Americans and Latin Americans create a style called breakdancing. They improvise complex routines to hip-hop music. Fancy footwork is combined with daring leaps and headspins.

c.2000

The Golden Age of Piracy

During the 16th century, the ports and the seas between Europe, Africa, and the Americas teemed with ships, many of them loaded up with valuable treasures. The rise in seafaring trade led to an increase in piracy. Ships and towns were raided for bountiful booty, and cutthroats, swashbucklers, and criminals sailed the seas in a Golden Age of Piracy.

The Pirate Round

The Indian Ocean is relatively pirate-free until Thomas Tew decides to sail around the Cape of Good Hope in Africa to plunder in a route that became known as the Pirate Round. His success leads many other pirates to follow in his path.

BEFORE

Piracy wasn't always a crime. In 1557, England's Queen Mary gave sailors known as privateers permission to attack and raid enemy ships. They shared their proceeds with the crown. Explorers often pilfered treasures to bring home. By the early 15th century, the vast amount of valuables carried across the oceans attracted seafaring criminals.

Safe haven

Pirates are invited to make Port Royal in Jamaica their home base, giving their protection to the town. Soon it is packed with pirates, and described as the richest and wickedest city in the world.

End of privateering

Some greedy privateers get out of hand, breaking the rules set down by their governments. The Dutch officially suspend any privateering in 1673, and the English in 1680. The French follow in 1697.

c. 1620 — **1657** — **1670** — **1673** — **1690** — **c.1693**

Buccaneer

The French welcome buccaneers to settle on Tortuga, off the island of Haiti. The word "buccaneer" comes from the French word for barbecuing—pirates would cook fish by heating them on wooden planks.

Sir Henry Morgan

Morgan leads many a pirate rampage with his leadership skills and formidable fleet. He captures and sacks Panama in 1671, bringing the second-largest city in the Western Hemisphere to its knees.

Jolly Roger

The black flag with a grinning skull is hoisted over a French pirate ship while it is being chased by an English navy vessel. Raising the Jolly Roger becomes the terrifying signal that a pirate attack is underway.

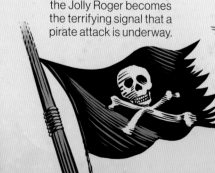

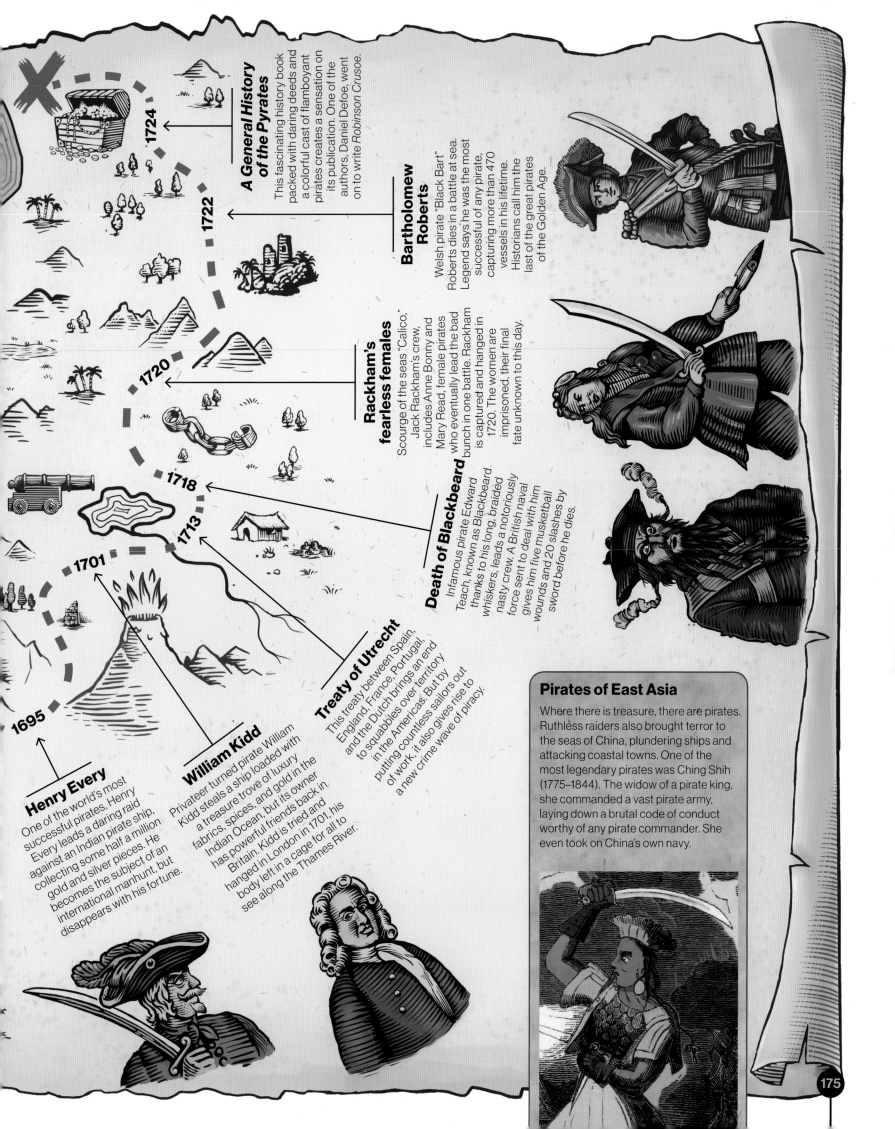

1724

A General History of the Pyrates

This fascinating history book packed with daring deeds and a colorful cast of flamboyant pirates creates a sensation on its publication. One of the authors, Daniel Defoe, went on to write *Robinson Crusoe*.

1722

Bartholomew Roberts

Welsh pirate "Black Bart" Roberts dies in a battle at sea. Legend says he was the most successful of any pirate, capturing more than 470 vessels in his lifetime. Historians call him the last of the great pirates of the Golden Age.

1720

Rackham's fearless females

Scourge of the seas "Calico," Jack Rackham's crew, includes Anne Bonny and Mary Read, female pirates who eventually lead the bad bunch in one battle. Rackham is captured and hanged in 1720. The women are imprisoned, their final fate unknown to this day.

1718

Death of Blackbeard

Infamous pirate Edward Teach, known as Blackbeard, thanks to his long, braided whiskers, leads a notoriously nasty crew. A British naval force sent to deal with him gives him five musketball wounds and 20 slashes by sword before he dies.

1713

Treaty of Utrecht

This treaty between Spain, England, France, Portugal, and the Dutch brings an end to squabbles over territory in the Americas. But by putting countless sailors out of work, it also gives rise to a new crime wave of piracy.

1701

William Kidd

Privateer turned pirate William Kidd steals a ship loaded with a treasure trove of luxury fabrics, spices, and gold in the Indian Ocean, but its owner has powerful friends back in Britain. Kidd is tried and hanged in London in 1701, his body left in a cage for all to see along the Thames River.

1695

Henry Every

One of the world's most successful pirates, Henry Every leads a daring raid against an Indian pirate ship, collecting some half a million gold and silver pieces. He becomes the subject of an international manhunt, but disappears with his fortune.

Pirates of East Asia

Where there is treasure, there are pirates. Ruthless raiders also brought terror to the seas of China, plundering ships and attacking coastal towns. One of the most legendary pirates was Ching Shih (1775–1844). The widow of a pirate king, she commanded a vast pirate army, laying down a brutal code of conduct worthy of any pirate commander. She even took on China's own navy.

THE AGE OF REVOLUTION

1750-1914

The Age of Revolution

Between 1750 and 1850, the world was transformed. The US War of Independence was the first in a series of political revolutions in which old governments were overthrown and new nations formed. During the Industrial Revolution, people left the countryside and flooded into towns and cities to work in factories. The steam engine and electricity transformed people's everyday lives, and offered new modes of transportation such as trains and cars.

1756–1763
The Seven Years' War between Britain and France in Europe spreads to colonies in North America.

1775–1783
Thirteen colonies in North America break away from British rule in the US War of Independence.

1788
A fleet of ships carrying convicts and their guards lands in Australia to start a British colony.

1804
Napoleon Bonaparte declares himself Emperor of France, leading to the Napoleonic Wars.

1755
A devastating earthquake destroys almost two-thirds of the city of Lisbon, capital of Portugal.

1769
James Watt's invention of a more efficient steam engine paves the way for the Industrial Revolution.

1789
Peasants march on the Bastille prison in Paris, kickstarting the French Revolution.

1803
The US doubles its territory when it acquires land from France in the Louisiana Purchase.

The United States
Thirteen colonies in North America rebelled against British rule, leading to a revolutionary war and the founding of the US (see pages 190–191).

Factory work
With the development of factories and new technology that powered the Industrial Revolution (see pages 194–195), working lives were transformed.

Australia
Britain sends convicted criminals to Australia (see pages 196–197) to establish colonies there. The first colonists land near the site of modern-day Sydney.

The French Revolution
The French people rose up against their monarchy. The French Revolution (see pages 200–201) led to a period known as the "Reign of Terror."

Stephenson's Rocket

George Stephenson's steam locomotive *Rocket* won the Rainhill Trials, a competition held in 1829 by the Liverpool and Manchester Railway company in England to find the best locomotive design.

1815
Napoleon is defeated at the Battle of Waterloo.

1831
Many American Indians die in a forced march to new territories known as the Trail of Tears.

1861–1865
The issue of slavery causes a civil war in the US between the northern and southern states.

1884–1885
A meeting between Europe's most powerful nations marks the start of major colonization in Africa.

1903
The Wright Brothers' historic manned flight begins the history of aviation.

1811
A revolution in Venezuela is the first of a series of uprisings that will see the end of Spanish rule in South America.

1858
Britain takes direct control over its territories in India.

1867
Three provinces in North America unite to form the Dominion of Canada within the British Empire.

1893
New Zealand becomes the first country in the world to give women the right to vote.

1912
The RMS *Titanic* sinks with great loss of life on its first and only voyage.

Latin America
The people of Central and South America fought for independence from Spain (see pages 206–207) in a series of conflicts that saw the end of Spanish colonial rule.

US expansion
As the US gained more territory, pioneering settlers moved into the new lands. This led to conflict with American Indian peoples (see pages 214–215).

The US Civil War
Southern states attempted to break away from the US over the issue of slavery. A devastating civil war followed (see pages 222–223), ending in victory for the North.

Colonial Africa
Competing for access to the continent's resources, a number of European nations took control of most of Africa (see pages 224–225).

The Enlightenment

In the 17th and 18th centuries, European thinkers began to question traditional religious and political teachings, believing that individuals should draw their own conclusions about society and nature. They conducted scientific experiments and wrote many books and essays, and their ideas directly inspired the American and French Revolutions.

Age of Reason

French philosopher René Descartes publishes *Discourse on the Method*, in which he argues that reason (conscious thought) is the source of all knowledge. His starting point is to doubt everything, even his own existence.

1637

Laws of physics

English mathematician Isaac Newton's *Principia Mathematica* describes his ideas on the laws of motion and gravity. Newton's work transforms people's understanding of the physical universe.

1687

Basic rights

In *Two Treatises of Government*, English philosopher John Locke argues that people possess certain basic rights such as the right to life, the right to own property, and the right to rebel against an unjust government.

1690

Science of plants

Swedish scientist Carl Linnaeus devises a system of plant classification that is still in use today. It means that scientists in different countries can be certain that they are describing the same plants.

1735

Man of letters

French writer and philosopher Voltaire (whose real name was François-Marie Arouet) completes his best-known work, *Candide*—a story that criticizes some of the philosophical and political ideas of his day.

Will of the people

In *The Social Contract*, French philosopher Jean-Jacques Rousseau challenges traditional views of society by arguing that laws are strong only when they are supported by the will of the people who must live under them.

Founding father

Thomas Jefferson drafts the Declaration of Independence. His ideas concerning liberty, government, and the rights of individuals are deeply influenced by Locke, Montesquieu, and other Enlightenment thinkers.

Wealth of Nations

Adam Smith publishes *The Wealth of Nations*, the first modern book on money matters. Smith is a leading figure of the Scottish Enlightenment in Edinburgh at a time when the city is a center of scientific and philosophical debate.

Human nature

According to Scottish philosopher David Hume in *A Treatise of Human Nature*, all knowledge comes from the experiences of our senses, instincts, and feelings, not from reason.

Useful knowledge

American thinker Benjamin Franklin founds the American Philosophical Society in Philadelphia with the aim of "promoting useful knowledge" and spreading Enlightenment ideas in North America.

Separation of powers

In his *Spirit of the Laws*, Charles de Montesquieu of France argues that the duties of government should be split into different branches to keep a small group of people from gaining too much power.

Encyclopedia

In France, Denis Diderot compiles the *Encyclopedia*, a mammoth work attempting to catalog all knowledge. It is 17 books in total and contains thousands of articles by the leading French thinkers of the day.

1739   **1743**   **1748**   **1751–1765**

Idealism

In *The Critique of Pure Reason*, German thinker Immanuel Kant asks challenging questions about how we think and how we know things. He believes that nobody can say for certain what reality is.

Chemistry

French nobleman and scientist Antoine Lavoisier's *Elements of Chemistry* lays the foundations for the modern study of the subject. However, in 1794 he is executed by guillotine during the French Revolution.

The female citizen

Playwright and feminist activist Olympe de Gouges publishes a pamphlet during the French Revolution declaring that women are equal to men and have the same rights of citizenship. She is executed two years later.

The Rights of Woman

In *A Vindication of the Rights of Woman*, English feminist writer Mary Wollstonecraft calls for educational reform, arguing that if girls were allowed the same education as boys, it would benefit all of society.

THE GREAT LISBON EARTHQUAKE

The disaster that shakes Europe

On the morning of November 1, 1755, the people of Lisbon gathered in the city's many churches, chapels, and cathedrals to celebrate All Saints' Day. Meanwhile, deep below the waves of the Atlantic Ocean, an earth-shattering force was about to unleash a series of events that would leave the city devastated.

> **"First we heard a rumble, like the noise of a carriage, it became louder... until it was as loud as the loudest noise of a gun, immediately after that we felt the first tremble."**

Christian Staqueler,
in an account of the Great Lisbon Earthquake of 1755

Unsuspecting citizens

On **November 1, 1755**, the Roman Catholic population flock to the churches and cathedrals of Lisbon. They are in a celebratory mood as they mark All Saints' Day in the capital of the kingdom of Portugal. After midnight mass, King Joseph I of Portugal leaves Lisbon with his family to celebrate outside the city. At **9:30 a.m.**, the morning mass is underway and thousands of people gather in the religious area of Lisbon. Across the city, solemn offerings are presented and ceremonial candles are lit to honor the saints of the Roman Catholic Church.

The world shakes

At **9:40 a.m.**, the first of three earthquakes shakes the city. Buildings crumble as thousands of churchgoers panic in the mayhem. Over the course of the morning, two more earthquakes hit the city. The second, more powerful shock lasts for three and a half minutes, followed less than 10 minutes later by a third. Shaking is felt as far away as North Africa, more than 400 miles (600 km) from Lisbon. The center is built on soft soil, so the quake

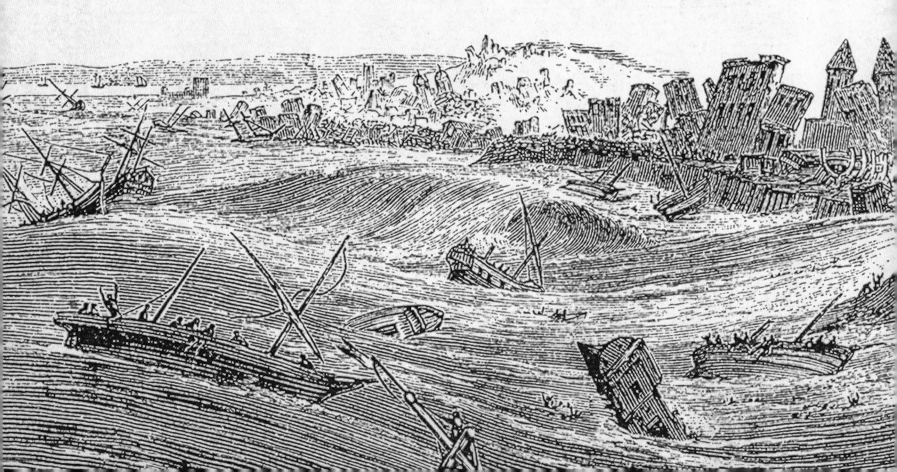

instantly destroys the foundations of the city. Large cracks up to 13 ft (4 m) wide tear across the streets and the religious heart of Lisbon collapses, killing thousands of celebrating churchgoers. People flee through the shuddering streets, heading toward the seemingly safe harbor to seek refuge on departing boats.

Waves of destruction

The people of Lisbon gather at the harbor and witness a curious marine event. The sea withdraws away from the city, revealing sunken shipwrecks scattered across the exposed seabed. Intrigued, more people gather to watch the strange phenomenon. At around **10:30 a.m.**, a 16–32 ft (5–10 m) ocean wave called a tsunami suddenly rushes toward the crumbling city. A series of devastating waves arrive with tremendous impact, flooding the harbor and city streets, and drowning the crowd. Overcrowded boats traveling out to sea and up the Tagus River capsize as the ocean surge swells the river, killing even more people.

Fires rage

As Lisbon crumbles and floods, the religious candles in churches and homes tumble with the falling debris. Fires start to break out across the city. Broken buildings block the network of narrow streets and prevent the survivors from putting out the growing flames. Soon the fires spread and build into a searing inferno that rages out of control for five days (from **November 2–6**). More than two-thirds of the city of Lisbon is destroyed.

Stillness returns

On **November 6**, a stillness falls over the city, the fires burn out, and the survivors of the disaster return to count their dead. Around 60,000 citizens of Lisbon are estimated to have lost their lives in the catastrophe. The earthquake was so strong, it was felt throughout Europe and North Africa. The quake was also destructive in Morocco, where approximately 10,000 people were killed. The church proclaims the disaster "an act of God" to punish the sinful. However, as Lisbon starts to rebuild, people struggle to understand why so many churchgoing people had suffered, and they can't explain what their citizens had done to deserve such dramatic punishment. Some scholars across Europe start to question the cause of the devastation and discuss earthquakes as "natural disasters," which leads to the beginnings of the scientific study of earthquakes, known as seismology.

The Great Dying

The worst mass extinction in Earth's history—the Great Dying—occurs just before the Age of Dinosaurs. Around 95 percent of the planet's species vanishes over a period of about 80,000 years. The cause is a mystery.

Toba supervolcano

The Toba supervolcano erupts in Sumatra, blasting 672 cubic miles (2,800 cubic km) of rock into the sky and cooling Earth's climate for up to 10 years. It is the largest explosive volcanic eruption in the last 25 million years.

Entombed in ash

Mount Vesuvius in Italy erupts, burying the town of Pompeii in ash and killing thousands. Centuries later, the site is rediscovered. Hollows in the ash are filled with plaster, revealing the dead.

Lisbon earthquake

A catastrophic earthquake hits the city of Lisbon in Portugal, triggering tsunamis and fires that cause further devastation. The city is almost completely demolished and 60,000 people are killed.

252 million years ago

66 million years ago

74,000 BCE

C. 1640 BCE

79 CE

1556

1775

1815

Dinosaur extinction

An asteroid at least 6 miles (10 km) wide hits the Yucatán Peninsula in Central America, blasting rock into the sky and blocking sunlight for years. Nearly all large animals are wiped out, including all types of dinosaur except birds.

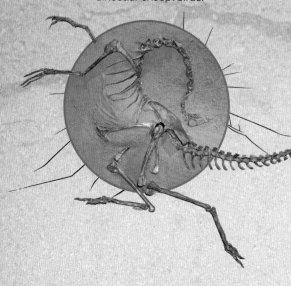

Greek tragedy

Much of the Greek island of Thera (modern-day Santorini) is destroyed by a massive volcanic eruption. The city of Akrotiri is buried under ash, and the eruption triggers tsunamis and earthquakes that devastate surrounding islands.

Record earthquake

The deadliest earthquake on record hits northern China, killing about 850,000 people. The death toll is very high because the traditional dwellings in the area are artificial caves excavated from loose, dusty soil.

Year without summer

Mount Tambora in Indonesia erupts, expelling vast dust clouds that lower global temperatures by 5.4°F (3°C). Crops fail to grow, causing mass starvation. The following year, Europe and North America experience a "year without summer", with heavy snow in June, July, and August.

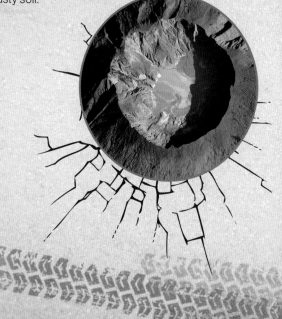

"It takes an earthquake to remind us that we walk on the crust of an unfinished planet."
American journalist Charles Kuralt

Natural disasters

The forces of nature that shape our planet can be spectacular in their destructive power. Earthquakes, volcanic eruptions, tsunamis, and hurricanes have occurred throughout history, and their unpredictable fury reminds us that we are small and vulnerable. But history also shows that these natural phenomena only rarely clash with human populations on a disastrous scale.

Storm surge

A massive hurricane hits the village of Coringa on the coast of India. It causes a disastrous storm surge, raising sea levels by 40 ft (12 m) and submerging the land with seawater. Around 300,000 people are killed.

Loudest eruption

Two-thirds of the island of Krakatoa in Indonesia is obliterated by a volcanic eruption that can be heard more than 3,000 miles (4,800 km) away, making it the loudest eruption in recorded history. More than 35,000 people die.

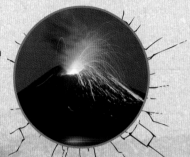

1839

1883

1906

1876

China floods

Heavy rain causes three major rivers to flood 70,000 square miles (182,000 square km) of land in China—an area about the size of Florida. Between 1 million and 4 million people die.

Famine in China

A prolonged drought in northern China leads to three years of failed crops and widespread famine. At least 10 million people die of starvation— about 10 percent of the local population.

San Francisco earthquake

More than 80 percent of the city of San Francisco is destroyed by an earthquake that kills 3,000 people and renders most of the city's population homeless.

1931

1925

1960

2004

Chile earthquake

The most powerful earthquake on record hits Chile. It lasts 10 minutes, kills several thousand people, and leaves 2 million homeless. Tsunamis caused by the quake hit Hawaii, Japan, and the Philippines.

Asian tsunami

An earthquake on the seabed off the coast of Sumatra sends a series of tsunamis across the Indian Ocean, causing devastation in Indonesia, Malaysia, Thailand, Sri Lanka, and India. More than 280,000 people are killed.

Tristate tornado

The deadliest tornado in US history carves a 151-mile (243-km) path of destruction through the states of Missouri, Illinois, and Indiana, killing 695 people and destroying 15,000 homes.

The story of music

Music around the world is as varied as the people who populate it. European music developed during the Middle Ages, but other traditions can be traced to much earlier dates. All forms of music are used to express emotion, to mark religious ceremonies or important events, and, above all, as a source of pleasure.

Japanese court music
Officials from Japan travel to China to learn about its culture. The Japanese blend Chinese court music with Korean and other Asian styles to create their own classical orchestral music, gagaku.

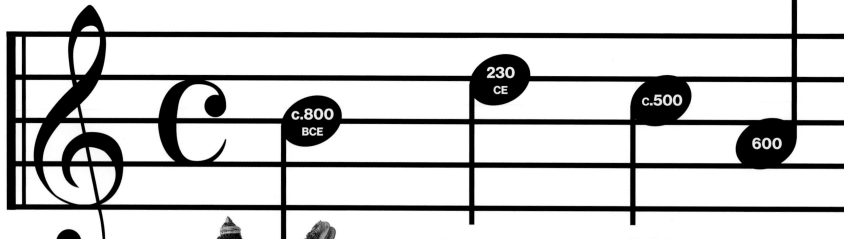

c.800 BCE

230 CE

c.500

600

Indian ragas
The Indian classical music form, the raga, is first referred to in the *Upanishads* (ancient texts of Hinduism). Ragas are particular patterns of notes, associated with certain moods and times of day.

Gamelan
An Indonesian gamelan orchestra consists of metallophones (tuned metal bars) hit with mallets, hand-played drums, gongs, and xylophones. Gamelan music is played in traditional ceremonies and on formal occasions.

Religious music
The rise of Christianity spreads music throughout Europe. Plainsong (a single unaccompanied melody with free rhythm) is sung in church services. Music is learned by ear and is largely performed from memory.

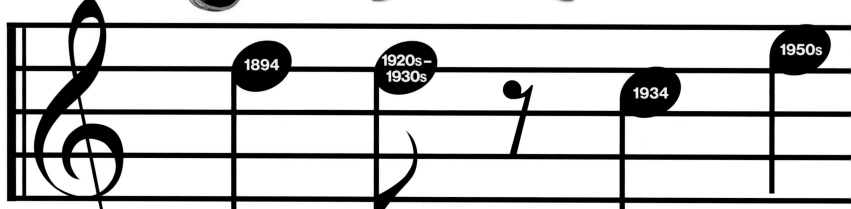

1894

1920s–1930s

1934

1950s

Modern music
Frenchman Claude Debussy composes *Prélude à l'après-midi d'un faune*, which is considered to be the start of modern Western music. His works use new kinds of harmony, and create moods and atmospheres, like the art movement known as Impressionism (see page 142).

Jazz Age
America's new music, jazz, becomes more popular. It is a blend of African and European styles, and features improvisation, where performers each play the music in their own unscripted way.

Umm Kulthum
Egyptian Umm Kulthum sings in the first broadcast on Radio Cairo. Her expressive vocal style makes her one of the most popular artists of the Arab world.

Rock and Roll
Guitar-based popular music, known as "Rock and Roll," emerges in the US. It makes big stars of performers such as Bill Haley & His Comets, Elvis Presley, and Chuck Berry.

Chinese opera

Emperor Xuanzong founds the first opera school in China, called the Pear Garden. Today, opera performers (which include singers, musicians, dancers, and acrobats) are still known as "Children of the Pear Garden."

Johann Sebastian Bach

German composer Bach is considered one of the greatest of the Baroque era. Music of this period is dramatic and powerful. Bach is the master of "counterpoint," where different melodies are weaved together.

Ludwig van Beethoven

German composer Beethoven writes his Ninth Symphony, which revolutionizes this type of orchestral piece by including the human voice. Despite being totally deaf, he conducts its first performance. He has to be turned around to see the enthusiastic applause from the audience.

Clara Schumann

Influential German Clara Schumann is one of the most respected pianists of the Romantic era. She has a 60-year career at a time when women rarely perform in public. Works of this period are longer, richer in sound, and full of emotion.

730

c.1400–1600

1685–1750

1762

1824

1819–1896

The Renaissance

Music in the West becomes more complex, with two or more melodies sung or played at the same time ("polyphony"). Developments in instrument-making, and the availability of printed music, allow more people to play music.

Wolfgang Amadeus Mozart

Gifted Austrian pianist Mozart begins a concert tour of Europe at the age of six. He becomes one of the leading composers of the Classical period, in which music has a new simplicity. His many works include the operas *Don Giovanni*, *The Marriage of Figaro*, and *The Magic Flute*.

The stave

The stave is a set of five horizontal lines that Western composers use to write their music. Notes are placed either on the lines or in the spaces in between. The position determines how high or low the note is ("pitch").

1963

2016

2018

"Beatlemania"

British pop group The Beatles attract huge crowds wherever they go, and 73 million people watch them on *The Ed Sullivan Show*. Fans often scream and faint at their concerts.

Beyoncé

Pop singer Beyoncé's popularity makes her the highest-paid black musician in history. Her album *Lemonade* encompasses a range of musical styles, such as reggae, hip hop, and funk. She and the album win many awards.

Multitalented musician

British composer Kerry Andrew specializes in works for the voice, experimenting with the different sounds that it can make. She also sings in a folk group and plays in a jazz-influenced band.

Imperial Russia

Under the Romanov family, Russia gained a vast empire, stretching from Alaska in the west to Poland in the east. But compared to nations in western Europe, Russia was stuck in the past—its economy was based on peasant farmers, and there was little industry. Although some czars tried to modernize Russia, failure to reform led to revolutionary movements that eventually toppled the dynasty.

Crimean War

Russia, attempting to seize territory from the declining Ottoman Empire, is defeated in the Crimean War against Britain, France, and Turkey. The defeat reveals the weaknesses of Russia's military.

1853–1856

Officers revolt

After Alexander I's sudden death, army officers, returning from the Napoleonic Wars with Western ideas, stage a revolt. They demand a constitutional monarchy and freedom for the serfs— peasant farmers controlled by landowning lords. The revolt is crushed by the new czar, Nicholas I.

December 1825

Fighting Napoleon

Under Alexander I, the country is drawn into the Napoleonic Wars, switching sides twice. Napoleon's 1812 invasion of Russia ends in a French disaster. Russia then plays a leading role in Napoleon's final defeat.

1805–1815

Catherine the Great

Following the murder of Czar Peter III, his German wife rules as Catherine II. She continues to westernize Russia, reforming the legal system. Russia seizes parts of Poland and Turkey, as well as Lithuania, Belarus, and Crimea.

1762–1796

St. Petersburg

The city of St. Petersburg, founded by Peter the Great in 1703, is proclaimed capital of Russia and the new seat of government. By Peter I's death in 1725, the city has 40,000 inhabitants.

1712

Peter the Great

Peter I becomes czar, meaning emperor. He introduces Western methods of education. He increases governance, making military spending the dominant power in the Baltic Sea.

1682–1725

The Imperial Crown

From Catherine the Great (1762) until Nicholas II (1896), every czar wore the Imperial Crown, decorated with 4,936 diamonds, at their coronation.

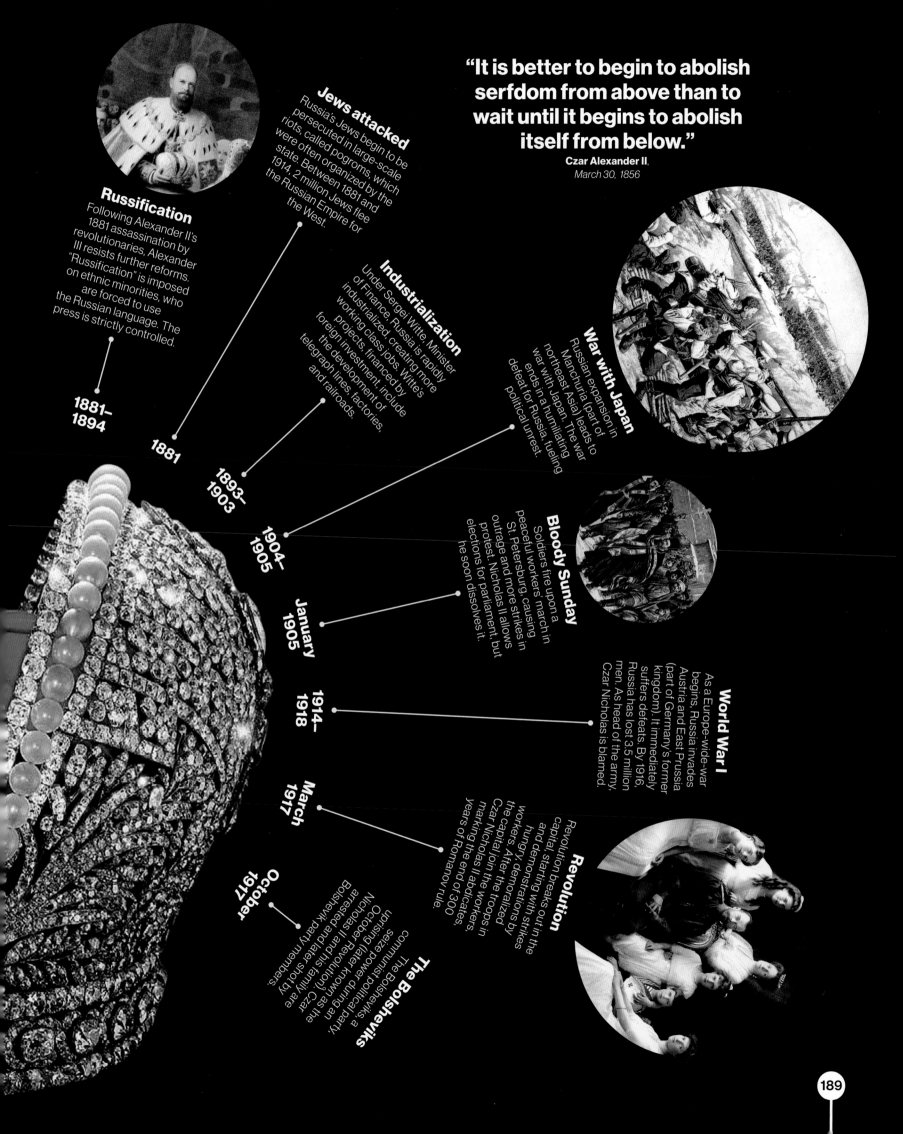

Russification

Following Alexander II's 1881 assassination by revolutionaries, Alexander III resists further reforms. "Russification" is imposed on ethnic minorities, who are forced to use the Russian language. The press is strictly controlled.

1881–1894

Jews attacked

Russia's Jews begin to be persecuted in large-scale riots, called pogroms, which were often organized by the state. Between 1881 and 1914, 2 million Jews flee the Russian Empire for the West.

"It is better to begin to abolish serfdom from above than to wait until it begins to abolish itself from below."

Czar Alexander II,
March 30, 1856

Industrialization

Under Sergei Witte, Minister of Finance, Russia is rapidly industrialized, creating more working class jobs. Witte's projects, financed by foreign investment, include the development of telegraph lines, factories, and railroads.

1881

1893–1903

War with Japan

Russian expansion in Manchuria (part of northeast Asia) leads to war with Japan. The war ends in a humiliating defeat for Russia, fueling political unrest.

1904–1905

Bloody Sunday

Soldiers fire upon a peaceful workers' march in St. Petersburg, causing outrage and more strikes in protest. Nicholas II allows elections for parliament, but he soon dissolves it.

January 1905

World War I

As a Europe-wide war begins, Russia invades Austria and East Prussia (part of Germany's former kingdom). It immediately suffers defeats. By 1916, Russia has lost 3.5 million men. As head of the army, Czar Nicholas is blamed.

1914–1918

Revolution

Revolution capital, starting with the hungry, demoralized workers. After the troops in the capital join the workers, Czar Nicholas II abdicates, marking the end of 300 years of Romanov rule.

March 1917

The Bolsheviks

The Bolsheviks, a communist political party, seize power during an October Revolution (later known as the October Revolution). Nicholas II and his family are arrested, and later shot by Bolshevik party members.

October 1917

Birth of the US

The American Revolution (1775–1783) came from growing tensions between the residents of the 13 colonies (see pages 160–161) and their British rulers. The colonists were unhappy about British taxes and felt that the government didn't respect their rights.

Crossing the Delaware
On Christmas night, George Washington leads boats across the icy Delaware River to launch a surprise attack on German troops fighting for Britain. Their victory gives the Continental Army new hope.

Saratoga
A turning point in the Revolutionary War, the second of two Battles of Saratoga sees British forces surrender. France enters the war, and will recognize US independence with an alliance in 1778.

Molly Pitcher
There is a legend that a woman called Molly Pitcher brings water to the American wounded on the battlefield at Monmouth, New Jersey. Mary Ludwig Hays may be the real woman behind this legend.

| September 1776 | December 1776 | June 1777 | October 1777 | April 1778 | June 1778 |

Submarine attack!
In the one-person submarine *Turtle*, Sergeant Ezra Lee tries to attach a bomb to the hull of British admiral Richard Howe's ship in New York Harbor. Lee can't drill through the ship's thick hull, and the bomb explodes harmlessly.

Stars and Stripes
The Second Continental Congress adopts the Stars and Stripes flag. Its 13 stripes and 13 stars represent the 13 colonies.

Dollar sign
The dollar sign $ begins to appear, possibly as an abbreviation for pesos used in trade with Spain. In 1792, the US will start producing the first dollar coins.

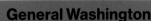

Founding Fathers

Representatives of the colonies, including George Washington, John and Samuel Adams, and Patrick Henry, meet as the First Continental Congress to set out their complaints about British rule.

General Washington

The Second Continental Congress names George Washington as Commander of the Continental Army, which will become the foundation of the US army. The first major battle of the war takes place at Bunker Hill.

Independence

On July 4, the Second Continental Congress votes to adopt the Declaration of Independence, which announces that the 13 American colonies now see themselves as independent from Britain.

March 1770   **September 1774**   **April 1775**   **June 1775**   **January 1776**   **July 1776**

Boston Massacre

In Boston, a mob of unruly American colonists attacks British soldiers, who then shoot and kill several people. This inflames anti-British feeling, giving the patriots (who oppose British rule) a boost of support.

Lexington and Concord

The first conflicts of the Revolutionary War take place in the towns of Lexington and Concord. British troops try to capture and destroy the colonists' supply of weapons, but the colonists have been warned of the attack.

"Common Sense"

Patriot Thomas Paine writes this anonymously published essay in Philadelphia, arguing in favor of American independence. Every rebel against British rule gets a copy.

Yorktown

After a stalemate in the north, the battlefront moves south. British forces surrender at Yorktown in Virginia, trapped by French warships off the coast and overpowered by the Continental Army.

American Constitution

Representatives of the 13 American states meet to approve an official Constitution. Called "the supreme law of the land," the Constitution establishes the government of the United States.

New capital

Washington commissions French architect L'Enfant to design a grand city to become the capital of the new nation. The city is named Washington in the president's honor.

July 1781   **October 1781**   **September 1783**   **May 1787**   **January 1789**   **July 1790**

James Armistead Lafayette

Born a slave, African-American Armistead works as a spy for the Continental Army. He will help them to secure a victory at Yorktown.

Treaty of Paris

This treaty formally ends the Revolutionary War and sets the boundaries of the United States. Britain agrees to recognize US independence, and British troops leave for home.

First US president

US representatives vote unanimously to elect George Washington as the first US president. In April 1789, he will take his oath in New York City, the capital at the time.

Crossing the Delaware River

On December 25, 1776, George Washington led his troops across the icy Delaware River to deliver a surprise attack on Trenton, New Jersey, captured in this iconic painting. Washington hoped that a quick victory would boost morale within his army following a series of defeats during the Revolutionary War. Despite the dangerous conditions, they crossed successfully and marched into Trenton the following morning, achieving an important victory over the troops fighting for Britain.

Seed sower

Jethro Tull's mechanical seed drill permits large-scale planting in neat rows. This innovation is part of the wider Agricultural Revolution, in which new farming methods and technology are used to increase crop productivity across Europe.

1701

Spinning jenny

James Hargreaves, a British carpenter and weaver, invents the spinning jenny. The machine spins more than one ball of yarn or thread at a time, making it easier and faster to make cloth.

1764

Steam engine

Scottish engineer James Watt patents a steam engine that is more efficient than existing machines. As well as draining water from mines, Watt's engine can be used in iron, cotton, and paper mills.

1769

Child labor

Britain's first Factory Act improves conditions for children working in factories. Now, children cannot work until they are nine, and the number of hours older children can work is limited. Children who are 9 to 13 go to school for 2 hours each day.

1833

Trains

British engineer George Stephenson wins the speed contest on the new Liverpool to Manchester railroad with his steam engine *Rocket*. In this year, the first 51 miles (82 km) of railroad track in the world is laid down in Britain.

1829

Mining

A series of innovations allows coal to be mined on a bigger scale than ever before, providing more fuel for industrial machines and transportation.

1815

The Industrial Revolution

One of the most important periods of change in human history was the Industrial Revolution. This was an exciting time of machines and manufacturing that transformed the way people lived and worked. It brought developments in technology that revolutionized farming, factories, and travel. These changes began in Britain in the 1760s and rapidly swept across the globe.

Town life

The results of the British census show that, for the first time, more people are living and working in towns than in the countryside.

1846

Sewing machines

American inventor Elias Howe patents the modern sewing machine. Now, clothes can be made in large factories, meaning that people no longer have to make clothes by hand.

1851

Factory towns

British industrialist Richard Arkwright builds a village to house workers for his cotton spinning mill in Cromford, England. It eventually includes a school, market, and church.

1771

Canal mania

Originally built to transport coal from mines to Manchester, England, the Bridgewater Canal is extended to connect to Liverpool. The success of this long-distance canal kicks off a period of construction known as "canal mania."

1776

Power loom

British inventor Edmund Cartwright builds the first power loom, a weaving machine that is driven by water instead of workers. It is later powered by the new steam engines.

1785

Worker riots

Textile laborers attack factories and destroy the machines they fear will replace them.

1811–1816

Safety lamp
1815: *The Geordie lamp and the Davy lamp are created. A piece of gauze covers the lamp's flame, preventing explosions.*

Mines Act
1842: *Britain's Mines Act bans women and young children from working underground.*

Dynamite
1867: *Swedish chemist Alfred Nobel invents dynamite, which provides a safer way to blast holes in mountains or the ground rather than simply lighting black powder. Dynamite is important in clearing paths to build things such as roads and railroad tracks.*

1875

Worker health

Britain's Public Health Act requires the government to ensure that housing and sewer systems are clean and safe.

Night shift

American inventor Thomas Edison creates a light bulb that lasts longer than other designs. Edison's light bulbs allow factories to continue operating after dark.

1879

Power stations

The first central electrical power station is completed in Deptford, England, due to increasing demand for power in industrialized central London.

1889

Aboriginal Australia

Australian Aboriginal people have one of the oldest continuous cultures on Earth. They were relatively undisturbed by outsiders until Europeans landed in the 17th century.

c.63,000 BCE First humans
The first inhabitants of Australia arrive by boat across the sea from Southeast Asia. They take advantage of the sea levels being much lower at this time.

45,000 BCE Megafauna
More than 85 percent of Australian megafauna (huge mammals) have been wiped out in Australia by this time. It is likely that humans prey on them, but a change in climate about 70,000 years ago may also have contributed. These creatures included tortoises as big as a small car and carnivorous kangaroos.

41,000 BCE Mungo Man
The oldest human remains ever discovered in Australia were of an ancient hunter from the southeast coast who is given the name "Mungo Man." Mungo Man's body was carefully laid out, the earliest example of Aboriginal burial traditions.

8000 BCE Uluru
Aboriginal people start to live around Uluru, a great rock in the Australian desert. The rock dates back 600 million years, and it is revered as a sacred site by Aboriginal people.

50,000 BCE Dreamtime
The new settlers are hunter-gatherers that live in groups with shared culture, beliefs, and art. Their core belief is that the land dates back to creation in an ancient period called the "Dreamtime."

45,000 BCE Rock engraving
Aboriginal engravings are found on rocks in Murujuga, featuring ancient pictures and symbols of animals, figures, and ceremonies.

38,000 BCE Didgeridoo
The didgeridoo is invented in the Northern Territory of Australia. It is believed to be the world's oldest musical instrument. It is played by blowing into one end of a long tube to produce deep, resonant sounds.

Aboriginal rock art

Aboriginal artists have painted images from their lives and mythology on rock for tens of thousands of years. Red pigments are made from iron-rich clays, and are brushed or blown from the mouth to color the rock surface.

Settling in Australia

Life for both jailers (on the left) and convicts (on the right) was tough in Australia, especially in the early years of the colony. At the end of a convict's sentence (which was usually seven years long), they were given a Certificate of Freedom. This meant they were allowed to leave to return to Britain, or stay on the colony and start life anew. Many decided to stay, and as the colony grew, it offered them a better standard of living than they could have hoped for back in Britain.

The colonization of Australia

The first Europeans turned Australia into a jail—a place for British convicts to serve time. In the process, Aboriginal inhabitants of the land were mistreated, a legacy that is still felt today.

1606 First Europeans
Dutch explorer Willem Janszoon becomes the first European to set foot on Australia. Another Dutchman, Abel Tasman, sails around it in 1642, but mistakes it for another place. Tasman calls the continent "New Holland."

1768 Cook's orders
On the orders of the British government, James Cook sets sail on his ship *Endeavour* to explore the area.

1770 Records and maps
While the *Endeavour* is anchored in Botany Bay, Australia, botanist Joseph Banks records new species of plant and animal life. Cook maps eastern Australia for the first time, and claims the land for Britain.

1787 First Fleet
Britain decides to send its convicts to Australia, and the First Fleet of 11 ships sets off for the new continent. It lands a year later, near modern-day Sydney.

1788 First contact
Conflict erupts between Europeans and Aboriginal people almost from the start. The Aboriginal people will be forced into hard labor in 1810. From 1822 onward, renewed violence will end in hundreds of Aboriginal casualties.

1789 Deadly diseases
European diseases decimate Aboriginal people, who have no immunity to them. Within the first century of settlers arriving, 90 percent of the Aboriginal population will be wiped out by disease and conflict.

1824 Australia
The name New Holland is officially replaced with "Australia." The country achieves independence from Britain on January 1, 1901.

1851 Gold rush
Life is looking up for the colonists when coal miners discover gold. The population grows and becomes more prosperous.

1905–1968 Stolen children
Children of Aboriginal descent are forcibly removed from their families by the government and Church and given to white families. The policy causes untold suffering to Aboriginal people. The government will issue an apology in 2008.

1976 Land rights
The government introduces laws that recognize the Aboriginal system of land ownership, meaning some land is handed back to them.

THE STORMING OF THE BASTILLE

A revolution begins

During a summer of unrest in 1789, thousands of angry French people crowded around a fortified prison called the Bastille in eastern Paris. The Bastille's governor held firm in his towering stronghold, but the tense standoff turned into a violent battle that would kick-start the French Revolution and end the King's reign.

A symbol of terror

In **1370**, during the bloody conflict known as the Hundred Years' War, the French king Charles V reinforces Paris's walled defenses and builds the imposing Bastille to guard the capital's eastern approach. Over the next 400 years, the towering fortress becomes a prison for high-ranking captives and develops a reputation for torture and terror.

Summer of rebellion

In the **summer of 1789**, France is in turmoil as taxes rise and food is in short supply. French commoners—people who are not members of the aristocracy—demand political change. In angry opposition to the nearly bankrupt King Louis XVI, they form a revolutionary organization that they call the National Assembly and demand changes to the French constitution.

The search for gunpowder

On **July 11, 1789**, Louis XVI dismisses the finance minister Jacques Necker, who is seen as sympathetic to the revolutionaries. French troops move into strategic positions around Paris as the monarchy tries to reinforce its grip on power. On **July 12**, the Bastille receives delivery of 250 barrels of gunpowder. Meanwhile, around Paris, rioters raid armories and weapon stores.

In the early morning of **July 14**, a mob of commoners loots the Hôtel des Invalides, searching for weapons. Unchallenged, the mob leaves with thousands of rifles but very little gunpowder, rendering the weapons useless. A soldier tells the mob about the 250 barrels of gunpowder delivered to the Bastille, so the mob marches 2.5 miles (4 km) east to the prison.

A firm standoff

In the **late morning**, the mob surrounds the Bastille and demands gunpowder and weapons. The prison's governor, the Marquis de Launay, stands firm inside the heavily defended stronghold. The 120 elderly soldiers of the Bastille's garrison position themselves around the ramparts and prepare to man the 18 cannons. Delegates from the swelling crowd of commoners surrounding the Bastille are turned away by the marquis as the angry governor refuses to listen to the mob's demands. By **early afternoon**, with frustration and impatience spreading through the crowd, a small group of raiders gain entry into the prison's courtyard.

The governor surrenders

Fearful of losing his grip on the fortress, the marquis orders his men to fire on the invading force. The gunfire angers the crowd, and more people join the assault, including defecting French troops. A battle begins as the mob storms the building, bolstered by several cannons. The Marquis de Launay, sensing defeat, threatens to light his stock of gunpowder and blow up the Bastille and most of Paris, but the revolutionaries call his bluff. At **5:00 p.m.**, as the Bastille's garrison switches sides, the fortress is lost and the governor surrenders. The Bastille—for years a symbol of tyranny and terror—is liberated by the victorious masses. The few prisoners that were imprisoned are released as the mob loots the armory and gunpowder stores.

Not a rebellion... a revolution

The Marquis de Launay is transported to the Hôtel de Ville to stand trial, but en route he is captured by the furious crowd and is beaten and killed. King Louis XVI doesn't hear of the uprising until later in the day. In **August 1789**, the National Assembly abolishes feudalism—a social system that gives the aristocracy control over commoners. On **September 3, 1791**, King Louis XVI is forced to agree to a constitutional monarchy, limiting his powers, but this lasts only a year. In **September 1792**, France is proclaimed a republic, its power held by the people instead of the monarchy. The transition to a republic does not go smoothly, and France descends into a dark period of further uprisings and violence known as the Reign of Terror.

The French Revolution

France experienced troubled times during the 18th century, as the divide between the rich rulers and poor peasants grew wider and wider. King Louis XVI was the target of national anger, with riots and marches on the streets. This eventually led to a bloody revolution that saw the country move from more than 1,000 years of royal rule to the formation of a new republic.

"Liberty, equality, fraternity!"
Slogan of the French Revolution

National Assembly

After King Louis XVI refuses to give the common people power, a group establishes itself as the National Assembly. Its members are angry with the wealthy ruling classes for letting the rest of the population struggle and starve. They start holding regular meetings to plot the king's downfall.

Equal rights

The Declaration of the Rights of Man is written, which states that all men are equal under law. This landmark document becomes an important legacy of the French Revolution.

New radicals

The most radical leaders of the French Revolution form the Jacobin Club, led by Maximilien Robespierre. Inspired by the US Declaration of Independence in 1776, this ambitious politician is determined to topple the king and create a new republic.

July 14, 1789

June 17, 1789

October 5, 1789

June 20, 1791

August 26, 1789

October 1789

Storming of the Bastille

A mob of angry French rioters attacks the Bastille prison, a medieval fortress in Paris. They release the prisoners and take the prison's ammunition. This event marks the start of the French Revolution.

Bread riots

High grain prices cause small-scale bread riots in France. About 7,000 armed female protesters march on the Palace of Versailles, calling for bread to feed their hungry families. King Louis XVI gives in to their demands.

King's capture

The National Assembly abolishes the ruling classes. Under cover of darkness, King Louis XVI and his wife Marie Antoinette try to escape, but they are seized and imprisoned.

Republic replacement

The government abolishes the monarchy and charges the former king with treason. History is made as France becomes a republic, with a new republican calendar and standard system of measurements.

Date with death

As the public become sick of Robespierre's brutality, his rivals arrest him. He tries to shoot himself but only manages to shatter his lower jaw, and is later executed at the guillotine. His death weakens the power of the Revolution.

January 21, 1793

November 10, 1799

September 22, 1792

July 28, 1794

Reign of Terror

The Jacobins take over the government, as the former king is executed at the guillotine. Marie Antoinette will be executed nine months later. Many thousands of enemies of the Revolution are also killed.

Emperor Napoleon

Military leader Napoleon Bonaparte takes charge of France and becomes First Consul. The French Revolution is over. In 1804, Napoleon crowns himself emperor of France and starts to wage war across Europe.

The guillotine

Introduced in 1792, the guillotine was used to behead about 17,000 people during the French Revolution. This death machine was named after Doctor Joseph-Ignace Guillotin, who wanted executions to be as quick and painless as possible. Public executions by guillotine became a gruesome form of popular entertainment, drawing huge crowds of spectators.

Medicine

Medicine began almost 10,000 years ago, when our prehistoric ancestors practiced crude forms of surgery. Later, the ancient Egyptians used honey in the belief that it could heal wounds, and created artificial body parts from pieces of wood. Today, technological developments and our advanced understanding of the body have redefined medicine and could save the lives of millions of people.

"First, do no harm."
Hippocrates, c.400 BCE

Lady with the lamp
Florence Nightingale was known as the "lady with the lamp."

Avicenna
Persian scholar Ibn Sina, better known as Avicenna, publishes *The Canon of Medicine*. This textbook is adopted by many medical schools and remains one of the most important works in the history of medicine.

Hearing heartbeats
The first stethoscope is a basic wooden tube created by French doctor René Laënnec to listen to heartbeats and breathing. Two earpieces are later added to the original design.

Bloodletting
At this time, it is wrongly thought that having too much blood causes illnesses, so doctors use bloodsucking leeches to remove blood from patients. Hospitals in London use 7 million leeches a year.

Nursing pioneer
British nurse Florence Nightingale sees soldiers dying from disease rather than injuries in the military hospitals of the Crimean War. She reforms hospital care, improving survival rates. Nursing becomes a new profession.

1025

1816

1833

1854

400 BCE

1796

1818

1849

1859

Father of medicine
Hippocrates is the most celebrated physician of ancient Greece. He is the first to suggest that diseases aren't caused by the supernatural, and stresses the importance of a healthy diet and regular exercise.

First vaccination
English doctor Edward Jenner intentionally infects a young boy with the mild disease cowpox to make him immune to the killer disease smallpox. This is the world's first vaccination, bringing an end to smallpox in 1979.

Blood transfusion
When British doctor James Blundell transfers blood from a donor to a patient using a syringe, it is the first successful blood transfusion. Unfortunately, many of the earliest transfusions caused the death of patients.

First female doctor
Many medical schools turn Elizabeth Blackwell (1821–1910) down on the basis of her gender, but she eventually graduates from Geneva Medical College as the first woman with a medical degree.

Germ theory
Instead of bad air being the cause of infections, French microbiologist Louis Pasteur shows that bacteria and other microscopic germs cause disease. He soon develops vaccinations against the deadly diseases anthrax and rabies.

Surgery

A series of groundbreaking moments in the history of surgery has resulted in operations becoming much safer and more comfortable for patients.

1860s First antiseptic
Surgeon Joseph Lister cleans wounds with carbolic acid, stopping infections.

1890s Sterilization
Infection rates drop when surgeons start boiling their instruments to remove bacteria from them.

2014 3D-printed skull
Dutch doctors replace half of a patient's skull with a 3D-printed plastic version.

1846 Ether
Dentist William Morton finds the chemical ether can make a patient lose consciousness.

1967 First heart transplant
Surgeon Christiaan Barnard puts the heart of a traffic accident casualty into another patient.

Penicillin

Scottish scientist Alexander Fleming is studying bacteria in petri dishes when he spots mold growing there. This mold had killed the surrounding bacteria, and this first antibiotic, known as penicillin, is mass produced by the late 1940s.

Body scanner

The first full body scanner is designed by American professor Raymond Damadian. The magnetic resonance imager (MRI) scanner creates a picture of the body's internal workings using the principles of magnetism, allowing it to help identify diseases and trouble spots.

First IVF baby

The first baby is born following *in vitro* fertilization (IVF). England's Louise Brown is the world's first "test-tube baby," born from an embryo created in a laboratory dish.

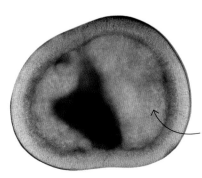

Cell division
Stem cells have the potential to grow into any type of cell.

Stem cell advances

Scientific research reveals that stem cells can be altered to become different types of cells. This breakthrough provides the potential to transplant stem cells to treat a range of blood and bone diseases.

1928

1977

1978

1999

1895

1965

1981

2015

Medical X-rays

German physicist Wilhelm Röntgen discovers energy waves he calls X-rays that pass through skin but not bone. X-rays are still used to locate broken bones and spot problem areas inside the body.

Battery-powered defibrillators

In the 19th century, scientists found that an electric shock can start a stopped heart, leading to the invention of the defibrillator—a device that passes an electric current through the heart. In 1965, British doctor Frank Pantridge designs a defibrillator small enough to fit inside ambulances.

Nanoscale technology

The Scanning Tunneling Microscope (STM) is invented by German scientists Gerd Binnig and Heinrich Rohrer. This invention allows scientists to work at the nanoscale, moving even the tiniest atoms.

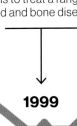

Growing kidneys

Scientists grow a functioning kidney in a laboratory and transplant it into a living organism. Tests show the replacement kidney works successfully in rats and pigs, but further research is needed for humans to receive artificial kidney transplants.

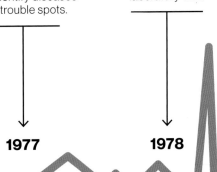

The Napoleonic Wars

Having become Commander of the French army in 1796, ambitious officer Napoleon Bonaparte led his nation into the French Revolutionary Wars and sought to take control of Europe. Britain and France signed the Peace of Amiens treaty to end the conflict. When France failed to keep the agreement, Britain declared war in 1803, marking the start of the bloody Napoleonic Wars.

Battle of Austerlitz

One of Napoleon's greatest victories occurs on December 2nd at Austerlitz (in the modern-day Czech Republic), where 68,000 French troops beat the combined forces of nearly 90,000 Austrian and Russian troops.

Feeding armies

In 1795, Napoleon offers a financial reward for budding inventors to find a way to preserve food for his army. A French confectioner claims the prize in 1809 for his design for sealed bottles. A year later, British merchant Peter Durand patents the tin can.

Emperor of France

As the French Republic comes to an end (see page 201), Napoleon announces himself the new emperor at the Notre Dame Cathedral in Paris. This historic moment sees Napoleon become the first Frenchman to take the title of emperor for 900 years.

Battle of Trafalgar

At this naval battle off the southwest coast of Spain on October 21st, the French and Spanish navies are beaten by the British navy, led by Admiral Horatio Nelson, who dies while fighting. With the French navy greatly weakened, France can't invade Britain.

European Empire

Much of Europe is now controlled by Napoleon and the French army. After 1,000 years, the Holy Roman Empire (see page 98) finally ends as France conquers Italy and parts of Germany.

1804

1805

1805

1806

1810

War horses
Huge numbers of horses were used in the Napoleonic Wars.

End of Peninsular War

1814 sees the end of a six-year war, in which the French fought the Spanish, Portuguese, and British for control of the Iberian Peninsula. French defeat at the Battle of Vitoria in 1813 eventually leads to the end of the war.

1821

1815

1815

1814

1812

Hundred Days

The Hundred Days sees Napoleon and a small army head for Paris to overthrow King Louis XVIII, who had been restored to the throne in 1814.

Battle of Waterloo

The Napoleonic Wars finally end at the Battle of Waterloo, near Brussels. Napoleon's army is beaten by the British and Prussian armies. King Louis XVIII returns to the French throne.

Bitter end

Failed invasions and battles result in Napoleon being sent into exile for a second time. He spends six years imprisoned on the remote island of St. Helena before his death.

Invasion of Russia

Napoleon launches a disastrous invasion of Russia, so other countries declare war on the now weakened France. Napoleon will be sent into exile in 1814, only to escape and return to France seeking control of Europe again.

Napoleon's life

Like the wars he waged, Napoleon's personal life was turbulent and testing. He divorced his first wife and spent two long periods in exile. His ambitions drove him to military success, but ultimately ended in failure.

1796
Rising through the ranks, he soon becomes Commander of the French army.

1804
Declaring himself emperor of France, he introduces the Napoleonic Code to give new rights to the poor.

1810
After ending his marriage to Joséphine, he marries Marie-Louise, daughter of the Austrian emperor.

1815
At the Battle of Waterloo near Brussels, Napoleon is defeated in the last military battle of the Napoleonic Wars.

1769
Napoleon Bonaparte is born on August 15th in Ajaccio, on the island of Corsica off France.

1796
Napoleon marries socialite Joséphine de Beauharnais.

1805
Napoleon is defeated at the Battle of Trafalgar, but achieves one of his greatest victories at Austerlitz.

1811
Napoleon's son is born on March 20th and named Napoleon II.

1821
Following six years in exile, Napoleon dies on May 5th.

> ## "Death is nothing, but to live defeated and inglorious is to die daily."
> **Napoleon Bonaparte**,
> letter to General Lauriston, 1804

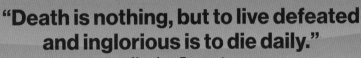

French cavalry
French soldiers, in blue and white uniforms, charge against the British troops.

Battle square
British soldiers stand in a tight square formation for defense.

Central and South American independence

In 1800, almost all of Central and South America was ruled by Spain and Portugal. However, when those two nations were invaded by the French emperor Napoleon I in the early 1800s, their rule in the continents was weakened. Demands for independence increased, and by 1825, most formerly Spanish countries in Central and South America had become independent nations, and Brazil was no longer part of Portugal.

Venezuela rises

Venezuelan revolutionaries Francisco de Miranda and Simón Bolívar form a republic (a form of government in which citizens choose the leaders) in Venezuela. However, the republic soon collapses, and Bolívar goes into hiding.

Mexican revolt

A Mexican priest, Miguel Hidalgo, leads a revolt in Mexico (which is ruled by Spain). He is executed in 1811, but the war for Mexican independence continues.

Argentinian independence

A group of Argentinian rebels declare that their region, the United Provinces of the River Plate (modern-day Argentina, Uruguay, and part of Bolivia), is independent.

Army of the Andes

José de San Martín leads an army of 3,500 Argentinians on a 25-day journey over the Andes mountains into Chile. They win the Battle of Chacabuco against Spanish forces and will go on to take Chile's capital, Santiago.

Freedom for Chile

Victory at the Battle of Maipú frees Chile from Spanish rule. Bernardo O'Higgins, a Chilean of Irish descent, becomes the country's first independent ruler.

1810

1811

1816

1817

1818

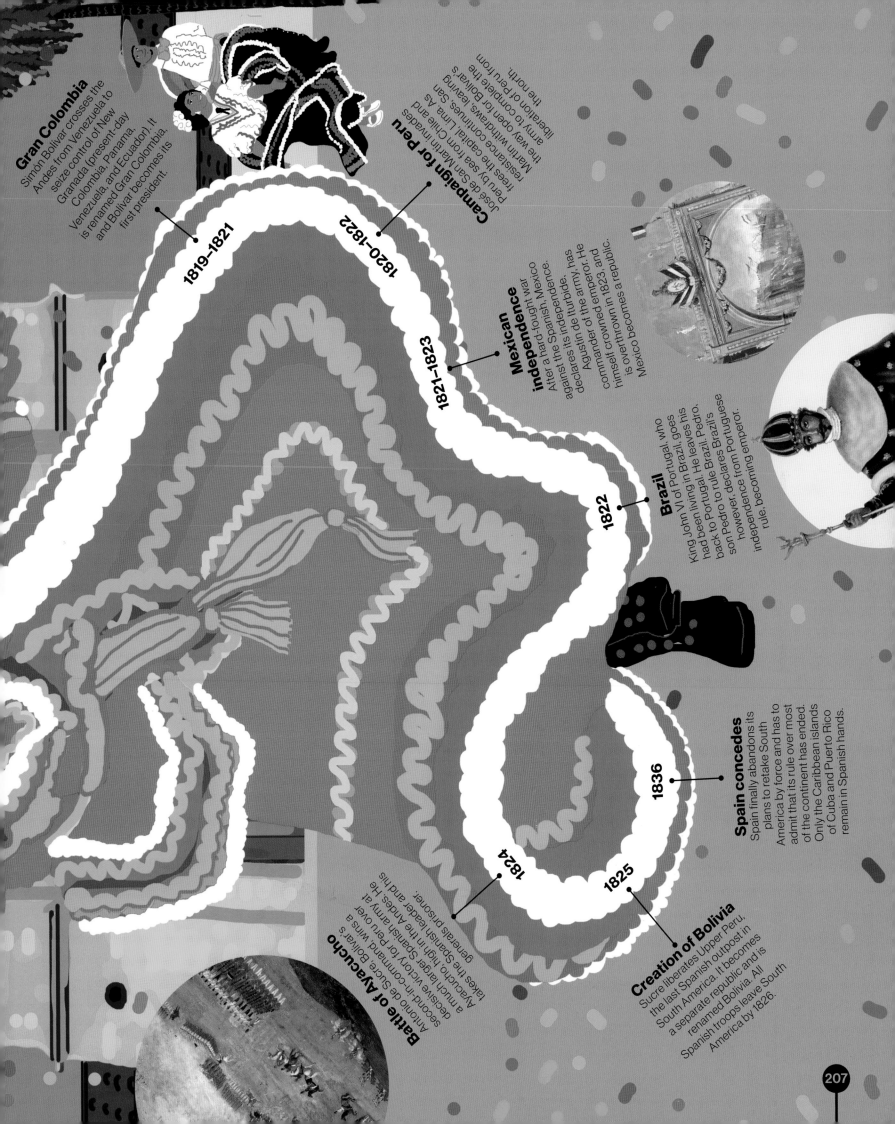

Gran Colombia
Simón Bolívar crosses the Andes from Venezuela to seize control of New Granada (present-day Colombia, Panama, Venezuela, and Ecuador). It is renamed Gran Colombia, and Bolívar becomes its first president.

1819–1821

Campaign for Peru
José de San Martín invades Peru by sea from Chile and frees the capital, Lima. As resistance continues, San Martín withdraws, leaving the way open for Bolívar's army to complete the liberation of Peru from the north.

1820–1822

Mexican independence
After a hard-fought war against the Spanish, Mexico declares its independence. He Agustín de Iturbide, has commanded emperor. He himself crowned in 1823, and is overthrown in 1823, and Mexico becomes a republic.

1821–1823

Brazil
King John VI of Portugal, who had been living in Brazil, goes back to Portugal. He leaves his son Pedro to rule Brazil's independence from Portuguese rule, becoming emperor.

1822

Battle of Ayacucho
Antonio de Sucre, Bolívar's second-in-command, wins a decisive victory for Peru over a much larger Spanish army at Ayacucho, high in the Andes. He takes the Spanish leader and his generals prisoner.

1824

Creation of Bolivia
Sucre liberates Upper Peru, the last Spanish outpost in South America. It becomes a separate republic and is renamed Bolivia. All Spanish troops leave South America by 1826.

1825

Spain concedes
Spain finally abandons its plans to retake South America by force and has to admit that its rule over most of the continent has ended. Only the Caribbean islands of Cuba and Puerto Rico remain in Spanish hands.

1836

Trains

Trains have come a long way since early horse-drawn wagons. The first railroads were short links between neighboring towns. Over time, they extended their reach across nations and continents. Whether going deep underground or overhead on monorails, rail is now one of the world's top modes of transportation.

Early locomotive

English inventor Richard Trevithick develops the first steam locomotive. It carries 70 people and nine tons of coal along a railroad track at 5 mph (8 kph).

Wagonways

Basic railroads called wagonways are used for the first time in European mines to transport heavy rock and coal. Carts are pulled along wooden rails by horses.

c.1550

1804

Steam demon

The speediest steam train ever, the *Mallard*, reaches a record-breaking 126 mph (203 kph) in England. It will travel nearly 1.5 million miles (2.4 million km) before retiring in 1963.

Epic railroad

Completed in 1904, Russia's Trans-Siberian Railway becomes the world's longest rail system. The route from Moscow to Vladivostok stretches 5,772 miles (9,289 km).

The Orient Express

The most famous passenger train in history makes its first direct journey from Paris in France to Istanbul in Turkey. It becomes a byword for luxury travel.

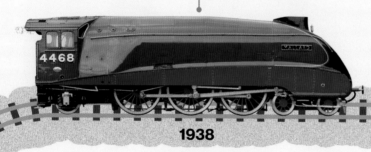

1938

1904

1889

Bullet train

Japan's Shinkansen train service, nicknamed the bullet train, opens to provide a high-speed link between Tokyo and Osaka. The 332 mile (535 km) trip takes less than four hours thanks to a top speed of 124 mph (200 kph).

Fastest on wheels

At a time when most trains are powered by diesel engines, France's *Train à Grande Vitesse* (TGV) service uses electric motors to reach the world's highest speeds for wheeled trains. Regularly topping 200 mph (320 kph), the TGV is both speedy and silent.

1964

1981

First passenger trains

The world's first public railroad opens in England. The Stockton and Darlington Railway carries passengers in horse-drawn carriages at first, but these are replaced with steam locomotives in 1833.

Stephenson's Rocket

English engineer Robert Stephenson designs the *Rocket*, the most advanced steam engine of its day. Able to reach 30 mph (48 kph), it is the first vehicle faster than a horse.

Intercity link

The first intercity railroad opens, connecting Liverpool and Manchester in England. English politician William Huskisson becomes the first person to be killed by a passenger train when he is run over by Stephenson's *Rocket* at the opening event.

1825   **1829**   **1830**

Fast track

The renowned English engineer Isambard Kingdom Brunel masterminds the first high-speed railroad—the Great Western—linking London with the west of England and Wales. Trains reach speeds of 60 mph (96 kph) on the network, slashing journey times.

Transcontinental

The First Transcontinental Railroad opens in the US, linking the east and west coasts via a 1,777-mile (2,860-km) track. A ceremonial 18-karat gold spike is hammered into the track to mark its completion.

Going underground

The world's first underground rail system opens in London, with wooden carriages pulled by steam engines. It will eventually grow into a 253-mile (408-km) network under the city.

1869   **1863**   **1835–1838**

The Channel Tunnel

The Channel Tunnel opens, connecting the UK and France via three underwater tunnels bored out of chalk under the English Channel. Two tunnels are for trains, while the third is for maintenance and emergencies.

Sky high

The world's highest railroad opens. The Qinghai–Tibet Railway runs from Tibet to China and reaches a height of 16,640 ft (5,072 m). Passengers are provided with an oxygen supply to help them breathe in the thin mountain air.

Magnetic magic

Maglev (magnetic levitation) trains in Japan achieve a record speed of 375 mph (603 kph) during testing. Instead of rolling on wheels, maglev trains float in the air, held off the tracks by powerful electromagnets.

1994   **2006**   **2015**

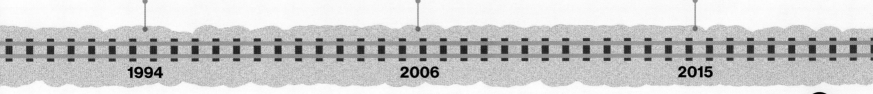

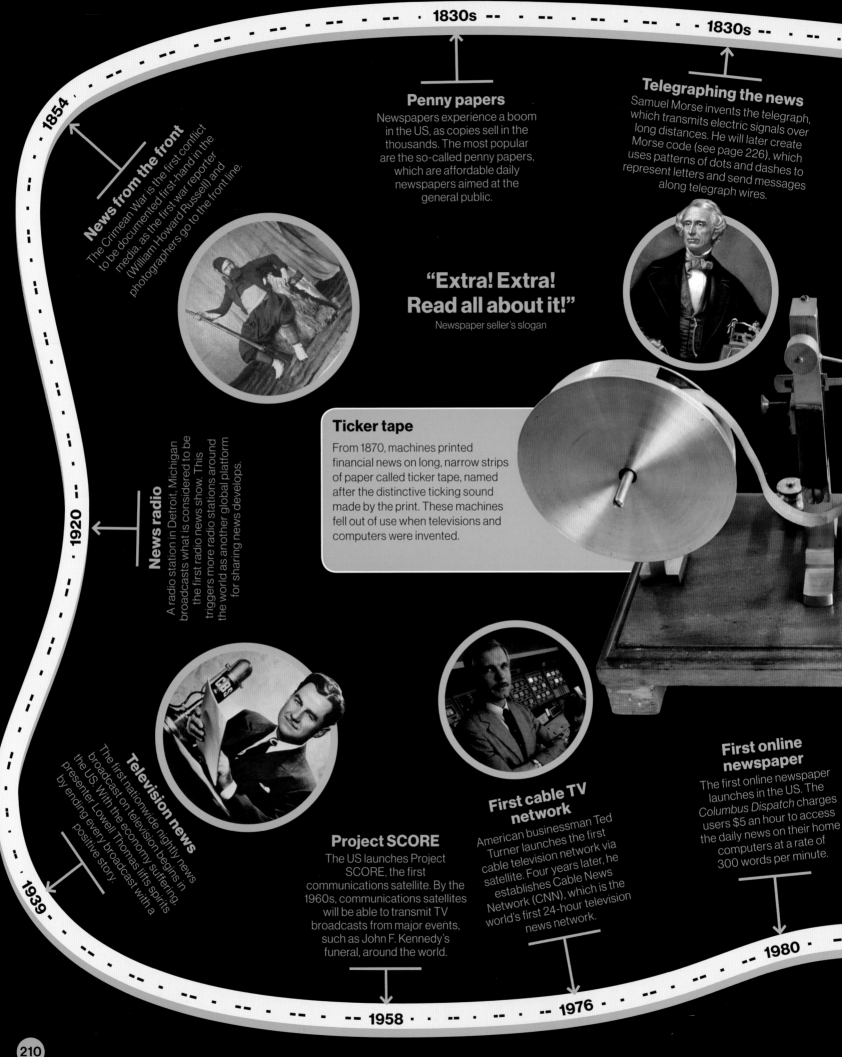

Telegraphing the news

Samuel Morse invents the telegraph, which transmits electric signals over long distances. He will later create Morse code (see page 226), which uses patterns of dots and dashes to represent letters and send messages along telegraph wires.

Penny papers

Newspapers experience a boom in the US, as copies sell in the thousands. The most popular are the so-called penny papers, which are affordable daily newspapers aimed at the general public.

News from the front

1854

The Crimean War is the first conflict to be documented first-hand in the media, as the first war reporter (William Howard Russell) and photographers go to the front line.

"Extra! Extra! Read all about it!"

Newspaper seller's slogan

Ticker tape

From 1870, machines printed financial news on long, narrow strips of paper called ticker tape, named after the distinctive ticking sound made by the print. These machines fell out of use when televisions and computers were invented.

News radio

1920

A radio station in Detroit, Michigan broadcasts what is considered to be the first radio news show. This triggers more radio stations around the world as another global platform for sharing news develops.

Television news

1939

The first nationwide nightly news broadcast on television begins in the US. With the economy suffering, presenter Lowell Thomas lifts spirits by ending every broadcast with a positive story.

Project SCORE

1958

The US launches Project SCORE, the first communications satellite. By the 1960s, communications satellites will be able to transmit TV broadcasts from major events, such as John F. Kennedy's funeral, around the world.

First cable TV network

1976

American businessman Ted Turner launches the first cable television network via satellite. Four years later, he establishes Cable News Network (CNN), which is the world's first 24-hour television news network.

First online newspaper

1980

The first online newspaper launches in the US. The *Columbus Dispatch* charges users $5 an hour to access the daily news on their home computers at a rate of 300 words per minute.

1792 · · **1791** · **17th century** · **1440s**

Semaphore
French inventor Claude Chappe develops the semaphore system for military communications. This is a line of hilltop towers with hinged arms that can be moved into different positions to "spell" words and letters.

Freedom of the press
The First Amendment to the US Constitution (see page 191) guarantees the freedom of the press. This is the right to report news or share opinions without being censored by the government.

First newspapers
The first newspaper is printed in Strasbourg, France, in 1605. For the next 20 years, newspapers appear all over Europe. In 1618, the Dutch publish the first large-format newspaper, called a broadsheet.

Printing press
German inventor Johannes Gutenberg devises the movable type printing press. This makes printing cheaper, and means pamphlets can be used to spread the news at a rapid rate.

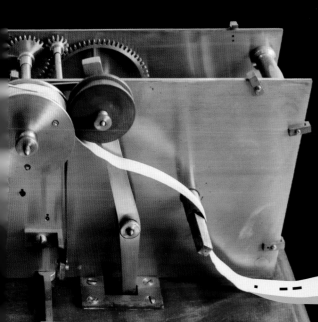

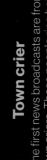

11th century

Town crier
The first news broadcasts are from town criers. These people ring bells and call out "Hear ye" to share the news. This role becomes essential, because most people at the time can't read.

Postal service
The Persian emperor Cyrus develops a postal service to carry mail across his huge empire. His successor Darius improves the system, placing horse-and-rider stations along the route.

Pigeon post
Pigeons, which were first domesticated by the ancient Egyptians, are used to carry messages home from Baghdad in modern-day Iraq. This helps speed up long-distance communications.

540 BCE · · **11th century CE**

Spreading the news

As empires expanded and civilizations spread, people tried all kinds of methods of spreading news, from messengers on horseback to town criers. The invention of the printing press made printing much cheaper and gave people national news in daily newspapers before both television and radio brought the news directly into their homes. Thanks to today's technology, such as communications satellites, cable TV, and the internet, global news is now accessible 24 hours a day, seven days a week.

Citizen journalism
The rise of the internet enables anyone with a connection to upload personal blogs, images, videos, and news, in a movement called citizen journalism. Sharing opinions online becomes more commonplace.

Wherever you are
CNN becomes the first news organization to stream its 24-hour news coverage online and via mobile applications, known as apps. This means global news is now available anywhere and at any time.

2000s · · · · **2011**

Engineering

Building large and complex structures such as bridges, tunnels, and skyscrapers would be impossible without engineers. An engineer uses scientific knowledge and mathematical calculations to ensure that buildings can support their own immense weight, keeping them stable and safe. As history demonstrates, well-engineered buildings can stay standing for centuries.

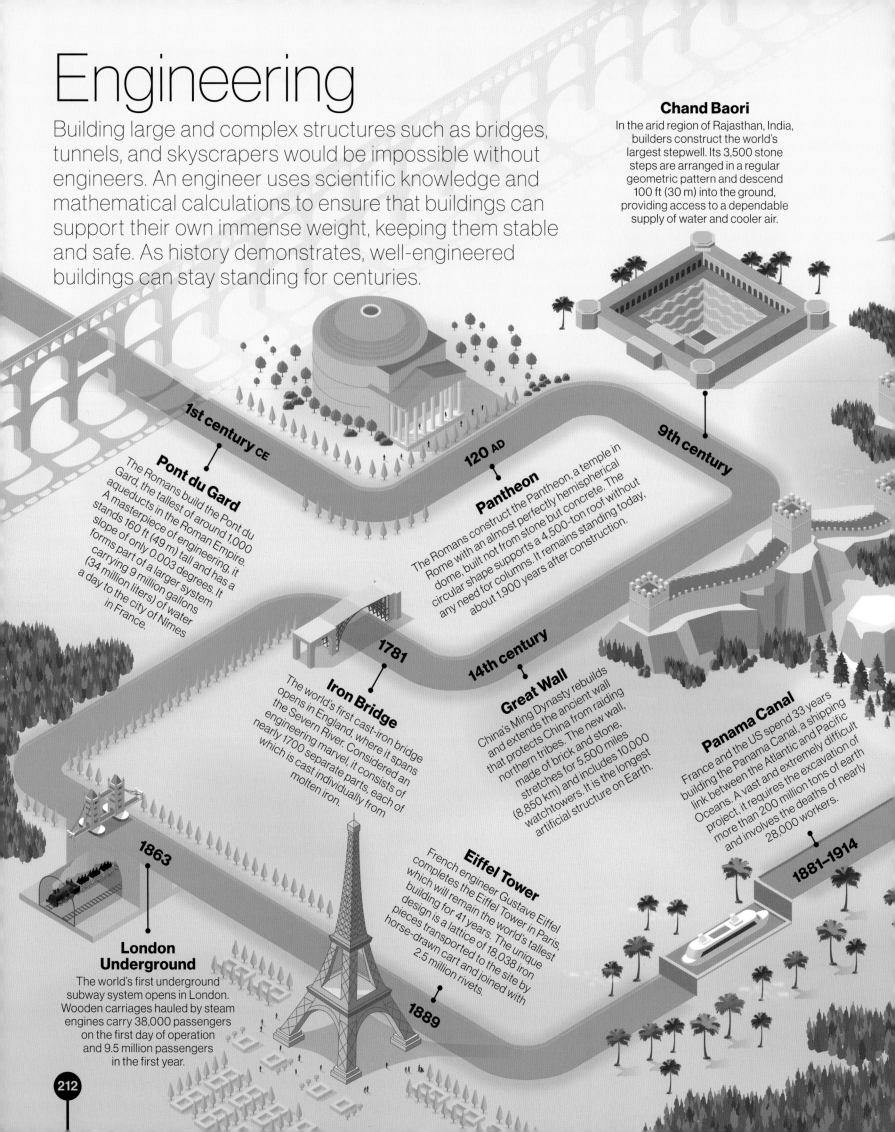

Chand Baori

9th century

In the arid region of Rajasthan, India, builders construct the world's largest stepwell. Its 3,500 stone steps are arranged in a regular geometric pattern and descend 100 ft (30 m) into the ground, providing access to a dependable supply of water and cooler air.

Pont du Gard

1st century CE

The Romans build the Pont du Gard, the tallest of around 1,000 aqueducts in the Roman Empire. A masterpiece of engineering, it stands 160 ft (49 m) tall and has a slope of only 0.003 degrees. It forms part of a larger system carrying 9 million gallons (34 million liters) of water a day to the city of Nîmes in France.

Pantheon

120 AD

The Romans construct the Pantheon, a temple in Rome with an almost perfectly hemispherical dome, built not from stone but concrete. The circular shape supports a 4,500-ton roof without any need for columns. It remains standing today, about 1,900 years after construction.

Iron Bridge

1781

The world's first cast-iron bridge opens in England, where it spans the Severn River. Considered an engineering marvel, it consists of nearly 1700 separate parts, each of which is cast individually from molten iron.

Great Wall

14th century

China's Ming Dynasty rebuilds and extends the ancient wall that protects China from raiding northern tribes. The new wall, made of brick and stone, stretches for 5,500 miles (8,850 km) and includes 10,000 watchtowers. It is the longest artificial structure on Earth.

Panama Canal

1881–1914

France and the US spend 33 years building the Panama Canal, a shipping link between the Atlantic and Pacific Oceans. A vast and extremely difficult project, it requires the excavation of more than 200 million tons of earth and involves the deaths of nearly 28,000 workers.

Eiffel Tower

1889

French engineer Gustave Eiffel completes the Eiffel Tower in Paris, which will remain the world's tallest building for 41 years. The unique design is a lattice of 18,038 iron pieces transported to the site by horse-drawn cart and joined with 2.5 million rivets.

London Underground

1863

The world's first underground subway system opens in London. Wooden carriages hauled by steam engines carry 38,000 passengers on the first day of operation and 9.5 million passengers in the first year.

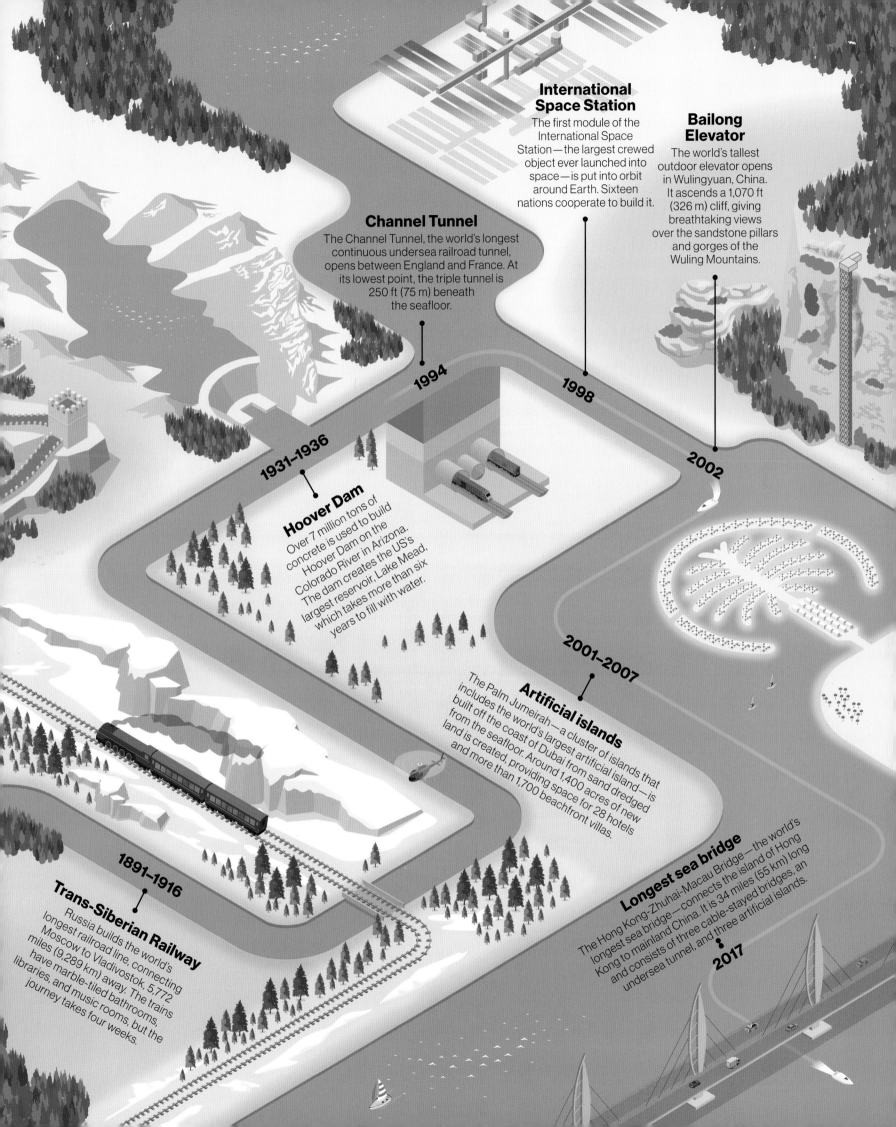

International Space Station

The first module of the International Space Station—the largest crewed object ever launched into space—is put into orbit around Earth. Sixteen nations cooperate to build it.

Bailong Elevator

The world's tallest outdoor elevator opens in Wulingyuan, China. It ascends a 1,070 ft (326 m) cliff, giving breathtaking views over the sandstone pillars and gorges of the Wuling Mountains.

Channel Tunnel

The Channel Tunnel, the world's longest continuous undersea railroad tunnel, opens between England and France. At its lowest point, the triple tunnel is 250 ft (75 m) beneath the seafloor.

1994

1998

2002

1931–1936

Hoover Dam

Over 7 million tons of concrete is used to build Hoover Dam on the Colorado River in Arizona. The dam creates the US's largest reservoir, Lake Mead, which takes more than six years to fill with water.

2001–2007

Artificial islands

The Palm Jumeirah—a cluster of islands that includes the world's largest artificial island—is built off the coast of Dubai from sand dredged from the seafloor. Around 1,400 acres of new land is created, providing space for 28 hotels and more than 1,700 beachfront villas.

1891–1916

Trans-Siberian Railway

Russia builds the world's longest railroad line, connecting Moscow to Vladivostok, 5,772 miles (9,289 km) away. The trains have marble-tiled bathrooms, libraries, and music rooms, but the journey takes four weeks.

Longest sea bridge

The Hong Kong-Zhuhai-Macau Bridge—the world's longest sea bridge—connects the island of Hong Kong to mainland China. It is 34 miles (55 km) long and consists of three cable-stayed bridges, an undersea tunnel, and three artificial islands.

2017

The US frontier

Huge numbers of Americans and Europeans pushed westward in North America looking for opportunity, adventure, and land. They were explorers, trappers, traders, and ordinary people. The frontier ideas of individualism and self-reliance are still influential today.

1739 Rocky Mountains
Two French fur traders, Pierre and Paul Mallet, make an epic journey into the American interior. They are the first Europeans to see the Rocky Mountains.

1769 Spanish settlements
Junipero Serra, a Spanish priest and monk, establishes a string of settlements along the Californian coast, starting at San Diego.

1803 Louisiana Purchase
President Jefferson buys the Louisiana Territory for 15 million dollars from France, doubling the size of the US.

1830s Oregon Trail
The very first wagon trains of settlers make their way along what will be known as the Oregon Trail, an overland route across the Rocky Mountains to the west.

1845 Manifest destiny
"Manifest destiny," an influential concept that claims that Americans are the "chosen ones" and it is their right to take over the entire continent, is first used.

1803 Lewis and Clark
Meriwether Lewis and William Clark lead an expedition across America's rivers and waterways. Their task is to map the Louisiana Territory. They will later be joined by Sacagawea, an American Indian woman who will act as an interpreter and guide.

1848 Gold Rush
After the discovery of gold in a stream behind a lumber mill, fortune seekers from across the globe head to California. Some 80,000 will make the trek in the first year of the Gold Rush.

1858 Transportation
The first nonstop stagecoach from St. Louis arrives in Los Angeles. The journey takes 20 days. In 1860, the Pony Express mail service completes its first delivery from St. Louis to Sacramento in 11 days.

1866 Outlaws
Jesse and Frank James start their criminal career with a bank robbery. The history of the "Wild West" will be full of deadly outlaws and their run-ins with the law.

1869 Transcontinental railroad
The first cross-country railroad is completed at Promontory Summit, Utah. It joins Sacramento, California to Council Bluffs, Iowa (itself connected to the east-coast train lines).

Frontier towns

As more and more people moved westward, frontier towns such as Tonopah, Nevada (above) spring up all over the west. Land is cheap, but settlers have to work hard, often with very little help from the government. Criminal gangs and American Indians loot trains, farms, and towns, and getting basic supplies is always difficult.

The Battle of Little Bighorn

Sitting Bull has a vision of soldiers falling into the native camps "like grasshoppers from the sky," which inspires Lakota Sioux, Arapaho, and Cheyenne warriors. In 1876, they inflict a major defeat on the US army, led by Colonel George Custer, by the Little Bighorn River, Montana.

Frontier wars

Almost from the start, relations between European settlers in the US and American Indian tribes were difficult. Both cultural differences and the settlers' insatiable demand for food and land caused conflict. The settlers eventually seized the land, but only after a series of bloody wars and massacres.

1622 Powhatan Confederacy
The Powhatan American Indians, frustrated by English demands for food and land, launch a surprise attack, killing almost 350 settlers. Warfare will continue for a decade.

1610 Pocahontas
Pocahontas, a Powhatan tribeswoman, helps bring peace between her people and the English settlers. She marries an Englishman in 1614 and travels to London, England in 1616.

1636 Pequot War
Settlers kill 500 members of the Pequot tribe in Connecticut, in retaliation for Pequot attacks. The tribe is practically wiped out.

1680 Pueblo Revolt
Spanish authorities in New Mexico try to stamp out the Pueblo people's religion. The Pueblos rebel, and successfully plunder the Spanish settlements.

1831 Trail of Tears
American Indians suffer from exposure, starvation, and disease as they are forced into their new territories. Their long walk will be known as the "Trail of Tears."

1830 Removal Act
President Andrew Jackson orders native tribes to move to unsettled land west of the Mississippi River. A few tribes go peacefully to the specially designated "Indian territory" across the Mississippi, but many resist.

1862 Sioux Uprising
Broken treaties, hunger, and stress cause the Sioux people to rebel against settlers. They will be defeated, and 38 of them hanged.

1864 Sand Creek Massacre
Tensions between settlers and American Indians in Colorado's plains rise as people pour into the area in search of gold. The situation explodes when the US army and settlers massacre hundreds of tribespeople in Sand Creek, Colorado.

1869 Sitting Bull
The bravery of Sitting Bull leads him to become the leader of the Lakota Sioux people. Other native peoples, such as the Arapaho and Cheyenne, soon follow him.

1890 Wounded Knee
The massacre of Sioux people in South Dakota marks the end of the long war between tribes and settlers. More than 150 Sioux men, women, and children are killed, with many more injured.

The 1848 Revolutions

In 1848, a wave of revolutions spread across the cities of Europe. Demands varied. In France, protestors called for economic reform and the right to vote. In Prussia and Germany, they wanted a democratic constitution (set of laws) and German unification. In parts of the Austrian Habsburg Empire, they demanded independence. Their governments promised reforms, but very little changed.

BEFORE

After the defeat of Napoleon in 1815, the Congress of Vienna creates the German Confederation and brings harsh rule back to Europe. The conservative monarchies of Austria, Russia, and Prussia form the Holy Alliance, making more liberal rule less likely.

January 1848

January 12
Uprising in Sicily

Independent state

Following an uprising in Sicily, which has been united with the Kingdom of Naples since 1815, Sicilian nobles set up an independent state. This state will end in May 1849, when King Ferdinand of Sicily and Naples orders his ships to bomb the island, earning him the nickname "Re Bomba" ("King Bomb").

February 1848

Political uproar

February 21
Communist Manifesto

The Communist Manifesto is published in London. Written in German by Karl Marx and Friedrich Engels, it calls for a revolution of the working class. As copies spread through Europe, it encourages angry people to protest against their governments.

February 22–23
REVOLUTION IN PARIS

Anger over the banning of political protest brings the people of Paris out on the streets. Soldiers fire shots into the crowd, killing 52. The rioters overthrow King Louis Philippe and declare the Second French Republic.

March 1848

GERMAN AND AUSTRIAN RIOTS

March 13–22
Prince Metternich resigns

Riots in Vienna force Prince Metternich, Chancellor of Austria and a hated symbol of repression, to resign. Hungary demands independence and is granted its own parliament. Street fighting breaks out in Milan, capital of Austrian-ruled Italy.

March 18–19
CALLS FOR GERMAN UNITY

Protestors in the German Confederation (an organization of separate German states) call for German national unity. After two days of street fighting in Berlin, the king of Prussia agrees to create a national assembly and promises a new constitution, but protests continue.

April 1848

April 10
RALLY IN LONDON

Votes for all men

Britain's working-class Chartist movement organizes a mass meeting in London to demand that all men (but not women) should be given the right to vote. Fearing revolution, the government calls in the army, but the protest is peaceful.

May 1848

May 18
FRANKFURT PARLIAMENT

Hopes for liberal reform

Following the March revolutions, representatives of the states of the German Confederation meet for the first time in Frankfurt. Their task is to create a constitution for Germany and make plans for German unification.

Revolution in Europe

The 1848 Revolutions broke out across a wide area of Europe, from Berlin in northern Germany to Palermo in Sicily. This map shows the location of the revolutions that are mentioned on this timeline.

BELGIUM
PRUSSIA
Berlin
Paris
POLAND
FRANCE
Vienna
Milan
Budapest
AUSTRIAN EMPIRE
PAPAL STATES
Rome
OTTOMAN EMPIRE
Mediterranean Sea
KINGDOM OF THE TWO SICILIES
Palermo

KEY

— Boundary of the German Confederation

December 1848

A NEW ERA BEGINS

December 2
Emperor resigns

Although never a target of the protestors, the weak Austrian emperor Ferdinand I is persuaded to resign in favor of his 18-year-old nephew Franz Joseph I, who will reign for the next 68 years.

December 10
FRENCH PRESIDENT

In the first national election ever held in France, Prince Louis-Napoleon Bonaparte, nephew of Napoleon I, is elected president of the Republic. He promises to restore order and prosperity to the country.

AFTER

In April 1849, the Frankfurt parliament offers Frederick William I of Prussia the imperial crown of Germany. He refuses, saying he would not accept "a crown from the gutter." His decision dashes all hope of liberal reform in Germany.

June 1848

June 23–26

MORE TROUBLE IN PARIS

June Days uprising

In France, the new government of the Second Republic closes the National Workshops that were set up in March to provide work for the unemployed. Thousands of workers take to the streets in a protest now known as the June Days uprising. The army puts a brutal stop to the uprising.

October 1848

October 6–31

OCTOBER REVOLUTION

Street battles in Vienna

Anger at the Austrian government's attempts to crush reforms in Hungary leads to street battles in Vienna, forcing the emperor to flee the city. After the army has retaken control, the leaders of the uprising are executed.

November 1848

November 15

ROME UPRISING

Minister assassinated

The Pope flees Rome after a minister of the Papal States (the parts of Italy ruled by the Pope) is assassinated. Protesters fill the streets demanding social reform and a democratic form of government. This will lead to the short-lived Roman Republic of February 1849.

Biology

Our interest in the natural world began more than 40,000 years ago, when prehistoric people first depicted animals on cave walls. Over time, zoology, the study of animals, and botany, the study of plants, combined to form a new science known as biology. More recently, the focus of biology has shifted to studying ourselves, with geneticists looking inside the human body to uncover the secrets of life.

c.39,000 BCE

Cave paintings

Evidence of prehistoric humans' interest in animals is seen in paintings on the walls at the Cave of El Castillo (Cave of the Castle) in Spain. These artworks are the first sophisticated representation of wildlife found anywhere in the world.

Covered meat — **Uncovered meat**

1674

Work of art
This bison is among the Cave of El Castillo's many animal paintings, alongside ibex, mammoths, and goats.

Circle of life

Italian biologist Francesco Redi (1626–1697) disproves the idea of "spontaneous generation"—that living things, such as flies and fleas, appear from dust or rotting meat. He realizes that flies lay their eggs on uncovered meat, which later hatch into maggots.

Magnifying microscope

Dutch textile merchant Antonie van Leeuwenhoek (1632–1723) makes a breakthrough in microbiology when he further develops the microscope by improving its magnification. This allows him to see tiny organisms in water.

c.330 BCE

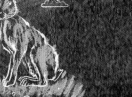

Classifying nature

The ancient Greek philosopher Aristotle (384–322 BCE) travels across Greece and Turkey to study wildlife. He organizes plants and animals into categories and names different species. This classification of nature is the start of zoology and botany.

1668

1735

First microscope

Dutch eyewear-maker Zacharias Janssen (1580–1638) invents the first compound microscope. The invention helps scientists across all areas of biology study their subjects in much greater detail.

Latin names

Swedish botanist Carl Linnaeus (1707–1778) devises taxonomy, a way of grouping together related plant and animal species. In his book *Systema Naturae*, he uses Latin names for genus (subfamily) and species.

1543

1595

Human dissection

Flemish scientist Andreas Vesalius (1514–1564) dissects (cuts up) human bodies and creates detailed drawings of the blood and nervous systems. The publication of his *De Humani Corporis Fabrica* revolutionizes the field of anatomy, the study of the human body.

Pumping blood
By studying the human heart, Vesalius learned how blood flows around the body.

Two names
Canis lupus (gray wolf) and Canis familiaris (domestic dog) are examples of the two-name Latin system still used today.

1838

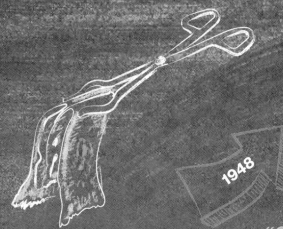

DNA discovery

Using pus-covered bandages from a nearby surgical clinic, Swiss chemist Friedrich Miescher (1844–1895) is the first to identify what he calls "nuclein" inside human white blood cells. Nuclein carries a person's genetic information. Today, it is better known as deoxyribonucleic acid (DNA).

1869

Mobile genetics

American scientist Barbara McClintock (1902–1992) studies corn and discovers jumping genes (transposons)—genes that can change position in the DNA of cells. By studying these jumping genes, she finds that genes can be switched on or off, changing the characteristics of the corn.

1948

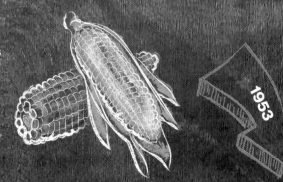

1953

"One general law leading to the advancement of all organic beings—namely, multiply, vary, let the strongest live and the weakest die."

Charles Darwin
On the Origin of Species, 1859

The secret of life

The work of scientists Franklin, Crick, and Watson combines to create the first DNA model. Called "the secret of life," their model reveals the chemical information existing inside all living creatures.

Double helix
DNA is made up of two twisted strands.

Genetics

Austrian monk Gregor Mendel (1822–1884) grows pea plants in his monastery garden and discovers that the plants pass on characteristics like color and size in a simple pattern to their young. This leads to the discovery of genes.

1996

Darwin's finches
Finches have evolved different-shaped beaks to suit the food available where they live.

1866

Natural selection

English naturalist Charles Darwin (1809–1882) publishes *On the Origin of Species*, his theory of "natural selection." After studying wildlife in South America, he realizes animals with the best characteristics for the environment survive and pass these traits on to their young.

Dolly the Sheep

History is made when scientists successfully clone an animal for the first time by duplicating a version of its DNA. The newborn lamb, named Dolly, is an exact copy of another sheep.

Sharing DNA
To create Dolly, DNA from one sheep was placed into another sheep's egg cell.

1859

2003

Cell theory

German botanist Matthias Schleiden (1804–1881) discovers that all plants are made of cells. A year later, German zoologist Theodor Schwann (1810–1882) realizes all animals are also made of cells.

Command center
The nucleus controls the cell and contains all of its genetic information.

Human Genome Project

The Human Genome Project is completed, showcasing the sequence of human DNA. A huge team of international scientists had mapped and identified the role of more than 20,000 genes that make up human DNA.

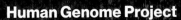

Trade beginnings

A group of London merchants establish the East India Company to profit from the valuable trade in silk and spices with India and the East Indies (modern-day Southeast Asia).

American colony

After an earlier settlement in modern-day North Carolina fails to thrive, the British occupy the land of the native Powhatan people to establish Jamestown (in modern-day Virginia) as their first permanent colony in North America.

Sugar and slaves

Britain captures the Caribbean island of Jamaica from the Spanish. As exports of sugar from the island increase rapidly, British traders begin forcibly transporting slaves from Africa to work on the sugar plantations there (see page 164).

1600

1607

1655

The British Empire

The origins of the British Empire were in trade with the East, but its ambition soon spread to other areas of the world. Over time, its mission expanded beyond commerce to total political control, eventually making it the largest empire in history. But the empire went into decline after World War I, when it became clear that people were no longer willing to accept British rule.

New Zealand

Britain takes control of New Zealand with the signing of the Treaty of Waitangi. It guarantees the native Maori people possession of their lands in return for giving up their rights of sovereignty.

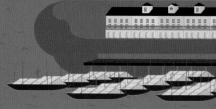

1840

1857–1858

Direct rule in India

After suppressing a revolt by sepoys in the armies of the East India Company, Britain rules India directly. Queen Victoria becomes Empress of India in 1870, although she never visits.

South African War

The Boers, settlers of Dutch descent, fight a bitter war against Britain for control of lands in Transvaal. Their defeat will lead to the creation of the Union of South Africa in 1910.

The birth of Canada

Three British provinces in North America—New Brunswick, Nova Scotia, and Canada (modern-day Ontario and Quebec)—unite to form a single country, the Dominion of Canada, within the British Empire.

African expansion

The empire grows as it takes huge expanses of territory in Africa from native peoples, including Egypt and Sudan in the north, Gambia and Ghana in the west, and most of mineral-rich southern Africa.

1867

1880–1900

1899–1902

Power in India

The East India Company builds Fort William in Calcutta (modern-day Kolkata). From there, it uses its private army of Indian soldiers, called "sepoys," to take control of much of India.

War in the colonies

The Seven Years' War in Europe turns global as fighting spreads to overseas colonies. At the end of the war, Britain gains New France (modern-day Canada) and other French territories.

American independence

The 13 colonies in North America revolt against British rule. They declare their independence on July 4, leading to the creation of the United States of America.

1702

1756–1763

1776

Colony in Australia

Twenty years after Captain Cook claimed Australia for Britain, a fleet arrives at Port Jackson (modern-day Sydney). Prisoner labor is used to establish a colony there. By the mid-1800s, there are nearly 400,000 settlers in Australia.

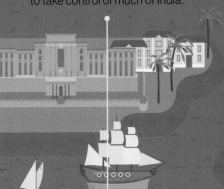

Foothold in Africa

The British seize the Cape of Good Hope on the southern tip of Africa, which has been a Dutch colony since 1652. They will lose it again, but win it back in 1806, when it then becomes the first British presence in Africa.

Singapore

British colonialist Sir Stamford Raffles founds a trading port on the island of Singapore in Southeast Asia, on the main trade route between India and China. It becomes a British colony in 1824.

1819

1795

1788

Irish uprising

After hundreds of years of British rule in Ireland, nationalists rebel in Dublin on Easter in 1916. The "Easter Rising" is quickly put down, but the fight against British rule continues. The Irish Free State, forerunner of the Republic of Ireland, will be founded in 1922.

World War I settlements

In the peace treaties concluding World War I, Britain gains control over former German colonies in Africa and in the Middle East following the division of the Ottoman Empire.

Partition of India

India wins independence as two new countries: the mainly Hindu India, and Pakistan, which is mainly Muslim. The Partition of India, as it is known, forces millions of people to migrate, leading to riots and thousands of deaths.

1916

1919–1920

1947

AFTER

Nearly all Britain's colonies and possessions became independent states between 1957 and 1980. Many joined the Commonwealth of Nations, a voluntary association of states with previous ties to the empire. Others operated as individual republics.

The American Civil War

Years of conflict over slavery and the rights of individual states eventually led to the American Civil War. From 1861 to 1865, the country was torn apart. More than 625,000 American soldiers died in the Civil War. This was more than the combined total of American soldiers that had died in all other wars to date.

Belle Boyd

Confederate spy Belle Boyd—one of several female spies in the Civil War—passes on information that helps Confederate general Stonewall Jackson's army recapture Front Royal, Virginia.

Gettysburg

This Pennsylvania battle is a turning point, finally ending Confederate hopes of invading the Union states. It is the bloodiest multiday conflict in the history of the Civil War.

Confederate states

To protect their economy based on slave labor (see pages 164–165), seven southern states leave the United States to create their own Confederate government, with Jefferson Davis as president. The Confederates see themselves as a separate nation. A month later, Abraham Lincoln will become US president.

First Battle of Bull Run

The Union is defeated in this Virginian battle (also known as the Battle of Manassas). Washington D. C. is fortified for protection. In August 1862, the Confederates will win the Second Battle of Bull Run.

July 1863

September 1862

May 1862

July 1861

April 1861

February 1861

The war begins

Lincoln refuses to hand over all military property in Confederate states to their new government. Confederate forces attack Fort Sumter in South Carolina, and the Civil War begins. Four more states leave the United States (known as the Union during the Civil War).

Napoleon Field Gun

Named after the French emperor Napoleon III, this type of cannon was widely used in the Civil War. It could hit a target up to 5,250 ft (1,600 m) away and fire a cannonball at 1,440 ft (439 m) per second.

Antietam

The bloodiest single day of the war sees some 23,000 soldiers dead, wounded, or missing. After a Union victory, Lincoln introduces the Emancipation Proclamation, an order to free every slave in the Confederate states.

Gettysburg Address

President Lincoln delivers his most famous speech at the dedication of the Soldiers' National Cemetery in Gettysburg. He declares that the Civil War is a struggle for freedom and equality.

Surrender meeting

After an attempt to break through Union lines fails, Confederate commander Robert E. Lee meets Union general Ulysses S. Grant at Appomattox Court House to sign a document of surrender.

Conscription and protests

There are riots in New York City because the Union started conscription in March, and people feel the system for drafting men into fighting favors the rich. The first African-American regiment of soldiers sees combat.

Escape

More than 100 captive Union officers escape from a Confederate prison after weeks of digging a tunnel. Around half are recaptured, but the others make their way back north.

November 1863

February 1864

November 1864

April 1865

May 1865

July 1863

Submarine warfare

Confederate submarine CSS *Hunley* torpedoes and sinks the Union warship USS *Housatonic*. The *Hunley* is the first combat submarine to sink an enemy warship, but it doesn't survive the attack and also sinks.

March to the Sea

Union general William Sherman and his troops march from the captured city of Atlanta to the port of Savannah, bringing devastation to Confederate states.

Lincoln assassinated

At a play in Washington, D. C., President Lincoln is shot by John Wilkes Booth, an actor hoping to avenge the Confederates. Lincoln dies the next morning.

War is over

The rest of the Confederate armies give up the fight. Both sides agree on surrender terms as new president Andrew Johnson declares the official end of the Civil War.

Key battles

From the first shots to the final surrender, the American Civil War divided the country. No side seemed to have a clear advantage at the outset. The Union had more soldiers and money, but the Confederates had cunning and strategic generals.

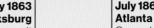

March 1862
Monitor* vs. *Virginia
This clash between two ironclad ships has plenty of flying cannonballs, but no victor.

December 1862
Fredericksburg
This is a low point for the Union as the Confederate army defeats them.

April – May 1863
Chancellorsville
The outnumbered Confederate army achieves a strategic win.

May 1864
Spotsylvania
Neither side claims victory in this brutal Virginia fight.

April 1862
Shiloh
The battle blazes for two days in Tennessee before a Union victory.

May – July 1863
Vicksburg
The Union army is victorious as it surrounds this Mississippi town.

July 1864
Atlanta
General Sherman and his troops seize control of this Georgia city.

Colonialism in Africa

In 1870, although the slave trade (see pages 164–165) had ravaged Africa for centuries, European powers controlled just 10 percent of the continent. The next 30 years saw European nations compete for control of Africa. By 1900, they had seized 90 percent of African land from local communities. It would take more than half a century for these countries to gain their independence.

Scramble for Africa

This map shows the domination of European powers in Africa by the end of the 19th century. France and Britain colonized the largest areas of land across the continent. Only Liberia and Ethiopia held onto their independence.

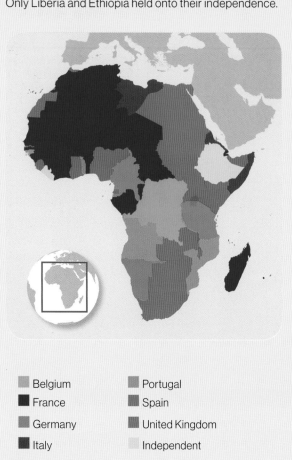

- ■ Belgium
- ■ France
- ■ Germany
- ■ Italy
- ■ Portugal
- ■ Spain
- ■ United Kingdom
- ■ Independent

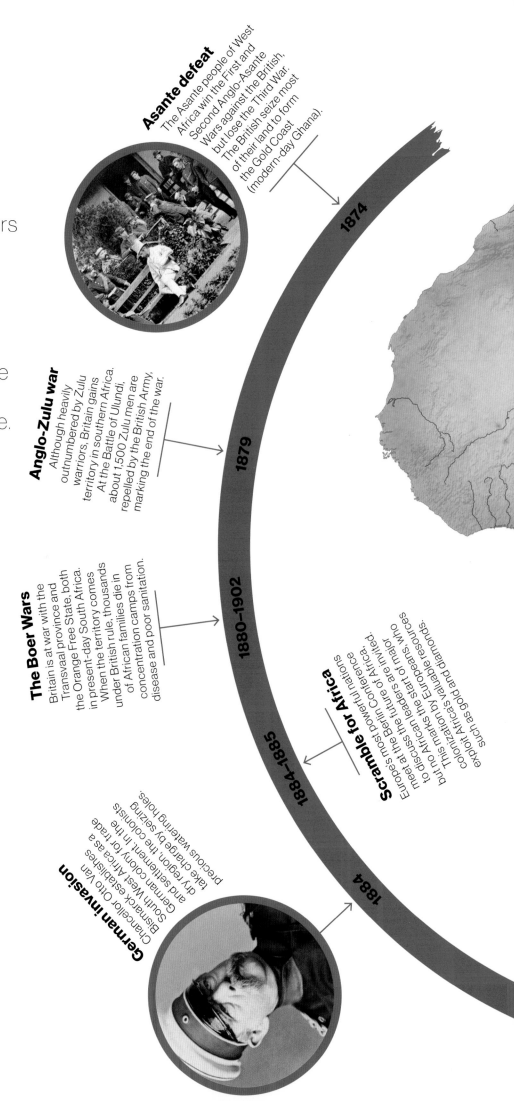

Asante defeat

The Asante people of West Africa win the First and Second Anglo-Asante Wars against the British, but lose the Third War. The British seize most of their land to form the Gold Coast (modern-day Ghana).

1874

Anglo-Zulu war

Although heavily outnumbered by Zulu warriors, Britain gains territory in southern Africa. At the Battle of Ulundi, about 1,500 Zulu men are repelled by the British Army, marking the end of the war.

1879

The Boer Wars

Britain is at war with the Transvaal province and the Orange Free State, both in present-day South Africa. When the territory comes under British rule, thousands of African families die in concentration camps from disease and poor sanitation.

1880–1902

Scramble for Africa

Europe's most powerful nations meet at the Berlin Conference. Leaders of major African nations are invited to discuss the future of Africa, but no African leaders start off as colonists who the Europeans resources. This marks the start of major colonization by Europeans. Africa's valuable resources, exploit Africa's gold and diamonds such as gold and diamonds.

1884–1885

German invasion

Chancellor Otto van Bismarck establishes German West Africa as a dry region, the colonists and settlement. In the precious watering holes. South West Africa as a take charge by seizing

1884

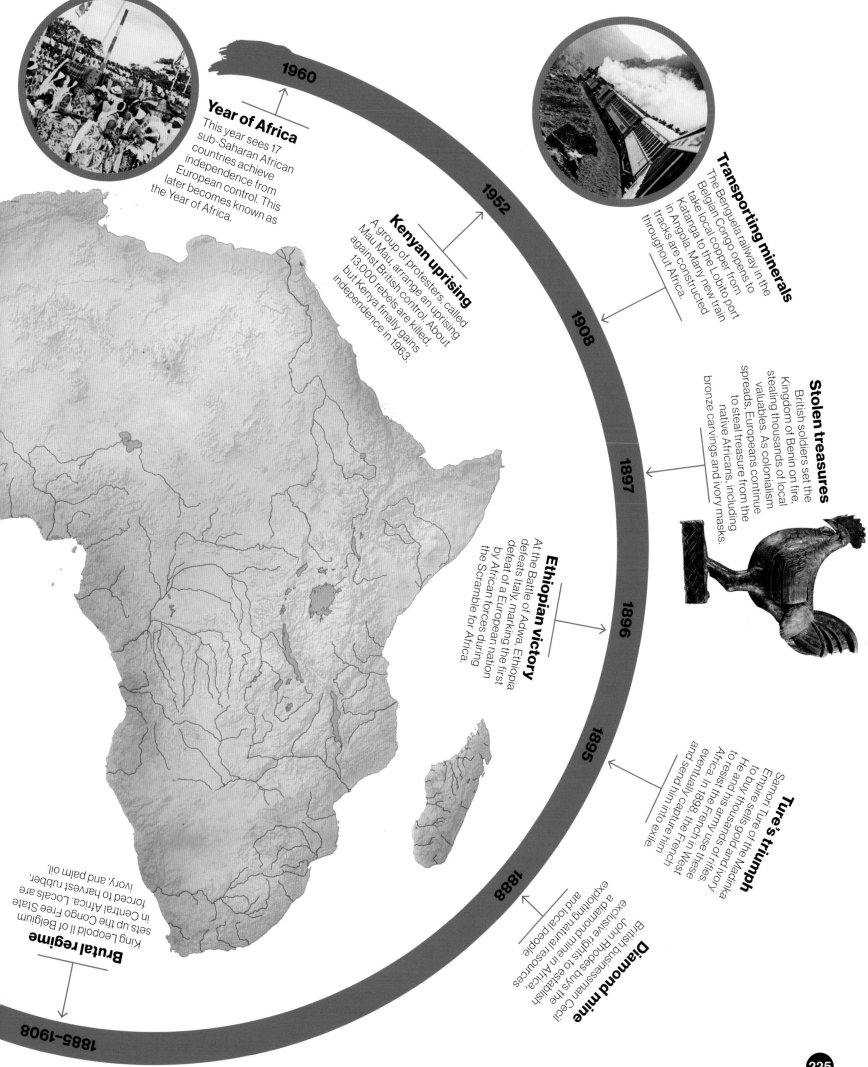

Year of Africa
This year sees 17 sub-Saharan African countries achieve independence from European control. This later becomes known as the Year of Africa.

1960

Kenyan uprising
A group of protesters called Mau Mau arrange an uprising against British control. About 13,000 rebels are killed, but Kenya finally gains independence in 1963.

1952

Transporting minerals
The Benguela railway in the Belgian Congo opens to take local copper from Katanga to the Lobito port in Angola. Many new train tracks are constructed throughout Africa.

1908

Stolen treasures
British soldiers set the Kingdom of Benin on fire, stealing thousands of local valuables. As colonialism spreads, Europeans continue to steal treasure from the native Africans, including bronze carvings and ivory masks.

1897

Ethiopian victory
At the Battle of Adwa, Ethiopia defeats Italy, marking the first defeat of a European nation by African forces during the Scramble for Africa.

1896

1895

Ture's triumph
Samori Ture of the Empire sells gold and ivory to buy thousands of rifles. He and his army use these to resist the French in West Africa. In 1898, the French eventually capture him and send him into exile.

1888

Diamond mine
British businessman Cecil John Rhodes buys the exclusive rights to establish a diamond mine in Africa, exploiting natural resources and local people.

Brutal regime
King Leopold II of Belgium sets up the Congo Free State in Central Africa. Locals are forced to harvest rubber, ivory, and palm oil.

1885–1908

225

Telecommunications

Communication has come a long way since ancient times, when messages were sent by smoke signals, beacons, and carrier pigeons. With the invention of the telegraph, telephone, radio, and the internet, people could send messages and converse across countries, and even continents, for the first time. The television transported scenes into the homes of millions, shaping the way people spend their free time today.

Electrical messaging

The invention of an electrical telegraph by British inventors William Fothergill Cooke and Charles Wheatstone makes long-distance messages possible. Electric signals are sent along wires attached to needle pointers, which can be made to point to specific letters and numbers on a plate to form a message. The messages sent by telegraphs are known as telegrams.

Continental cables

A new era of cross-continent communication dawns when the very first telegraph cable is laid across the Atlantic Ocean. By 1902, cables have been placed under the Pacific Ocean too, allowing telegrams to be sent all around the globe.

Tesla's transmission

Serbian-American engineer Nikola Tesla is the first person to produce and transmit radio waves. He is also the brains behind many inventions, including the electric motors that power modern machines.

1837

1876

1895

1844

1792

1858

1888

1897

Morse code

American inventor Samuel Morse creates a code to interpret the electric signals being sent along telegraph wires. It uses different lengths of signal to create patterns of dots and dashes, which represent different letters and numbers.

Radio waves

German scientist Heinrich Hertz is the first person to discover radio waves. He recognizes the potential of these electromagnetic waves to transfer information.

Telegraph system

French inventor Claude Chappe devises a system of movable wooden arms, the position of which indicates letters or numbers. These arms are placed on tall masts so they can be seen from far away, allowing messages to be passed from town to town. He calls this new system a telegraph, which means "to write at a distance."

Telephone call

Scottish inventor Alexander Graham Bell experiments with sending sounds through telegraph wires. These can be heard at the other end, in an early version of a telephone call. The first call is from Bell to his assistant Thomas Watson, when he says: "Mr. Watson—come here—I want to see you."

Marconi's message

Italian inventor Guglielmo Marconi sets up his own company to investigate radio waves. He devises a wireless telegraph, which uses radio waves to send Morse code through the air without any wires.

Voice for radio

Canadian-American inventor Reginald Fessenden is the first human voice to be broadcast via radio. This sparks the construction of radio transmitters to create an exciting new form of entertainment that many people can enjoy, gathered around their radios in their own homes.

Color vision

The first color television is unveiled in 1928, but it is not until the 1950s that color televisions become affordable. People begin to enjoy programs in their own homes.

First mobile phone

The first mobile telephone is launched, but it is too large and expensive for people to use. The first mobile phone call is made on a phone that weighs a massive 2.4 lbs (1.1 kg) and takes 10 hours to charge.

Early email

Electronic messaging across computers, called email, begins when US computer programmer Ray Tomlinson sends the first ever email—a test message to himself. Email will become one of the world's most popular forms of communication.

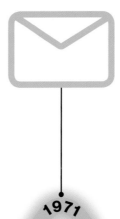

World Wide Web

British scientist Tim Berners-Lee creates the World Wide Web—a way of connecting internet resources across the world. This information-sharing system of linked webpages can be accessed from any computer.

> **"In the new era, thought itself will be transmitted by radio."**
> **Guglielmo Marconi**, *New York Times*, 1931

1906

1925

Early 1950s

1970s

1962

1971

1989

1984

2000s

Space communications

The first communications satellite is *Telstar 1*, sent into orbit by the US. This satellite receives radio signals from Earth and bounces them back to receivers on the ground, resulting in the transmission of television and telephone communications.

Heavyweight phone

The DynaTAC becomes the world's first commercial mobile phone. Nicknamed "The Brick," this device goes on the market for a jaw-dropping $4,000 (equivalent to around $9,000 today), which few can afford. The battery lasts only half an hour.

Mechanical television

British inventor John Logie Baird creates the world's first mechanical television, which uses rotating discs to generate a video signal. He constructs this from random objects including knitting needles, cookie tins, and a tea chest. It is unveiled in London in 1926.

Digital TV

Analog television technology, which manipulates electrical signals to create sound and color, is replaced by plasma screens and digital technology, which provides high-definition images and a huge choice of channels. The first digital television broadcasts take place in the early 2000s.

Photography

Imagine a world without photos—no selfies, no breaking news shots, and no way of recording the most important events in our lives. When photography began in the early 1800s, it changed the way people saw and understood the world around them. Less than 200 years later, technological advances have seen cameras shrink from large, bulky boxes into tiny digital devices that we carry around in our smartphones.

1855

War photography
British photographer Roger Fenton takes the first pictures of conflict while visiting the battlefields of the Crimean War. He makes 350 images that generate huge public interest.

1861

Color photography
Scottish physicist James Clerk Maxwell projects three separate exposures of a tartan ribbon through red, green, and blue filters to create a color photograph.

1888

Mass photography
Photography becomes an accessible, popular pastime, as Kodak launches its easy-to-use, roll-film camera. Twelve years later, the mass-produced, one-dollar "Brownie" box camera goes on sale.

1950s

The first SLR camera
SLR (single-lens reflex) cameras reach the mass market during the 1950s. SLR cameras, like this Nikon F shown above, allow photographers unprecedented control over their camera's settings.

1964

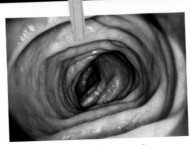

Inside the body
The invention of the fiberscope lets doctors see hard-to-reach places inside the body. This photograph was taken inside the gut. Made of thin, flexible glass cables, the device transmits light from the lens to the eyepiece.

1980s

Point and shoot
Kodak introduces its new Instamatic camera, which makes the process of changing film easier. It is the first of a new generation of smart "point and shoot" cameras that automatically select the correct settings for taking an image.

1826

The first photograph
French inventor Joseph Nicéphor Niépce takes the oldest surviving photo, capturing this rooftop view using light-sensitive chemicals. The exposure (light making a picture on film) takes several hours.

1838

First photo of a human
Louis Daguerre photographs this street scene using his invention, the daguerrotype. The only person to appear is a man having his shoes cleaned, as he stays still for the seven minutes it takes to capture the exposure.

1839

Portrait photography
American photographer Robert Cornelius takes the first self-portrait photograph, using a daguerreotype camera. To take the exposure, he must sit still for 15 minutes.

1895

First X-ray
German physicist Wilhelm Röntgen takes an X-ray image of his wife's hand, which shows that X-rays can penetrate (travel through) skin and muscle, but are stopped by bone.

1920s

Photojournalism
The golden age of photojournalism begins, as technological advances make cameras more portable. In the US, magazines such as *Time* and *Life* start to include "photo essays," which reveal social injustices.

1947

Polaroid cameras
After his three-year-old daughter asks why she must wait for a picture, Edwin Land invents the Polaroid 95 instant camera, which develops photographs in 60 seconds. By 1956, more than a million Polaroids have sold.

1991

Digital cameras
The first commercial digital camera goes on sale, 16 years after it was first invented by American engineer Stephen Sasson. Digital cameras store images as electronic data, getting rid of the need for film.

2000

Selfies
The first mobile phones with built-in digital cameras are released in South Korea and Japan. "Selfies" become a global phenomenon, as everyone from celebrities to political leaders takes and posts self-portraits online.

The dark room
Before images were stored as electronic data on digital cameras, photographic film was used to record images (known as exposures). The film was developed into a photograph with the use of chemicals in a dark room, lit only by a shaded bulb. The resulting prints were then hung up to dry.

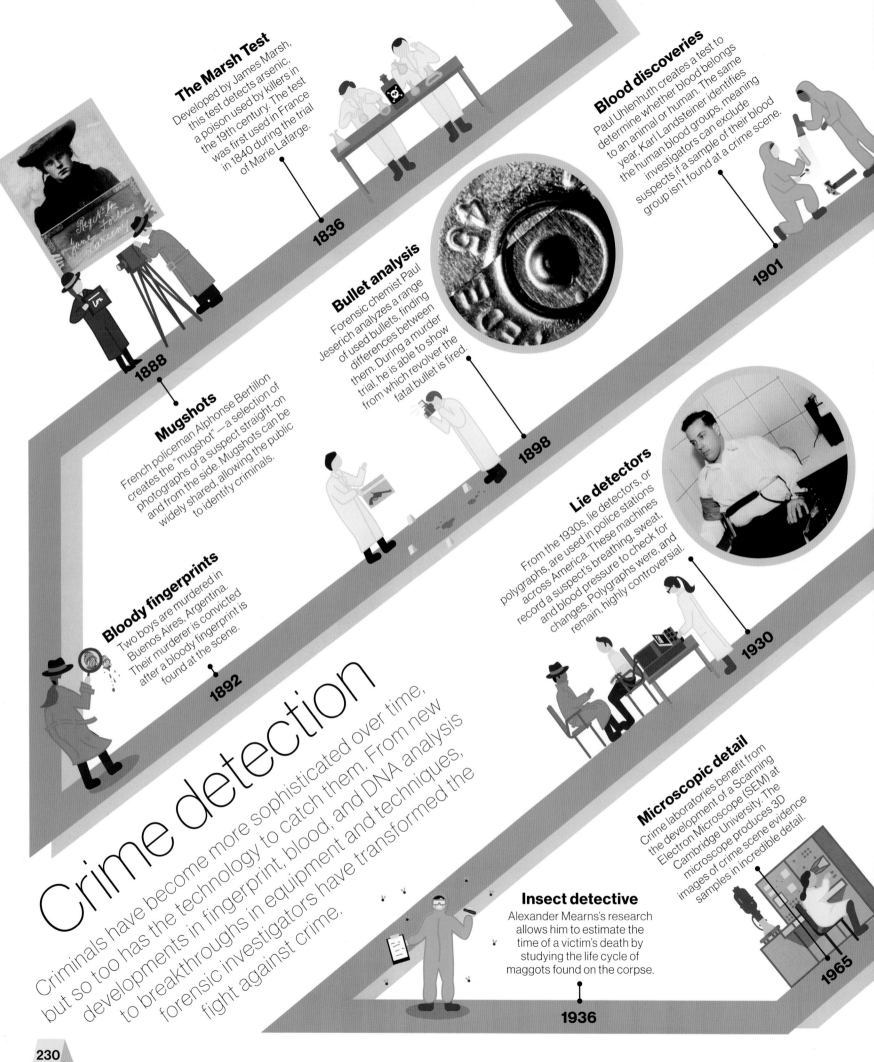

The Marsh Test

Developed by James Marsh, this test detects arsenic, a poison used by killers in the 19th century. The test was first used in France in 1840 during the trial of Marie Lafarge.

1836

Blood discoveries

Paul Uhlenhuth creates a test to determine whether blood belongs to an animal or human. The same year, Karl Landsteiner identifies the human blood groups, meaning investigators can exclude suspects if a sample of their blood group isn't found at a crime scene.

1901

Bullet analysis

Forensic chemist Paul Jeserich analyzes a range of used bullets, finding differences between them. During a murder trial, he is able to show from which revolver the fatal bullet is fired.

1898

Mugshots

French policeman Alphonse Bertillon creates the "mugshot"—a selection of photographs of a suspect straight-on and from the side. Mugshots can be widely shared, allowing the public to identify criminals.

1888

Lie detectors

From the 1930s, lie detectors, or polygraphs, are used in police stations across America. These machines record a suspect's breathing, sweat, and blood pressure to check for changes. Polygraphs were, and remain, highly controversial.

1930

Bloody fingerprints

Two boys are murdered in Buenos Aires, Argentina. Their murderer is convicted after a bloody fingerprint is found at the scene.

1892

Crime detection

Criminals have become more sophisticated over time, but so too has the technology to catch them. From new developments in fingerprint, blood, and DNA analysis to breakthroughs in equipment and techniques, forensic investigators have transformed the fight against crime.

Microscopic detail

Crime laboratories benefit from the development of a Scanning Electron Microscope (SEM) at Cambridge University. The microscope produces 3D images of crime scene evidence samples in incredible detail.

1965

Insect detective

Alexander Mearns's research allows him to estimate the time of a victim's death by studying the life cycle of maggots found on the corpse.

1936

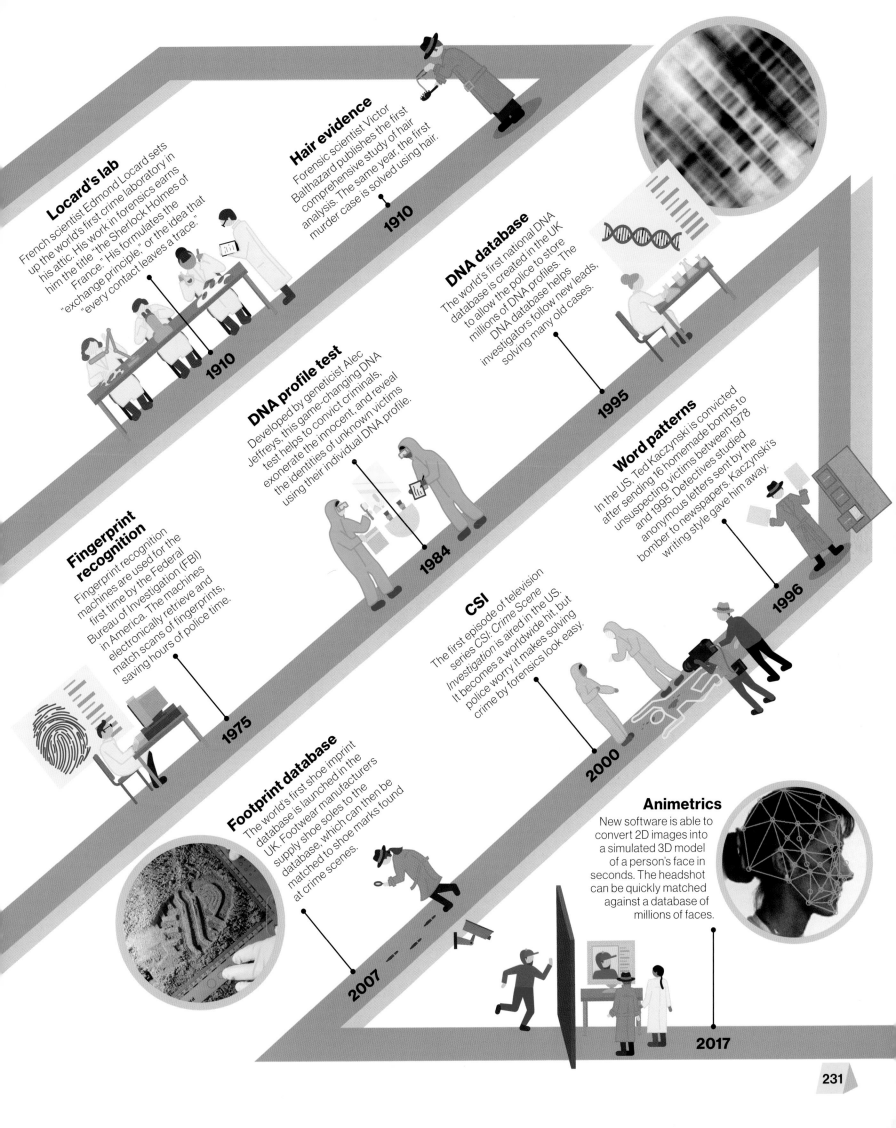

Locard's lab

French scientist Edmond Locard sets up the world's first crime laboratory in his attic. His work in forensics earns him the title "the Sherlock Holmes of France." His formulates the "exchange principle," or the idea that "every contact leaves a trace."

1910

Hair evidence

Forensic scientist Victor Balthazard publishes the first comprehensive study of hair analysis. The same year, the first murder case is solved using hair.

1910

DNA database

The world's first national DNA database is created in the UK to allow the police to store millions of DNA profiles. The DNA database helps investigators follow new leads, solving many old cases.

1995

DNA profile test

Developed by geneticist Alec Jeffreys, this game-changing DNA test helps to convict criminals, exonerate the innocent, and reveal the identities of unknown victims using their individual DNA profile.

1984

Word patterns

In the US, Ted Kaczynski is convicted after sending 16 homemade bombs to unsuspecting victims between 1978 and 1995. Detectives studied the anonymous letters sent by the bomber to newspapers. Kaczynski's writing style gave him away.

1996

Fingerprint recognition

Fingerprint recognition machines are used for the first time by the Federal Bureau of Investigation (FBI) in America. The machines electronically retrieve and match scans of fingerprints, saving hours of police time.

1975

CSI

The first episode of television series CSI: Crime Scene Investigation is aired in the US. It becomes a worldwide hit, but police worry it makes solving crime by forensics look easy.

2000

Footprint database

The world's first shoe imprint database is launched in the UK. Footwear manufacturers supply shoe soles to the database, which can then be matched to shoe marks found at crime scenes.

2007

Animetrics

New software is able to convert 2D images into a simulated 3D model of a person's face in seconds. The headshot can be quickly matched against a database of millions of faces.

2017

Aircraft and aviation

In the 15th century, Italian artist Leonardo da Vinci sketched designs for flying machines, which he based on his studies of birds. For the next four centuries, inventors continued to set their sights on the skies, but it was not until the Wright Brothers' historic flight at the dawn of the 20th century that true aviation history began.

Up, up, and away!
French brothers Joseph and Etienne Montgolfier send a sheep, a chicken, and a duck soaring in a hot air balloon. The Montgolfiers' balloon will later be used for the first human flight.

1783

Battle of Britain
During World War II, members of the British Royal Air Force (RAF), flying in *Supermarine Spitfires*, fight in the skies with the German Luftwaffe in close-range aerial combats that become known as "dogfights."

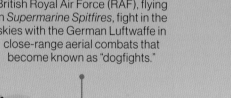

1940

Modern helicopter
The first practical helicopter is invented by Russian-American Igor Sikorsky, and takes to the skies. Like modern helicopters, the design features a main rotor on top and a tail rotor for balance.

1939

Jet power
The world's first fully functioning jet-powered aircraft, the *Heinkel He 178*, takes off for the first time. The design, by German Hans von Ohain, reaches speeds of 400 mph (644 kph).

1939

Commercial jet
After three years of testing, the world's first commercial jet airliner takes off. *De Havilland DH106 Comet* can carry more people around the world more quickly than any other aircraft.

1949

Twin-rotor choppers
American aircraft innovator Frank Piasecki invents twin-rotor helicopters, including the famous *Chinook* design. These are used to carry soldiers into conflict and take part in rescue missions.

1960s

Jump Jet
The *Harrier Jump Jet* takes flight, becoming the world's first vertical takeoff plane. This style of takeoff suits fast exits from battle zones.

1966

Hydrogen airship

The world's first powered airship is built by Frenchman Jules Henri Gifford. The hydrogen-filled, steam-powered design completes a controlled journey of 16.8 miles (27 km).

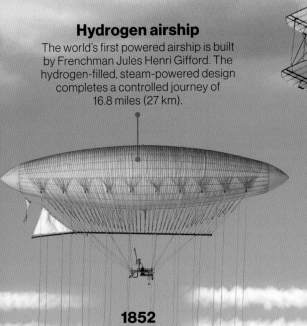

1852

Wright flight

Orville Wright completes the world's first powered, heavier-than-air flight. It lasts for 12 seconds and he covers a distance of 120 ft (36.5 m).

1903

Crossing the Channel

French inventor Louis Blériot becomes the first person to cross the English Channel by air. It takes him 37 minutes in his *Blériot XI*.

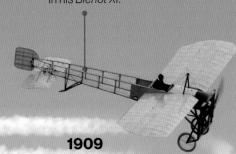

1909

Jet engine

British engineer Frank Whittle designs plans for the jet engine. He patents the design and makes this first working version seven years later.

1930

Around the world

Four *Douglas World Cruisers*, specially designed aircraft operated by the US Army Air Service, become the first planes to circumnavigate the Earth. The around-the-world trip covers 27,500 miles (44,250 km) in about six months.

1924

Atlantic crossing

The first nonstop flight across the Atlantic Ocean is completed by British aviators John Alcock and Arthur Brown, who cross 1,890 miles (3,040 km) in less than 16 hours.

1919

Supersonic flight

British-French turbojet-powered supersonic passenger jet airliner *Concorde* takes off for the first time. Traveling at up to twice the speed of sound, it remains in service until 2003.

1969

Aboard the Airbus

The world's biggest and heaviest passenger aircraft, the *Airbus A380*, takes to the skies for the first time. Powered by four Rolls-Royce engines, it has room for up to 853 passengers.

2005

Pilotless drones

With no pilot on board, flying machines known as drones are controlled by a handheld remote control. Today, there is widespread use of drones for military purposes, surveillance, and recreation.

21st century

Getting the vote

The ancient Greeks first held elections 2,500 years ago. In the 17th century, the idea of representative government emerged—that the public should vote for, and be represented by, elected officials. Having the right to vote is known as "suffrage," but who should be given this right? In many countries, the "electorate" (those with the right to vote) has expanded over time, as people have fought for their voices to be heard.

1789

1789

"All men..."
The US Constitution, which sets out America's laws, comes into effect. The decision about who can and can't vote is left to the states. Most states only give the right to vote to white males who own property.

The Rights of Man
The *Declaration of the Rights of Man*, written by France's National Constituent Assembly, states that all men, not just those with money and property, can vote and participate in lawmaking.

New democracies
When the Soviet Union collapses, a new wave of democracy sweeps across Europe. With more people going to the polls, teams of international observers begin to monitor elections to keep them fair.

1989

1965

Civil rights progress
The hard-earned 1965 Voting Rights Act is a result of the US Civil Rights Movement campaigning for change. It outlaws discrimination against African-American voters, such as turning people away on election day, or making voters pass literacy tests.

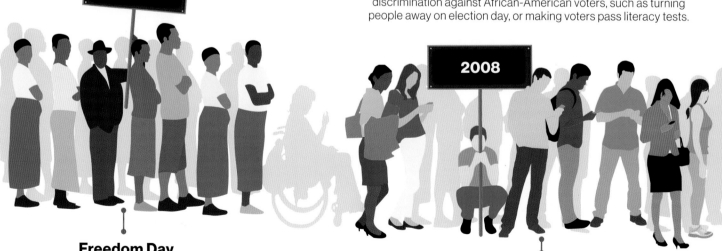

1994

2008

Freedom Day
South Africa holds its first election with universal suffrage, meaning all people regardless of their race now have the right to vote. Previously, South Africa's system of racial separation, known as "apartheid," meant that black people could not vote.

Young voters
Austria becomes the first country in the European Union to open the vote to 16-year-olds. A handful of countries allow 16-year-olds to vote, but in most states, voters are 18 or over.

Great Reform Bill

After widespread rioting in Britain about unfair elections, parliament tries to make voting fairer. This Bill expands the number of property-owning men allowed to vote and standardizes voting practices across the country.

The 15th Amendment

Although slavery was abolished in the US in 1865, African-Americans in the southern states still can't vote. The 15th Amendment makes it illegal to deny the vote based on skin color, but African-American voters still face discrimination.

Compulsory voting

Belgium starts the world's first compulsory voting system, but only men can vote. Those over the age of 18 must pay a fine if they don't vote, and if they fail to four times in a row, they lose the right. Women's votes will become compulsory in 1949.

The 19th Amendment

After decades of struggle and protest, US women get the vote. Campaigners like Elizabeth Cady Stanton, Susan B. Anthony, and Alice Paul have worked for years to improve opportunities for women in education and employment, as well as for the right to vote.

Campaigning for change

Emmeline Pankhurst founds the Women's Social and Political Union in England. Its motto, "Deeds, not words," is a call to action for suffragettes, who use shock tactics to win support. In 1918, women over 30 get the right to vote; in 1928, women of all ages do.

Female pioneers

After a long equal rights campaign, New Zealand becomes the first country to give women the vote. Australia follows in 1902, then women gain the right to vote in Scandinavia, Canada, and parts of Europe.

Progress for women

More than 200 years after women in New Zealand won the right to vote, women in Saudi Arabia are allowed to vote in local elections for the first time.

> "Voting is the most precious right of every citizen, and we have a moral obligation to ensure the integrity of our voting process."
>
> **Hillary Rodham Clinton**

Physics

For more than 2,500 years, scientists have studied the behavior of matter, forces, and energy in an attempt to understand how the Universe functions. As theories were proposed over the centuries, the principles of physics were established. We know more today about the Universe than the ancient physicists did, but there is still much more to discover.

c. 600 BCE

Static electricity

The ancient Greeks discover static electricity, meaning electricity that does not move. Thales of Miletus (624–546 BCE) realizes that rubbing amber (fossilized tree resin) with fur attracts lightweight objects, including hair, straw, and grass.

Sun
The Sun produces rays of light, which travel through space and hit objects on Earth.

1514

Original optics

Arab physicist Alhazen ibn al-Haytham (965–1040) disproves the idea that the human eye can see because it creates its own light. Instead, he realizes that sunlight bounces off an object and is reflected into the eye, allowing us to see it.

Light
Light from the Sun bounces off the flower and is reflected into the eye.

Earthly rotation

At a time when Earth was thought to be at the center of the Universe, Polish astronomer Nicolaus Copernicus (1473–1543) uses mathematical models to show that the Universe is heliocentric, meaning the Sun is at the center and the planets rotate around it.

c. 400 BCE

EUREKA!

c. 1000

1604

Tiny particles

Greek philosopher Democritus (460–370 BCE) theorizes that the Universe is made up of tiny moving particles, although he can't prove this. He calls these particles atoms, but his ideas have little to do with what we know as atoms today.

Galileo's theory

Galileo (1564–1642) experiments with gravity and motion. He drops cannonballs of different sizes from great heights and shows that they all hit the ground at the same time. He also theorizes about inertia—the idea that objects will keep going or stay still unless a force is acting on them.

c. 250 BCE

Eureka!

Greek mathematician Archimedes (287–212 BCE) has a "Eureka!" ("I've found it!") moment while in the bathtub. Water spills out as he climbs in, leading him to formulate the principle of buoyancy, which explains why objects float in water.

Falling objects
Objects made from the same material are pulled down by gravity at the same rate.

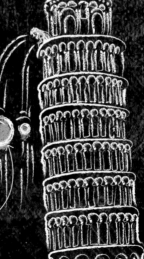

Gravitational waves

First predicted by Einstein, gravitational waves are detected in space. These tiny ripples reveal information about the Universe, including black holes and the Big Bang.

2015

Electromagnetism

Scottish scientist James Clerk Maxwell (1831–1879) realizes that electricity and magnetism are not separate phenomena, but a single force, and that light is a type of electromagnetic radiation. His work leads to the discovery of radio waves, which are used in many types of technology.

1861

1895

The "God particle"

The particle that gives all matter its mass is discovered by scientists. The Higgs boson, nicknamed the "God particle," advances unified field theory, which aims to explain particles and forces.

Electric experiment

During a thunderstorm, American politician and experimenter Benjamin Franklin (1706–1790) flies a kite attached to a metal key. When a lightning strike causes sparks to fly from the key, it proves that lightning is a type of electricity.

X-ray invention

German physicist Wilhelm Röntgen (1845–1923) produces the first X-ray after discovering electromagnetic radiation can penetrate solid objects. X-rays revolutionize medical science, allowing doctors to see inside living bodies.

2012

Schrödinger's Cat

As part of a theoretical experiment, Austrian physicist Erwin Schrödinger (1887–1961) imagines a cat inside a box with radioactive material. As the cat can't be seen, it could be alive or dead, or both. Similarly, scientists can't know what a particle is doing until they observe it.

1752

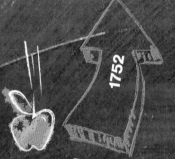

New elements
Polonium was named after Poland, where Marie Curie was born.

84
Po
Polonium
(209)

88
Ra
Radium
(226)

1898

Radioactive elements

Pierre and Marie Curie discover the radioactive elements polonium and radium. Radioactive elements are very unstable, as their atoms can split apart all by themselves. When an atom splits, it gives off radioactivity, either as tiny chunks of particle or waves of energy.

1935

Newton's gravity

English physicist Isaac Newton (1643–1727) publishes his landmark work *Principia Mathematica*, in which he explores motion and explains how the force of gravity holds the Universe together.

Latin origins
Radium is the Latin word for "ray."

Famous equation
Einstein realized that you can calculate the energy an object produces if you multiply its mass by the speed of light.

$$E = mc^2$$

1905

Space and time

German scientist Albert Einstein (1879–1955) proposes that gravity exists because heavy objects bend space and time. Imagine placing Earth onto a sheet of stretchy rubber, making it dip in the middle. When the Moon rolls past, it gets stuck circling Earth and can't climb out of the dip.

Expanding Universe

Belgian physics professor Georges Lemaître (1894–1966) proposes his theory that the Universe is expanding and later suggests that the Universe began with an explosion, the so-called Big Bang.

1687

1927

Cars

Wheels first got vehicles moving in about 3500 BCE, allowing horse-drawn carts to carry heavy loads. But it took more than 5,000 years for the first horseless carriages to hit the road. The real breakthrough was the invention of the internal combustion engine, which allowed cars to run on gas. Mass production followed, forever changing the way we travel.

Steam machine

French engineer Nicolas-Joseph Cugnot builds the first automobile, a three-wheeled cart powered by steam from a wood burner at the front. It can reach speeds of 2 mph (3 kph) and has to be refilled with wood every 15 minutes.

1769

Traffic lights

The first electric traffic lights are installed in Cleveland, Ohio, with red and green indicating stop and go.

Assembly line

Ford introduces a moving assembly line to his factories, using a conveyor belt to haul parts past teams of workers. A Model T can now be assembled in 90 minutes. By 1927, 15 million will have been sold.

Tin Lizzie

American businessman Henry Ford starts the Ford Motor Company. He sells 1,700 cars in the first year. Five years later, the Model-T, nicknamed Tin Lizzie, is produced at Ford's factory in Detroit and becomes the world's first affordable car.

1914   **1913**   **1903**

First diesel car

The German car manufacturer Mercedes-Benz brings the first diesel passenger car to the market. The 260-D model is displayed at an automobile show in Berlin and soon has a year-long waiting list of buyers.

Seatbelt safety

The modern seatbelt is introduced by Swedish manufacturer Volvo. In the interest of safety, Volvo makes the patent open so that all car manufacturers can use it.

Robot workers

The first industrial robot is used in car construction. Unimate is a robotic arm that welds parts and stacks metal on the production line at US car giant General Motors.

1936   **1959**   **1961**

Combustion engine

Swiss inventor Francois Isaac de Rivaz devises an engine that uses an explosion of hydrogen inside a cylinder to push a piston out. He uses the engine to drive a carriage a short distance. It is the world's first automobile driven by an internal combustion engine.

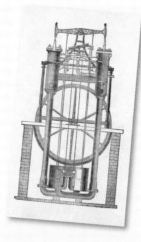

Explosive design

English engineer Samuel Brown patents an internal combustion engine fueled by hydrogen. He mounts the engine on a cart and drives it up a hill in Greenwich, London, in front of a watching crowd.

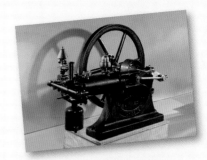

Four-step cycle

German engineer Nikolaus Otto invents the four-stroke engine, an internal combustion engine that cycles through four steps: sucking in fuel; compressing it; burning it; and expelling it.

1807   **1823**   **1876**

Inflatable tires

Scottish inventor John Boyd Dunlop invents pneumatic (inflatable) rubber tires for his 10-year-old son's tricycle. Inflatable tires are later adapted for automobiles and become a huge success.

First road trip

German engineer Karl Benz masterminds the Motorwagen, the first commercial gas-powered automobile. In 1888, his wife, Bertha, takes it on the world's first long-distance automobile journey, acting as both driver and mechanic.

Speed demon

The first speeding ticket is given in England to Walter Arnold for driving at 8 mph (13 kph)—more than four times the speed limit of 2 mph (3 kph).

1896   **1888**   **1885**

Driverless cars

Nevada becomes the first US state to allow driverless cars to be tested on public roads. Driverless cars use a computer assisted by a GPS unit, laser sensors, cameras, and other devices to find their way without human intervention.

Sporty numbers

Italian car manufacturer Lamborghini is established by Ferruccio Lamborghini. Luxury sports cars become popular on both sides of the Atlantic, but only a small number of people can afford them.

Hybrid cars

The Toyota Prius—one of the earliest and most successful hybrid cars—goes on sale. It is powered by both a gas engine and an electric motor, improving efficiency and reducing toxic emissions. Within the next decade, more than one million hybrid cars will be sold.

1963   **1997**   **2011**

Great adventures

The 20th century saw a burst of daring feats and great adventures, as pioneering explorers pushed against the limits of human capabilities. Although scientific and technological advances helped to make these endeavors possible, their ultimate success was due to the inspiring courage and resilience of extraordinary men and women.

Lift off
American Orville Wright flies the first powered plane, which he designed with his brother Wilbur Wright. The fabric-covered aircraft looks like a box kite with propellers. It flies for just 12 seconds, 20 ft (6 m) above a beach in North Carolina.

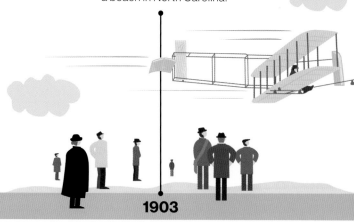

1903

Everest conquered
Edmund Hillary from New Zealand and Tenzing Norgay from Nepal successfully climb Mount Everest, the world's highest mountain, for the first time. It is a dangerous and grueling mission to reach the top of the world.

1953

Mysterious disappearance
Amelia Earhart takes off from Oakland Airport, California, on the first leg of her journey to become the first woman to circumnavigate the globe. En route, she goes missing, and the mystery surrounding her disappearance becomes legend.

1937

Pioneering flight
American Charles Lindbergh flies solo across the Atlantic Ocean nonstop in his plane the *Spirit of St. Louis*. Traveling for almost 34 hours, from New York to Paris, his achievement makes him famous around the world.

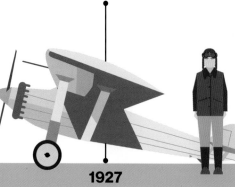

1927

Deep down
Jacques Piccard from Switzerland and Don Walsh from the US, in their submarine *Trieste*, are the first humans to reach Challenger Deep, the oceans' deepest-known point. Their 6.8-mile (11-km) descent into the Mariana Trench in the western Pacific Ocean takes almost five hours. They spend just 20 minutes on the ocean floor.

1960

The Flying Housewife
American Geraldine "Jerrie" Mock, famous for her pearls and hairstyle, becomes the first woman to fly solo around the world. The flight takes 29 days with 21 stopovers.

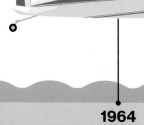

1964

Historic swim
At the age of 64, endurance swimmer Diana Nyad becomes the first person to swim the 60 mile (96.5 km) distance from the Bahamas to Florida, encountering crocodiles, jellyfish, and sharks along the way.

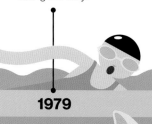

1979

Finding the way

Sailing in a small fishing boat, famous Norwegian explorer Roald Amundsen and his crew find a way through the Northwest Passage, the waterway that links the Arctic and Pacific Oceans.

1903–1906

Claiming the North Pole

American Robert E. Peary and his team claim to be the first people to reach the North Pole. Later, experts argue that Peary missed the pole by about 30 miles (48 km), but it remains an incredible story of courage.

1908–1909

Into the jungle

British geographer Colonel Percy Fawcett disappears in Brazil while looking for a lost city that he calls "Z." The unsolved mystery of his disappearance makes international headlines.

1925

Endurance

British explorer Ernest Shackleton, in his ship *Endurance*, aims to cross Antarctica via the South Pole. Disaster strikes when *Endurance* gets stuck in ice. The crew survives thanks to Shackleton's extraordinary leadership skills.

1914–1917

Race to the South Pole

Five years after navigating the Northwest Passage, Roald Amundsen sets off on a race against Britain's Robert F. Scott to reach the South Pole. Amundsen gets there first and Scott dies on the harrowing journey home.

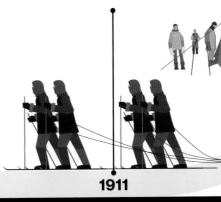

1911

Walking the Amazon

British explorer Ed Stafford walks the length of the Amazon River, 6,000 miles (9,656 km) in total from its source to the ocean. The journey takes him two and a half years.

2010

The highest jump

American Alan Eustace travels to the edge of space in a balloon. He detaches himself from the balloon and plummets to earth, opening his parachute shortly before landing. His descent to Earth is faster than the speed of sound and takes 15 minutes.

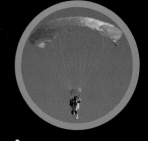

2014

THE VOYAGE OF R.M.S. *TITANIC*

The "unsinkable" sinks

On April 10, 1912, the colossal steamship R.M.S. *Titanic* set sail on its maiden voyage from Southampton, England. With around 2,200 passengers and crew on board, the world's biggest ship cut through the waters of the Atlantic Ocean, heading for New York City. The journey was expected to take seven days, but the *Titanic*, which had been proclaimed "unsinkable," was unknowingly sailing toward a catastrophic finale.

Harboring bad omens

At the beginning of **April 1912**, before R.M.S. *Titanic*'s scheduled departure for its first ever voyage, the crew reports a fire in a coal bunker below deck. Unable to put out the blaze, and after the *Titanic* is judged seaworthy, the crew is ordered to control the flames until the ship reaches New York. On **April 10**, as the *Titanic* leaves Southampton, suction created by the power of the propellers causes the mooring chains of the docked S.S. *City of New York* to break. It drifts into a collision course with the *Titanic*. The quick thinking of Captain Smith and the use of several tugboats help prevent a disastrous departure.

Icy warnings

The *Titanic* makes good time across the Atlantic Ocean. On **April 12**, the crew receives the first ice warning from R.M.S. *Empress of Britain*. More warnings then come through in the evening from the French ship, S.S. *la Touraine*. Two days later, on **April 14**, more iceberg warnings are received. At **11:00 a.m.**, Captain Smith cancels the first scheduled lifeboat drill. At **2:00 p.m.**, he tells the managing director of White Star Line, the owner of the *Titanic*, Joseph Bruce Ismay, who is on board for the celebratory maiden voyage, about the ice warnings.

A moonless night

On the evening of **April 14**, the temperature drops close to freezing. More warnings come in, but Captain Smith is dining with the passengers, so doesn't receive the news until later. At **11:00 p.m.**, a final warning comes in from the S.S. *Californian*, informing the *Titanic* crew it has decided to stop sailing for the evening due to the ice. The message is ignored by the operator, who is busy transmitting passenger messages to shore. At **11:40 p.m.**, on a moonless, calm night, the lookout fails to spot an iceberg until it is only 1,000 yds (900 m) away. First Officer William Murdoch orders the engines into reverse and the

Titanic steers sharply to avoid collision. Traveling at 23 mph (40 kph), the *Titanic* strikes the iceberg, which tears through the starboard (right) side of its hull, destroying five watertight compartments.

Women and children first

Just **before midnight** on **April 14**, Captain Smith and the ship's designer, Thomas Andrews, investigate the damage. Andrews predicts the unimaginable—the *Titanic* will sink in a couple of hours. **At midnight**, Titanic's first distress call is missed by the S.S. *Californian*, which is only 5 miles (8 km) away. At **12:20 a.m.** on **April 15**, Captain Smith orders use of the lifeboats. The *Titanic* is fitted with 20 lifeboats, which altogether only have room for around 1,200 people, so the crew prioritizes evacuating women and children. Five minutes later, R.M.S. *Carpathia* responds to the distress call, but it is 67 miles (107 km) away. In the chaos of the evacuation, the lifeboats launch with only 705 on board. At **2:20 a.m.**, the "unsinkable" *Titanic* sinks below the icy waters, with more than 1,500 passengers and crew following it to a watery grave.

Rescue and relief

At **4:10 a.m.**, the *Carpathia* arrives and at around **8:00 a.m.**, with all 705 survivors on board, it sets sail for New York, arriving three days later on **April 18**. Survivors disembark amid crowds of eagerly awaiting family, friends, and photographers who followed the story that shook the world.

Lessons learned

After several months of news reports, theories, and an official inquiry, the disaster is deemed an accident. The high speed that the colossal steamship was traveling at is judged as "standard practice," removing blame from Captain Smith and his crew. After the inquiry, it is recommended that on future voyages, the number of places on board lifeboats should match the number of passengers on board.

> **"There is no danger that *Titanic* will sink. The boat is unsinkable."**
>
> **Phillip Franklin,**
> White Star Line vice-president

THE MODERN WORLD

After 1914

The Modern World

In the first half of the 20th century, tensions between international powers exploded into two world wars. European nations were weakened by the cost and destruction of these conflicts, and lost control of their overseas empires. In the late 20th century, new rivalries sparked new conflicts. At the same time, technology leapt forward. Humans ventured into space, while the invention of computers led to a digital age that continues in the 21st century.

1924
Joseph Stalin becomes leader of the ruling Communist Party in the Soviet Union.

1933
Adolf Hitler comes to power in Germany.

1936–1939
Spain descends into civil war between the government and nationalists led by General Franco.

1945
The US drops atomic bombs on the Japanese cities of Hiroshima and Nagasaki, ending World War II.

1948
The United Nations creates the nation of Israel in Palestine as a homeland for the Jews.

1914–1918
War between the powers of Europe spreads to become World War I.

1929
The crash of the US stock market on Wall Street leads to the Great Depression.

1939
World War II breaks out when Hitler invades Poland.

1941
The Japanese attack on Pearl Harbor brings the US into World War II.

1948
The Soviet Union blocks transportation links to West Berlin, starting the Cold War.

1949
Mao Zedong proclaims the communist People's Republic of China.

World War I
Beginning in Europe, World War I (see pages 248–249) quickly spread to colonies around the world. The war cost the lives of 20 million people.

The Soviet Union
A communist revolution in Russia transformed the country into the Soviet Union (see pages 254–255). Under Joseph Stalin, its people faced great hardships.

World War II
When Adolf Hitler of Germany invaded Poland, World War II (see pages 258–267) engulfed the globe. Fifty million people died as a result of the war.

Decolonization
After World War II, many colonies in Africa and Asia successfully fought for independence from Europe (see pages 268–269).

The Difference Engine

As early as the 19th century, English mathematician and inventor Charles Babbage had designed a machine to perform complicated mathematical computations. But it wasn't until the late 20th century that the age of computers really got underway. Babbage was never able to construct a finished machine—the one shown here was made in the 1980s from his original designs for the Difference Engine #2.

1950
North Korea invades South Korea, starting the Korean War.

1955
African-American Rosa Parks refuses to give up her seat on a bus for a white man, igniting the US Civil Rights Movement.

1964
The US formally enters the Vietnam War on the side of the South.

1962
The Cold War threatens to get hot when the Soviet Union and the US clash over Soviet missiles installed in Cuba.

1989
English engineer Tim Berners-Lee creates the World Wide Web.

1989
The fall of the Berlin Wall marks the start of the collapse of the Soviet Union.

1994
Nelson Mandela is elected the first black president of South Africa.

2004
A tsunami (tidal wave) devastates Southeast Asia.

2001
Terrorist attacks on sites in the US lead to the start of the "War on Terror."

2017
President Robert Mugabe of Zimbabwe is forced to resign.

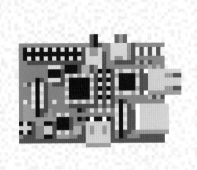

The Middle East

The interference of the West in the affairs of the Middle East (see pages 272–273) led to decades of conflict in the region. It remains unresolved to this day.

The Cold War

The US and the Soviet Union were on different sides of a "Cold War" (see pages 282–283) that was played out in other nations around the world.

Civil Rights

More than a century after the end of slavery in the US, African-Americans sought legal equality through the Civil Rights Movement (see pages 290–291).

The digital age

The development of computers, the internet, and smartphones (see pages 298–299) has led to a digital age where information is readily available.

World War I

At the turn of the 20th century in Europe, nations competed for land and power, with each country forming both military alliances and hostile rivalries. The stage was set for war. Between 1914 and 1918, Russia, France, and Britain fought against Austria-Hungary and Germany, with both sides using devastating new weaponry and tactics. World War I became one of the bloodiest conflicts in history.

Gallipoli Campaign
British, French, Australian, and New Zealand troops mount a huge attack on the Gallipoli Peninsula hoping to capture Turkey, but the plan is a failure. Two hundred thousand Allied troops are killed or wounded.

Western Front
The German advance across western Europe is halted by Allied troops. Both sides dig trenches, which form the Western Front, a line that eventually stretches from the Swiss border to the North Sea, 400 miles (645 km).

War erupts
Austria-Hungary blames Serbia for the Archduke's assassination and declares war. Russia sends troops to defend Serbia, leading Germany to declare war on Russia. Country after country rushes to defend their allies and declare war on their rivals.

War in the skies
World War I is the first major war during which aircraft are used. From early 1915, planes are used for reconnaissance and taking photographs. They are later deployed to drop bombs and fight against one another in the skies.

BEFORE
In 1882, Germany, Italy, and Austria-Hungary sign a Triple Alliance. Germany's rising power alarms Britain and Russia. In 1907, Britain joins a Triple Entente with Russia and France.

September 1914

January 1915

April 25, 1915– January 9, 1916

1 August 1914

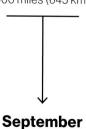

June 28, 1914

August 26– 30, 1914

December 25, 1914

April 22, 1915

Assassination
The heir to the Austro-Hungarian throne, Archduke Franz Ferdinand, is assassinated on a visit to Sarajevo, Bosnia. The killer, Gavrilo Princip, is a nationalist who believes that Bosnia should be part of Serbia, not Austria-Hungary.

Battle of Tannenberg
On the Eastern Front (Central and Eastern Europe), the Russian army invades Germany, but they suffer a crushing defeat. The Russian commander commits suicide and the army never really recovers.

The Christmas Truce
By the end of 1914, both sides on the Western Front have reached a stalemate. A spontaneous truce is called at Christmas. Soldiers enter "No Man's Land" between the trenches to play soccer, sing carols, and swap simple gifts.

Poison gas
The German army unleashes a new weapon—poisonous chlorine gas. The first attack takes place near the Belgian city of Ypres. Five thousand soldiers die as gas seeps into the trenches, and 10,000 are injured.

Battle of Jutland

The only naval battle of the war is fought off the Jutland Peninsula in Denmark between the British and German navies. There are heavy losses on both sides. The German navy withdraws for the duration of the war.

U-boats

Germany announces it will use U-boats (submarines), to fire torpedoes at unarmed British merchant ships carrying vital supplies of food and ammunition.

Passchendaele

After relentless heavy rainfall, this four-month battle campaign near Ypres sees 600,000 casualties. The Allies gain only 5 miles (8 km) of land. The battle is remembered for the horrendous conditions and terrible death toll.

Peace

With US troops now helping the Allies, the Germans are overwhelmed. Both sides agree to end the war. The fighting stops officially on the 11th hour of the 11th month. Red poppies go on to be symbols of the tragic waste of World War I.

May 31–June 1, 1916

January 31, 1917

July 31– November 6, 1917

November 11, 1918

February 21– December 16, 1916

July 1– November 18, 1916

April 6, 1917

March 21, 1918

AFTER

World War I costs the lives of almost 10 million military personnel and six million civilians. The Treaty of Versailles, signed in 1919, ends the Austro-Hungarian and Turkish Empires. It also leaves Germany humiliated and angry. Despite all leaders promising peace, by 1939 the world is at war again.

USA joins the war

America has stayed neutral, but the German sinking of the passenger liner *Lusitania* on May 7, 1915, killing Americans on board, changes public opinion. When America discovers that Germany is urging Mexico to start a war with them, America joins the Allies.

Battle of Verdun

The war in France is at a stalemate. The Germans plan a major offensive in the French city of Verdun. More than 700,000 men lose their lives in the ensuing battle, which is the longest of the war.

Battle of the Somme

Tanks are used, and British soldiers climb out of their trenches toward the German line in a "big push." They are met with unrelenting artillery fire. More than 19,000 British troops die on the opening day.

The Spring Offensive

After Russia surrenders, Germany focuses on a series of huge attacks against the Allied forces, which now include US soldiers. The Germans hope to achieve a quick victory, but fail in their attempted "knockout blow."

The 1920s

After the horrors of World War I, the Roaring Twenties proved to be a more carefree and hopeful time, especially in the US. An economic boom there meant people had money to enjoy the finer things in life—from cars to culture. Music, writing, and fashion all buzzed with new ideas, and the powerful artistic medium of film began.

1920 Prohibition
Alcohol is prohibited in the US. Criminal gangs grow rich by illegally making and selling their own alcohol and running bars called speakeasies. The ban on alcohol will be lifted in 1933.

1923 The Charleston
The Charleston (see page 172)—named after a song composed in 1923—is the dance of the era. The dance is deemed indecent, which makes young people love it even more!

1926 Birth of television
The Scottish inventor John Logie Baird demonstrates the first television images to scientists in London. Television is born.

1927 *The Jazz Singer*
The first film to feature synchronized sound is *The Jazz Singer*. The film is a hit, and signals the beginning of the end of the silent era of movies.

1929 Academy Awards
The Academy of Motion Picture Arts and Sciences (AMPAS) hand out the first awards (soon to be called "Oscars") in a small ceremony in Hollywood, California.

1922 The Jazz Age
Originating with African-Americans in New Orleans, jazz music really takes off, so much so that the 1920s become known as the Jazz Age. Jazz music features strong rhythms and improvisation.

1925 Boom!
Factories that had increased production for World War I switch to making consumer goods. People buy cars and luxury items on credit (paying for the item in installments). The economy experiences a boom as a result.

1927 Ford Model T
The last Model T cars roll out of the Ford Motor Company's factories. 16.5 million units were sold worldwide. Its success is down to mass production and the economic boom.

1929 The Wall Street Crash
Billions of dollars are wiped off the value of the American stock market on Wall Street, as the economic boom turned into a bust. The Wall Street Crash will prove to be the biggest economic catastrophe in US history.

Flappers

The flapper craze takes Western fashion for women by storm. Flappers wear shorter skirts, bob their hair, and listen to jazz—all things that are seen as rebellious by older generations.

The 1930s

The Wall Street Crash spelled the end of the Roaring Twenties. The 1930s were to prove a decade of hardship and conflict like no other before, with dire consequences for almost every part of the world. There were some positive aspects, however. The "New Deal" got the US economy back on track, and comic books entertained people all over the world.

1930 Great Depression
The Wall Street Crash causes American businesses to stop investing and importing things from Europe. This loss of business triggers the worldwide Great Depression. Millions lose their jobs, homes, and ability to pay for basic things, such as food. Europe in particular is hit hard.

1931 Crisis in Europe
Germany and Austria's economies are thrown into chaos. Austria's largest commercial bank collapses in May, and this triggers a financial panic throughout Europe. In Germany, people burn worthless banknotes for warmth.

1932 Hoovervilles
More than two million Americans are homeless, and 25 percent are out of work. Slums—mockingly called "Hoovervilles" after President Herbert Hoover, who fails to help—start popping up.

1933 Hitler and fascism
Adolf Hitler comes to power in Germany with promises to fix the country's economic woes. Hitler and his Nazi party are fascists: an extreme right-wing ideology that emphasizes nationalism and has contempt for democracy and minorities.

1933 New Deal
Franklin D. Roosevelt becomes US president, and promises a "New Deal" for the American people. This includes jobs and a huge social welfare package to help ease the Great Depression.

1934 Dust Bowl
Years of severe drought across the prairies of the US and Canada cause winds to whip up the light, dry soil into dust storms, destroying agriculture and worsening the problems of the Great Depression.

1936 Spanish Civil War
Spanish nationalists, led by General Francisco Franco, rebel. Pro-government supporters unite against the nationalists, and a civil war breaks out. It will last for three years before the nationalists win.

1938 Superheroes rise!
The "Golden Age of Comic Books" begins when superheroes such as Superman and Wonder Woman appear for the first time.

1939 World War II
World War II begins when Hitler invades Poland, forcing Britain and France to declare war on Germany.

Lining up for food

The economic crash leaves millions without homes, jobs, or both, and forces many to rely on charity to survive. Long lines gather at bakeries and soup kitchens in order to receive free food. Many dress professionally to give the impression to neighbors that they are off to work for the day.

Archaeology

Archaeology is the study of the past through the objects, buildings, and human remains left by those who have lived before us. Around the world, archaeologists have uncovered entire buried towns, discovered the existence of long forgotten civilizations, and unearthed spectacular treasures. Their findings have revealed fascinating details, not just about the lives of past kings and queens, but of everyday people, too.

Uncovering Pompeii

In Italy, workers begin digging at Pompeii, a town buried under a volcanic eruption in 79 CE. Their aim is to find works of art. Later, Pompeii's streets, shops, houses, and temples are revealed, as well as the empty spaces left by the decayed corpses of those buried in ash during the eruption.

1748

1797

Decoding hieroglyphics

Jean-François Champollion uses the Rosetta Stone, discovered in Egypt in 1799, to decipher Egyptian hieroglyphics. The stone has the same inscription in Greek, hieroglyphics, and demotic (an everyday Egyptian script).

1822

Layers of history

Historian John Frere uses stratigraphy for the first time to describe a Stone Age site at Hoxne in Suffolk, UK. Stratigraphy, the study of layers, is based on the idea that the lowest layers are the oldest.

The city of Uruk

William Loftus discovers and excavates the Sumerian city of Uruk in modern-day southern Iraq. Uruk, founded in around 4500 BCE, is the world's oldest city.

Assyrian treasures

In modern-day Iraq, Henry Layard discovers and excavates the Assyrian palaces of Nimrud and Nineveh. He finds statues of gods that have human heads, bird wings, and the bodies of lions or bulls.

Three-age system

Danish historian Christian Thomsen divides prehistory into the Stone, Bronze, and Iron Ages, based on human tool use. He reasons that the earliest tools used by humans were initially made of stone, then bronze, and later, iron.

1836

1849–1854

1845–1851

Royal tombs

Seeking to find the truth behind the Greek legends of the Trojan War, German Heinrich Schliemann excavates Troy, Mycenae, and Tiryns. In the royal tombs of Mycenae, he discovers beautiful gold masks.

1871–1890

The Gokstad ship

Norwegian historian Nicolay Nicolayson excavates the 9th century Gokstad ship burial. The ship is 76 ft (23 m) long and perfectly preserved. It holds the body of a Viking ruler.

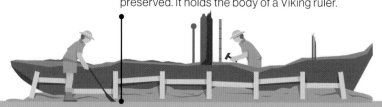

1880

The Terracotta Army

Chinese archaeologists begin excavating pits holding an army of 7,000 life-size terracotta warriors. They were buried in 210 BCE to protect the tomb of China's First Emperor.

1974

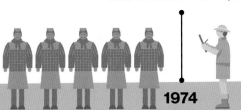

Tollund Man

Two brothers cutting turf at Tollund in Denmark discover the perfectly preserved body of a man, who died 2,000 years ago. His stomach held his last meal, a gruel of barley and chamomile.

1950

Inscribed bones

The Chinese archaeologist Li Ji excavates Anyang, capital of the Shang Dynasty, which ruled northern China from 1600–1046 BCE. He finds many thousands of animal bones, inscribed with the earliest known Chinese writing.

1928–1937

King Pacal's tomb

In Palenque, Mexico, Alberto Ruz Lhuillier digs beneath a Mayan pyramid temple and discovers the tomb of King Pacal (ruled 615–683). Pacal's skeleton was found wearing a beautiful jade mosaic mask.

1948–1952

The Indus civilization

In India, John Marshall excavates the cities of Harappa and Mohenjo-Daro. He reveals the existence of the forgotten Indus, or Harappan, civilization, which flourished here from 2500–1800 BCE.

1921–1922

Tombs of Ur

Leonard Woolley excavates the Sumerian royal tombs at Ur, dating from c.2750–2400 BCE. Among the treasures is a golden and lapis lazuli (a semiprecious blue stone) statue of a goat.

1927

Machu Picchu

In the Andes of Peru, Hiram Bingham finds the lost Inca citadel (fortress) of Machu Picchu. Built on a mountain ridge 7,970 ft (2,430 m) above sea level, Machu Picchu was abandoned in the 16th century.

1911

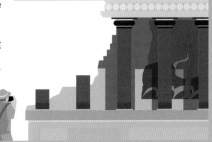

Pharaoh's tomb

Howard Carter discovers the tomb of Pharaoh Tutankhamun, the only unrobbed Egyptian royal burial ever found. The king was buried in 1327 BCE wearing a solid gold mask, inlaid with blue glass.

1922

Sequence dating

In Egypt, Flinders Petrie develops sequence dating. By documenting changing styles of pottery from the cemetery at Naqada, he is able to work out the dates of those graves.

1880–1901

The Minoan Civilization

Arthur Evans excavates the Palace of Knossos in Crete, Greece, revealing a previously unknown Bronze Age civilization, at its height from 2000–1500 BCE. He calls it Minoan, after Minos, the legendary king of Crete.

1900–1905

The Soviet Union

In the early 20th century, Russia transformed—its monarchy ended, and there were two revolutions and a civil war. Reborn as the Soviet Union (or the USSR), it became the world's first communist state, believing that the government should take control of resources such as land and farms and share wealth created by these resources among the people. From the 1940s, the Soviet Union occupied many countries in Europe, forcing them to become communist, too.

Start of the Cold War

The UK, US, and French zones of Germany unite into a new country, West Germany, and East Germany remains Soviet. The USSR cuts off transportation links to West Berlin to threaten West Germany. The West drops supplies into West Berlin by air, beginning the Cold War conflict between East and West.

1948–1949

The Great Terror

Stalin gets rid of any Communist Party members, army leaders, or peasants who might oppose him. Around 20 million Soviets are sent to gulags (labor camps), and thousands die.

1936–1938

1939

World War II

The USSR and Germany sign a pact and invade Poland, starting World War II. Soon, however, Germany turns on the USSR. Battles ensue between the two sides, but ultimately the Nazis in Germany are defeated. Germany and its capital, Berlin, are divided into four zones, each placed under control of the UK, the US, France, or the USSR.

Great Famine

Collective farms prove a failure. Grain is taken from the countryside to feed people in the cities, and the peasants starve. It leads to a devastating famine in which up to 8 million people die, many in Ukraine.

1932

Five-year Plan

To industrialize the country, Stalin plans to increase coal, metal, and oil production over 5 years. Land is taken from peasants (kulaks) and combined into huge collective farms.

1928–1932

The rise of Stalin

When Russia's communist leader Vladimir Lenin dies, Joseph Stalin takes over. Stalin has risen to power by murdering his rivals and putting his supporters in powerful positions.

1924

From czar to USSR

From the 19th century, Russians began to demand a better way of life. Huge famine led to multiple revolutions, in which the czar (emperor) lost power. The Bolsheviks, a communist political party, seized power. In the wake of this political upheaval, the Soviet Union was formed in 1922.

March 1917
Further mass protests force the czar to abdicate.

1918
The Bolsheviks execute anyone disloyal to them. They become the Russian Communist Party.

1905
Czar Nicholas II gives his people an elected government.

November 1917
The Bolsheviks, led by Vladimir Lenin, seize power.

1922
The Russian Communist Party founds the Soviet Union.

Stalin dies

Stalin dies after a stroke. He was a ruthless dictator, responsible for millions of deaths, yet he made the Soviet Union very powerful across Central and Eastern Europe.

1953

Glasnost and perestroika

Leader Mikhail Gorbachev introduces policies of openness, or *glasnost,* and restructuring, known as *perestroika.* This encourages warmer relations with the West.

1970s

1985

Economic stagnation

Under leader Leonid Brezhnev, the economy stops growing. There is widespread corruption, little to buy in stores, and poor living conditions. This damages the public's faith in the government.

Revolutions of 1989

Soviet-imposed communist governments are toppled in Central and Eastern Europe, beginning in Poland, as people seek independence from Soviet rule.

1989

The fall of the Berlin Wall

The Berlin Wall, built to divide West Berlin from East Germany, is broken down on one momentous night, marking the end of communist rule in Europe.

1989

The fall of the Soviet Union

Boris Yeltsin becomes the first popularly elected president of Russia and bans the Soviet Communist Party. The Soviet Union is disbanded.

1991

The story of skyscrapers

From the very first high-rises in the 19th century to the super-tall glass towers of today, skyscrapers have become powerful symbols of modern life. They continue to reach greater heights, made possible by exciting developments in building materials and construction methods. Many of today's architects and engineers are now challenging themselves to design spectacular buildings that are environmentally friendly, too.

"The skyscraper is the point where art and the city meet."

Ada Louise Huxtable,
The Tall Building Artistically Reconsidered, 1984

Dynamic Tower

In the United Arab Emirates, construction of the Dynamic Tower starts in 2020. With wind turbines between each pair of floors, the building will be able to produce all of its own energy. Each floor will rotate independently, giving occupants constantly changing views.

Jeddah Tower

This skyscraper in Saudi Arabia is scheduled to open in 2020. It will be the first building in the world to reach more than 3,200 ft (1 km).

Shanghai Tower

Topping out in 2013, this twisting tower in China is 2,073 ft (632 m) tall. Its elevators are the fastest in the world, traveling at speeds of 45.9 mph (74 kph). The building also captures rainwater to be used in its air conditioning and heating systems.

Burj Khalifa

In 2010, the Burj Khalifa opens in Dubai. Standing at 2,717 ft (828 m) tall, it can be seen from 60 miles (100 km) away. In response to the attack on the World Trade Center, the Burj Khalifa is designed with refuge areas on each floor, to provide protection in case of fire.

Twin Towers

Engineers learn more about the effect of wind on tall, solid structures, making it possible for buildings they design to reach greater heights. In New York in 1971, the Twin Towers of the World Trade Center, symbols of the city's wealth and power, are completed. In 2001, both collapse after terrorists fly planes into them.

Petronas Towers

Construction on these twin skyscrapers in Kuala Lumpur, Malaysia, finishes in 1998. They are 1,483 ft (452 m) high and connected by a skybridge. The designers were influenced by Islamic art.

Empire State Building

This high-rise, opened in 1931, is a symbol of hope for New York during a period of economic turmoil, offering employment to those without work. At 102 stories high, for 40 years, it is the world's tallest building.

Chrysler Building

American businesses compete to build the tallest company headquarters in New York. Racing against the Bank of Manhattan, car manufacturer Chrysler hoists a stainless-steel spire to the top of its building in 1930, making it 1,046 ft (318 m) high.

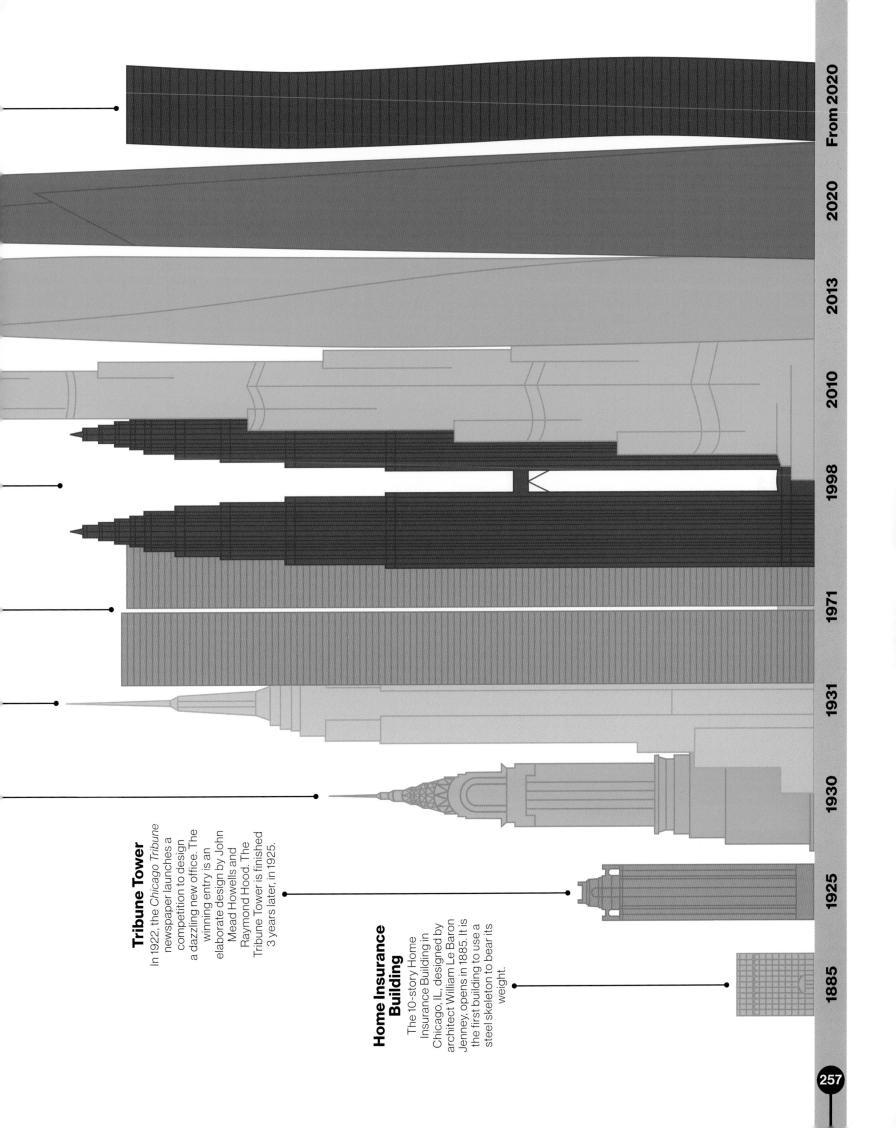

Tribune Tower

In 1922, the *Chicago Tribune* newspaper launches a competition to design a dazzling new office. The winning entry is an elaborate design by John Mead Howells and Raymond Hood. The Tribune Tower is finished 3 years later, in 1925.

Home Insurance Building

The 10-story Home Insurance Building in Chicago, IL, designed by architect William Le Baron Jenney, opens in 1885. It is the first building to use a steel skeleton to bear its weight.

From 2020

2020

2013

2010

1998

1971

1931

1930

1925

1885

257

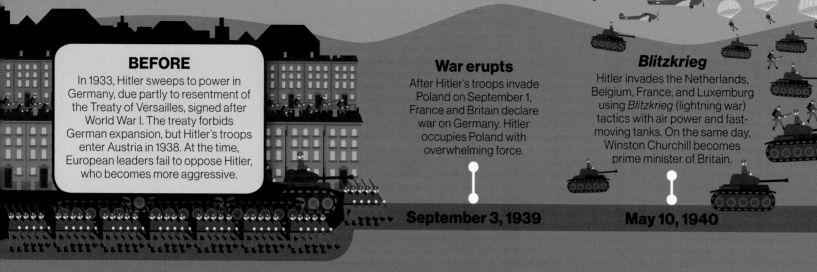

BEFORE

In 1933, Hitler sweeps to power in Germany, due partly to resentment of the Treaty of Versailles, signed after World War I. The treaty forbids German expansion, but Hitler's troops enter Austria in 1938. At the time, European leaders fail to oppose Hitler, who becomes more aggressive.

War erupts

After Hitler's troops invade Poland on September 1, France and Britain declare war on Germany. Hitler occupies Poland with overwhelming force.

September 3, 1939

Blitzkrieg

Hitler invades the Netherlands, Belgium, France, and Luxemburg using *Blitzkrieg* (lightning war) tactics with air power and fast-moving tanks. On the same day, Winston Churchill becomes prime minister of Britain.

May 10, 1940

Battle of the Atlantic

Britain relies on oil, food, and raw materials arriving by sea from America, but German U-boats (submarines) attack and sink supply ships. Allied ships start to sail in escorted convoys (groups).

1940–1941

The Blitz

For almost 40 weeks, Germany targets British towns and cities with nighttime bombing raids, nicknamed the Blitz, to cripple Britain's war effort. People take cover in underground shelters and children are evacuated to areas less at risk of attack.

September 1940– May 1941

World War II in Europe

Fought between 1939 and 1945, World War II was the most costly and destructive war in history—many millions of people were killed and injured. One by one, countries joined the conflict and the world divided into the Axis powers (led by Germany, Italy, and Japan) and the Allies (made up of Britain, France, the Soviet Union, and, later, the USA).

January 22–December 10, 1941   **April 6, 1941**   **June 22, 1941–February 2, 1943**   **November 8, 1942**

Tobruk siege

The Allies take Tobruk in Libya, North Africa, and then resist German attacks in a nine-month siege. This dogged defense prevents any German advance into Egypt.

Invasion of the Balkans

German, Italian, and Bulgarian troops attack Yugoslavia. After terrible losses, Yugoslavia surrenders. The Battle of Greece ends with the fall of Athens on April 27. Hitler now has direct access to the Mediterranean Sea.

Russia invaded

Germany attacks Russia with a huge force, but after almost two years of fighting, Germany is defeated at the Battle of Stalingrad on February 2, 1943 after a bitter winter. The Battle of Stalingrad is a crucial turning point in the war.

Operation Torch

When President Franklin D. Roosevelt brings America into the war, his soldiers help in the successful invasion of North Africa. After seven months of fighting, German and Italian troops are forced to surrender.

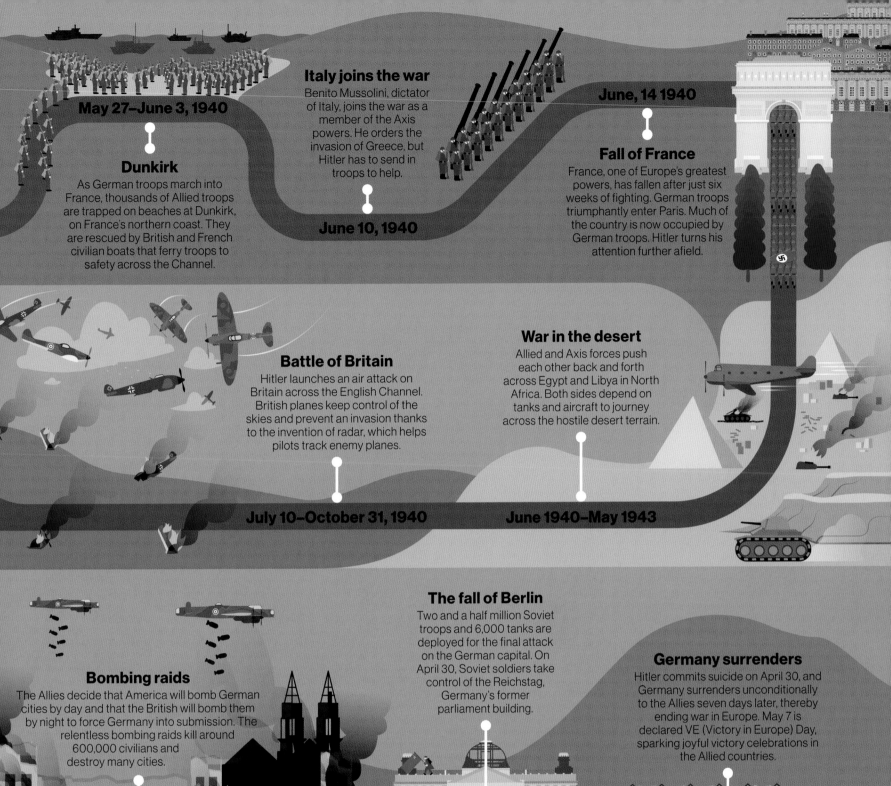

May 27–June 3, 1940

Dunkirk

As German troops march into France, thousands of Allied troops are trapped on beaches at Dunkirk, on France's northern coast. They are rescued by British and French civilian boats that ferry troops to safety across the Channel.

Italy joins the war

Benito Mussolini, dictator of Italy, joins the war as a member of the Axis powers. He orders the invasion of Greece, but Hitler has to send in troops to help.

June 10, 1940

June, 14 1940

Fall of France

France, one of Europe's greatest powers, has fallen after just six weeks of fighting. German troops triumphantly enter Paris. Much of the country is now occupied by German troops. Hitler turns his attention further afield.

Battle of Britain

Hitler launches an air attack on Britain across the English Channel. British planes keep control of the skies and prevent an invasion thanks to the invention of radar, which helps pilots track enemy planes.

July 10–October 31, 1940

War in the desert

Allied and Axis forces push each other back and forth across Egypt and Libya in North Africa. Both sides depend on tanks and aircraft to journey across the hostile desert terrain.

June 1940–May 1943

Bombing raids

The Allies decide that America will bomb German cities by day and that the British will bomb them by night to force Germany into submission. The relentless bombing raids kill around 600,000 civilians and destroy many cities.

June 10, 1943

The fall of Berlin

Two and a half million Soviet troops and 6,000 tanks are deployed for the final attack on the German capital. On April 30, Soviet soldiers take control of the Reichstag, Germany's former parliament building.

June 6, 1944

April 23, 1945

Germany surrenders

Hitler commits suicide on April 30, and Germany surrenders unconditionally to the Allies seven days later, thereby ending war in Europe. May 7 is declared VE (Victory in Europe) Day, sparking joyful victory celebrations in the Allied countries.

May 7, 1945

D-Day

After four years of planning, "Operation Overlord" begins: the Allied invasion of France. Around 150,000 troops land on the French coast, and after six weeks of fighting German forces, they start to push across France, liberating towns and cities from Nazi occupation as they go.

AFTER

At the Potsdam Conference on July 17, 1945, the Allies divide Germany, and Berlin, into controlled zones. The United Nations is created, with the aim of finding peaceful solutions to conflict. Although the war is over, Europe faces an enormous refugee crisis.

BRITAIN PREPARES

June

War is coming

With war looming, air raid shelters are built, blackout curtains are put up, and hospitals get ready to treat the injured. The Women's Land Army (WLA), which played a crucial role during World War I, is re-established to provide extra labor for farms.

Evacuation

September 1

Anticipating Nazi bombing raids, the British government moves almost three million people, mostly children, to rural areas as well as overseas, as part of Operation Pied Piper. In France, the entire population of Strasbourg is evacuated to avoid German bombs.

Gas masks

September

Many people remember the horror of gas attacks during World War I and the bombing of cities by aircraft during the Spanish Civil War (1936–1939). Millions of gas masks are given to British families for protection.

DOING WITHOUT

August

Rationing introduced

Supply shortages mean that all around the world people must adjust to "doing without." Germany introduces food rationing, but Hitler, fearing a drop in public morale, keeps the restrictions to a minimum. In Britain, bacon, butter, and sugar are rationed in January 1940.

War at home

World War II wasn't just fought between soldiers on the battlefield: it involved millions of ordinary civilians, too. Men, women, and children had to adjust to wartime conditions and their daily lives changed dramatically. Food was rationed, children were evacuated, and cities were bombed.

1940

July 3

Shelter from the bombs

UK civilians are thrust into the front line when Germany begins bombing its urban areas. Cardiff is the first city to experience bombing. In London, the first of many air attacks, known as the "Blitz," takes place on September 7. The raids force people to seek cover in air raid shelters and underground rail stations.

September 15

Polish pilots

Polish pilots escape to Britain to fight with the Royal Air Force (RAF). During the Battle of Britain, the Polish pilots fight heroically.

1940

UK UNDER SIEGE

June

Battle of the Atlantic

German U-boats sink three million tons of vital supplies carried by Allied merchant ships traveling from North America to Britain. The country normally imports much of its food, but with ships struggling to make the journey across the Atlantic, the British population is in danger of starvation.

FREE FRANCE

June 18

Launching resistance

After the Nazi occupation of France, Charles de Gaulle, a junior general, flies to London and makes an appeal on the radio for France to resist the Nazi invaders. It is the beginning of "Free France," the exiled government of France.

1941

SOVIET PROPAGANDA

June

When Germany enters the Soviet Union, the Soviets use propaganda to rally the population against the Nazi invaders. Soviet posters urge young men to join the military, encourage workers to produce more for the front, and inspire civilians to carry out acts of sabotage to halt the invasion.

SKIRTED SOLDIERS

December 7

When America enters the war after the Japanese attack on Pearl Harbor, Hawaii, US women are recruited into the military. The step is controversial; many at the time believe this type of work is only suitable for men.

1942

The Final Solution

January 20

The Nazi party wants to destroy the Jewish population of Europe. At a conference in Wannsee, near Berlin, they formalize a plan to transport Jewish people from all over Europe to death camps in Poland, where they will be killed or forced to carry out hard labor.

Dangerous work

At the height of the war, each country depends on keeping its war machine going with ammunition, tanks, guns, and explosives. In munitions factories, women take over the roles of men who have left for the front line. They work as mechanics, welders, engineers, drivers, and machine operators.

1943

German war industry

February

Hitler is forced to introduce "total war measures". Both the economy and the whole of society are mobilized for war production. Germany brings in workers from Nazi-occupied countries to be used as slave labor.

French Resistance

1943–1944

The French movement to undermine their Nazi occupiers reaches its height. Ordinary French people join resistance groups across the country. Resistance fighters spread anti-Nazi propaganda, support stranded Allied pilots, and use sabotage and guerrilla warfare tactics to fight back against Nazi occupation.

1945

Hiroshima and Nagasaki

August 6–9

The US drops the world's first atomic bombs on the Japanese cities of Hiroshima and Nagasaki. 120,000 people are killed instantly. The unprecedented attacks force Japan to surrender, but the bombings have devastating humanitarian consequences.

The Blitz

During the Blitz (September 1940–May 1941), Germany launches 71 nighttime bombing raids on London. Air raid wardens and civilians search for survivors in the wreckage of destroyed buildings.

The Holocaust

From 1933 to 1945, Germany was ruled by the Nazi Party, an anti-Semitic (anti-Jewish) political organization that blamed Jewish people for the country's misfortunes. The Nazis built thousands of concentration camps, where they imprisoned and killed 6 million Jews, and 5 million homosexuals, disabled people, Romanies, and political prisoners.

Anne Frank

Anne Frank was a young Jewish girl living in the Netherlands when World War II broke out. She later died in Bergen-Belsen concentration camp. Her diary survived, though, recording her thoughts and experiences while she was hiding from the Nazi regime. Her writing is a reminder of the constant fear and hardship felt by many who lived under Nazi occupation.

Auschwitz, Poland

Railway tracks lead right up to the entrance to Auschwitz-Birkenau concentration camp. During the Holocaust, more than 1 million people were killed at Auschwitz. Today, the camp is preserved as a memorial.

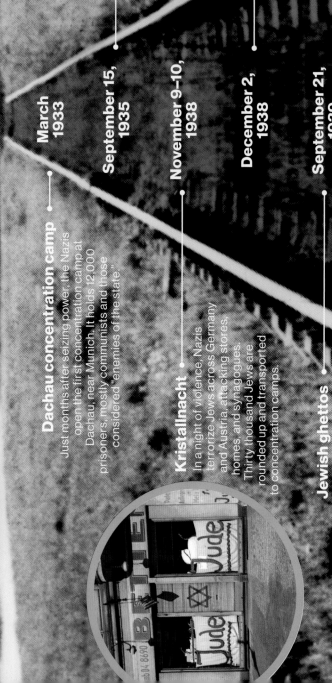

March 1933

Dachau concentration camp

Just months after seizing power, the Nazis open the first concentration camp at Dachau, near Munich. It holds 12,000 prisoners, mostly communists and those considered "enemies of the state."

September 15, 1935

Nuremberg race laws

At its annual rally in Nuremberg, the Nazi Party passes more anti-Semitic laws, that further restrict the rights of Jewish people. The laws mean that Jews lose their citizenship and can no longer marry non-Jews.

November 9–10, 1938

Kristallnacht

In a night of violence, Nazis terrorize Jews across Germany and Austria, attacking stores, homes, and synagogues. Thirty thousand Jews are rounded up and transported to concentration camps.

December 2, 1938

Kindertransport

After Kristallnacht, many Jews try to leave Germany, but some countries refuse to accept them. As part of a rescue effort known as Kindertransport, 10,000 Jewish children escape to Britain, leaving their parents behind.

September 21, 1939

Jewish ghettos

When Nazi troops invade Poland, Polish Jews are forced to move into ghettos, restricted areas controlled by Nazi troops. Food and water are scarce, and living conditions are very cramped.

Auschwitz opens

The first prisoners arrive at Auschwitz concentration camp in Poland. The prisoners, mostly Polish political rebels, are tattooed with numbers in order of their arrival.

June 14, 1940

Star of David

From this date, Jewish people over the age of 6 in Nazi-occupied Europe are gradually made to wear a badge in the shape of the Star of David (a traditional Jewish symbol), so that they can be easily identified.

September 1, 1941

The final solution

High-ranking Nazis meet to discuss the "Final Solution," their plan to exterminate Europe's Jews, who they see as *Untermenschen* (subhumans) and a problem to be solved. They agree to deport all Jews to Poland, where they will be killed in death camps.

January 20, 1942

The death camps

Six "death camps" are established across Nazi-occupied Poland. Jews from all over Europe are rounded up. They are transported by train in appalling conditions to the camps, where they are selected for slave labor or immediate execution.

1942

Gas chambers

The Nazis use increasingly systematic methods to commit mass murder. They release poison gas into sealed shower rooms, which are full of prisoners. The bodies are buried in mass graves or cremated.

February 15, 1942

Liberation

As Allied troops march toward Germany, they liberate the concentration camps from Nazi control. The soldiers are appalled by the death and devastation they find. Prisoners are weak, starving, and sick. After liberation, thousands continue to die from illnesses they caught while imprisoned.

July 1944–May 1945

The Nuremberg Trials

After World War II ends in September 1945, the Allies seek to bring those responsible for the Holocaust to justice. The trials are fully televised, and for the first time, the public learns the horrific extent of Nazi war crimes.

1945–1949

A Jewish homeland

After the horrors of the Holocaust, the international community faces pressure to find land for Jewish survivors to establish a homeland. The new state of Israel is created in the Middle East.

May 14, 1948

The D-Day landings

On June 6, 1944 — "D-Day" — the Allied forces of Britain, the US, Canada, and France launched the largest naval, land, and air operation in history. Troops landed on the beaches of Normandy, France, including the code-named Omaha Beach, seen here. By the end of D-Day, more than 150,000 troops had landed in Normandy. They moved inland, allowing more troops to land over the next few days. This marked the first step towards freeing Europe from Nazi occupation.

The Pacific War

Although World War II began in Europe, by 1941, conflict had erupted worldwide. Much of the fighting took place in Asia and the Pacific between the Allied forces and Japan, supported by the Axis powers Germany and Italy. Hitler's invasion of France and the Netherlands in 1940 had left European-controlled territories in Southeast Asia vulnerable as Japan attempted to expand its empire in the region.

Battle of the Coral Sea

Allied forces halt Japanese plans to invade New Guinea. This is the first sea battle in which neither side's ships catch sight of the other. Instead, the battle is fought between planes sent out from aircraft carriers.

Australia attacked

Japanese planes bomb the port of Darwin, on the north Australian coast. Most of the city's military structures are destroyed.

Japanese victories

With astonishing speed, Japanese forces attack Hong Kong, the Philippines, Malaya, Thailand, Guam, and Wake Island, taking vast areas of land.

Military alliance

Japan enters into a military alliance with Germany and Italy, signing a document known as the Tripartite Pact. Germany and Italy promise Japan an empire that stretches across Asia.

September 1940

December 7, 1941

December 1941

February 15, 1942

February 19, 1942

February 27– March 1, 1942

May 4–8, 1942

Battle of the Java Sea

After defeating Allied naval forces in the Java Sea, Japan conquers the Dutch East Indies (modern-day Indonesia). It is another devastating victory against the Allied forces, and Japan now dominates the air and sea.

Singapore surrenders

Japanese forces continue to advance. The fall of Singapore and the loss of 138,000 British Commonwealth troops marks a humiliating defeat for Britain.

Pearl Harbor

Japanese forces bomb the US naval base at Pearl Harbor in Hawaii. Americans are shocked by the surprise attack. The US and Allies declare war on Japan; Germany declares war on the US.

Fighting in the skies
Japanese planes were faster than those of the US. They ruled the skies until 1943, when American air capabilities improved, overtaking Japan's.

Battle of Iwo Jima
US troops land on Iwo Jima, meeting fierce resistance from Japanese troops hiding in tunnels that criss-cross the island. Japanese soldiers refuse to surrender, but the US declares victory.

Atomic bombs
The cities of Hiroshima and Nagasaki are destroyed when the US drops two atomic bombs. Tens of thousands are killed immediately, and tens of thousands more die later from the effects of radiation.

Island hopping
The tide starts to turn as US forces fight back and begin to defeat Japanese troops one island at a time. Many Japanese soldiers refuse to be taken prisoner, choosing to commit suicide instead.

August 15, 1945

August 6 and 9, 1945

March 9–10, 1945

February–March 1945

October 1944

August 1942–February 1943

June 4–7, 1942

Japan surrenders
Despite the devastation caused by the atomic bombs, Japan's military leaders and parts of the government refuse to surrender. Emperor Hirohito pressures them to admit defeat, and after 4 years of bloodshed, the war finally ends.

Japan under siege
US forces begin a bombing campaign designed to cut off essential supplies to the mainland. Japanese cities are attacked, too. A raid on Tokyo creates a firestorm that kills 100,000 people.

Kamikaze attacks
Japanese pilots adopt extreme tactics during battle, flying their planes into the decks of US warships. These suicide missions, known as "kamikaze" attacks, destroy dozens of warships.

Battle of Midway
The Japanese navy's attempts to take control of Midway Island in the Central Pacific are defeated by Allied forces. Japan suffers the loss of 3,500 troops and four aircraft carriers in its first major setback.

War at sea
Aircraft carriers became the most important elements in each country's naval forces, allowing planes to take off and land in the heat of battle.

Burma and India
Expecting the Indian population to rise up against its British colonial rulers, Japan tried to invade India from Burma. The British fought back, however, and the jungle conflict became one of the bloodiest of World War II.

Indian independence

Britain had controlled India since the 1820s, but by the late 19th century, Indians began demanding the ability to make their own way in the world, free from British rule.

Migration

The partition of the colony in 1947 turns millions of Muslims in India, and Hindus and Sikhs in Pakistan, into religious minorities. What follows is the largest mass-migration of people in history. More than 14.5 million people leave their homes and most of their possessions to make it across the new borders. Violence on the way claims about one million of these refugees. These Sikhs are leaving Pakistan to make it to East Punjab, in northern India.

1885 The INC
The Indian National Congress (INC) forms to campaign for Indian independence. As the INC is mainly Hindu, Indian Muslims form the Muslim League in 1906 to campaign for them.

1930 Salt March
Gandhi walks 242 miles (390 km) to protest at the British taxes on basics such as salt. Many are arrested, but the march draws more attention to the independence movement.

1939 World War II begins
The British Empire declares India's entry into World War II without consulting India's leaders. Although 2.5 million Indian soldiers fight, the decision only increases Indian resentment.

1945 End of World War II
For Britain, the cost of victory in World War II is high. It simply did not have the ability or the desire to attempt to hold on to India, and so it sets about negotiating an end to its control.

1947 Independence
Pakistan gains independence, with Jinnah as its first governor-general. A day later, India finally achieves its freedom. Nehru becomes its first prime minister.

1909 British concessions
The British pass laws in 1909, 1919, and 1935 that give Indians more control over their country. Both the INC and Muslim League feel that these concessions don't go far enough, and the independence campaign rolls on.

1915 Gandhi
The Indian nationalist and activist Mohandas Gandhi begins organizing opposition to British rule in the country through nonviolent means, such as disobeying British laws.

1942 Quit India Movement
Gandhi and Jawaharlal Nehru (the INC leader) call for the British to leave in the Quit India Movement. Gandhi is arrested and the movement is banned, but this only increases its support.

1946 Riots
Muhammad Ali Jinnah, leader of the Muslim League, demands a separate Muslim state, which the INC rejects. Riots break out in Calcutta, leading to the deaths of 4,000 people. It is later agreed that the largely Muslim populations in the northeast and northwest will become Pakistan.

1948 Early struggles
Gandhi is assassinated by a Hindu extremist who believes the leader is responsible for partition. Later on, India and Pakistan go to war over the disputed Kashmir region.

Ghana's first president

Kwame Nkrumah becomes the first president of an independent Ghana in 1957. He immediately sets about improving conditions in the country by opening schools and establishing a social welfare system. Perhaps one of his most enduring ideas is his promotion of Pan-Africanism—an intellectual movement dedicated to studying, understanding, and communicating African culture.

African independence

After World War II, the European colonial powers found it increasingly difficult to hold on to their colonies. Some African countries fought for freedom, but others were granted it democratically.

1952 Kenyan uprising
A group of Kenyan protesters, called the Mau Mau, rebel against British control. About 13,000 of them are killed, but Kenya will finally gain independence in 1963.

1957 Ghanaian freedom
Ghana demands freedom from British rule, and it is immediately granted. Kwame Nkrumah becomes the first president of the new nation.

1962 Algerian agreement
Years of war between the Algerian people and the ruling French army end when French president Charles de Gaulle grants Algeria its independence. Rwanda also gains freedom from Belgium, and Uganda its independence from Britain this year.

1964–1968 Leaving the British Empire
In four years, six countries leave the British Empire. In 1964, Malawi and Zambia go, followed by Botswana and Lesotho two years later. Mauritius and Swaziland gain independence in 1968, along with Equatorial Guinea, which cedes from Spain.

1952 Egypt
Although officially independent since 1922, Egypt was still occupied by Britain. The British Empire's grip on the country is finally loosened by a revolution led by Colonel Gamal Abdel Nasser, who becomes the country's first president.

1956 Morocco and Tunisia
Two former French colonies in North Africa break free from French power within weeks of each other. Morocco achieves independence after a short period of unrest, but Tunisia's transition comes in a largely peaceful fashion.

1960 African independence
Seventeen sub-Saharan African countries, including 14 former French colonies, achieve independence from European control. It will become known as the "Year of Africa."

1963 African unity
The Organization of African Unity is established by 32 African states. It aims to improve the lives of ordinary Africans through cooperation and discussion between member states.

1974–1975 Portuguese colonies
The dictatorship that had led Portugal since 1933 is overthrown in 1974. Angola, São Tomé, and Príncipe, Mozambique, and Cape Verde, all seize their opportunity and gain independence from Portugal.

Ancient spies

Some of the earliest spies operate during the war between the ancient Egyptians and the Hittite Empire. The Hittites send people in disguise to feed the Egyptians false information, hoping to lead them into an ambush.

1274 BCE

The Art of War

In his book *The Art of War*, the ancient Chinese general Sun Tzu advises that spying is necessary in warfare. Using spies allows you to learn as much as you can about your enemy and their battle plans.

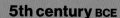

5th century BCE

Invisible ink

Organized by an American major, the spy network known as the Culper Ring uses invisible ink to write hidden messages. The ink helps Americans communicate in secret during the Revolutionary War.

1778

The Cabinet Noir

Cardinal Richelieu, chief minister to King Louis XIII of France, sets up the Cabinet Noir ("black room"). This French intelligence service intercepts the letters sent between French nobles, so that threats to the king can be thwarted.

1628

New technology

The invention of photography and telegrams allows for new methods of surveillance during the Civil War. Spies can now photograph military defenses and camps and intercept telegrams.

1860

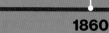

Enigma machine
The cracking of the German Enigma code helped to lead the Allies to victory in World War II.

Codebreaking

During World War I and World War II, communication technology becomes increasingly complex, as new codemaking machines are created. As a result, improving codebreaking techniques becomes crucial for deciphering secret messages.

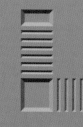

1914–1945

The story of spying

For thousands of years, spies have worked to uncover secret information. Most spies work for governments, finding out the secrets of enemies or potential enemies. The most important part of spying, or espionage, is to keep the activity secret, and over the centuries, spies have devised ingenious ways to conceal their work.

Today

The age of digital spies

A USB flash drive is able to store vast amounts of data on a tiny stick, making it easier than ever to obtain secret information and keep it hidden.

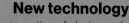

Early codes

In order to avoid their communications being read by the enemy during the Peloponnesian War, the Spartans develop the scytale. This was one of the earliest systems for coding and decoding secret messages.

431–404 BCE

1467 CE–1603 CE

Masters of infiltration

Using great stealth and speed, the shinobi (later known as ninja) are trained secret agents employed by powerful Japanese warlords. They use espionage, sabotage, and assassination to attain their goals.

Shuriken
Also known as throwing blades, shuriken could be thrown at a shinobi's enemy or used by hand to slash.

Hiding in plain sight

The writing of the Florentine Codex is finished, and reveals that Aztec merchants, called Pochteca, often acted as spies. Their extensive travels make them perfect for this task, because they can learn much about the Aztec Empire.

1585

The first spy network

Frances Walsingham becomes the principal secretary and spymaster of Queen Elizabeth I of England. Walsingham builds up a network of spies whose aim is to uncover plots to overthrow the queen.

1573

The Spymaster
Walsingham had conspirators tortured in order to get them to confess to their plots.

The French Resistance

Angry about German occupation, groups emerge within France to sabotage enemy activity. The Resistance sets up escape routes for airmen and escaped prisoners of war, and attacks German transportation and communications.

1940

Pencil fuses
Used during World War II, these time-delayed pencil fuses allowed the person setting the bomb to escape before the attached explosives detonated.

First modern spy agencies

World War II sees the creation of new intelligence services to help win the war, including Britain's Special Operations Executive (SOE) and the US Office of Strategic Services (OSS).

1940–1942

Public surveillance

East Germany's State Security Ministry, known as the Stasi, is formed. Secret agents use impressive technology, such as tiny cameras concealed in everyday items, to observe people of interest.

1950

Formation of the CIA

In order to improve its intelligence gathering after World War II and with the Cold War beginning, the US creates the Central Intelligence Agency (CIA), a foreign intelligence service.

1947

Formation of the KGB

The Soviet Union creates an intelligence agency called the Committee for State Security, or the KGB. It becomes one of the world's most effective intelligence organizations.

Video surveillance

CCTV cameras can be used to monitor traffic and crime, but are also an important tool for spies and intelligence agencies, who use them to track the movements of people of interest.

1974

1954

Camera
Stasi spies would use this secret camera to gather intelligence.

Middle East conflicts

Although the Middle East is home to many identities, Muslim Arabs make up the majority of its people. After World War I, European empires that had power in the region collapsed, and the Arabs regained control. But soon after World War II, Jews were granted the state of Israel in Palestine. Age-old tensions, Arab–Israeli conflict, and intervention by the West, have combined to make the Middle East a volatile region.

BEFORE

From the 1890s, a political campaign known as Zionism called for a Jewish homeland in Palestine. In the Balfour Declaration of 1917, Britain pledged to help create this nation of Jews. However, Muslim Arabs had lived in Palestine for centuries. After the horrors inflicted on the Jewish people during the Holocaust (see pages 262–263) the United Nations (UN) decided that Arabs and Jews would share Palestine, fueling Arab anger.

1940s–1960s

May 14, 1948

Israel is created

The UN divides Palestine between Jews and Arabs by creating a new Jewish state called Israel. A war immediately breaks out between Israel and its Arab neighbors. The conflict ultimately leads to Israel gaining more land.

1948–1960s

Palestinian displacement

In the year following the creation of Israel, more than 750,000 Palestinians flee or are expelled from their homes, becoming refugees. Both sides blame each other. Over the next decade, Jewish immigrants from Muslim countries and 250,000 Holocaust survivors settle in Israel.

1960s–1970s

June 5–10, 1967

Six-Day War

Arab forces from Egypt, Jordan, and Syria attack Israel, but Israel emerges victorious, capturing swathes of Arab territory. The Palestinian areas of the West Bank and Gaza Strip become known as the "occupied territories."

October 6–26, 1973

Yom Kippur War

Attacks on Israel by its Arab neighbors Egypt and Syria on Yom Kippur, a Jewish holy day, take Israel by surprise. However, Israel strikes back and its troops enter Syria. The conflict ends when the UN calls for a ceasefire.

January 1978– February 1979

Iranian Revolution

The monarch of Iran, Mohammad Reza Shah, is overthrown and forced to leave the country in the Iranian Revolution, also known as the Islamic Revolution. The nonreligious way of life he promoted is replaced by a new regime based on strict Islamic law, headed by Muslim leader Ayatollah Khomeini.

March 26, 1979

Israel and Egypt peace deal

Hosted in the US by President Carter, the leaders of Israel and Egypt attend peace talks. They sign a deal in which Israel returns Egyptian land it captured in the Six-Day War of 1967.

1980s

September 22, 1980–August 20, 1988

Iran–Iraq War

Fearing an uprising in his own country following the Iranian Revolution, Saddam Hussein, president of Iraq, invades Iran. A brutal eight-year war begins, and tensions increase across the region.

June 6, 1982

Israel invades Lebanon

In an attempt to attack Palestinian rebel forces in Lebanon, Israel invades the country. The Palestinians, led by Yasser Arafat and the Palestine Liberation Organization (PLO), flee to Tunisia.

December 9, 1987–September 13, 1993

The First Intifada

The Palestinians living in the West Bank and Gaza launch an intifada (popular uprising) against Israeli occupation. Israeli soldiers sent to stop the rebellion kill more than 300 civilians within its first year.

November 15, 1988

Independence for Palestine

The PLO issues a declaration of independence for a Palestinian state. Within days, more than 25 countries around the world offer their support to the unofficial Palestinian government. The PLO says it wants peace.

1990s

August 2, 1990–February 28, 1991

War in the Gulf

Iraq invades and occupies Kuwait, a nation rich in valuable oil resources. Six months later, a military operation, led by the US and supported by forces from 35 nations, is launched to expel Iraq. After great effort from the US and its allies, Saddam Hussein is defeated.

1993

The Oslo Accords

In a historic breakthrough, Israel agrees to withdraw from some of the Arab territories it has occupied if the PLO rejects violence against Israel. Jordan also signs a peace deal with Israel.

2000s

September 28, 2000–February 8, 2005

The Second Intifada

A period of violence erupts after Ariel Sharon, an Israeli politician, visits a site known to Muslims as Haram al-Sharif, and to Jews as Temple Mount. The visit to an Islamic holy place is seen as an insult by Palestinians.

From September 11, 2001

The War on Terror begins

The terrorist group al-Qaeda carries out attacks against high-profile targets in the US, leading to the destruction of the World Trade Center in New York. Believing that the Taliban, another terrorist group, is supporting al-Qaeda, the US intervenes in Afghanistan to bring down the Taliban regime.

March 20–May 1, 2003

Weapons of mass destruction

The US, the UK, Australia, and Poland attack Iraq because they believe Iraq holds weapons of mass destruction that could be a threat to the Islamic world. Western intervention in the Islamic world only increases anger against the West.

July 12–August 14, 2006

July War

War erupts in Lebanon after Hezbollah, a powerful Lebanese military group, captures Israeli soldiers and Israel fights back. More than 1,000 Lebanese people and around 165 Israeli people are killed in 34 days of fighting.

AFTER

Palestinians continue to call for independence for the occupied territories, and conflict still rages across the region. In 2010, a period of uprisings across the Middle East known as the Arab Spring challenged leadership and called for democracy. The worst violence was in Syria, which descended into brutal civil war.

Understanding the Middle East

There are many different groups involved in conflicts across the Middle East. Some of the key players are listed here, with the year they were founded.

1897 Zionism
This movement aims to create a permanent Jewish national state in Palestine.

1987 Hamas
This Islamic military group is dedicated to destroying Israel and creating an Islamic state in Palestine.

1988 Al-Qaeda
Formed by Osama Bin Laden, al-Qaeda wants to rid Islamic countries of Western influence.

2013 ISIL
Also known as ISIS, this terrorist organization seeks an Islamic state across Iraq, Syria, and beyond.

1964 PLO
The Palestine Liberation Organization aims to liberate Palestine and destroy the state of Israel.

1994 Taliban
An extreme Islamic political and religious movement, the Taliban is founded in Afghanistan.

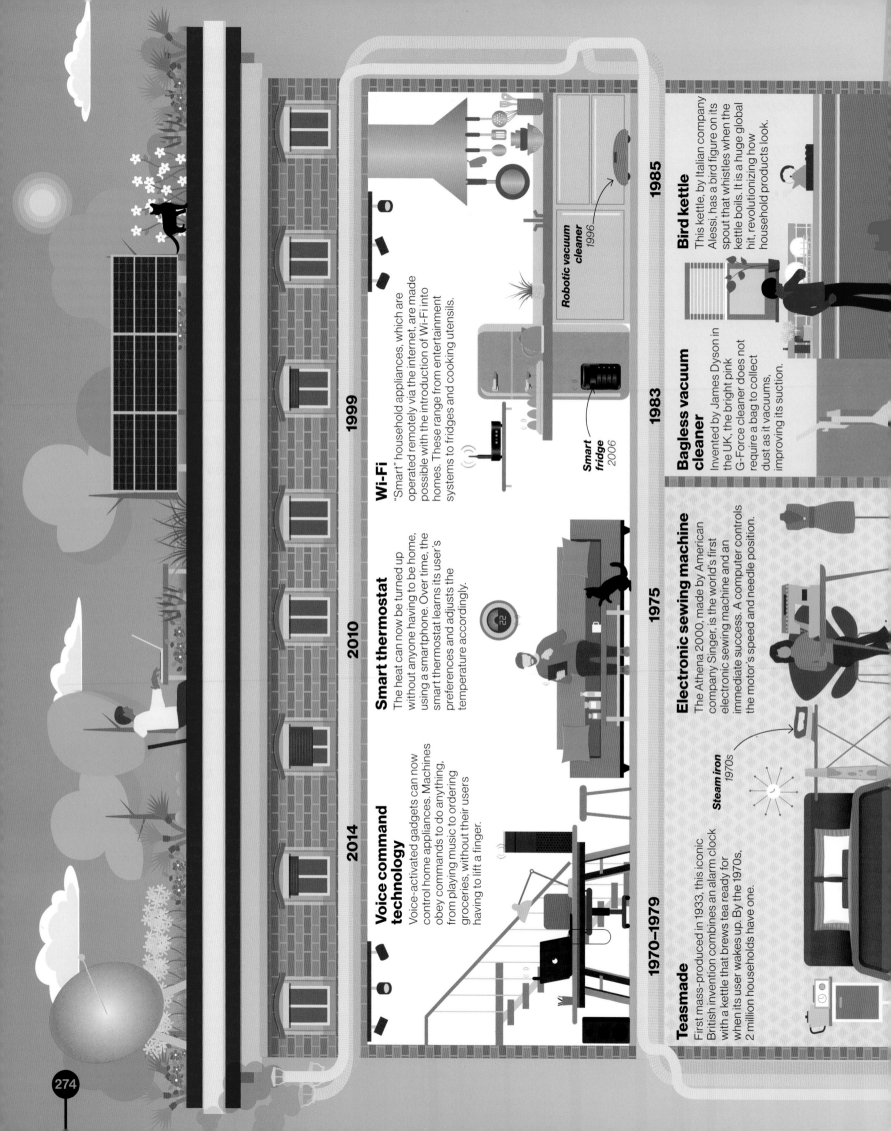

2014

Voice command technology

Voice-activated gadgets can now control home appliances. Machines obey commands to do anything, from playing music to ordering groceries, without their users having to lift a finger.

2010

Smart thermostat

The heat can now be turned up without anyone having to be home, using a smartphone. Over time, the smart thermostat learns its user's preferences and adjusts the temperature accordingly.

1999

Wi-Fi

"Smart" household appliances, which are operated remotely via the internet, are made possible with the introduction of Wi-Fi into homes. These range from entertainment systems to fridges and cooking utensils.

Smart fridge 2006

Robotic vacuum cleaner 1996

1985

Bird kettle

This kettle, by Italian company Alessi, has a bird figure on its spout that whistles when the kettle boils. It is a huge global hit, revolutionizing how household products look.

1983

Bagless vacuum cleaner

Invented by James Dyson in the UK, the bright pink G-Force cleaner does not require a bag to collect dust as it vacuums, improving its suction.

1975

Electronic sewing machine

The Athena 2000, made by American company Singer, is the world's first electronic sewing machine and an immediate success. A computer controls the motor's speed and needle position.

Steam iron 1970s

1970–1979

Teasmade

First mass-produced in 1933, this iconic British invention combines an alarm clock with a kettle that brews tea ready for when its user wakes up. By the 1970s, 2 million households have one.

Household appliances

In the early 20th century, electricity revolutionized everyday life. A whirlwind of labor-saving devices transformed the home, relieving people of domestic drudgery. Appliances such as vacuum cleaners and washing machines freed women from spending so much time doing housework, as society expected of them, allowing them to work or pursue hobbies. In the 21st century, new devices have evolved to save time and effort for women, men, and children.

1872

Modern radiator

In the 1800s, plumbing is a sign of wealth, so pipes are shown off. The Bundy Loop, a cast-iron, steam-heated radiator, becomes fashionable.

1882

Electric iron

People have been pressing creases out of clothes for centuries, but Henry Seely of New York is the first to power an iron using electricity.

1907

Vacuum cleaner

American inventor James Spangler invents the portable vacuum cleaner, which has a rotating brush and a bag to collect dust.

1908

Washing machine

Introduced by the Hurley Machine Company of Chicago, IL, the Thor is the first electric washing machine.

1913

Electric fridge

American engineer Fred W. Wolf creates the first electric refrigerator suitable for the population at large. It's known as the Domelre.

Electric kettle
1922

1967

Microwave

Despite being invented in the 1940s, it isn't until 1967 that a microwave oven small and cheap enough to be used easily in homes is developed.

1938

Clothes dryer

American inventor J. Ross Moore, tired of hanging his clothing outside, especially during winter, invents a clothes dryer that can run on gas and electricity.

1929

Electric toaster

The introduction of presliced bread in 1928 advances the use of electric toasters.

Stovetop coffee maker
1933

1929

Air conditioning

American company Frigidaire creates one of the first air conditioning units small enough for use in regular homes. It is shaped like a radio cabinet.

1929

Dishwasher

Originally invented in the 1880s by American Josephine Cochrane, German company Miele improves the dishwasher by creating an electric version.

Advertising

After World War II, advertising promoted labor-saving devices that promised to cut the time spent doing household chores. Most of this was aimed at women, but as society has begun to develop a more equal attitude toward women and men, advertising has made some progress in representing men in household roles, too.

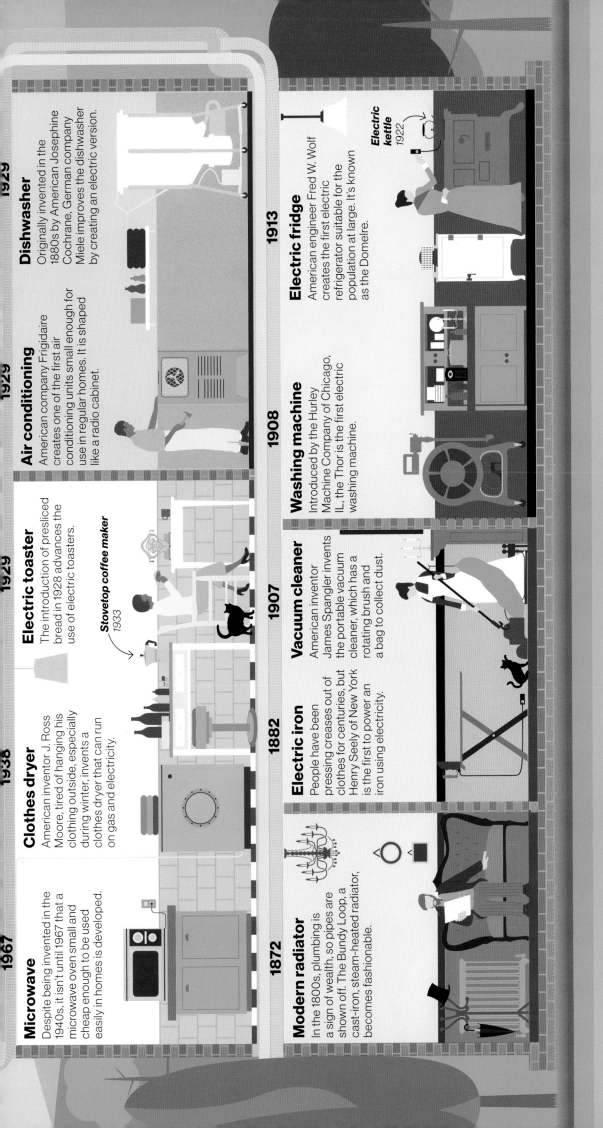

The Korean War

In 1950, conflict between North and South Korea threatened to explode into a much wider war. It became an international concern when the US supported the South Koreans, and the communist countries of China and the Soviet Union championed the North Koreans.

1947 Truman Doctrine
US president Harry Truman announces that the US will seek to stop the spread of communism in places it had not spread to yet—a policy known as the "Truman Doctrine."

1948 After World War II
The Korean peninsula was under Japanese rule before World War II. After Japan's defeat in the war, the Soviet Union occupies the north of the country, while the US controls the south.

1948 Partition
Korea is partitioned into two countries, but both communist North Korea and democratic South Korea hope to overthrow the other, and reunite the country.

1950 North Korea invades
Communist North Korea strikes first and invades the South. The North makes great gains, and captures the South Korean capital, Seoul.

1950 US and China join
Through the United Nations (UN), the US sends troops to help South Korea in July, turning the tide in the South's favor. By October, they have driven the North back and have even taken the North's capital city, Pyongyang. China enters the war to help the North.

1951 Stalemate
China's intervention drives the South Korean and UN troops south. A stalemate emerges, with each side's territory reverting back to the prewar borders. Peace talks begin, but don't achieve anything.

1953 Truce
The two sides agree to a truce, which ends the fighting. The border between the two countries stays where it was before the war, and a demilitarized zone is set up between them.

1954 The Geneva talks
The US and China meet to talk about uniting the two Koreas, but they can't reach an agreement. The Korean peninsula remains divided to this day—with a communist North and a democratic South.

Refugees

The back-and-forth nature of the war creates a huge refugee crisis as people flee to find safety. By 1951, about 500,000 refugees crowded into the South Korean city of Busan, with the overall number of refugees created by the war believed to be between four and six million.

A difficult war

The US found fighting in Vietnam to be incredibly difficult. The Vietnamese communists were guerilla fighters, which meant their attacks were sporadic and unpredictable. They used the terrain much better than the Americans, and slowly demoralized them by dragging them into a complex and seemingly endless struggle.

The Vietnam War

One of the major conflicts of the late 20th century, the Vietnam War raged for almost 20 years. It destroyed large swathes of the country and led to the deaths of millions of soldiers and civilians. As the conflict dragged on, an international antiwar movement protested what seemed to be a senseless, bloody war.

1945 Ho Chi Minh
The defeat of the Japanese in World War II leaves a power vacuum in Vietnam. Communist leader Ho Chi Minh declares North Vietnam independent, and his Viet Minh guerrilla fighters take on France, Vietnam's old colonial masters.

1950 US support
The US steps up its military and financial help to France, and President Truman authorizes $15 million in aid. The People's Republic of China (formed in 1949) and the Soviet Union support North Vietnam.

1959 Ho Chi Minh Trail
North Vietnam builds a supply route called the Ho Chi Minh Trail to South Vietnam. They use this to support pro-communist rebels in the South, known as the National Liberation Front.

1954 Withdraw and partition
The French completely withdraw after a huge defeat at the battle of Dien Bien Phu. Vietnam is divided in half, with Ho Chi Minh taking control of the North, and anticommunist, US-supported Ngo Dinh Diem ruling in the South.

1964–1965 Gulf of Tonkin
North Vietnam attacks two US warships. In response, the US issues the Gulf of Tonkin Resolution, committing the country to defending itself and South Vietnam. The USSR increases support of North Vietnam.

1962 Agent Orange
The US sprays Agent Orange, a deadly herbicide, to kill the foliage sheltering communist fighters and to destroy their food supplies. This causes long-lasting health issues for civilians and troops on both sides, and ruins large swathes of Vietnamese soil.

1965 First protests
The first antiwar marches happen in the US, with mounting casualties and the massive cost of fighting angering many. More than 100,000 people march on Washington DC in 1967.

1968 Tet Offensive
The communists launch the Tet Offensive—a coordinated series of attacks across South Vietnam. Initially surprised by the assault, the South Vietnamese and US forces regroup and retaliate.

1971 Pentagon Papers
The *Washington Post* publishes the Pentagon Papers. These show the government felt the war to be unwinnable, but had lied about it. The US had begun to pull out troops in 1969, and secret peace talks began in 1970.

1975 Fall of Saigon
A ceasefire is announced in 1973, and US troops are withdrawn. North Vietnam launches another attack and the South's capital, Saigon, falls. Vietnam is united as a communist state soon after.

Bay of Pigs invasion

The CIA attempts to remove Cuba's communist leader Fidel Castro from power. The CIA-backed rebel invaders are defeated by Castro's army in what became known as the Bay of Pigs invasion.

Cuban missile crisis

The Soviet Union installs nuclear missiles in Cuba, and the US demands their removal. The world fears full-scale nuclear war, but, after 13 days, the Soviet Union offers to remove the weapons in return for a US promise not to invade Cuba.

Nuclear disarmament

In London, thousands protest against nuclear weapons, especially the testing of hydrogen bombs by the US and Soviet Union. The protest is led by the Campaign for Nuclear Disarmament (CND) organization.

President John F. Kennedy

John F. Kennedy becomes the youngest-ever US president in the tightest election since 1884. He promises to fight for world freedom.

Anti-segregation sit-ins

African American students launch a series of "sit-in" protests against segregation (separating of blacks and whites) by refusing to leave "whites only" counters at diners.

1962

1963

1961

1960

1969

1968

1967

The 1960s

The 1960s saw great change take place. The Cold War (see pages 282–283) took hold, with continuing conflict in Vietnam, and nuclear war was a constant threat. But there was also a fresh optimism. New attitudes about freedom of expression and equality were reflected in music, fashion, and politics, and anything and everything seemed possible.

Woodstock

A 3-day music festival is held in the Catskill Mountains in New York. It is attended by more than 400,000 people, causing massive traffic jams and road closures. Musicians such as Jimi Hendrix, Janis Joplin, and Ravi Shankar perform.

Revolution

Protests across the world break out when people demand political change and better rights. In Paris, France, more than 10 million students and workers go on strike.

Stonewall Riots

A police raid of the Stonewall Inn, a gay club in New York City, turns violent. This inspires the formation of several gay, lesbian, and bisexual civil rights organizations to protect against social and political discrimination.

Dr King assassinated

Dr Martin Luther King, Jr. is shot in Memphis, TN. A few days later, his wife, Coretta, and their children lead a huge crowd on a silent remembrance march through Memphis.

The Feminine Mystique

Betty Friedan launches the modern feminist movement with a book that discusses the role of women in society and promotes equality. It sells millions of copies.

"I have a dream"

The campaign for civil rights in the US is led by Dr Martin Luther King, Jr. He calls for equality in his passionate "I have a dream" speech to demonstrators in Washington, DC.

Kennedy assassination

President John F. Kennedy is shot and killed in Dallas, TX. His death devastates the country. Lyndon B. Johnson is quickly sworn in as the new president.

1964

British invasion

British bands such as The Beatles, The Who, and The Rolling Stones storm the US charts, achieving fame and changing music forever.

Vietnam War

The US becomes involved in a long war in Vietnam to prevent it from falling under communist rule. The loss of life on both sides leads to mass protests around the world.

Pop art

Taking inspiration from comic books and advertising, the pop art movement flourishes. Artist Andy Warhol is the most distinctive pop artist, using bold images and bright colors to depict everyday objects.

1965

Fashion revolution

Teenagers begin to have their own money to buy clothes, and they feel less pressure to dress like their parents. This causes a revolution in the fashion world, with designs aimed at these new customers.

1966

Underground press

New publications develop for young people who don't agree with the traditional views of their parents. These include *Oz*, *International Times*, and *Ink*, and are dedicated to poetry, music, and promoting political change.

Hippies

A movement of young people known as "hippies" emerges in San Francisco. They are recognizable by their long hair and colorful clothing, and they promote ideas of nonviolence and love.

Summer of Love

Young people reject the violence seen in news broadcasts and call for peace, love, and understanding across the world. They are influenced by music and Eastern religions such as Buddhism and Hinduism.

Postcolonial Africa

In the 1950s and 1960s, African nations gained independence from colonial rule with varying degrees of success. Although there was freedom in many places, there was also corruption, military coups, civil war, and division among different ethnic groups. However, in the 21st century, optimism is growing, with greater wealth and improving political stability.

Rwandan Genocide
More than a million people of the Tutsi ethnicity in Rwanda are killed by members of the neighboring ethnic group, the Hutus. The international community fails to stop this.

Ghanaian independence
Kwame Nkrumah becomes the country's first independent prime minister after years of British colonial rule. In an emotional speech, he tells tens of thousands of Ghanaians: "your beloved country is free forever."

"In the end, the ballot must decide, not bullets."
Jonas Savimbi, Angolan politician, in a speech in 1975

President Nelson Mandela
After decades of apartheid (racial segregation) in his country, and 27 years of imprisonment for protesting against this, Nelson Mandela is elected the first black president of South Africa. This ends 300 years of white rule.

1957	1960–1965	1963	1971–1979	1975–2002	1984–1985	1994	1994

Congo Crisis
The Congo (modern-day Democratic Republic of Congo) dissolves into crisis after becoming independent from Belgium in June 1960. A breakaway state of Katanga exists until the United Nations (UN) intervenes in 1963. The army seizes power in 1965.

Idi Amin
Ugandan president Amin expels Asian minorities from Uganda and launches attacks on his Tanzanian enemies. He abuses human rights and uses violence against other ethnic groups. He is overthrown in 1979.

African Unity
Following the independence of many African nations from European rule, the Organization of African Unity is established by 32 African states to encourage and protect Africa's interests.

Ethiopian famine
Decades of war and extreme drought cause starvation in Ethiopia, where more than 400,000 people die and millions more are left hungry and poor. Many are forced to leave their homes and resettle elsewhere.

Angolan Civil War
The Republic of Angola, rich in diamonds and oil, becomes independent from Portugal in 1975, but becomes impoverished by a civil war. This will be one of Africa's longest-running conflicts.

Economic boom

Africa is predicted to have the largest economic growth of any continent over the next decade, thanks to younger populations, access to water, and less poverty and disease.

Kofi Annan

Kofi Annan from Ghana becomes the Secretary-General of the United Nations. He expands the UN's work into protecting the environment, fighting against HIV/AIDS in Africa, and improving human rights.

Polite politics

Nigeria votes out President Goodluck Jonathan in favor of Muhammadu Buhari. Jonathan's politeness in defeat allows a peaceful transfer of power, which is inspirational across Africa.

Civil war in Sudan

Civil war begins in the Darfur region of Sudan between rebel groups and the government. Several hundred thousand people are killed and millions flee their homes in a conflict that remains unresolved today.

Independence for South Sudan

South Sudan votes to break away from Sudan after a bloody civil war between the mainly Christian south and the Arab Muslim north. Much of the world recognizes the new nation, but it remains one of the poorest areas in the world.

HIV/AIDS vaccine trial launched

5,400 South African men and women sign up for a trial of a new HIV/AIDS vaccine, hoping for a breakthrough against the disease. Seven million South Africans are living with the virus.

| 1997 | 2003 | 2004 | 2010 | 2010 | 2011 | 2011 | 2015 | 2014–2016 | 2016 | 2017 |

Prize for Kenya

Wangari Mathai, a Kenyan feminist and environmentalist, receives the Nobel Peace Prize. Her Green Belt Movement teaches women to grow trees in order to improve their living conditions.

Ebola

West Africa experiences the biggest outbreak of the Ebola virus ever known. Thousands die and the economies of many countries are damaged, some of which are still recovering from civil war.

World Cup

The World Cup comes to South Africa, the first time an African nation has held such a prestigious worldwide event. Many people's perceptions of the country and continent are changed for the better.

Rwandan reform

Rwanda manages to rebuild its economy after its devastating civil war. Life expectancy, the number of children attending school, and the amount of money spent on health care have all improved.

Robert Mugabe steps down

Robert Mugabe, president of Zimbabwe since 1980, loses his grip on power and resigns after the military take control. He is blamed for economic chaos, preventing political freedom, and the abuse of human rights.

Berlin blockade

The USSR flexes its muscles by preventing road and rail access to West Berlin, threatening West Germany. Britain and the US drop millions of tons of supplies into West Berlin from planes until the Soviets lift the blockade.

1948

A divided Europe

After World War II, the USSR takes control of areas of Eastern Europe, including East Germany, forming a communist "Eastern Bloc." The US helps to rebuild western European countries. Eastern Europe becomes cut off from the West.

1945

1949

NATO

The East-West divide becomes official when the US and Western European countries establish the North Atlantic Treaty Organization (NATO), promising that in times of conflict, these countries will help one another.

1949

George Orwell's *1984*

British author George Orwell writes *1984*, a novel that imagines the nightmare of living under a brutal government similar to a communist dictatorship. It inspires many books, movies, and music.

1949

First Soviet nuclear bomb

In response to the US nuclear bombs that ended World War II, the Soviets become a nuclear power by testing their own weapons. The US and USSR compete to have more powerful weapons than each other. Neither of them ever actually uses these because they fear mass destruction.

1972

World Chess Championship

In the "match of the century," American Bobby Fischer beats chess champion Boris Spassky of the USSR. This ends 24 years of Soviet domination of the World Chess Championship.

1983

"Star Wars"

US president Ronald Reagan calls the USSR an "evil empire." He reveals a plan, called "Star Wars," to put weapons in space. These would defend against a nuclear attack, and show off US wealth and technology. However, they are never built.

The Cold War

After World War II, the capitalist US and communist Soviet Union (the USSR) were the most powerful countries in the world. A period of great tension began, as each side tried to prevent the other from gaining too much power. The invention of nuclear weapons created an additional threat. This is known as the Cold War, because conflict was fought through political ideas rather than military force.

The hot wars

Although the Cold War never resulted in actual warfare between the USSR and US, it led to many smaller wars in other countries as the two sides tried to spread their influence. These were known as proxy wars, or hot wars.

1950–1953 Korean War

1956 Hungarian Revolution

1973 Chilean coup

1975 Angolan Civil War

1979–1990 Nicaraguan Revolution

1955–1968 Vietnam War

1959 Cuban Revolution

1968 Czechoslovakian Uprising

1979–1989 Afghan War

1951

McCarthyism

A scandal erupts when some US government officials are caught giving American secrets to the USSR. Senator Joseph McCarthy mounts a campaign to hunt down rebel US communists, but innocent people are prosecuted in the process.

1950–1954

Cambridge spies

After being recruited as Soviet spies while at Cambridge University in the UK, four British men are discovered to have been passing secret information to the USSR. Three of them are forced to move to the Soviet Union, and one shares Soviet secrets in exchange for his freedom.

1955

Warsaw Pact

The USSR unites the Eastern Bloc through the Warsaw Pact which, like NATO in the West, creates an agreement that the countries will support one another. It strengthens Soviet power over the Eastern Bloc, too.

1962

Cuban Missile Crisis

The USSR builds nuclear missile launch sites in communist Cuba, close to the US coast. The US demands that the sites be removed. Nuclear war seems inevitable. However, the Soviets withdraw at the last minute.

13 August 1962

The Berlin Wall

German communists erect a wall dividing East Berlin from West. It becomes an ugly symbol of division between the two Cold War political ideals. The wall separates many people from their families, homes, and jobs.

1960s

The internet

During the 1960s, the US government funds a project by DARPA (Defense Advanced Research Projects Agency) to develop a way to share information between military computers quickly, and so the internet is born.

1957–1969

Space Race

The US and USSR compete to advance their space exploration. Their progress represents the scientific and economic power of each country. It ends when American spacecraft *Apollo 11* lands on the Moon.

1985–1991

Glasnost and *Perestroika*

Soviet leader Mikhail Gorbachev begins to make changes in the USSR. *Perestroika* ("restructuring") improves the economy, while *glasnost* ("openness") allows freedom of the press and political expression.

10 November 1989

Fall of the Berlin Wall

As the USSR weakens, East Germans are astonished to finally be allowed to travel freely to West Germany. The wall is knocked down, and Germany is reunited. This marks the end of communist rule in Eastern Europe.

1991

The Soviet Union collapses

For the first time in its history, Russia elects a president. The Communist Party is defeated and ordered to end its rule. The world looks on in amazement as the USSR disintegrates into 15 separate countries.

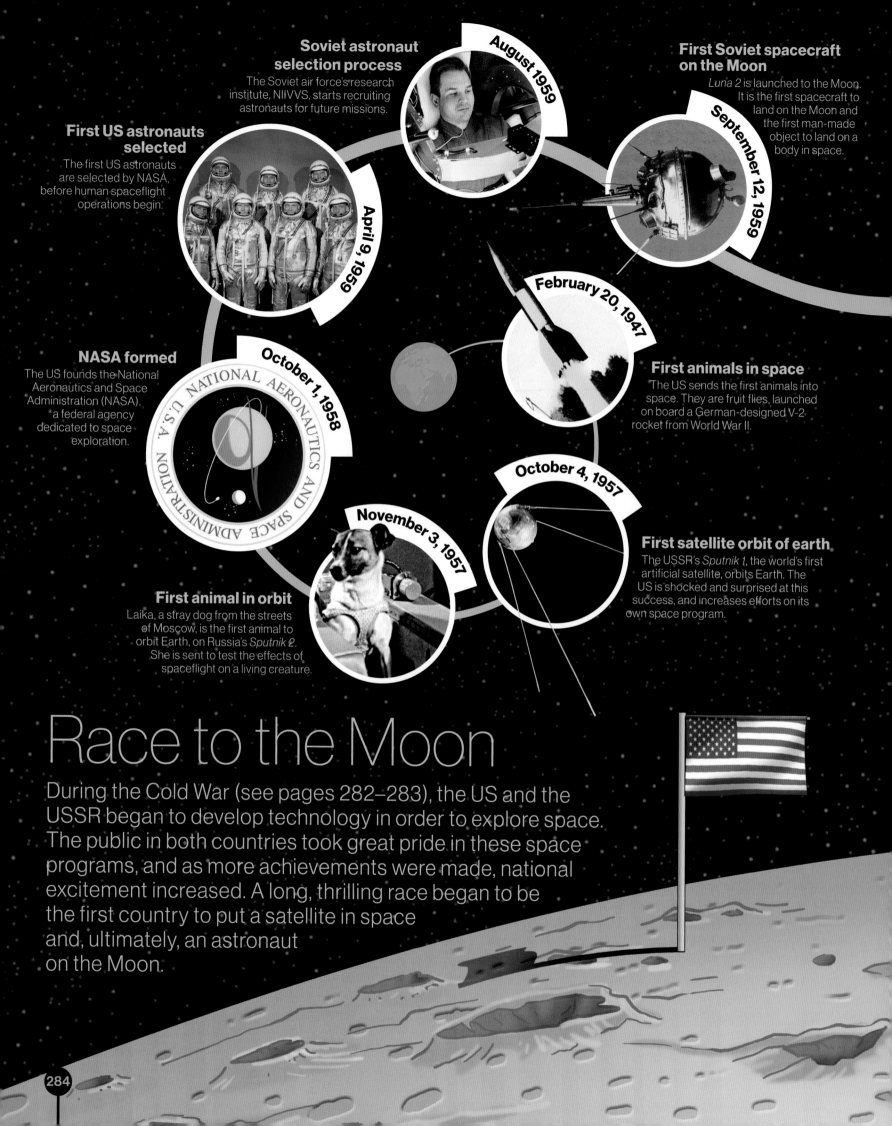

Soviet astronaut selection process

The Soviet air force's research institute, NIIVVS, starts recruiting astronauts for future missions.

August 1959

First Soviet spacecraft on the Moon

Luna 2 is launched to the Moon. It is the first spacecraft to land on the Moon and the first man-made object to land on a body in space.

September 12, 1959

First US astronauts selected

The first US astronauts are selected by NASA, before human spaceflight operations begin.

April 9, 1959

February 20, 1947

First animals in space

The US sends the first animals into space. They are fruit flies, launched on board a German-designed V-2 rocket from World War II.

NASA formed

The US founds the National Aeronautics and Space Administration (NASA), a federal agency dedicated to space exploration.

October 1, 1958

NATIONAL AERONAUTICS AND SPACE ADMINISTRATION U.S.A.

October 4, 1957

November 3, 1957

First satellite orbit of earth

The USSR's *Sputnik 1*, the world's first artificial satellite, orbits Earth. The US is shocked and surprised at this success, and increases efforts on its own space program.

First animal in orbit

Laika, a stray dog from the streets of Moscow, is the first animal to orbit Earth, on Russia's *Sputnik 2*. She is sent to test the effects of spaceflight on a living creature.

Race to the Moon

During the Cold War (see pages 282–283), the US and the USSR began to develop technology in order to explore space. The public in both countries took great pride in these space programs, and as more achievements were made, national excitement increased. A long, thrilling race began to be the first country to put a satellite in space and, ultimately, an astronaut on the Moon.

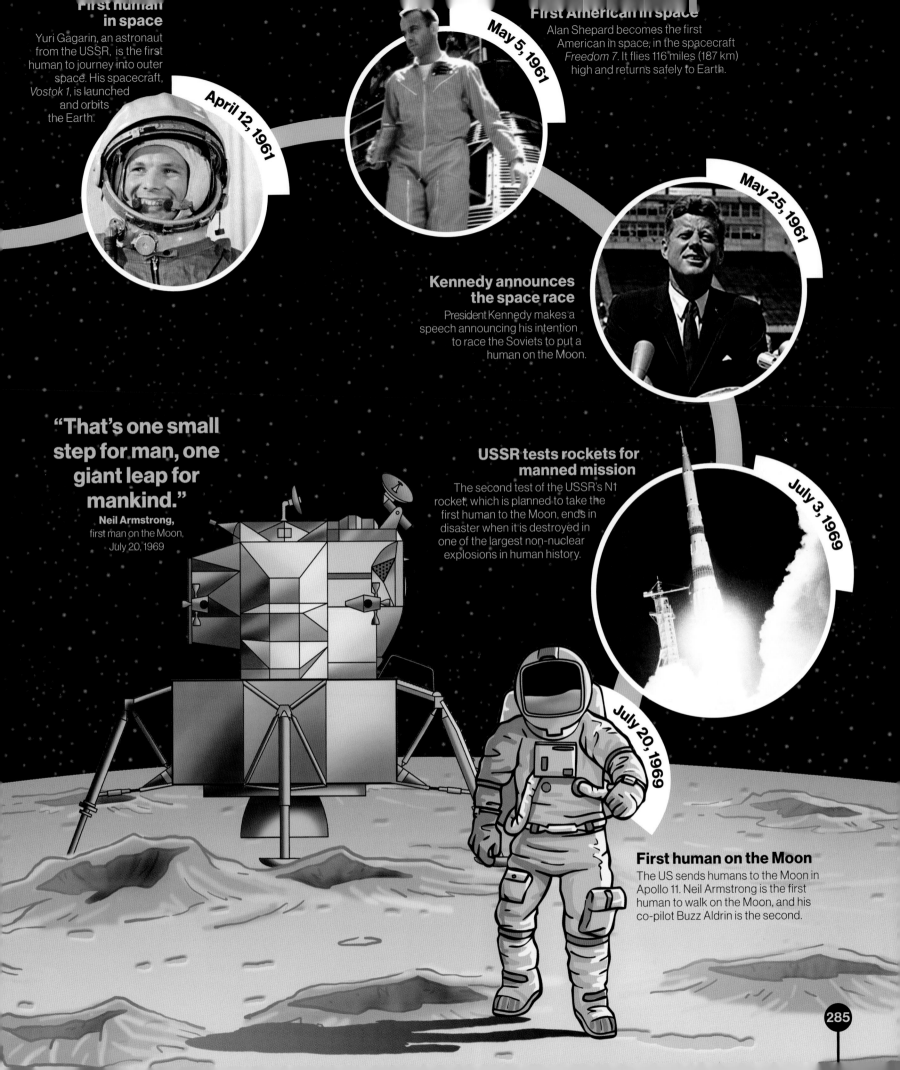

First human in space

Yuri Gagarin, an astronaut from the USSR, is the first human to journey into outer space. His spacecraft, *Vostok 1*, is launched and orbits the Earth.

April 12, 1961

May 5, 1961

First American in space

Alan Shepard becomes the first American in space, in the spacecraft *Freedom 7*. It flies 116 miles (187 km) high and returns safely to Earth.

May 25, 1961

Kennedy announces the space race

President Kennedy makes a speech announcing his intention to race the Soviets to put a human on the Moon.

"That's one small step for man, one giant leap for mankind."

Neil Armstrong,
first man on the Moon,
July 20, 1969

USSR tests rockets for manned mission

The second test of the USSR's N1 rocket, which is planned to take the first human to the Moon, ends in disaster when it is destroyed in one of the largest non-nuclear explosions in human history.

July 3, 1969

July 20, 1969

First human on the Moon

The US sends humans to the Moon in Apollo 11. Neil Armstrong is the first human to walk on the Moon, and his co-pilot Buzz Aldrin is the second.

Apollo launches

Apollo 11 was the first crewed mission to land on the Moon. The astronauts' journey would not have been possible without the extremely powerful *Saturn V* rocket. On the morning of July 16, 1969, the huge three-stage rocket, towering 361 ft (110 m) above its launch pad in Florida, lifted *Apollo 11* away from Earth and into low Earth orbit. Its upper stage then blasted the craft on its epic 950,000-mile (1.5 million-km) journey to the Moon.

THE CUBAN MISSILE CRISIS

A world on the brink of war

In the fall of 1962, the global superpowers of the United States and the Soviet Union were in a diplomatic deadlock. This began when the Soviets installed nuclear missiles on the Caribbean island of Cuba, close to the US. As letters, official statements, and threats passed between the two rival nations, the rest of the world looked on for 13 tense days as fragile global peace teetered on the brink of nuclear war.

Old comrades, new rivals

During the **1950s**, former World War II allies the United States and the Soviet Union become rival superpowers, and they each slowly build up a stock of nuclear weapons. As this "Cold War" develops, in **1952**, the US secretly backs a military coup in Cuba, around 100 miles (160 km) off the coast of Florida. This allows military dictator Fulgencio Batista to regain power. Seven years later, in **1959**, a revolution led by Cuban nationalist Fidel Castro overthrows Batista, and Cuba becomes the first communist state in the West.

An invasion fails

In **1960**, US president Dwight D. Eisenhower halts trade and aid to Cuba. Cuba's isolation encourages Castro to seek new allies and, by **December 1960**, Castro has accepted military and diplomatic support from the Soviet Union. In **1961**, John F. Kennedy becomes the new president of the US, and he approves a plan to overthrow Castro's government. This is put in motion on **April 17, 1961**, when a force of exiled Cubans living in the US invades western Cuba at the Bay of Pigs. The US-backed rebellion fails, and Castro's military forces are triumphant, killing 100 and capturing about 1,200 of the invading exiles.

Missiles in place

Relations between the US and the Soviet Union continue to decline with disagreements over Allied-occupied Berlin in Germany. Then, in **April 1962**, the US finalizes a deal to make ready their nuclear weapons in Turkey, close to the Soviet border. In **July**, in retaliation for this threat to his country, the Soviet Union's premier Nikita Khrushchev strikes a deal with Castro to build Soviet missile bases on the island. On **August 31**, US senator Kenneth Keating warns his government of the Soviet military presence in Cuba. On **September 21**, Soviet Minister of Foreign Affairs Andrei Gromyko urges the US to back away from Cuba or else face the possibility of war.

The crisis begins

On **October 14, 1962**, after ordering a U-2 spy plane to fly over Cuba, evidence is presented to President Kennedy and the Executive Committee, known as ExComm. Eight days of discussions and analysis lead to President Kennedy addressing the nation at 7:00 p.m. on **October 22**, stating that he has evidence of Soviet nuclear missiles on Cuba. The US sends its navy to surround the Caribbean island and block any other ships from approaching. The military is ordered to increase their readiness for war.

Tensions rise

On **October 23, 1962**, Premier Khruschev replies to President Kennedy, claiming that all weapons on Cuba are defensive. On **October 24**, tensions rise as Soviet ships approach the US naval blockade, with Soviet submarines close behind. The US reacts by making ready its airbases in Florida, and by placing US Strategic Air Command on high alert for the first time in its history. Over the next two days, communications flow between Kennedy and Khrushchev through the United Nations. A deal to end the standoff is close until a US spy plane is shot down over Cuba on **October 27**.

The world holds its breath

Nations around the world watch as nuclear war looms. Then, on **October 28**, a deal is struck to end the crisis. The US promises not to invade Cuba, and to withdraw its missiles from Turkey in exchange for the removal of all missiles from Cuba. The US naval blockade finally ends on **November 20**, as the last Soviet ship leaves the Caribbean. A month later, on **December 24**, the US sends food and medical supplies to Cuba in exchange for those captured in the Bay of Pigs invasion. A year later, on **August 30, 1963**, the US and the Soviet Union establish a "hotline" between their leaders to allow for immediate diplomatic discussions in the future.

"We were eyeball to eyeball and the other fellow just blinked."
US Secretary of State Dean Rusk on hearing that the Soviet ships had turned back, October 1962

The Civil Rights Movement

The Civil War brought an end to slavery, but the African American struggle for equal rights was only just beginning. In many parts of the country, racism and unequal treatment for black people were supported by law. During the 1950s and 1960s, people joined together as the Civil Rights Movement to fight for equality.

February–July 1960

DINERS PROTEST

Greensboro sit-in

College students in Greensboro, North Carolina, take their seats at a white-only Woolworth's lunch counter. Soon, peaceful "sit-in" protests like this one take place all over the south.

May 17, 1954

INTEGRATED SCHOOLS

Brown vs. Board of Education

An all-white elementary school in Topeka, Kansas, rejects 8-year-old African American student Linda Brown, so her father files a lawsuit. The case ends up in the US Supreme Court, which decides that segregating (separating) black and white children in public schools is unconstitutional.

December 1, 1955

ROSA PARKS ARRESTED

Bus boycott

Police arrest Rosa Parks in Montgomery, Alabama, after she refuses to give up her bus seat to a white man. A young Dr. Martin Luther King, Jr. leads black townspeople in a year-long bus boycott before the Supreme Court rules segregation on buses is illegal.

1957

Law change

**September 3
Little Rock Nine**

Some states ignore the new rules. When nine African-American high school students enroll in an all-white school in Little Rock, Arkansas, the governor calls the National Guard to stop them. Later, the US government sends troops to escort the Little Rock Nine to school.

**September 9
Civil Rights Act of 1957**

The US government responds to the growing movement with the Civil Rights Act of 1957, the first civil rights law in more than 80 years. The legislation helps to protect the voting rights of African-Americans and signals support for change.

May–December 1961

FREEDOM RIDERS

Campaigners attacked

Black and white college students show their support for civil rights by riding on buses together in segregated areas. When these "Freedom Riders" are met with violence, the photos are shown around the globe.

1963

RIOTS

May 11
Birmingham riots

A protest following a night of bombings targeted at civil rights leaders turns into 8 days of riots in Birmingham, Alabama. Local police respond violently, stunning the country. Media coverage of the riots sparks a national debate.

August 28
"I have a dream"

At the end of a march attended by 250,000 people in Washington DC, civil rights leader Martin Luther King, Jr. delivers his famous speech from the steps of the Lincoln Memorial. King's powerful words convince many Americans that now is the time for change.

1964

BALLOT OR BULLET?

April 3
Malcolm X gives speech

Activist and religious leader Malcolm X gives a fiery speech in which he promotes change by any means necessary, whether it's the ballot box or the bullet. Rivals assassinate him in 1965.

FREEDOM SUMMER

June
Register to vote

In Mississippi, thousands of volunteers work together to register as many African American voters as possible. The volunteers face harassment and intimidation.

Equal rights

July 2
Civil Rights Act of 1964

After a summer of protests, the US government proposes legislation to end segregation in public places and give everyone equal access to jobs regardless of a person's race, color, or religion. The act is signed into law by President Lyndon B. Johnson.

March 7–25, 1965
Selma

March to Alabama

With Martin Luther King, Jr., thousands of marchers walk 50 miles (80 km) from Selma to the state capital of Montgomery. The march leads to the passing of the Voting Rights Act in August 1965.

1968

VIOLENCE

April 4
Luther King, Jr. shot

A sniper assassinates Martin Luther King, Jr. in Memphis, Tennessee. Shock spreads quickly, and riots break out in several US cities. President Johnson asks Americans to reject violence and puts pressure on Congress to pass new legislation quickly.

EQUAL ACCESS

April 11
Civil Rights Act of 1968

Congress signs this act to give everyone fair and equal access to housing. The impact of civil rights legislation like this is huge, but the march for equality continues.

Selma

The march in Alabama from Selma to Montgomery was organized to draw attention to the difficulties African Americans faced when registering to vote. Although African Americans had the right to vote, state officials tried to stop them from registering. Registration offices were rarely open, and officials made people complete unnecessary literacy tests, fill in long forms, and pay fees.

3150 BCE–30 CE

Ancient Egyptians
The Egyptians live in a hot climate, so they make nearly all their clothes from lightweight linen woven from flax plants grown beside the Nile River. Both men and women wear makeup and wigs.

c.750–323 BCE

Ancient Greeks
A simple chiton (a long sleeveless shirt tied with a belt) is worn by men, women, and children. It can be short or long, printed or plain, gathered or loose, and topped with a cloak for extra warmth.

509 BCE–476 CE

The Romans
Most people wear simple tunics and togas made from wool and linen. The colors of these clothes mark the wearer's rank in society. Purple, for example, is worn by the ruling classes.

1400s

Middle Ages
The most common item of medieval clothing is the tunic. Rich people wear fancy versions of this. Hose (thin, fitted trousers with feet, much like tights) begin to become popular for men. These are an early version of pants.

c.1450–1600

Renaissance
Clothing moves from being loose to fitted. Men and women start to wear different items of clothing. As wealthy people begin to travel the world, fashions from different countries influence each other. Many copy the style of Queen Elizabeth I of England, known for her full-skirted dresses and large ruffs.

Fashion

People have always been interested in what they wear, from the ancient Egyptians and their carefully crafted wigs, to today's shoppers, who can buy the latest fashions online. Fashion has changed as many times as you've changed your socks. Its history is as long and colorful as some of its most sensational creations.

2000s

Fast fashion
Fashion becomes accessible, with high-end stores cheaply recreating catwalk trends. However, concerns grow about working conditions in factories, and the environmental impact of cheap, disposable clothes.

1980s

Designer decade
In the 1980s, fashion designers became superstars, and models became celebrities. The internet makes fashion truly global. If a celebrity appears in a dress, it can sell out in moments on the other side of the world.

1970s

Flares and heels
Trousers are more popular with women than ever before, and flares get wider for men and women. Platform shoes step into fashion, influenced by performers such as David Bowie and Elton John.

1960s

Youthquake
Teenagers, now with their own money to spend, break free from the fashions of their parents. Young designers lead the way, such as Mary Quant, who shocks older generations when she designs the miniskirt in 1964.

1950s

Leisure time
After World War II ends, travel and leisure, once just for the wealthy, become more affordable. Swimwear, sandals, and sunglasses become popular. The bikini is invented in 1946, and rises in popularity in the 1950s.

c.1500–1700

Ottoman finery
The Ottoman Empire, stretching from southern Europe to Asia, inspires European fashion. This includes turbans and long, flowing robes, crafted from beautiful, expensive fabrics.

1600s

European fashions
France (and to a lesser extent, England) leads the way in fashion, with the rest of Europe following. More than ever, clothes demonstrate wealth and position in society. The rich splurge on the latest fashions in hand-decorated silk and velvet.

1603

Kimono
The Edo period in Japan (see pages 158–159) sees a rise in the kimono, a robe with flowing sleeves and a wide belt. Wealthy people compete for the richest fabrics, expressing their status and style.

1700s

Rococo
An artistic movement known as rococo inspires lighter, more flowing clothes. Fitted dresses are replaced by full-skirted gowns known as mantuas, and later by open robes and petticoats. Men wear coats and breeches (short pants) in a move away from tight-fitting hose.

1800s

Sportswear
The introduction of vacation in the 1800s gives people more leisure time to do sports. Rich people adopt outfits for sports such as hunting, riding, and archery. Sporty fashion is for both women and men.

1940s

Wartime fashion
During World War II, money and material is in short supply, meaning few can afford new suits or dresses. Many men and women are inspired to join the armed forces by the smart uniforms.

1930s

Film star fashion
A financial crash puts an end to the fun of the jazz age. Unable to buy into fashion, normal people instead admire the clothes of glamorous film stars such as Fred Astaire and Ginger Rogers. The women wear long, fitted dresses, and men's suits have narrow waists and wide shoulders.

1920s

Jazz age
Following World War I, practical, comfortable clothes become popular. Skirts become shorter, and many young women, known as flappers, cut their hair short, smoke, and dance to jazz to rebel against old-fashioned society.

T-shirts
The US Navy introduces this iconic item of clothing, meant to be worn as an extra layer under a shirt. It is stretchy and holds its shape, as well as being easy to clean and inexpensive.

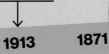

1913

1871

Blue jeans
The first jeans are invented by Jacob W. Davis and Levi Strauss in the US. The jeans have metal fastenings at the seams, making them tough and long-lasting. They become popular with laborers across the US, and by the mid-20th century will become a key feature of wardrobes across the world.

1846

African prints
A new printing technique is developed, which prints fabric with wax to create colorful patterns. This printed fabric is a huge hit in Ghana, and soon is being used to make clothes across much of West and Central Africa. The patterns are used to create pictures that tell stories and ideas.

Space exploration

The desire to explore space has led to many incredible developments. In 1969, humans first landed on the Moon. Twenty years later, all the planets in the solar system had been explored by spacecraft. Now, the next era of space exploration is beginning, with ambitious plans to expand space tourism and send humans to Mars.

First satellite

The Soviet Union triggers the Space Age with the launch of *Sputnik 1*, the first artificial satellite, into space. *Sputnik 1* takes about 98 minutes to travel around Earth. Its success shocks the US, causing the country to speed up its own space program.

Sputnik 1
This simple satellite is about the size of a basketball.

Viking 1
One of two Viking spacecraft sent to Mars by NASA, Viking 1 takes pictures and gathers scientific data.

Mission to Mars

NASA's *Viking 1* lands on the surface of Mars after a 10-month journey. It is the first spacecraft to not only land on another planet, but also take photos and collect data that can be sent back to Earth.

1957

1965

1976

1990

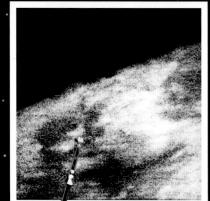

Images of Mars

The first close-up photos of the planet Mars are beamed back to Earth. Taken by US spacecraft *Mariner 4*, they aren't quite what the world is expecting. Rather than showing aliens on Mars as people hoped, the grainy pictures show barren, gray craters.

Hubble space telescope
This historic telescope circles Earth every 96 minutes.

Space telescope

NASA's Hubble Space Telescope is launched, and becomes the most famous space observatory ever flown. It can observe objects more than 13.4 billion light-years from Earth.

Mariner 4
This spacecraft records images as it flies past Mars. It is the first craft to photograph a planet other than Earth.

Humans in space

For as long as humans have looked up at the stars, we have dreamed of exploring the universe. In 1961, the first person entered space in his spacecraft, marking the beginning of an extraordinary journey for humans venturing into space.

1965
Soviet Alexey Leonov walks in space.

1969
American Neil Armstrong walks on the Moon.

2001
Businessman Dennis Tito is the first space tourist.

1961
Soviet Yuri Gagarin is the first person in space.

1998
The International Space Station (ISS) is built.

2003
The first piloted Chinese space mission is launched.

Juno
Space probe Juno is roughly the size of a basketball court.

Interstellar space exploration

NASA's *Voyager 1* probe is the first artificial object to travel to the edge of the solar system and head off into interstellar space (the space between stars). No spacecraft has gone there before.

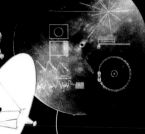

Golden record
Voyager 1 carries a record of sounds and images of life on Earth, in case of encounters with aliens.

Jupiter mission

Juno travels more than 1.7 billion miles (2.7 billion km) from Earth to Jupiter, a giant planet with a diameter around 11 times the size of that of Earth. Juno investigates how Jupiter formed 4.6 billion years ago.

2012

2014

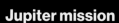

2016

2017

Comet landing

The *Philae* is the first spacecraft ever to land on the surface of a speeding comet. As it hurtles toward the comet, it sends back information about the solar system and life on Earth.

Philae
This giant robot is packed with cameras and sensors to probe the secrets of space.

Mission to Saturn ends

Launched in 1997, *Cassini* ends its 20-year mission exploring Saturn and its moons. The craft breaks up as it plows into Saturn's cloud tops in a dramatic end to one of NASA's most successful missions.

Cassini
The probe slips between Saturn and rings to send stunnin images back to Earth

Booming nations

After World War II, many East and Southeast Asian countries progressed from poverty to extreme wealth. This development began in the 1960s, as Asian countries, starting with Japan, began to produce high-tech items such as cameras and computers. As these goods were exported to other continents, the economies of these countries grew until they were some of the largest in the world.

1964

Bullet train
The world's first high-speed train, nicknamed a "bullet" train, is built in Japan. It reaches speeds of around 186 mph (300 kph) and runs between Japanese cities Tokyo and Osaka, cutting the travel time between them from seven hours to four.

1965

Singapore develops
After becoming independent from neighboring Malaysia, Singapore sees massive economic growth. Factories and companies are encouraged to develop, attracting huge investments from abroad. Many international companies build offices here.

1974

Ten projects
On the island of Taiwan, a series of improvements gets underway known as the Ten Major Construction Projects. Some projects are industrial, but six of them focus on improving transportation by building new roads, railroads, ports, and airports.

1978

Changing China
Deng Xiaoping becomes leader of China after Mao's death and makes huge changes to the economy. Foreign firms are invited to invest in China for the first time in many years. Almost every organization undergoes extensive change, transforming China beyond recognition.

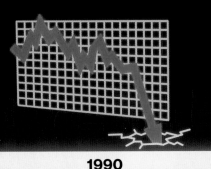

1990

Japanese crash
Japan has risen from the ruins of World War II to become the world's second-largest economy. However, in 1990, the economy crashes, leading to what is known as the "lost decade," in which the country struggles to make money.

1993

High aspirations
The Petronas Towers are built in Kuala Lumpur in Malaysia. These twin skyscrapers, inspired by Islamic art, will be the world's tallest buildings until 2004, standing at 1,482 ft (452 m) tall. They symbolize Malaysia's economic success.

1997

Hong Kong
The control of Hong Kong is transferred from Britain to China after more than 150 years of British rule. Skilled workers use the business skills they have acquired during British rule to help the Hong Kong economy grow.

2003

Three Gorges Dam
China builds a giant dam across the Yangzte River, 1.4 miles (2.3 km) long and 607 ft (185 m) tall. It is an incredible feat of engineering, but China is criticized for forcing more than a million people to leave their homes to make room for it.

1979   1981   1983   1988

The Walkman
Japanese company Sony releases a portable cassette tape player, called the Walkman. It enables people to listen to music while on the move. It sells out in Japanese stores and soon becomes a worldwide phenomenon.

High poverty
Although business and technology is rapidly improving in Asia, most people's living conditions are not. East Asia has the highest poverty rate in the world, with 77 per cent living on less than $1.25 a day, according to the World Bank.

Gaming revolution
Japanese company Nintendo launches what will become the best-selling game console of all time, known as the Famicom. It revolutionizes how people spend their free time and makes Nintendo a leader in the new gaming industry.

Korean cars
After a decade of growth in its automobile industry, South Korea exports half a million cars to the rest of the world in a single year. By the early 21st century, South Korea is one of the world's largest car manufacturers.

2004   2008   2011   2015

Tsunami
An earthquake (the third-largest ever recorded) under the Indian Ocean near Indonesia sets off a devastating tsunami, producing waves of nearly 100 ft (30 m). Across 14 different countries, 230,000 people die, and millions lose their homes.

Beijing Olympics
China hosts the Summer Olympic Games in Beijing across 37 venues. It is a chance for China to impress the rest of the world—more than 4.7 billion people watch the events on televisions around the world.

Nuclear disaster
An earthquake and tsunami on the coast of Japan kills thousands, but the crisis worsens when sea water damages the Fukushima nuclear plant. The plant melts, explodes, and leaks lethal radiation, meaning over 100,000 people have to be evacuated.

Chinese boom
The World Bank, an international bank, ranks China as the world's largest economy, overtaking the United States. Its decision is based on the comparison of the size of incomes in countries across the world.

Computing

Before 1935, the word "computer" referred to a person whose job it was to do mathematical calculations. Today, a computer is a machine that takes input, stores and processes data, and gives output. Computers were initially built from mechanical components such as levers and gears until electronic parts were used in the 20th century. Early computers were so huge they filled entire rooms. Now, the computing power of the smartphone in your pocket is just as powerful.

1946

ENIAC
John Mauchly and J. Presper Eckers, scientists at the University of Pennsylvania, build one of the first general-purpose computers, called ENIAC. This massive 30-ton computer glowing with 18,000 tubes is intended to make more calculations than all of humanity has up to this point.

1936

Turing machine
British computer scientist Alan Turing has an idea for a machine that can solve any problem that is solvable, leading to the development of the modern computer. During World War II, he devises a range of codebreaking tools to break Nazi codes.

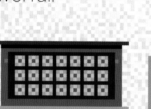

1890

Punch card
American inventor Herman Hollerith designs a machine to calculate the size of the population in the 1890 US census. It uses electricity to read a pattern of holes punched in a card. His invention saves both time and millions of dollars.

1843

Ada Lovelace invents programming
Babbage shows math whiz Ada Lovelace his idea for a mechanical computer. She works out how the computer can manipulate letters and symbols as well as numbers. Her idea was decades ahead of its time. Historians consider her the first computer programmer.

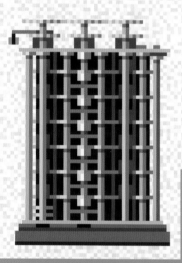

1822

Babbage's Difference Engine
British inventor Charles Babbage draws up plans for his Difference Engine—a mechanical device that can do complicated calculations. He imagines that this machine will store data in the future, anticipating the computer technology that is to come. Construction begins on the engine but is never completed.

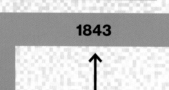

"A computer... is the most remarkable tool we have ever come up with. It's the equivalent of a bicycle for our minds."
Steve Jobs, in a 1990 documentary

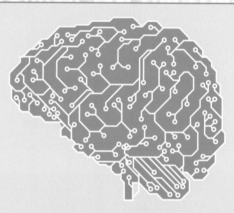

Artificial intelligence
As early as 1950, Alan Turing wanted to know if machines could ever think as intelligently as humans. He put together a test to decide when this AI (artificial intelligence) was achieved. Nowadays, computer scientists and inventors with access to even faster and more powerful machines are coming closer to achieving Turing's goals of creating a machine with the intelligence of a human.

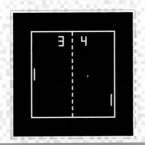

 1958

 1959

 1971

 1976

First computer game

Hundreds of people line up to play in New York, when physicist William Higinbotham serves up what is said to be the first ever computer game. Two players use buttons and dials to bat a blob of light across a virtual court.

Computer language

While working for the US Navy, math expert Grace Hopper develops the first computer language, which becomes known as COBOL. This language is still in use today.

Floppy disk

Engineers at tech company IBM invent the floppy disk, a small plastic envelope housing a bendy mylar (plastic) disk that lets users share data quickly. Billions of disks a year are sold.

Cray supercomputer

The world's fastest computer is built. Its "C" shape reduces the time signals take to travel through the machine. It takes a year to assemble and costs about $9 million.

 1994

 1984

 1982

 1976

First smartphone

IBM's Simon Personal Communicator is the world's first smartphone, created years before there is a name for the device. A touchscreen allows users to make calls, email, and manage schedules.

Mac attack

Apple launches its Macintosh, the first successful computer controlled with a mouse. A drop-down menu makes it simple to use. Microsoft releases a mouse-friendly Windows operating system the next year.

Rise of the PC

The Commodore 64 makes personal computers popular. Thousands of software programs, such as word processors, spreadsheets, and games, are released for the machine, which is one of the highest-selling computers ever.

Apple I and Apple II

Steve Wozniak, Ron Wayne, and Steve Jobs create and sell one of the first desktop computers, Apple I, as a kit for computer enthusiasts. Apple II is created a year later, and appeals to a wider audience with its keyboard, game controllers, and the video game *Breakout*.

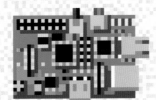

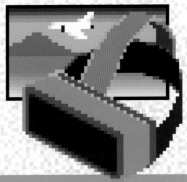

2012

 2010

 Raspberry Pi

 2016

First tablet

Microsoft releases the first tablet computer. The device features a touchscreen, and can access games, music, email, and the internet, putting the power of a much larger machine in the user's hands.

Raspberry Pi

This tiny and inexpensive computer introduces a generation of kids to computer programming through fun and easy projects that young coders upload and share with each other online.

AR/VR goes mainstream

Smartphone users can add digital elements to a view on their camera with augmented reality (AR) technology, and can immerse themselves in artificial digital environments with virtual reality (VR).

Sor Juana Inés de la Cruz

This Mexican nun is known as the first feminist writer of the Americas. Her work *La Respuesta* (*The Answer*) is a letter written in response to a priest who has attempted to silence her and other women, and deny them education.

Mary Wollstonecraft

A Vindication of the Rights of Woman by British writer and philosopher Mary Wollstonecraft is published. It sets out the reasons why women and men are equal and deserve equal rights and opportunities. Its arguments are still relevant today.

US campaign for suffrage

The National American Woman Suffrage Association (NAWSA) is created to campaign for women's suffrage in the US (see pages 234–235). Two million people will join, and it will play a key role in passing the 19th Amendment, which will guarantee women's right to vote in the US in 1920.

International Women's Day

A day is created to promote women's rights and support suffrage. It is initially only marked in a few European countries, but will soon spread across the world.

UK suffragists

The National Union of Women's Suffrage Societies (NUWSS) forms in the UK, under the leadership of Millicent Fawcett. The NUWSS supports a peaceful campaign for women to get the vote. It believes that a nonviolent approach will show that women are respectable and responsible enough to participate in politics.

c.1399   1691   1792   1848   1860   1869   1897   1905   1911

Christine de Pisan

French poet and author de Pisan supports her family through her writing. She writes some of the first feminist works of literature, which argue for equal rights and treatment, and celebrate female heroines from history.

Seneca Falls

The first-ever women's rights convention in the US meets at Seneca Falls in New York. More than 200 women, led by Elizabeth Cady Stanton and Lucretia Mott, meet to discuss rights for women.

Anna Filosofova

Russian women's rights leader and social campaigner Anna Filosofova leads a movement to provide women with work, education, and low-cost housing. Her work is revolutionary for its time.

Feminism

Feminism is the belief that women and men are equal, and should have equal rights and opportunities. However, historically, men have been given more powerful roles than women. Many feminists protest and campaign to achieve equal rights and power. Early feminists focused on getting women the right to vote, but over time the movement has come to address the role of women in many more areas, from politics and home life to music and sports.

UK suffragettes

Emmeline Pankhurst rallies British women, known as suffragettes, around the slogan "Deeds not Words," which describes their tactic of demanding, not asking, for the right to vote. They march, stage hunger strikes, break windows, and chain themselves to railings outside important buildings.

Indian women's movement

India becomes independent from British rule, and the government writes a new set of laws, with the involvement of women. These support freedom and nondiscrimination for all, helping to inspire a women's movement in India.

Dora Shafik

The feminist movement in Egypt finds its voice in Dora Shafik, a writer and editor. In 1951, she storms the Egyptian parliament with a group of women, demanding the right to vote. A week later, a bill is passed allowing women to vote and become members of parliament.

International rights

The UN agrees on a list of rights that women should have across the world, in a treaty called CEDAW. By 2017, 189 countries will sign the treaty, making it one of the most important agreements on human rights in history.

> "We cannot all succeed when half of us are held back."
>
> **Malala Yousafzai,**
> in a speech to the UN, 2013

Women's March

In response to sexist language and abuse of power, people take to the streets in Washington D.C., and many places across the world. It is a show of support for women's rights, and equality more generally, across gender, race, religion, and more. It is estimated that seven million people take part worldwide.

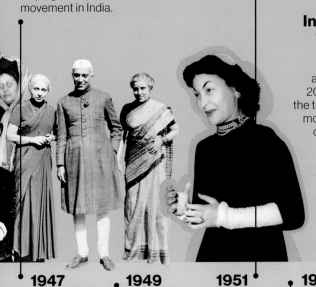

1947 **1949** **1951** **1963** **1973** **1979** **1990s** **2014** **2017**

The Feminine Mystique

American writer Betty Friedan discovers that many women in the US are unhappy being housewives (married women who work in the home, looking after their children and the household). She writes *The Feminine Mystique*, a book that insists women deserve to go to college and have successful careers, just as much as men.

Riot Grrrls

This feminist musical movement begins in the state of Washington. Frustrated with being surrounded by all-male bands, women begin to form their own bands. They make music, create magazines, and hold meetings to express and discuss their thoughts on feminism and politics.

Simone de Beauvoir

French philosopher Simone de Beauvoir writes *The Second Sex,* a book that discusses the treatment of women throughout history. It attempts to define what it means to be female, inspiring generations to follow.

Billie Jean King

Tennis star Billie Jean King founds the Women's Tennis Association, which campaigns to give female tennis players equal pay to male players. It is a start in breaking a trend in sports where female athletes are paid less than men. However, this inequality still exists in many sports today.

Malala Yousafzai

Malala Yousafzai, a Pakistani activist for girls' education, wins the Nobel Peace Prize. She is known for writing about the Taliban (see pages 272–273) banning girls from attending school, and surviving an attempt by the Taliban to kill her when she was 15 years old.

The internet

The internet began in the US more than 50 years ago, when the government tried to think up a foolproof way for computers to talk to each other. In its early years, the internet was a tool for scientists and the military to share information. Who knew that it would evolve to be used by almost anyone for nearly everything? Now, about half the world's population has internet access, and an estimated 4 billion people use the internet.

1971

First email
Ray Tomlinson invents the email program, which sends messages from one computer to another. He introduces the use of the @ symbol in email addresses.

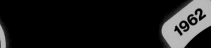

1961

ARPANET
Computer scientist Leonard Kleinrock figures out a way of enabling computers to talk to each other by breaking information into small blocks. This is known as ARPANET, and is a predecessor of the internet.

1962

Modem
Researchers at Bell Labs produce the first commercial modem. This is a device that converts digital signals to electrical ones and back again, so that computers can communicate via telephone lines.

1998

Rise of the search engine
PhD students Larry Page and Sergey Brin build the hugely successful Google search engine. Google makes access to information on the web faster and easier.

1996

Viral video
A 3D animation of a baby dancing goes "viral" via forwarded email chain messages. This is probably the first ever viral video, and a precursor to the meme.

2001

Online encyclopedia
Jimmy Wales and Larry Sanger launch Wikipedia, an online encyclopedia. More than 20,000 entries fill its pages in the first year, and it becomes the largest reference site on the internet.

2004

Rise of social media
A student at Harvard University, Mark Zuckerberg, launches facebook.com. It will go on to become the world's biggest social networking site.

2003

Music on the go
Apple launches its iTunes music store, sparking a trend for downloading music. People can now play their favorite music on their computer or portable music player. More than a million songs are sold in the first week.

2005

Video-sharing
YouTube is created, and becomes one of the fastest-growing sites on the internet. The first video on the site is a 19-second clip about elephants.

1973
Hello, internet
Computer networking becomes international, as University College London and the Royal Radar Establishment in Norway connect to ARPANET. The term "internet" isn't used until 1974.

1983
Domain names
The system for naming websites with phrases such as .com, .edu, or .org is created. This makes it much easier for people to know which website they are visiting.

> ## "The internet is the first thing that humanity built that humanity doesn't understand."
> **Eric Schmidt,** former head of Google, in a speech at the Internet World Trade Show, 1999

1989
World Wide Web
The World Wide Web begins as a project at the European Organization for Nuclear Research (CERN). It is led by British scientist Tim Berners-Lee. The first web browser and the world's first website go live at CERN in 1990. The World Wide Web opens to the public 3 years later.

1995
Online shopping
1995 sees the rise of what will become some of the world's largest online shops. Amazon.com, a huge internet bookstore, launches. The online shopping site eBay, originally called Auction Web, lists its first item for sale (a broken laser pointer).

1991
Fresh coffee
Researchers rig up a live shot of a coffee machine so they can see on their computer screens when a fresh pot has been brewed. This is thought of as the first webcam.

2017
The Internet of Things
There are more devices connected to the internet than there are people in the world. Around 8.4 million devices are in use. The "Internet of Things" describes all the physical objects in the world connected to the internet.

2011
Internet politics
Social media sites such as Twitter and Facebook enable communication during a period of revolutionary protests and demonstrations across the Middle East known as the Arab Spring. Protesters can quickly organize demonstrations and spread information on the sites.

2007
Online voting
Estonia is the world's first country to use internet voting in a governmental election. This makes it easier for many people to vote, encouraging more people to participate in the election.

2017
Face pay
Facial recognition technology allows users to pay for goods with their faces in China. A scanner analyzes users' faces and matches them to a database of photos.

Youth culture

A shift in thinking during the 20th century resulted in a new wave of youth movements that changed and challenged mainstream society. Young free spirits made their mark on the world by defying convention and forming their own ideas about how society should be run. Each movement introduced a fresh political idea together with a cultural identity that influenced music, fashion, and sports.

1901
Wandervogels
A group of German students establish a back-to-nature youth movement that emphasizes freedom and the spirit of adventure. It is known as the Wandervogel movement, which means "wandering bird."

1970s
Hip-hop
From the streets of New York comes this gritty urban movement. African-Americans start the new musical style of hip-hop, featuring rapping (rhyming speech to an instrumental beat). The music inspires breakdancing, a new and athletic form of dance.

1970s
Afrobeat
This musical movement is made popular by Nigerian musician and activist Fela Kuti, and is influenced by West African funk, jazz, and soul music. The rebellious lyrics send a strong message to the continent's governments from disenchanted youths.

1970s
Punk
Beginning in the UK and the US and spreading across the world, this movement began as an aggressive, loose style of music, which spread into politics and fashion, too. Its rebellious, antigovernment message causes much controversy in the media.

1960s
Hippies
The hippie movement in the US promotes nonviolence and tolerance of others, and is inspired by the spirituality of religions such as Buddhism and Hinduism. Many hippies live together in communes, grow their hair long, and wear flowing, colorful clothing.

1920s

Flappers

Groups of women across the West scandalize society by dismissing its expectations of women. They cut their hair into bobs, wear knee-length skirts (short for the time), and dance to jazz music.

1930s

Sapeurs

In the Congo in Africa, local young African men rebel against the dominant European colonizers by emulating their elegant, colorful, and expensive clothing.

1950s

The Beat Generation

A group of writers in New York City start a movement challenging mainstream society. They live an alternative lifestyle inspired by books, poetry, and jazz music.

1950s–1960s

Surfers

Inspired by Polynesian culture, surfing is popular on the coasts of Australia, Hawaii, and California. It influences clothing, music, and even language. Skateboarding and snowboarding develop so that people can "surf" on any terrain.

1960s

Mods and Rockers

Britain experiences a battle between youth cultures when Mods and Rockers clash, sometimes violently, over their opposing fashions and interests. Mods are scooter-riding, stylish soul fans while the Rockers are leather-clad bikers preferring rock and roll.

1970s

Goth

The term "Goth" comes from a genre of literature known as "Gothic horror." Goths are associated with melancholy music, dark dress, and the color black. This movement represents detachment from mainstream culture.

1980s

Cosplay

This term combines the words "costume" and "play," and describes a hobby in which enthusiasts dress up as different characters. It is first coined by Japanese reporter Nobuyuki Takahashi at WorldCon, an annual science-fiction convention held in Los Angeles, California.

1990s

Riot Grrrl

Started in Washington, this feminist movement focuses on sexism in punk rock music. Calling for girl power, Riot Grrrl encourages young women to enjoy their independence through music, clothing, and shared beliefs.

1990s

Harajuku

A rainbow of colorful clothing splashes the streets of Tokyo's Harajuku district. Art students lead the charge by expressing themselves in flamboyant fashions, inspired by cartoon culture, to revolutionize Japanese street style.

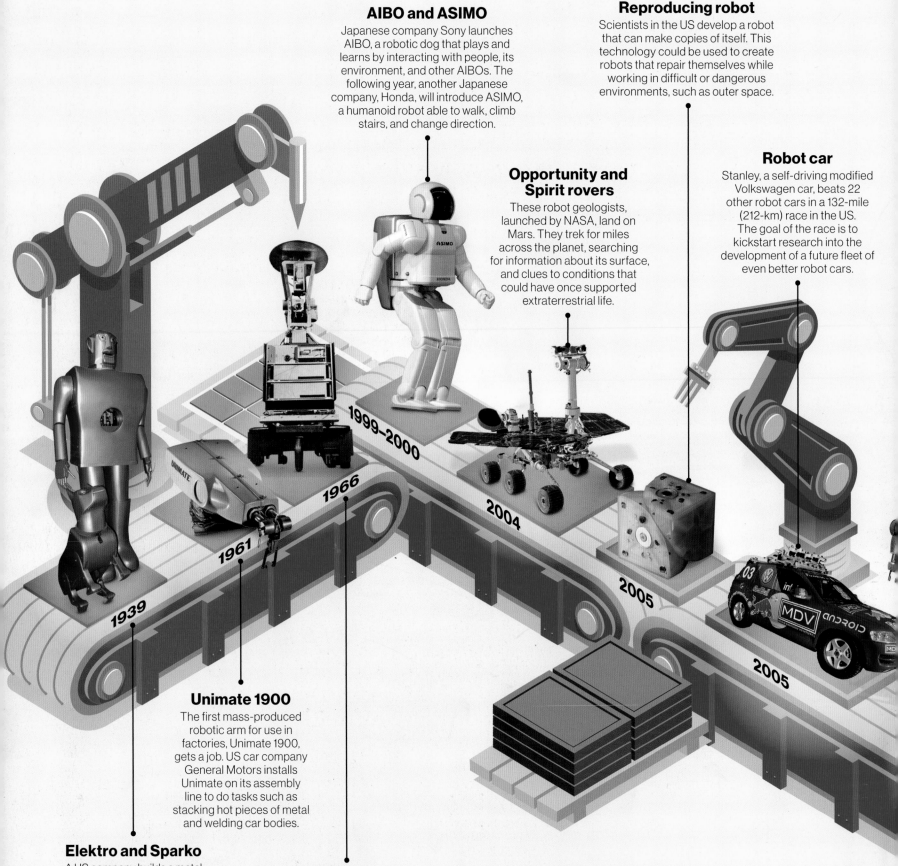

AIBO and ASIMO

Japanese company Sony launches AIBO, a robotic dog that plays and learns by interacting with people, its environment, and other AIBOs. The following year, another Japanese company, Honda, will introduce ASIMO, a humanoid robot able to walk, climb stairs, and change direction.

Reproducing robot

Scientists in the US develop a robot that can make copies of itself. This technology could be used to create robots that repair themselves while working in difficult or dangerous environments, such as outer space.

Opportunity and Spirit rovers

These robot geologists, launched by NASA, land on Mars. They trek for miles across the planet, searching for information about its surface, and clues to conditions that could have once supported extraterrestrial life.

Robot car

Stanley, a self-driving modified Volkswagen car, beats 22 other robot cars in a 132-mile (212-km) race in the US. The goal of the race is to kickstart research into the development of a future fleet of even better robot cars.

1939

1961

1966

1999–2000

2004

2005

2005

Elektro and Sparko

A US company builds a metal person, Elektro, for the New York World's Fair. Standing 7 ft (2.1 m) tall, it rolls on wheels, moves its fingers and arms, and has a 700-word vocabulary (prerecorded on vinyl records). Its robot dog, Sparko, begs, barks, and wags its tail.

Unimate 1900

The first mass-produced robotic arm for use in factories, Unimate 1900, gets a job. US car company General Motors installs Unimate on its assembly line to do tasks such as stacking hot pieces of metal and welding car bodies.

Shakey

Basic artificial intelligence allows this mobile robot to see and move around in its environment. A 1970 magazine article calls it, perhaps over-ambitiously, "the first electronic person," but the robot named for his wobbly walk becomes iconic.

> ## "I visualize a time when we will be to robots what dogs are to humans."
>
> **Claude Shannon**, mathematician, in an article in *Omni Magazine*, 1987

The story of robotics

For centuries, people have been fascinated by the idea of mechanical devices that can be programmed to perform in a particular way: robots. In the 20th century, advances in technology launched a robot revolution. Inventors, many of them inspired by works of science fiction, created incredible, complex robots to help people at work and play.

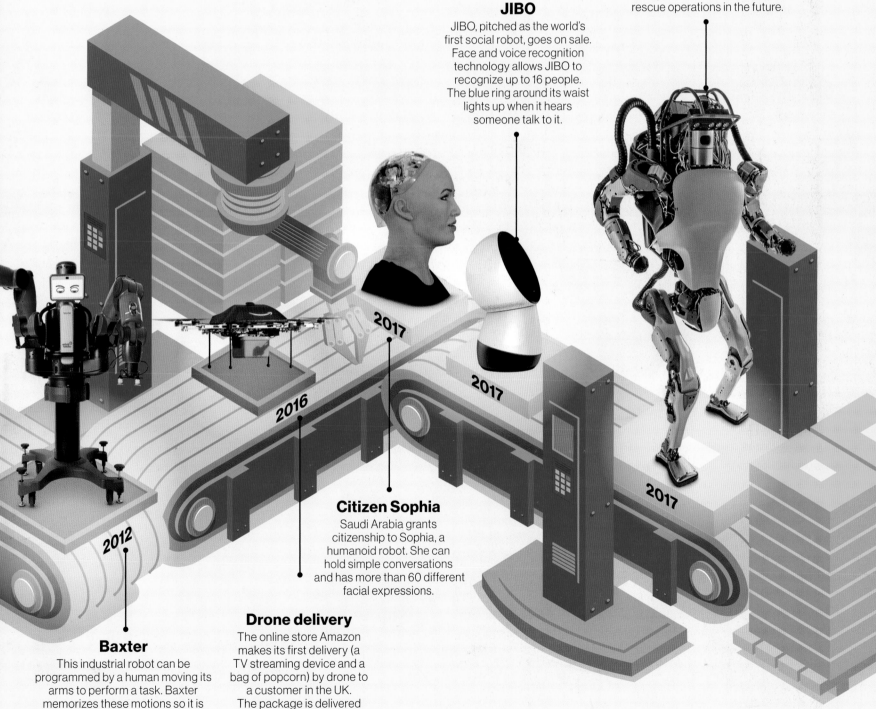

Robot backflip
Despite the difficulty of developing a humanoid robot capable of walking on two legs, US robotics company Boston Dynamics releases a video of its Atlas robot doing a backflip, signaling a new age of robot movement. They hope that Atlas's strength and agility can be put to use in search and rescue operations in the future.

JIBO
JIBO, pitched as the world's first social robot, goes on sale. Face and voice recognition technology allows JIBO to recognize up to 16 people. The blue ring around its waist lights up when it hears someone talk to it.

Citizen Sophia
Saudi Arabia grants citizenship to Sophia, a humanoid robot. She can hold simple conversations and has more than 60 different facial expressions.

Drone delivery
The online store Amazon makes its first delivery (a TV streaming device and a bag of popcorn) by drone to a customer in the UK. The package is delivered a mere 13 minutes after the order is placed.

Baxter
This industrial robot can be programmed by a human moving its arms to perform a task. Baxter memorizes these motions so it is able to repeat the task independently. It can be programmed by anyone.

2012

2016

2017

2017

2017

2017

US presidents

Since the office was created in 1789, there have been 44 presidents of the United States. To be eligible, a person has to be at least 35 years old and born either in the US, or overseas to US citizen parents.

George Washington
Led an army against the British in the War of Independence, then became the first president. He was unanimously elected.

1789–1797

John Adams
Helped draft the Declaration of Independence. Established the naval department, so he is remembered as the "Father of the Navy."

1797–1801

Thomas Jefferson
The main author of the Declaration of Independence, which stated that the colonies would no longer accept British rule.

1801–1809

John Tyler
Vice-president who took the presidency on the death of William Henry Harrison, making him the first president to serve without being elected to office.

1841–1845

James K. Polk
Greatly expanded the territory of the US, adding three new states, and taking over land in the west that would become New Mexico and California.

1845–1849

Zachary Taylor
Successful military general who commanded US forces in the war against Mexico (1846–1848). Died of cholera a year after taking office.

1849–1850

Millard Fillmore
Tried to make a compromise between the anti-slavery states and the slave-owning states, but the peace was short-lived.

1850–1853

Franklin Pierce
Allowed new states to decide for themselves whether to allow slavery, which angered many and edged the US ever closer to civil war.

1853–1857

James Buchanan
Like previous presidents, he tried to make peace between states on the slavery issue, but by the end of his term, civil war was looming.

1857–1861

Grover Cleveland
The only president ever to serve two non-consecutive terms—he lost an election, then was voted back in again four years later.

1885–1889, 1893–1897

Benjamin Harrison
Grandson of President William Henry Harrison, during his term the country expanded and six new states were admitted to the Union.

1889–1893

William McKinley
Oversaw expansion of US territories, including Hawaii and Puerto Rico. Six months into his second term, he was assassinated.

1897–1901

Theodore Roosevelt
The youngest person to become president, at 42. Won the Nobel Peace Prize in 1906 for negotiating peace between Russia and Japan.

1901–1909

William H. Taft
A lawyer by profession, he set up the postal savings bank and passed a law allowing states to collect income tax.

1909–1913

Woodrow Wilson
Took the US into World War I in 1917. After the war, he proposed the formation of the League of Nations to try to prevent future conflict.

1913–1921

John F. Kennedy
His work to reform civil rights and promote racial equality was cut short when he was shot dead in Texas.

1961–1963

Lyndon B. Johnson
Brought in the Civil Rights Act, but faced opposition for sending more troops into the war in Vietnam.

1963–1969

Richard Nixon
Ended the Vietnam War and improved relations with the Soviet Union. His term ended in disgrace after political corruption was uncovered.

1969–1974

Gerald Ford
Unexpectedly became vice-president, then president, during an era of scandals. His honesty helped restore the image of the presidency.

1974–1977

Jimmy Carter
President during a difficult period for the US, both at home and abroad. After his term in office, he became a respected statesman.

1977–1981

Ronald Reagan
A former movie star, he helped end the Cold War. He was shot by a would-be assassin but recovered.

1981–1989

James Madison

Helped draw up the US Constitution, which explained government powers and guaranteed certain rights for citizens.

1809–1817

James Monroe

Remembered for the Monroe Doctrine, which declared that the US would resist attempts by other countries to establish colonies in the Americas.

1817–1825

John Quincy Adams

Son of president John Adams. After his presidency, he became a campaigner against slavery.

1825–1829

Andrew Jackson

Before he took office, he became a national hero for leading the army that defeated the British at the Battle of New Orleans.

1829–1837

Martin Van Buren

After financial panic and stock market crash led to economic depression, Van Buren became unpopular and was not reelected.

1837–1841

William Henry Harrison

The first president to die in office. He died of pneumonia only a month after he became president.

1841

Abraham Lincoln

Opposed to slavery, he led the country during four years of civil war. Days after the war ended, he was shot dead by John Wilkes Booth.

1861–1865

Andrew Johnson

Put on trial by the Senate for violating the Tenure of Office Act, he escaped being removed from office by a single vote.

1865–1869

Ulysses S. Grant

A hero of the Civil War, he was an inexperienced politician whose presidency was overshadowed by scandal and corruption.

1869–1877

Rutherford B. Hayes

After winning one of the closest presidential elections ever, he fought to end corruption in politics and public life.

1877–1881

James A. Garfield

Shot dead after only 200 days in office, before he could carry out his promise to reform the civil service and other public bodies.

1881

Chester A. Arthur

Brought in a law that meant that civil servants were hired purely for their ability rather than because of their political connections.

1881–1885

Warren G. Harding

An unpopular president who was dogged by rumors of financial wrongdoing. He died suddenly, before an investigation could begin.

1921–1923

Calvin Coolidge

Honest, hard-working, and modest, he was fondly nicknamed "Silent Cal." Under his presidency, the US economy boomed.

1923–1929

Herbert Hoover

Shortly after his election, the US entered an era of serious economic depression. Hoover was blamed and did not win a second term.

1929–1933

Franklin D. Roosevelt

Led the US through the Great Depression and World War II. He funded a plan to revive the US economy and help people out of poverty.

1933–1945

Harry S. Truman

Authorized the dropping of two nuclear bombs on Japan, which ended World War II. He took the US to war with Korea.

1945–1953

Dwight D. Eisenhower

Led the Allied armed forces in World War II. During his two terms of office, the US economy thrived.

1953–1961

George H. W. Bush

An oil tycoon and former head of the CIA, he took the US and its allies into the first Gulf War with Iraq (1990–1991).

1989–1993

Bill Clinton

Presided over a time of peace and prosperity, but his reputation was damaged by a scandal over a relationship with a White House intern.

1993–2001

George W. Bush

After the terrorist attacks of 9/11, he ordered the invasion of Afghanistan and declared the War on Terror.

2001–2009

Barack Obama

The first African-American president. His healthcare reforms were disliked by opponents, and led to stalemate in government.

2009–2017

Donald Trump

Before entering politics, Trump was a wealthy businessman, and a famous television personality.

2017–

British rulers

The history of England, and later Britain, is tied together by a string of kings and queens. Long ago, royals could start wars, break from the Church, and punish the country's leaders. Today, the Queen has little power but upholds long and popular traditions.

▶757–1066

Anglo-saxons

After the Romans left Britain in the 5th century CE, the land was attacked by invaders and split into warring kingdoms. The leader of one, Egbert, became the first king of England. Throughout the Saxon period, powerful kings fended off Viking raids, but England was ruled by Viking monarchs for more than 25 years.

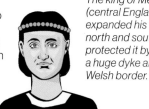

Offa 757–796
The king of Mercia (central England) expanded his kingdom north and south and protected it by building a huge dyke along the Welsh border.

757–796	Offa	959–975	Edgar
802–839	Egbert	975–978	Edward II "The Martyr"
839–856	AEthelwulf	979–1013	AEthelred II "The Unready"
856–860	AEthelbald	1014–1016	AEthelred II "The Unready"
860–866	AEthelbert	1013–1014	Svein
866–871	AEthelred I	1016	Edmund II "Ironside"
871–899	Alfred "The Great"	1016–1035	Canute
899–924	Edward "The Elder"	1035–1040	Harold I "Harefoot"
925–940	Athelstan	1040–1042	Hardicanute
940–946	Edmund I	1042–1066	Edward III "The confessor"
946–955	EAdred	1066	Harold II
955–959	EAdwig		

Egbert 802–839
Originally King of Wessex, Egbert increased the power and influence of his kingdom. His authority was recognized throughout most of England after he defeated Mercia and Northumbria.

1485–1603 ◀

Tudors

The Tudors ruled with an iron fist and were not always popular, but they fostered national pride and parliament grew in strength under them. The manufacturing and merchant classes rose in status, and architecture, literature, and theater blossomed. Playwright William Shakespeare was a leading light.

Elizabeth I 1558–1603
Strong-willed Elizabeth was a clever politician with loyal followers. Under her reign trade, exploration, and prosperity increased.

Mary I 1553–1558
Nicknamed Bloody Mary, Henry VIII's eldest daughter burned Protestants after she seized the throne, and restored the Roman Catholic Church.

Henry VIII 1509–1547
Famous for his six wives (he divorced two and beheaded two), Henry VIII made himself head of the Church in England and bankrupted his country.

1485–1509	Henry Vii Tudor
1509–1547	Henry Viii
1547–1553	Edward VI
1553	Lady Jane Grey
1553–1558	Mary I
1558–1603	Elizabeth I

1461–1485 ◀

Yorkists

This branch of the House of Plantagenets had a strong claim to the throne. After Richard of York was killed in the Battle of Wakefield (1460), his son Edward became the first Yorkist king.

1461–1470	Edward IV
1471–1483	Edward IV
1483	Edward V
1483–1485	Richard III

Richard III 1483–1485
The last English king to die on a battlefield, Richard III may have had a role in the death of his two nephews, the princes, in the Tower of London.

1399–1413	Henry IV
1413–1422	Henry V
1422–1461	Henry VI
1470–1471	Henry VI

Henry VI 1422–1461 and 1470–1471
After losing his father's gains in France, a failing mind cost Henry VI the throne for a time.

▶1603–1649

Stuarts

This dynasty was dominated by political battles between king and parliament, which ended with a civil war and a beheading. Although the Stuarts believed they had a god-given right to rule, they were tolerant of Catholics, and made peace with Spain. They were patrons of the arts and left a legacy of beautiful art and architecture.

James I 1603–1625
Scotland and England were united when this Scottish king took the throne.

Charles I 1625–1649
This stubborn king believed in his divine right to rule. Defeated by Oliver Cromwell in the Civil War, he was tried and executed by his parliament.

▶1649–1659

Commonwealth

For the first and only time in its history, England was a Commonwealth (or republic) without a king or queen. Ruled by puritan Oliver Cromwell and his parliament, the country took Jamaica from the Spanish and defeated the Dutch at sea.

1649–1653	Republic
1653–1658	Oliver Cromwell (Lord Protector)
1658–1659	Richard Cromwell (Lord Protector)

Oliver Cromwell (Lord Protector) 1653–1658
After Charles I was executed, this leading general established his own council of 15 and a parliament of 400. He was followed by his son Richard.

▶1660–1714

Stuarts

After Charles II was restored to the throne London suffered two disasters. A plague killed more than 100,000 people and a great fire destroyed most of the city. James II tried to restore the Catholic faith but fled when William of Orange was invited to restore rights in the Glorious Revolution.

1660–1685	Charles II
1685–1688	James II
1689–1694	William III of Orange and Mary II (jointly)
1694–1702	William III
1702–1714	Anne

Charles II 1660–1685
This "merry monarch" had many interests and many mistresses. He took a keen interest in architecture and science, and introduced yachting to England.

▶1714–1901

Hanoverians

The Hanoverian dynasty saw many changes. Robert Walpole became the first prime minister to German-speaking George I, and Britain developed into an industrial society. By the end of Queen Victoria's reign, Britain's economic power was challenged by Germany and the US.

1714–1727	George I
1727–1760	George II
1760–1820	George III
1820–1830	George IV
1830–1837	William IV
1837–1901	Victoria

George I 1714–1727
This German-born king faced rebellion in Scotland then scandal when a South Sea trading company went bust and ruined thousands of investors.

▶ 1066–1154

Normans

Originally Vikings who had settled in northwest France, the Normans were hungry for new land. William the Conqueror claimed the throne after he defeated Harold II at the Battle of Hastings. The Normans built castles and brought with them a feudal system of lords, who held land, and peasants, who worked it.

1066–1087	William "the Conqueror"
1087–1100	William II
1100–1135	Henry I
1135–1154	Stephen

Alfred "The Great" 871–899
The only English king to be known as "The Great," Alfred was almost overthrown by Viking raiders but fought back, captured London, and expanded his original Wessex kingdom.

Canute 1016–1035
This Viking king treated Danes and Saxons fairly and the country prospered. There is an old story that he proved he was an ordinary man by trying and failing to make the tide go back.

Harold II 1066
Harold II was appointed by his brother-in-law Edward the Confessor but his reign was short-lived. He died after being shot in the eye in the Battle of Hastings, and William I took the throne.

William "the Conqueror" 1066–1087
Called "the Conqueror" because he conquered England, William was crowned king on Christmas Day 1066. He built the Tower of London and ordered a survey of land and people called the Domesday Book.

1399–1461 ◀

Lancastrians

These three kings reigned through almost continual warfare. French territory was recaptured and then lost, and in the War of the Roses, the royal houses of Lancaster and York fought over the throne for 30 years.

Henry V 1413–1422
Henry V reclaimed lost territories in France when he defeated the French at the Battle of Agincourt.

Henry IV 1399–1413
Returning from exile in France, Henry IV reclaimed the throne from Richard II. His reign was marked by many rebellions.

Edward I "Longshanks" 1272–1307
This warrior king fought many battles to unite England and Scotland. A model parliament was formed during his reign.

Henry III 1216–1272
After provoking civil wars with his barons, Henry III was defeated by their leader de Montfort, who formed a parliament of lords, bishops, knights, and freemen.

John I 1199–1216
John lost most of the territories in France and taxed his country heavily. The Magna Carta (great charter) was drawn up to settle the rights of people, Church, and monarchy.

1154–1399 ◀

Plantagenets

Originating in Anjou in France, this dynasty took its name from a yellow flower (*Planta genista*) an ancestor wore in his hat. During much of their rule, England was at war with France and Scotland, and Wales and Ireland came under English rule. The Plantagenets laid the foundation for law and government by creating justices of the peace and the first parliament. They put the royal seal on a charter of rights called the Magna Carta.

1154–1189	Henry II
1189–1199	Richard I "The Lionheart"
1199–1216	John I
1216–1272	Henry III
1272–1307	Edward I "Longshanks"
1307–1327	Edward II
1327–1377	Edward III
1377–1399	Richard II

Richard I "The Lionheart" 1189–1199
This crusading king spent most of his reign fighting for Christianity in West Asia. Imprisoned by the Emperor of Germany, he was returned for a huge ransom and was eventually killed in France.

▶ 1901–1910

George III 1760–1820
The Americans won independence and England fought France in the Napoleonic Wars during George's reign.

William IV 1830–1837
Many more people got the vote under William IV, and slavery was abolished throughout the British Empire.

Victoria 1837–1901
This much-loved queen ruled for 64 years. After her husband Prince Albert died, she went into mourning but was coaxed back to public life.

Saxe-Coburg-Gotha

This dynasty of just one king is named after Queen Victoria's husband Prince Albert, who was the son of the Duke of Saxe-Coburg and Gotha. Edward became king at the age of 59 and reigned during the first years of the 20th century, when new inventions like the first automobile were taking Britain into the modern age.

Edward VII 1901–1910
Edward was a social king who enjoyed sports, parties, and travel. He helped restore relations between France and England and built a new royal estate at Sandringham in Norfolk.

▶ 1910–

Windsors

George V changed his surname to Windsor during the World War I because of the strong anti-German feelings of his people. After Edward VIII gave up the throne to marry a divorced woman in 1936, his younger brother George VI was king through World War II. Queen Elizabeth II has reigned for more than 60 years.

1910–1936	George V
1936	Edward VIII
1936–1952	George VI
1952–	Elizabeth II

George VI 1936–1952
George VI was a good athlete and soldier, but this shy man with a stammer had not expected to be king. He managed to overcome his speech impediment and became popular during and after the war.

Elizabeth II 1952–
The current queen remains head of the Commonwealth (former colonies) and is popular around the world. Prince William and Catherine, Duchess of Cambridge, and their children lead a new generation of royals.

Glossary

Terms defined elsewhere in the glossary are in italics.

abdication
Formally handing over power or responsibility to another.

abolition
The act of doing away with something completely.

anti-Semitism
Prejudice and hostility toward Jewish people.

apartheid
In South Africa, a government policy of racial *segregation* that lasted from 1948 to 1994.

aqueduct
A bridge or other structure built to supply water.

armistice
An agreement that is reached to end a conflict.

assassination
The murder of a key figure by surprise attack, carried out for political or religious reasons.

asteroid
An object in space, made from a mixture of rock and metals, that orbits (see *orbit*) the Sun.

atmosphere
The layer of air that surrounds Earth or another planet.

atom
The smallest part of an *element* that has the same chemical makeup as the element.

bacteria
Microscopic, single-celled (see *cell*) organisms (see *organism*), some of which are responsible for serious diseases.

barbarian
The name given by the Romans to tribes outside the Roman Empire.

BCE
Before Common Era. The years before 1 CE (start of the *Common Era*). This abbreviation has largely replaced BC (Before Christ).

blockade
The isolation of an area so as to prevent supplies from entering or leaving.

Bronze Age, the
A period of ancient history when people mostly used bronze for making tools and weapons.

caliph
The title of the religious and political leader of Islam (in the Islamic world).

capitalism
An economic system based on the private ownership of property and free competitive conditions for business.

CE
Common Era. The years from 1 CE to the present day. This abbreviation has largely replaced AD (Anno Domini, which is Latin for "in the year of the Lord").

cell
The basic unit from which all living organisms are made.

censorship
Limiting access to ideas or information that is seen as harmful to a country's national interest, particularly by government officials.

citizen
A person who belongs to a city or a bigger community such as a state or country.

city-state
A self-governing, independent state consisting of a city and its surrounding area.

civil rights
The rights of citizens (see *citizen*) to be socially and politically equal.

civil war
A war between opposing groups of people in the same country.

classical
Relating to the ancient Greek or ancient Roman world.

Cold War, the
The period of hostility between the *West* and the communist (see *communism*) countries dominated by the USSR. It lasted from shortly after World War II until 1989.

colonization
The act of sending settlers to establish a *colony* in another country, sometimes involving taking political control over the people already living there.

colony
An area under the political control of another state; or the group of people who have settled there.

communism
The political belief in a society in which ownership of property and wealth is shared.

Congress
The law-making branch of the US government.

conquistador
One of the Spanish conquerors of American Indian civilizations.

constitution
A set of laws or rules that determine the political principles of a government.

Counter-Reformation, the
The period of change in the Catholic Church after the Protestant *Reformation*. This included internal reform and opposition to *Protestantism*.

coup
The sudden violent or illegal seizure of power by a group.

Crusades, the
Eight military expeditions of the 11th to 13th centuries, in which Christian knights tried to seize back the city of Jerusalem from the Muslims (see *Muslim*).

culture
The customs, beliefs, and behavior shared by a society.

daimyo
A Japanese lord.

democracy
A form of government based on rule by the people, usually through elected representatives.

depression
In history, a period of drastic decline in economic activity, marked by widespread unemployment and hardship.

dictator
A leader who rules a country alone, with no restrictions on the extent of their power.

DNA
Deoxyribonucleic acid, the chemical that stores genetic information inside living cells (see *cell*).

domestication
The taming of wild animals to make them useful to humans.

dynasty
A royal family ruling a country for successive generations.

element
A substance in which all the atoms (see *atom*) are the same, which can't be broken down by another substance.

empire
A group of lands or peoples brought under the rule of one government or person.

Enlightenment, the
The period of European history, in the 1700s, when radical thinkers tried to reach a new understanding of society, government, and humanity, and then to reform them.

evolution
The gradual change of *species* over generations as they adapt to the changing environment.

exile
Forced absence from a person's home or country.

extinction
The disappearance on Earth of the last living representative of a *species*.

fascism
An ideology stressing *nationalism*, which places the strength of the state above individual citizens' welfare.

feudalism
A political system under which lords granted land to people of lower rank in return for loyalty, military assistance, and services.

fossil
The remains or impression of a prehistoric plant or animal, often preserved in rock.

glasnost
The Russian word for "openness." Used by Mikhail Gorbachev to describe his policies in the Soviet Union during the late 1980s.

gravity
The natural force that attracts one object to another and prevents things from floating off into space.

guerrilla warfare
A type of warfare in which small groups of fighters make surprise attacks against a larger force.

guild
An organization in 11th–14th-century Europe formed by skilled workers or merchants of the same craft or trade to protect its members and control business.

habitat
The area where an animal naturally makes its home.

heresy
Beliefs, held by a member or members of a larger religious group, that are considered to be in conflict with that group's established beliefs.

hominin
A member of the biological group that includes humans and their extinct ancestors and relatives.

hurricane
A violent tropical storm with winds that can reach more than 74 mph (119 kph).

invertebrate
An animal without a backbone, such as an insect, spider, worm, or jellyfish.

Iron Age, the
The historical period characterized by the use of iron for making weapons and tools.

jihad
Arabic word meaning "holy war" or "the struggle within oneself against sin."

martyr
A person who is killed for refusing to renounce his or her religious beliefs.

mass
The amount of matter in an object.

medieval period
Also known as the Middle Ages, the period in European history that lasted from about the 5th to the late 15th century CE.

Mesoamerica
"Middle America," the name for the region stretching from central Mexico in the north, to Guatemala in the south.

Mesopotamia
The region of modern-day Iraq lying between the Tigris and Euphrates rivers, where many of the earliest civilizations began.

missionary
A religious person who seeks to persuade others, often living in foreign lands, to adopt his or her religion.

molecule
A group of atoms (see *atom*) linked by chemical bonds.

monarchy
A type of government in which a king or queen is recognized as head of state, even though he or she may have no real power.

morality
Beliefs based on the principles of what is right and wrong.

Muslim
A follower of *Islam*.

nation
An independent country, or one or more countries whose people share historical, linguistic, or cultural (see *culture*) ties.

nationalism
The belief that the interests of one's nation are more important than the interests of other countries.

Neanderthal
An extinct species of early human closely related to our own species.

Neolithic
The later *Stone Age*, during which improved stone tools and weapons were made and the first farming began.

nomad
A person who moves from one place to another to find fresh pastures and water for livestock.

orbit
The path taken by an object—for example, a planet—that is circling around another.

organism
Any living thing, including an animal, a plant, or a microscopic life-form such as a bacterium (see *bacteria*).

paganism
A term used for the religious beliefs of the ancient Greeks and Romans and other early European peoples before the coming of Christianity.

pandemic
A sudden and widespread outbreak of disease.

patent
The exclusive rights held by an inventor or company to make use of a specific process or invention.

peasant
A worker on the land, usually an agricultural laborer.

perestroika
Russian word meaning "reconstruction." Used by Mikhail Gorbachev to describe his plans for improving the economy of the Soviet Union in the late 1980s.

persecute
To oppress or harass a person or group because of their origins or beliefs.

pharaoh
The title of the ruler of ancient Egypt, who was traditionally seen as both a king and a god.

philosophy
A set of ideas or beliefs.

photosynthesis
The use of sunlight energy by living organisms (see *organism*) to create organic molecules (see *molecule*) from carbon dioxide and water.

pilgrim
A religious follower who makes a journey to a holy place.

prehistory
The time before the development of civilizations, before the invention of writing.

propaganda
Information spread publicly to put forward political views; propaganda is sometimes used to cause deliberate harm to a person or group.

Protestantism
A form of Christianity, resulting from the *Reformation*, in which allegiance is no longer offered to the Pope.

recession
A decline in a country's economic activity, but less serious than a *depression*.

Reformation, the
The reform movement of the 16th century, in which many churches broke from the Catholic Church headed by the Pope in Rome.

Renaissance, the
A period of European history, beginning in the 14th century, when far-reaching changes occurred in the arts and intellectual life.

republic
A country without a hereditary monarch (see *monarchy*) or emperor. Modern republics are usually led by presidents.

revolt
An organized uprising intended to overthrow whoever is in authority.

revolution
A sudden and fundamental change in society brought about by an organized group of protestors.

samurai
A Japanese warrior who owes allegiance to a *daimyo* and follows a strict code of honor.

script
The written characters that make up a writing system, such as an alphabet.

secular
Nonreligious.

segregation
Separation, particularly of one race from another within a racist social system.

shogun
One of the military leaders who ruled Japan in the name of the emperor.

siege
To surround and *blockade* a city or fortress with the intention of capturing it.

slave
A person who is held as the property of another.

socialism
The belief that the government should have some control over the economy and be able to spread wealth more evenly among the people.

Solar System, the
The Sun, together with its orbiting (see *orbit*) planets, including Earth, and smaller bodies such as *asteroids*.

sovereign
A ruler or head of state exerting supreme power.

species
A type of *organism*, such as a horse or leopard. The members of a species can breed with each other, but usually not with other species.

stalemate
A situation where further action by either side in a conflict appears impossible.

stockade
A line of stout posts or logs set in the ground to form a defense against attack.

stock exchange
An organization that allows trading in shares of companies and other financial assets.

Stone Age, the
The period of *prehistory* when humans and their ancestors made tools out of stone.

sub-Saharan Africa
The part of Africa to the south of the Sahara desert.

suffrage
The right to vote.

suffragette
In the early 20th century, a person who fought for women to have the right to vote.

sultan
In some Islamic countries, the traditional title given to the ruler.

superpower
A powerful and influential country considered stronger than its allies.

treason
The crime of betraying one's country, especially by trying to overthrow its government.

treaty
An official, written agreement between warring parties to bring hostilities to an end.

tribute
Money or goods paid by one king to another, or by one state to another, as recognition of the other's superior status.

tsar
The title of the male rulers of Russia from the 15th century until 1917; a female ruler or the wife of a tsar was titled tsarina.

tsunami
A powerful, fast-moving wave caused by an earthquake or volcanic eruption under the sea. Tsunamis cause widespread destruction when they hit land.

Universe
All of space and everything it contains.

vaccination
Precautionary medical treatment, usually given by injection, that keeps people from contracting a disease.

virus
A tiny life-form that can invade body cells (see *cell*), where they multiply, causing illness.

West, the
Europe and North America or their ideals when seen in contrast to other civilizations.

Zionism
The movement to create and maintain a homeland for the Jewish people in Israel.

Index

Page numbers in bold indicate main entries.

York)

21,

246,
93

240

9

...owledgments

he following for
of this book:
av Parida, Sean
ssistance; Charvi
litorial assistance;
an and Baibhav
e Crozier at Butterfly
ing; Victoria Pyke
index.

nt Manager

ner and Education

Education and

he following for
photographs:

lter; f-far; l-left;

(tr/Chain mail).
Science Museum,
nce Museum (bc);
(cr); Gary Ombler /
cience & Society
9 Alamy Stock
ing Kindersley:
ndon (cl). Getty
ience Photo
Photo Library:
hoto: keith morris
/ The Science
DEA / A. DAGLI
n Hughes (bl).
br). 18-19 Science
23RF.com: prapan
Stock Photo:
Toon (t). Avalon:
k Photo: Classic
Archive (tc); Ian
: Charley Gallay
o: imageBROKER
mages: DEA /
Library: Kaj R.
to: Ancient Art and
rris (tr); Liquid Light
bc). Getty Images:
roup (bl).
lamy Stock Photo:
EA / G. LOVERA (cl).
ibler / Jonathan
neil setchfield - uk
r, Courtesy of
y (cr); Whipple
ridge (tl); Gary
on (br). Getty
to: age fotostock
bert Preston
s: Private Collection
). Getty Images:
A. DAGLI ORTI (tr).
gs (br). Alamy
rry Vincent (bc);
eman Images:
jes: DEA /
s: Erich Lessing (bc).
clb); Peter Horree (tl).
listory (bl). Dorling
y of Pennsylvania
ology (cla).
Getty Images.
my Stock Photo:
oto: robertharding
ollection / © Look
: Gary Ombler /
stime.com:
h Lessing (tc).
ical Picture Archive
Images: The Israel
t of Norbert
tock Photo: James
ges (br). Bridgeman
stime.com:
Photo: Granger
tty Images: Werner
). 44-45 Getty
ges: (tc). Alamy
). Bridgeman
s: DEA / A. DAGLI
Collector (cla).
ock Photo: Giulio
ction (tr). Bonhams
esy of Butter Lane
Images: azndc (br).
n Galella (bl).
Bowling pins);
r, cr/Table tennis, br);
ickgalichstudio (cr);
. iStockphoto.com:
RF.com: Khoon Lay
tisak Taramas (cl);
bl, br); macrovector
tudios (tl, tc).
Synelnychenko
Dreamstime.com:
RF.com: Volodimir
k Photo: IanDagnall
en (bc/right); Paul
ures from History (bl).
ess Ltd (bl); Pulsar
l Malie / AFP (bc/left).
lamy Stock Photo:
/ A. DAGLI ORTI
sing (c). 59 Alamy
stime.com: Andrei
(cr). Getty Images:
mages: Dario Mitidieri
s: Museo
Alamy Stock
rchive (c); Lordprice
Pictures from History
n History (cr). Dorling
ty of Pennsylvania
ology (tl). 68-69
g-images: (cr).

Alamy Stock Photo: robertharding (br). **Bridgeman Images:** Pictures from History (tr). **70-71 iStockphoto.com:** RapidEye (c). **70 Alamy Stock Photo:** neil setchfield - uk (tr). **Getty Images:** DEA PICTURE LIBRARY (clb, b); Science & Society Picture Library (tl). **71 Alamy Stock Photo:** dpa picture alliance (tl). **Getty Images:** DEA / A. DAGLI ORTI (crb); Science & Society Picture Library (br, cra, tc, tr). **72 Alamy Stock Photo:** colaimages (tl). **Bridgeman Images:** Louvre, Paris, France / Index (cl); Museum of Fine Arts, Springfield, Massachusetts / Pictures from History / Daderot (tr); Private Collection / © Look and Learn (clb). **Getty Images:** Photo 12 / UIG (bl). **72-73 123RF.com:** Sergio Barrios (background). **Alamy Stock Photo:** MuseoPics - Paul Williams (c). **73 Alamy Stock Photo:** The Granger Collection (tr). **Bridgeman Images:** Musei Capitolini, Rome, Italy (br). **Getty Images:** Ann Ronan Pictures / Print Collector (bl). **74 123RF.com:** Steven Heap (cra); Lefteris Papaulakis (cl). **Alamy Stock Photo:** Peter Horree (tr). **Dreamstime.com:** Stevanzz (bl). **Getty Images:** De Agostini Picture Library (clb). **74-75 iStockphoto.com:** phant (cb). **75 123RF.com:** Kirill Makarov (tl). **Getty Images:** Marka / UIG (br); Werner Forman / Universal Images Group (cr). **78-79 Bridgeman Images:** Bibliotheque de l'Opera Garnier, Paris. **iStockphoto.com:** tomograf (background). **80 123RF.com:** Khoon Lay Gan (tl, tr, cl, bc, br, c); Aleksey Vanin (bl). **Dreamstime.com:** Guillermain (cr). **81 123RF.com:** Khoon Lay Gan (tc, c, bl, bc, br). **Dreamstime.com:** Gunay Aliyevs (crb); Guillermain (tr, cra). **84-85 123RF.com:** ikonstudio; vilnarobotav3d (columns). **84 Alamy Stock Photo:** Peter Horree (cl). **Bridgeman Images:** Louvre, Paris, France (cr); Private Collection / Tallandier (t). **85 Alamy Stock Photo:** Peter Horree (tl). **Bridgeman Images:** Czartoryski Museum, Cracow, Poland (c); Fitzwilliam Museum, University of Cambridge (br); Louvre Museum, Paris / Pictures from History (br). **Getty Images:** DEA / A. DAGLI ORTI (cr); Ullstein bild Dtl. (tr). **87 Alamy Stock Photo:** World History Archive (crb). **Bridgeman Images:** Granger (tr). **Dorling Kindersley:** Alamy: Image Gap (cl). **iStockphoto.com:** RapidEye (bc). **88 Alamy Stock Photo:** ART Collection (br); Ian Dagnall (bl). **Dreamstime.com:** Jarnogz (bc/left). **89 Alamy Stock Photo:** Peter Horree (bc/right); INTERFOTO (tr); Image Gap (bc/left). **Bridgeman Images:** Pictures from History (bl). **90 Alamy Stock Photo:** ART Collection (tl); Granger Historical Picture Archive (bl, tr). **Bridgeman Images:** Pictures from History (br). **Getty Images:** Fine Art Images / Heritage Images (bc). **91 Alamy Stock Photo:** FLHC 16 (tl); Heritage Image Partnership Ltd (tr); The Picture Art Collection (bl). **Bridgeman Images:** Pictures from History (br). **Dorling Kindersley:** James Stevenson / National Maritime Museum, London (cr). **92 akg-images:** Universal Images Group (t). **Alamy Stock Photo:** Ian Dagnall (cl); PRISMA ARCHIVO (clb). **Bridgeman Images:** Gerard Degeorge (tl); San Diego Museum of Art, USA / Edwin Binney 3rd Collection (cla). **93 akg-images:** Science Source (cr). **Bridgeman Images:** Pictures from History (crb); With kind permission of the University of Edinburgh (t); Private Collection (cra). **94 Alamy Stock Photo:** David Hilbert (t); Tom Till (br). **Getty Images:** Oliver J Davis Photography (bl); Imágenes del Perú (cl); DEA PICTURE LIBRARY (cc). **95 Alamy Stock Photo:** James Wagstaff (tl). **Getty Images:** DEA PICTURE LIBRARY (bl); Print Collector (bl); MyLoupe (br). **Rex by Shutterstock:** Granger (tr). **96-97 Bridgeman Images:** Granger (c). **96 Getty Images:** DEA / A. DAGLI ORTI (bl); CM Dixon / Print Collector (t). **97 akg-images:** (br). **Alamy Stock Photo:** Granger Historical Picture Archive (cra). **100-101 Getty Images:** Universal Images Group. **iStockphoto.com:** tomograf (background). **102-103 Getty Images:** De Agostini / N. Cirani (c); Maria Swärd (background). **102 Alamy Stock Photo:** Sue Martin (br); World History Archive (tr). **Getty Images:** Bettmann (tl); Hulton Archive (tc); DEA / A. DAGLI ORTI (bl). **103 Alamy Stock Photo:** Historical Images Archive (bl). **104 akg-images:** Pictures From History (cra); Science Source (cr). **Alamy Stock Photo:** ART Collection (cla). **Getty Images:** De Agostini Picture Library (cl). **105 Alamy Stock Photo:** The Picture Art Collection (ca). **Getty Images:** Heritage Images (tr); Photo Josse / Leemage (cl); Universal History Archive (cr). **106 Alamy Stock Photo:** Peter Horree (r). **Bridgeman Images:** Bibliothèque Nationale, Paris, France / Archives Charmet (tl). **107 Alamy Stock Photo:** Jon Arnold Images Ltd (c); Mara Duchetti (l). **108-109 iStockphoto.com:** Mike Fuchslocher. **110 Alamy Stock Photo:** Paul Fearn (c); Granger Historical Picture Archive (b). **Bridgeman Images:** Pictures from History (t). **110-111 Dorling Kindersley:** Dave King / Durham University Oriental Museum (sword). **111 akg-images:** Pictures From History (cl); Science Source (cr). **Alamy Stock Photo:** ART Collection 2 (c); ART Collection (t). **114 Alamy Stock Photo:** Phil Degginger (br). **115 Alamy Stock Photo:** age fotostock (br); National Geographic Creative (tr, clb); Ivan Kuzmin (bl). **Bridgeman Images:** Dirk Bakker (tl); Thomas Gilcrease Museum, Tulsa, OK, USA / Dirk Bakker (c); De Agostini Picture Library / G. Cappelli (crb). **116-117 Dorling Kindersley:** Dreamstime: Rui Matos / Rolmat (background). **117 Alamy Stock Photo:** Portrait Essentials (tc); Peter Righteous (l). **Getty Images:** Heritage Images (cr); Hulton Archive (br). **118 Alamy Stock Photo:** Robert Hoetink (tl/ring, bl/ring, bc/ring); Peter Horree (tl). **Bridgeman Images:** Pictures from History (bl). **The Trustees of the British Museum:** (tr). **Getty Images:** Werner Forman / Universal Images Group (bc). **118-119 The Trustees of the British Museum:** (c). **119 Alamy Stock Photo:** Robert Hoetink (b/ring, tl/ring, tr/ring). **Bridgeman Images:** British Library, London, UK / © British Library Board. All Rights Reserved (tc). **Getty Images:** Photo taken by Alan (b); Werner Forman / Universal Images Group (tl). **120 Alamy Stock Photo:** IanDagnall Computing (tl). **121 Alamy Stock Photo:** Granger Historical Collection (c); Science History Images (tc). **Getty Images:** Werner Forman (tr). **124 Alamy Stock Photo:** Chronicle (br); Granger Historical Collection (tr); Science History Images (bl, c). **Getty Images:** Science Photo Library (tl). **124-125 123RF.com:** Irina Brinza. **126 Bridgeman Images:** De Agostini Picture Library (br); Prismatic Pictures (tl). **Dorling Kindersley:** Dave King / Warwick Castle, Warwick (bc). **127 Alamy Stock Photo:** Volodymyr Horbovyy (tr). **Bridgeman Images:** Cleveland Museum of Art, OH, USA / Gift of Mr. and Mrs. John L. Severance (bl); Granger (cr). **Dorling Kindersley:** Richard Leeney / Maidstone Museum and Bentliff Art Gallery (tl). **Getty Images:** DEA / A. DAGLI ORTI (bc). **129 Alamy Stock Photo:** ART Collection (tc); Niday Picture Library (bc); Heritage Image Partnership Ltd (c); GL Archive (cr/overlaid). **Getty Images:** Harald Sund (br). **130 Getty Images:** DEA / A. DAGLI ORTI (br); SuperStock (bc/left); Imagno (bc/right). **iStockphoto.com:** tomograf (bc/right, background). **131 Alamy Stock Photo:** ART Collection (br); Science History Images (bc/left); Alexander Helin (bc/right). **Bridgeman Images:** Library of Congress, Washington D.C. (bl). **iStockphoto.com:** tomograf (bl/background). **Science & Society Picture Library:** Science Museum (t). **132-133 iStockphoto.com:** Newbird (background). **132 akg-images:** (c). **Alamy Stock Photo:** FLHC 8 (cr). **Dreamstime.com:** Jacek Kutyba / Jacqu (br). **Getty Images:** DEA / A. DAGLI ORTI (bl). **133 Alamy Stock Photo:** Alfio Scisetti (tl). **Bridgeman Images:** American Museum of Natural History, New York, USA / Photo © Boltin Picture Library (cl). **Getty Images:** Science & Society Picture Library (tr). **134 Alamy Stock Photo:** Artokoloro Quint Lox Limited (bl); Niday Picture Library (cla); Granger Historical Picture Archive (crb). **Dorling Kindersley:** James Stevenson / National Maritime Museum, London (tr); James Stevenson / Tina Chambers / National Maritime Museum, London (cr). **Library of Congress, Washington, D.C.:** (c). **135 123RF.com:** Richard Pross / richardpross (bc). **Alamy Stock Photo:** George Atsametakis (tl); Jeanette Dietl (br). **Dorling Kindersley:** Gary Ombler / Fleet Air Arm Museum (c). **Getty Images:** Joe Scarnici / HISTORY (tc); Harald Sund (tr); Science & Society Picture Library (cl). **iStockphoto.com:** gmalandra (bl). **138-139 Alamy Stock Photo:** Panther Media GmbH. **138 Alamy Stock Photo:** GL Archive (tl). **Bridgeman Images:** De Agostini Picture Library (bc). **Getty Images:** DEA / G. DAGLI ORTI (cr); SuperStock (tc). **139 Alamy Stock Photo:** Chronicle (ftl); Science History Images (tl); North Wind Picture Archives (tr); The Granger Collection (ftr); GL Archive (c). **140-141 iStockphoto.com:** tomograf (background). **Science Photo Library:** Christian Jegou Publiphoto Diffusion. **142 akg-images:** (bc). **Alamy Stock Photo:** Ian Dagnall (tr); FineArt (tl). **Bridgeman Images:** British Library, London, UK / © British Library Board. All Rights Reserved (cl); Private Collection / © The Lucian Freud Archive / Private Collection / © The Lucian Freud Archive / Bridgeman Images (bl, bl). **Getty Images:** Universal History Archive (tc); VCG Wilson / Corbis (cr). **The Metropolitan Museum of Art:** Jacques and Natasha Gelman Collection, 1998 (br). **143 Alamy Stock Photo:** Art Directors & TRIP (tc); Ian Dagnall (br); FineArt (cb); GL Archive (clb); Heritage Image Partnership Ltd (tl). **Getty Images:** Asian Art & Archaeology, Inc. / CORBIS (cra); De Agostini Picture Library (cla, tr); Pascal Deloche / GODONG (ca). **Courtesy National Gallery of Art, Washington:** Gift of Victoria Nebeker Coberly, in memory of her son John W. Mudd, and Walter H. and Leonore Annenberg (crb). **The Metropolitan Museum of Art:** Jacques and Natasha Gelman Collection, 1998 (bl). **144-145 123RF.com:** Grigory Stepanov (Nails). **Dreamstime.com:** Ovydyborets (background, paper). **144 123RF.com:** nathanael005 (t/scroll background). **Alamy Stock Photo:** Chronicle (cl); INTERFOTO (t). **Getty Images:** Imagno (b). **145 123RF.com:** nathanael005 (t/scroll background). **akg-images:** De Agostini Picture Library (tr). **Alamy Stock Photo:** Chronicle (tl); PRISMA ARCHIVO (cl); Pictorial Press Ltd (br); Historical Images Archive (bl). **146-147 Dreamstime.com:** Ovydyborets (background). **147 Bridgeman Images:** Tarker (tr). **148-149 Alamy Stock Photo:** Lebrecht Music and Arts Photo Library. **150 Alamy Stock Photo:** Art Collection 3 (bl). **Bridgeman Images:** Pictures from History (tr). **151 Alamy Stock Photo:** Niday Picture Library (br). **Bridgeman Images:** Granger (cl). **Getty Images:** DEA / A. DAGLI ORTI (cr). **152 Alamy Stock Photo:** Richard Wainscoat (bl). **154 Alamy Stock Photo:** Aurelian Images (br); INTERFOTO (bl). **Bridgeman Images:** Apsley House, The Wellington Museum, London, UK / © Historic England (r). **Getty Images:** Fine Art Images / Heritage Images (tl); Fototeca Gilardi (bc). **154-155 Dreamstime.com:** Designprintck (background). **155 Alamy Stock Photo:** Everett Collection Historical (c); Lifestyle pictures (tl). **Getty Images:** Apic (br); Leemage (bl). **156-157 Alamy Stock Photo:** ART Collection. **158 Alamy Stock Photo:** Granger Historical Picture Archive (tr); V&A Images (tc). **Bridgeman Images:** Church of the Gesù, Rome, Italy (c); Private Collection (bl); Musee Guimet, Paris, France (cl). **158-159 Alamy Stock Photo:** age fotostock (cb). **159 Alamy Stock Photo:** Alfo Co., Ltd. (cl); Heritage Image Partnership Ltd (c). **Bridgeman Images:** Private Collection / Archives Charmet (cr); Private Collection / Pictures from History (br). **Getty Images:** Asian Art & Archaeology, Inc. / CORBIS (tr); Print Collector (tl). **160 Alamy Stock Photo:** Glasshouse Images (fbl). **Bridgeman Images:** Granger (br); Private Collection / © Look and Learn (t); Library of Congress, Washington D.C. (bl). **Getty Images:** Historical (fbr). **160-161 Dreamstime.com:** Ovydyborets (background paper). **161 akg-images:** (cr). **Bridgeman Images:** Granger (tl, tc, tr); Private Collection / © Look and Learn (br). **162 Alamy Stock Photo:** Paul Fearn (tl); Science History Images (tr); INTERFOTO (ca). **Wellcome Images http://creativecommons.org/licenses/by/4.0/:** (br). **163 Alamy Stock Photo:** The Granger Collection (tl); Lebrecht Music and Arts Photo Library (bl); Science History Images (cb). **Dorling Kindersley:** Whipple Museum of History of Science, Cambridge (tr). **Getty Images:** Universal History Archive (cr). **164 Bridgeman Images:** Pictures from History (br). **165 Bridgeman Images:** Pictures from History (br). **166 Alamy Stock Photo:** Dinodia Photos (tl, tc, tr); IndiaPicture (bl). **167 Alamy Stock Photo:** Granger Historical Collection (tl); Alexander Helin (tc); V&A Images (cr); Niday Picture Library (br). **168 Bridgeman Images:** National Palace Museum, Taipei, Taiwan (tl); Pictures from History (tc, b). **Dreamstime.com:** Songquan Deng / Rabbit75 (tr). **168-169 Dreamstime.com:** Designprintck (background). **169 Alamy Stock Photo:** ART Collection (bl); imageBROKER (tr); Everett Collection Historical (cb). **Dorling Kindersley:** Andy Crawford / British Museum (br). **Getty Images:** DEA PICTURE LIBRARY (bc); Universal History Archive (cra). **170-171 123RF.com:** Igor Zakharevich (background). **175 akg-images:** Science Source (br). **177 Alamy Stock Photo:** Granger Historical Picture Archive (tl); Prisma by Dukas Presseagentur GmbH (fcr). **Dorling Kindersley:** Simon Clay / National Motor Museum, Beaulieu (b). **Getty Images:** Photo Josse / Leemage (bl). **178 Alamy Stock Photo:** Chronicle (bc/right); Niday Picture Library (br). **Bridgeman Images:** 00596841 (bl). **179 Alamy Stock Photo:** Granger Historical Picture Archive (bl). **Dorling Kindersley:** Gary Ombler / National Railway Museum, York / Science Museum Group (t). **Library of Congress, Washington, D.C.:** (bc/left, bc/right). **182-183 Bridgeman Images:** Granger (b). **iStockphoto.com:** tomograf (background). **184 Alamy Stock Photo:** Enrico Della Pietra (tc). **Getty Images:** Stephen J Krasemann (br); Sergio Pigozzi (tr). **NASA:** (br); GSFC / METI / ERSDAC / JAROS, and U.S. / Japan ASTER Science Team (c). **185 Alamy Stock Photo:** Science History Images (bc). **Getty Images:** InterNetwork Media (bl); Tom Pfeiffer / VolcanoDiscovery (tc); Topical Press Agency / Hulton Archive (cr); STF / AFP (br). **186 Alamy Stock Photo:** AF archive (b); Dinodia Photos (cl). **Getty Images:** Hiroyuki Ito (tr). **187 123RF.com:** mikewaters (tc). **Alamy Stock Photo:** SPUTNIK (br). **Getty Images:** De Agostini Picture Library (cr); Michel Porro (tl); DEA / A. DAGLI ORTI (tr). **188-189 Bridgeman Images:** Kremlin Museums, Moscow, Russia (c). **188 Alamy Stock Photo:** Niday Picture Library (clb); The Print Collector (tr). **Getty Images:** Photo Josse / Leemage (bl); Jose Fuste Raga (cl). **189 Alamy Stock Photo:** Chronicle (tl); Chris Hellier (cra); Pictorial Press Ltd (cr); Hi-Story (br). **190 Alamy Stock Photo:** North Wind Picture Archives (c). **Bridgeman Images:** 00596841 (cr); Private Collection / © Look and Learn / Barbara Loe Collection (bc). **Getty Images:** Science & Society Picture Library (bl). **191 Alamy Stock Photo:** (crb); ART Collection (tl); IanDagnall Computing (tr); Science History Images (cra); Granger Historical Picture Archive (bl); The Granger Collection (br); North Wind Picture Archives (cla). **Bridgeman Images:** (clb). **Getty Images:** Hulton Archive (c). **192-193 Bridgeman Images:** Metropolitan Museum of Art, New York, USA. **196 123RF.com:** Martijn Mulder (c). **Alamy Stock Photo:** imageBROKER (bc); Penny Tweedie (r). **Getty Images:** Danita Delimont (tl); Werner Forman / Universal Images Group (ca). **197 Alamy Stock Photo:** Chronicle (l); Marc Tielemans (tc); The Picture Art Collection (cr); Photo 12 (cb). **198-199 iStockphoto.com:** tomograf (background). **199 Bridgeman Images:** Archives Charmet. **200 Alamy Stock Photo:** Chronicle (bc); Dennis Hallinan (br); Masterpics (tr). **Bridgeman Images:** Musee de la Ville de Paris, Musee Carnavalet, Paris, France (tl, tc). **201 Alamy Stock Photo:** Niday Picture Library (bl); PRISMA ARCHIVO (bc). **Bridgeman Images:** Musee de la Ville de Paris, Musee Carnavalet, Paris, France (cl). **202 Alamy Stock Photo:** Granger Historical Picture Archive (br). **Getty Images:** adoc-photos / Corbis (bl); De Agostini Picture Library (tl); Bettmann (tr). **203 Getty Images:** Business Wire (bl); David Silverman (tr); Science & Society Picture Library (br, tl). **204 Alamy Stock Photo:** ART Collection (tr). **205 Alamy Stock Photo:** Paul Fearn (tr); NMUIM (tl); Granger Historical Picture Archive (br). **Bridgeman Images:** Manchester Art Gallery, UK (bl). **206 Getty Images:** De Agostini Picture Library (b); Hulton Archive (t). **207 Alamy Stock Photo:** Granger Historical Picture Archive (tr). **Getty Images:** De Agostini Picture Library (bl); PHAS / UIG (cr). **208 Alamy Stock Photo:** Ed Buziak (crb). **Dorling Kindersley:** Mike Dunning / National Railway Museum, York (cl); Clive Streeter / The Science Museum, London (tr). **Getty Images:** Central Press / Hulton Archive (cr); Wolfgang Kaehler / LightRocket (ca). **Daniel Lu:** (bl). **209 Alamy Stock Photo:** Top Photo Corporation (bc). **Dorling Kindersley:** Gary Ombler / National Railway Museum, York / Science Museum Group (tc); Gary Ombler / Didcot Railway Centre (crb). **Dreamstime.com:** Yinan Zhang / Cyoginan (br). **Getty Images:** Science & Society Picture Library (tl, tr, c, bl). **Manuscripts and Archives, Yale University Library:** Yale Collection of Western Americana, Beinecke Rare Book and Manuscript Library, Yale University, New Haven, Connecticut (cl). **210 Alamy Stock Photo:** Everett Collection (bl); ZUMA Press, Inc. (br); The Granger Collection (tr). **Digital image courtesy of the Getty's Open Content Program:** (tl). **210-211 Alamy Stock Photo:** Prisma by Dukas Presseagentur GmbH (c). **211 Bridgeman Images:** Bibliotheque des Arts Decoratifs, Paris, France / Archives Charmet (r). **214 Alamy Stock Photo:** Lordprice Collection (bl); Science History Images (cl). **Getty Images:** American Stock Archive (r); Bettmann (t). **215 Alamy Stock Photo:** FineArt (cr); National Geographic Creative (tr). **Library of Congress, Washington, D.C.:** (l, br). **216 Alamy Stock Photo:** Chronicle (tr); Granger Historical Picture Archive (tl, bl); INTERFOTO (br). **217 Alamy Stock Photo:** Chronicle (bc/left); Classic Image (bl); Glasshouse Images (br). **Bridgeman Images:** Private Collection / © Look and Learn (bc/right). **218-219 123RF.com:** Igor Zakharevich (background). **222 Bridgeman Images:** Chicago History Museum, USA (cl). **Dorling Kindersley:** Dave King / Gettysburg National Military Park, PA (bl). **Library of Congress, Washington, D.C.:** (bc, tr, br). **223 Alamy Stock Photo:** ClassicStock (tr). **Bridgeman Images:** Private Collection (tl). **Getty Images:** Bettmann (c). **224 akg-images:** North Wind Picture Archives (cr). **Getty Images:** Hulton Archive (br); Popperfoto (cb). **225 Alamy Stock Photo:** Heritage Image Partnership Ltd (cr). **Getty Images:** Express Newspapers (tl); Paul Popper / Popperfoto (crb). **226 Alamy Stock Photo:** Pictorial Press Ltd (crb). **Bridgeman Images:** Photo © CCI (bc). **Getty Images:** Stefano Bianchetti / Corbis (tr); Photo 12 / UIG (clb); Araldo de Luca / Corbis (br). **227 123RF.com:** beaucroft (bl); klotz (tc). **Dreamstime.com:** Grzym (crb). **Getty Images:** Bettmann (tl); Science & Society Picture Library (clb); Bloomberg (br). **228 Alamy Stock Photo:** Ton Snoei (t). **Bridgeman Images:** Private Collection / Avant-Demain (cr). **Getty Images:** George Rose (br); Science & Society Picture Library (c, bl). **iStockphoto.com:** selvanegra (bc). **Library of Congress, Washington, D.C.:** (tl). **228-229 iStockphoto.com:** Rouzes (pegs and photo background). **229 Alamy Stock Photo:** Granger Historical Picture Archive (tl); World History Archive (tc, cl). **Bridgeman Images:** PVDE (cr). **Getty Images:** Science & Society Picture Library (bl). **iStockphoto.com:** kosamtu (br). **Library of Congress, Washington, D.C.:** (tr, c). **230 Alamy Stock Photo:** FOR ALAN (tl); Marmaduke St. John (tr); Pictorial Press Ltd (cr). **231 Alamy Stock Photo:** By Ian Miles-Flashpoint Pictures (bl). **Getty Images:** Science & Society Picture Library (tr); Stegerphoto (br). **232 Alamy Stock Photo:** David Osborn (br); Science History Images (cl). **Dreamstime.com:** Steve Mann / The_guitar_mann (bc); Gary Scott (cl). **Getty Images:** Bettmann (cr). **233 Getty Images:** Ross Land (tr); Science & Society Picture Library (tl); © Museum of Flight / CORBIS (c). **iStockphoto.com:** aapsky (br). **236-237 123RF.com:** Igor Zakharevich (background). **238 Alamy Stock Photo:** Granger Historical Picture Archive (br). **Daimler AG:** Mercedes-Benz Classic (bl). **Dorling Kindersley:** Gary Ombler / R. Florio (cr). **Getty Images:** Rykoff Collection (c). **Utah State Historical Society:** (cl). **Volvo Car Group:** (bc). **239 Alamy Stock Photo:** Heritage Image Partnership Ltd (cl). **Dorling Kindersley:** Simon Clay / National Motor Museum, Beaulieu (cr); James Mann / National Motor Museum Beaulieu (c); Matthew Ward (bl). **Getty Images:** Kim Kulish / Corbis (br); Science & Society Picture Library (tr). **Toyota UK:** (cb). **240 Alamy Stock Photo:** Everett Collection Historical (bl); Pictorial Press Ltd (ca). **TopFoto.co.uk:** (cb). **241 Alamy Stock Photo:** GL Archive (cl). **Getty Images:** Library of Congress / Corbis (tr); NY Daily News Archive (tr). **Paragon Space Development Corporation and Volker Kern:** (br). **242-243 Getty Images:** Bettmann. **iStockphoto.com:** tomograf (background). **245 Alamy Stock Photo:** David Parker (backdrop); Splash News (c). **Getty Images:** Agence France Presse (tl); Popperfoto (bl); Yamaguchi Haruyoshi (cr); Ralph Morse / The LIFE Picture Collection (tr). **246 Alamy Stock Photo:** Granger Historical Picture Archive (bl). **Getty Images:** Central Press / Hulton Archive (br); Heritage Images (tc); Bettmann (tr). **247 Dorling Kindersley:** Clive Streeter / The Science Museum, London (t). **Getty Images:** Agence France Presse (bc/right); Francoise De Mulder / Roger Viollet (bl). **248 Alamy Stock Photo:** Everett Collection Historical (tr). **Bridgeman Images:** © SZ Photo / Scherl (bl); Private Collection / Photo © Christie's Images (br). **Rex by Shutterstock:** Universal History Archive \ UIG (bc). **248-249 123RF.com:** Nuwat Chanthachanthuek (c). **249 Alamy Stock Photo:** Everett Collection Historical (br); Heritage Image Partnership Ltd (tr); Granger Historical Picture Archive (bc). **Bridgeman Images:** Private Collection / © Look and Learn / Elgar Collection (tl). **Getty Images:** Bettmann (bl). **iStockphoto.com:** Gojal (cr). **250 123RF.com:** andreadonetti (bl). **Alamy Stock Photo:** Granger Historical Picture Archive (tl); Tom Hanley (tc); Pictorial Press Ltd (cr). **Dorling Kindersley:** Gary Ombler / R. Florio (crb). **251 Alamy Stock Photo:** Ewing Galloway (l). **Getty Images:** Bettmann (tl); Hulton Archive (tc, br). **252 Alamy Stock Photo:** Hercules Milas (bl). **253 akg-images:** Album / J.Enrique Molina (cr); Erich Lessing (cla). **Alamy Stock Photo:** World History Archive (cl). **Getty Images:** De Agostini Picture Library (cb). **254 Getty Images:** Bettmann (t); Heritage Images (cl). **255 Alamy Stock Photo:** Sueddeutsche Zeitung Photo (cb); World History Archive (ca). **Getty Images:** Bettmann (tl); Sovfoto / UIG (c); Shepard Sherbell / Corbis (br). **260-261 Dorling Kindersley:** Dreamstime.com: Ovydyborets. **Getty Images:** Hulton-Deutsch Collection (background). **260 Bridgeman Images:** Archives de Gaulle, Paris, France (b). **Getty Images:** Fox Photos (cla); William Vandivert / The LIFE Picture Collection (tr); Popperfoto (cr); Keystone (c). **261 Alamy Stock Photo:** Prisma by Dukas Presseagentur GmbH (br). **Getty Images:** Margaret Bourke-White / The LIFE Picture Collection (c); Fox Photos (tl). **262 Bridgeman Images:** Pictures from History (b); SZ Photo (tl); SZ Photo / Scherl (tr). **262-263 Getty Images:** Hulton Archive. **263 Auschwitz-Birkenau Memorial & Museum:** (tl). **Bridgeman Images:** Galerie Bilderwelt (tr); SZ Photo (br). **Getty Images:** Galerie Bilderwelt (bl). **264-265 Alamy Stock Photo:** World History Archive. **266 Bridgeman Images:** SZ Photo / Scherl (r). **Getty Images:** (bl). **267 Alamy Stock Photo:** Military History Collection (br); Pictorial Press Ltd (tl). **Bridgeman Images:** PVDE (bc). **Getty Images:** Historical (bl); SuperStock (tr). **268 Alamy Stock Photo:** World History Archive (tl). **Getty Images:** Margaret Bourke-White / The LIFE Picture Collection (r); Central Press / Hulton Archive (tr); Keystone (bl). **269 Alamy Stock Photo:** Zoonar GmbH (br). **Getty Images:** Mark Kauffman / The LIFE Picture Collection (l); Keystone-France / Gamma-Keystone (cb); Popperfoto (tc). **270 Getty Images:** Science & Society Picture Library (bl). **271 123RF.com:** Burnel1 (tr). **Alamy Stock Photo:** Artokoloro Quint Lox Limited (ca); MARKA (br). **272 Alamy Stock Photo:** Everett Collection Historical (bl); Granger Historical Picture Archive (cl); World History Archive (c). **Getty Images:** AFP (br); Christine Spengler / Sygma (cr). **273 Alamy Stock Photo:** PCN Photography (tr); US Air Force Photo (c). **Getty Images:** Francoise De Mulder / Roger Viollet (b); David Rubinger / The LIFE Images Collection (cl). **275 Getty Images:** Apic / RETIRED (tr). **276 Alamy Stock Photo:** Everett Collection Historical (c); Keystone Pictures USA (r). **Getty Images:** Bettmann (bl); VCG Wilson / Corbis (cl). **277 Alamy Stock Photo:** FLHC 47 (ca); INTERFOTO (l). **Getty Images:** Bettmann (br); Underwood Archives (cb). **278 Alamy Stock Photo:** colaimages (c); World History Archive (tr); Susan Pease (bl). **Getty Images:** Bettmann (clb); Henry Diltz (bl/above); Reg Lancaster (br/above); Robert Abbott Sengstacke (br); Edward Miller (cla). **279 Alamy Stock Photo:** Everett Collection (bl); Tracksimages.com (cl); US Army Photo (cr); M&N (clb). **Getty Images:** B.Friedan (tl); The LIFE Picture Collection (tc); Bettmann (tr); Popperfoto (crb); Photolibrary (br); Francois LOCHON (c). **280 Alamy Stock Photo:** Allstar Picture Library (c). **Getty Images:** AFP (bl); Mark Kauffman / The LIFE Picture Collection (tl); William Campbell / Sygma (br); Patrick Robert / Sygma / CORBIS (tr). **281 Alamy Stock Photo:** imageBROKER (tr); David Parker (br). **Getty Images:** GIANLUIGI GUERCIA / AFP (cl); Santi Visalli (tl); PHILIP OJISUA / AFP (cra). **284 Alamy Stock Photo:** ART Collection (br); SPUTNIK (cb, tc); Chronicle (cl). **NASA:** (tl, cl, tr). **285 Alamy Stock Photo:** ITAR-TASS News Agency (tl). **John F. Kennedy Library Foundation:** Robert Knudsen. White House Photographs. John F. Kennedy Presidential Library and Museum, Boston (tr). **NASA:** (tc). **Martin Trolle Mikkelsen:** (cr). **286 Getty Images:** Ralph Morse / The LIFE Picture Collection (l, r). **287 Getty Images:** Ralph Morse / The LIFE Picture Collection (r, l). **288-289 Getty Images:** Bettmann (cl). **290 Getty Images:** Bettmann (cl, cr, tr). **290-291 Getty Images:** AFP. **291 Bridgeman Images:** Granger (cr); Underwood Archives / UIG (cl). **Getty Images:** Agence France Presse (cl/far). **292 Alamy Stock Photo:** The National Trust Photolibrary (tr/Queen Elizabeth); Trinity Mirror / Mirrorpix (br). **Bridgeman Images:** Castello della Manta, Saluzzo, Italy (tc/Middle ages); Victoria & Albert Museum, London, UK (tr). **Getty Images:** DEA / S. VANNINI / De Agostini (tl); Tim Graham (bl/Diana); DEA / A. DAGLI ORTI (tl/Greek); In Pictures Ltd. / Corbis (tc); Mark Kauffman / The LIFE Picture Collection (br/mini dresses); Michael Putland (bc). **293 Alamy Stock Photo:** Heritage Image Partnership Ltd (tr); MARKA (bc/left). **Bridgeman Images:** National Trust Photographic Library / John Hammond (tl/Baroque Europe); Photo © Historic Royal Palaces / Robin Forster (tr/Mantua dress). **Getty Images:** DEA / A. DAGLI ORTI (tl, cra); Galerie Bilderwelt (br). **iStockphoto.com:** BernardAllum (tc/Kimono). **300 Alamy Stock Photo:** Paul Fearn (cb); Granger Historical Picture Archive (cl); Lebrecht Music and Arts Photo Library (c/Wollstonecraft); Trinity Mirror / Mirrorpix (br/Pankhurst); Len Collection (br). **Carrie Chapman Catt Papers, Bryn Mawr College Library Special Collections:** (ca). **Getty Images:** Topical Press Agency / Hulton Archive (crb). **The National Library of Norway:** (cr). **301 Alamy Stock Photo:** Keystone Pictures USA (ca); World History Archive (cl); Splash News (br). **Getty Images:** Sam Morris (tr); Popperfoto (cb); RDA (clb). **302-303 Vecteezy.com:** (Icons). **306 Getty Images:** Ralph Crane / The LIFE Picture Collection (cl); Science & Society Picture Library (r); Yamaguchi Haruyoshi (t). **Professor Hod Lipson:** Jonathan Blutinger (photographer), Victor Zykov (designer) (crb). **307 Alamy Stock Photo:** Anton Gvozdikov (tc). **Courtesy of Boston Dynamics:** (r). **Getty Images:** NurPhoto (cr).

All other images © Dorling Kindersley
For further information see: www.dkimages.com